# YOU DECIDE!
## 2005

## Current Debates in American Government

### JOHN T. ROURKE
*University of Connecticut*

PEARSON

Longman

New York   Boston   San Francisco
London   Toronto   Sydney   Tokyo   Singapore   Madrid
Mexico City   Munich   Paris   Cape Town   Hong Kong   Montreal

Executive Editor: Eric Stano
Supplements Editor: Kristi Olson
Senior Marketing Manager: Megan Galvin-Fak
Cover Designer: John Callahan
Cover image courtesy of Getty Images, Inc.
Manufacturing Manager: Roy Pickering
Printer and Binder: Phoenix Color
Cover Printer: Phoenix Color

*You Decide! 2005—Current Debates in American Government* by John T. Rourke

For permission to use copyrighted material, grateful acknowledgment is made to the copyright holders on pp. 289–291, which are hereby made part of this copyright page.

Please visit our website at http://www.ablongman.com

ISBN 0-321-33343-8

1 2 3 4 5 6 7 8 9 10 - PBT - 07 06 05 04

# TABLE OF CONTENTS

Preface  xv

## 1. CONSTITUTION  2

### GUNS, SAFETY, AND THE CONSTITUTION:
### INDIVIDUAL RIGHT *OR* SUBJECT TO REGULATION?

**Guns, Safety, and the Constitution: Individual Right**

ADVOCATE:   Joyce Malcolm, Professor, Department of History, Bentley College and Senior Fellow, MIT Security Studies Program

SOURCE:   "Infringement," *Common Place*, July 2002

**Guns, Safety, and the Constitution: Subject to Regulation**

ADVOCATE:   Daniel A. Farber, Henry J. Fletcher Professor of Law and Associate Dean of Faculty and Research, University of Minnesota

SOURCE:   "Disarmed by Time: The Second Amendment and the Failure of Originalism," *Chicago-Kent Law Review*, 2000

*Also suitable for chapters on Courts, Civil Liberties, Criminal Justice Policy*

## 2. FEDERALISM  16

### DECIDING ABOUT GAY MARRIAGE:
### MAKE IT A FEDERAL ISSUE *OR* LEAVE IT TO THE STATES?

**Deciding about Gay Marriage: Make It a Federal Issue**

ADVOCATE:   Orrin Hatch, U.S. Senator (R-UT)

SOURCE:   *Congressional Record*, July 9, 2004

**Deciding about Gay Marriage: Leave It to the States**

ADVOCATE:   Patrick Leahy, U.S. Senator (D-VT)

SOURCE:   Statement during hearings on "A Proposed Constitutional Amendment" before the U.S. Senate Judiciary Committee, March 23, 2004

*Also suitable for chapters on Civil Rights, Courts, Constitution*

## 3. CIVIL RIGHTS  34

### BANNING D&X (PARTIAL-BIRTH) ABORTIONS:
### VIOLATING WOMEN'S RIGHTS *OR* PROTECTING FETAL RIGHTS?

**Banning D&X (Partial-Birth) Abortions: Violating Women's Rights**

ADVOCATE:   Center for Reproductive Rights

SOURCE:    Position paper, "Unconstitutional Assault on the Right to Choose: 'Partial-Birth Abortion' Ban Is an Affront to Women and to the U.S. Supreme Court," February 2003

**Banning D&X (Partial-Birth) Abortions: Protecting Fetal Rights**
ADVOCATE:    Kathi A. Aultman, MD, board certified obstetrician gynecologist, and Fellow, American College of Obstetricians and Gynecologists
SOURCE:    Testimony during hearings the "Partial-Birth Abortion Ban Act of 2002" before the U.S. Senate Committee on the Judiciary, Subcommittee on the Constitution, July 9, 2002

*Also suitable for chapters on Courts, American Political Culture/Ideology, Interest Groups*

---

### 4. CIVIL LIBERTIES    56

---

REQUIRING REGISTRATION TO ACCESS INTERNET PORNOGRAPHY: ABRIDGING FREE SPEECH *OR* SAFEGUARDING CHILDREN?

**Requiring Registration to Access Internet Pornography: Abridging Free Speech**
ADVOCATE:    Anthony M. Kennedy, Associate Justice, U.S. Supreme Court
SOURCE:    Opinion in *Ashcroft v. American Civil Liberties Union*, June 29, 2004

**Requiring Registration to Access Internet Pornography: Safeguarding Children**
ADVOCATE:    Stephen G. Breyer, Associate Justice, U.S. Supreme Court
SOURCE:    Opinion in *Ashcroft v. American Civil Liberties Union*, June 29, 2004

*Also suitable for chapters on Courts, Political Culture (freedom v. safety), Criminal Justice*

---

### 5. AMERICAN PEOPLE/POLITICAL CULTURE    72

---

IMMIGRATION AS A THREAT TO "WHO WE ARE": VALID CONCERN *OR* UNFOUNDED FEAR?

**Immigration as a Threat to "Who We Are": Valid Concern**
ADVOCATE:    John O'Sullivan, Editor-in-chief of the *National Interest*
SOURCE:    "Who We Are," *The American Conservative*, July 19, 2004

**Immigration as a Threat to "Who We Are": Unfounded Fear**
ADVOCATE:    Jim Sleeper, Lecturer in Political Science, Yale University
SOURCE:    Review of Samuel Huntington's *Who Are We?: The Challenges to America's National Identity*, History News Network, May 3, 2004

*Also suitable for chapters on Social Policy*

## 6. PUBLIC OPINION/PARTICIPATION   88

### POST-9/11 CRITICISM OF U.S. FOREIGN POLICY: UN-AMERICAN *OR* PATRIOTIC

**Post-9/11 Criticism of U.S. Foreign Policy: Un-American**

ADVOCATE:   Victor Davis Hanson, Shifrin Visiting Professor of Military History, U.S. Naval Academy, Annapolis

SOURCE:   "I Love Iraq, Bomb Texas," *Commentary*, December 2002

**Post-9/11 Criticism of U.S. Foreign Policy: Patriotic**

ADVOCATE:   Gore Vidal, novelist, playwright, and essayist

SOURCE:   "We Are the Patriots," *The Nation*, June 2003

*Also suitable for chapters on Civil Liberties, Foreign Policy*

## 7. MEDIA   104

### USE OF POLLS BY THE MEDIA: OUT OF CONTROL *OR* VALID REPORTING?

**Use of Polls by the Media:  Out of Control**

ADVOCATE:   Lori Robertson, Managing Editor, *American Journalism Review*

SOURCE:   "Poll Crazy," *American Journalism Review*, January/February 2003

**Use of Polls by the Media:  Valid Reporting**

ADVOCATE:   Bill McInturff and Lori Weigel, partners, Public Opinion Strategies, a national survey research firm

SOURCE:   "Servants of the People: Political Leadership and the Public Voice," *Public Perspective*, July/August 2001

*Also suitable for chapters on Elections, Public Opinion, and Policy Process*

## 8. INTEREST GROUPS   116

### ETHNIC FOREIGN POLICY LOBBYING: MISPLACED ALLEGIENCE *OR* ALL-AMERICAN TRADITION?

**Ethnic Foreign Policy Lobbying: Misplaced Allegiance**

ADVOCATE:   Geoffrey Wheatcroft, a British journalist

SOURCE:   "Hyphenated Americans," *Guardian Unlimited* online, April 25, 2000

**Ethnic Foreign Policy Lobbying: All-American Tradition**

ADVOCATE:   Yossi Shain, Aaron and Cecile Goldman Visiting Professor, Georgetown University; Professor of Political Science, Tel Aviv University

SOURCE:   "For Ethnic Americans, The Old Country Calls," *Foreign Service Journal*, October 2000

*Also suitable for chapters on Political Culture and Foreign Policy*

## 9. POLITICAL PARTIES    128

### THE ODDS-ON FAVORITE IN THE FUTURE:
### DEMOCRATS *OR* REPUBLICANS?

**The Odds-On Favorite in the Future: Democrats**

**ADVOCATE:**    John B. Judis, Senior Editor, *The New Republic*, and Ruy Teixeira, Senior Fellow, the Century Foundation

**SOURCE:**    "America's Changing Political Geography: Where Democrats Can Build a Majority," *Blueprint: Ideas for a New Century*, September/October 2002

**The Odds-On Favorite in the Future: Republicans**

**ADVOCATE:**    Daniel Casse, Senior Director, White House Writers Group

**SOURCE:**    "An Emerging Republican Majority?" *Commentary*, January 2003

*Also suitable for chapters on Elections*


## 10. VOTING/CAMPAIGNS/ELECTIONS    146

### THE ELECTORAL COLLEGE: ABOLISH *OR* PRESERVE?

**The Electoral College: Abolish**

**ADVOCATE:**    Becky Cain, President, League of Women Voters

**SOURCE:**    Testimony during hearings on "Proposals for Electoral College Reform: H.J. Res. 28 and H.J. Res. 43" before the U.S. House of Representatives Committee on the Judiciary, Subcommittee on the Constitution, September 4, 1997

**The Electoral College: Preserve**

**ADVOCATE:**    Judith A. Best, Professor of Political Science, State University of New York at Cortland

**SOURCE:**    Testimony during hearings on "Proposals for Electoral College Reform: H.J. Res. 28 and H.J. Res. 43" before the U.S. House of Representatives Committee on the Judiciary, Subcommittee on the Constitution, September 4, 1997

*Also suitable for chapters on Presidency, Federalism*


## 11. CONGRESS    158

### CONGRESSIONAL TERM LIMITS:
### PROMOTING CHOICE *OR* RESTRICTING CHOICE?

**Congressional Term Limits: Promoting Choice**

**ADVOCATE:**    Paul Jacob, Executive Director, U.S. Term Limits

**SOURCE:**    Testimony during hearings on "Limiting Terms of Office for Members of the U.S. Senate and U.S. House of Representatives," before the U.S. House of Representatives, Committee on the Judiciary, Subcommittee on the Constitution, January 22, 1997

**Congressional Term Limits: Restricting Choice**

ADVOCATE:    John R. Hibbing, Professor of Political Science, University of Nebraska

SOURCE:    Testimony during hearings on "Limiting Terms of Office for Members of the U.S. Senate and U.S. House of Representatives," before the U.S. House of Representatives, Committee on the Judiciary, Subcommittee on the Constitution, January 22, 1997

*Also suitable for chapters on Elections*


### 12. PRESIDENCY   170

PRESIDENTIAL WAR POWERS AND TERRORISM:
UNILATERAL AUTHORITY *OR* CONSTITUTIONAL CONSTRAINTS?

**Presidential War Power and Terrorism: Unilateral Authority**

ADVOCATE:    Douglas Kmiec, Dean of the Columbus School of Law, The Catholic University of America

SOURCE:    Testimony during hearings on "Applying the War Powers Resolution to the War on Terrorism," before the U.S. Senate Committee on the Judiciary, April 17, 2002

**Presidential War Power and Terrorism: Constitutional Constraints**

ADVOCATE:    Jane Stromseth, Professor of Law, Georgetown University Law Center

SOURCE:    Testimony during hearings on "Applying the War Powers Resolution to the War on Terrorism," before the U.S. Senate Committee on the Judiciary, April 17, 2002

*Also suitable for chapters on Constitution, Foreign Policy, National Security Policy*


### 13. BUREAUCRACY   186

THE DEPARTMENT OF EDUCATION AND TITLE IX:
CHAMPION OF EQUALITY *OR* OVERZEALOUS CRUSADER?

**The Department of Education and Title IX: Champion of Equality**

ADVOCATE:    Judith Sweet, Vice-President for Championships and Senior Women Administrator, National Collegiate Athletic Association

SOURCE:    U.S. Department of Education, Secretary's Commission on Opportunity in Athletics, Hearings, August 27, 2002

**The Department of Education and Title IX: Overzealous Crusader**

ADVOCATE:    Amanda Ross-Edwards, Visiting Professor of Political Science, Fairfield University

SOURCE:    "The Department of Education and Title IX: Flawed Interpretation and Implementation," an essay written for this volume, October 2003

*Also suitable for chapters on Civil Rights, Education Policy*

## 14. JUDICIARY   198

### LEGAL PHILOSOPHY AS A QUALIFICATION FOR THE BENCH: JUDICIOUS STANDARD *OR* OBSTRUCTIONIST BARRIER?

**Legal Philosophy as a Qualification for the Bench: Judicious Standard**

ADVOCATE:   Laurence H. Tribe, Professor, Harvard Law School

SOURCE:   Testimony during hearings on "Judicial Nominations, Filibusters, and the Constitution: When a Majority Is Denied Its Right to Consent," before U.S. Senate Committee on the Judiciary, May 6, 2002

**Legal Philosophy as a Qualification for the Bench: Obstructionist Barrier**

ADVOCATE:   Todd F. Gaziano, Senior Fellow in Legal Studies and Director, Center for Legal and Judicial Studies, The Heritage Foundation

SOURCE:   Testimony during hearings on "A Judiciary Diminished Is Justice Denied: The Constitution, the Senate, and the Vacancy Crisis in the Federal Judiciary" before U.S. House of Representatives, Committee on the Judiciary, Subcommittee on the Constitution, October 10, 2002

*Also suitable for chapters on Constitution, Congress*

## 15. ECONOMIC POLICY   226

### CONSTITUTIONALLY REQUIRE A BALANCED BUDGET: FISCAL SANITY *OR* FISCAL IRRESPONSIBILITY?

**Constitutionally Require a Balanced Budget: Fiscal Sanity**

ADVOCATE:   William Beach, Director, Center for Data Analysis, Heritage Foundation

SOURCE:   Testimony during hearings on the "Balanced Budget Amendment" before the U.S. House of Representatives Committee on the Judiciary, Subcommittee on the Constitution, March 6, 2003

**Constitutionally Require a Balanced Budget: Fiscal Irresponsibility**

ADVOCATE:   Richard Kogan, Senior Fellow, Center on Budget and Policy Priorities

SOURCE:   Testimony during hearings on the "Balanced Budget Amendment" before the U.S. House of Representatives Committee on the Judiciary, Subcommittee on the Constitution, March 6, 2003

*Also suitable for chapters on Constitution, Congress, Economic Policy*

## 16. CRIMINAL JUSTICE POLICY   238

### THE DEATH PENALTY: RACIALLY BIASED *OR* JUSTICE SERVED?

**The Death Penalty: Racially Biased**

ADVOCATE:   Julian Bond, Professor of History, University of Virginia and Distinguished Professor-in-Residence, American University

**SOURCE:** Testimony during hearings on "Race and the Federal Death Penalty," before the U.S. Senate Committee on the Judiciary, Subcommittee on Constitution, Federalism, and Property Rights, June 13, 2001

### The Death Penalty: Justice Served
**ADVOCATE:** Andrew G. McBride, former U.S. Associate Deputy Attorney General
**SOURCE:** Testimony during hearings on "Race and the Federal Death Penalty," before the U.S. Senate Committee on the Judiciary, Subcommittee on Constitution, Federalism, and Property Rights, June 13, 2001

*Also suitable for chapters on Civil Rights*

---

## 17. EDUCATION POLICY    250

### AFFIRMATIVE ACTION ADMISSIONS:
### PROMOTING EQUALITY *OR* UNFAIR ADVANTAGE?

### Affirmative Action Admissions: Promoting Equality
**ADVOCATE:** 41 College Students and 3 Student Coalitions
**SOURCE:** Amicus Curiae brief to the U.S. Supreme Court in *Grutter v. Bollinger* (2003)

### Affirmative Action Admissions: Unfair Advantage
**ADVOCATE:** 21 Law Professors
**SOURCE:** Amicus Curiae brief to the U.S. Supreme Court in *Grutter v. Bollinger* (2003)

*Also suitable for chapters on Constitution, Civil Rights*

---

## 18. FOREIGN POLICY    264

### TORTURING TERRORISTS:
### SOMETIMES JUSTIFIED *OR* ALWAYS ABHORRENT?

### Torturing Terrorists: Sometimes Justified
**ADVOCATE:** Robert G. Kennedy, Professor of Management, University of St. Thomas
**SOURCE:** "Can Interrogatory Torture Be Morally Legitimate?," paper presented at the Joint Services Conference on Professional Ethics. U.S. Air Force Academy, January 2003

### Torturing Terrorists: Always Abhorrent
**ADVOCATE:** Lisa Hajjar, Professor of Sociology, Law and Society Program, University of California-Santa Barbara
**SOURCE:** "Torture and the Future," *Middle East Report Online*, May 2004

*Also suitable for chapters on Civil Liberties, Criminal Justice, National Security Policy*

**CREDITS   289**

# EXTENDED TABLE OF CONTENTS

## WEB ISSUES

The following topics are available on the Web at:
http://www.ablongman.com/YouDecide/

### 19. DECIDING POLICY

### ADOPT DIRECT DEMOCRACY *OR* REMAIN A REPUBLIC?

**Deciding Policy: Adopt Direct Democracy**

ADVOCATE:  Harlan Hahn, Professor of Political Science, University of Southern California

SOURCE:  Testimony during hearings, "Voter Initiative Constitutional Amendment," before the U.S. Senate Committee on the Judiciary, Subcommittee on the Constitution, December 13, 1977

**Deciding Policy: Remain a Republic**

ADVOCATE:  Peter G. Fish, Professor of Political Science, Duke University

SOURCE:  Testimony during hearings, "Voter Initiative Constitutional Amendment," before the U.S. Senate Committee on the Judiciary, Subcommittee on the Constitution, December 13, 1977

*Suitable for chapters on Introduction, Constitution, Political Participation, Policymaking*

### 20. CONSTITUTIONAL AMENDMENTS

### LET STATES INITIATE *OR* KEEP CURRENT PROCESS?

**Constitutional Amendments: Let States Initiate**

ADVOCATE:  Nelson Lund, Professor, George Mason University School of Law

SOURCE:  Testimony during hearings, "Procedures for State Initiation of Constitutional Amendments," before the U.S. House of Representatives, Committee on the Judiciary, Subcommittee on the Constitution, March 28, 1988

**Constitutional Amendments: Keep Current Process**

ADVOCATE:  Representative Mickey Edwards (R-MA) and Louis Michael Seidman, Professor, Georgetown University Law Center, on behalf of Citizens for the Constitution, nonpartisan organization devoted to fostering public discussion concerning amendments to the Constitution

SOURCE:  Testimony during hearings, "Procedures for State Initiation of Constitutional Amendments," before the U.S. House of Representatives, Committee on the Judiciary, Subcommittee on the Constitution, March 28, 1988

*Suitable for chapters on Constitution, Federalism*

## 21. PROPORTIONAL REPRESENTATION

### ADVANCE OF DEMOCRACY *OR* DESTABILIZING IDEA?

**Proportional Representation: Advance of Democracy**

ADVOCATE:    Theodore S. Arrington, Professor of Political Science, University of North Carolina at Charlotte

SOURCE:    Testimony during hearings on the "H.R. 1173/States' Choice of Voting Systems Act" before the U.S. House of Representatives Committee on the Judiciary, Subcommittee on the Constitution, September 23, 1999

**Proportional Representation: Destabilizing Idea**

ADVOCATE:    Abigail Thernstrom, Senior Fellow, Manhattan Institute

SOURCE:    Testimony during hearings on "H.R. 1173/States' Choice of Voting Systems Act," before the U.S. House of Representatives Committee on the Judiciary, Subcommittee on the Constitution, September 23, 1999

*Suitable for chapters on Elections, Congress*

## 22. ANTI-TERRORIST LEGISLATION

### THREAT TO CIVIL LIBERTIES *OR* CONSTITUTIONAL SHIELD?

**Anti-Terrorist Legislation: Threat to Civil Liberties**

ADVOCATE:    Bob Barr, former member of the U.S. House of Representatives (R-GA)

SOURCE:    Testimony during hearings on, "America after 9/11: Freedom Preserved or Freedom Lost?" before the U.S. Senate Committee on the Judiciary, November 2003

**Anti-Terrorist Legislation: Constitutional Shield**

ADVOCATE:    James B. Comey, Deputy Attorney General of the United States

SOURCE:    Testimony during hearings on "Preventing And Responding to Acts of Terrorism: A Review of Current Law" before the U.S. Senate Committee on the Judiciary, April 2004

*Also suitable for chapters on Courts, Political Culture (freedom v. safety), Criminal Justice, National Security*

## 23. REGULATING THE CAMPAIGN FINANCE ACTIVITY OF NONPROFIT ORGANIZATIONS

### NEEDED REFORM *OR* OPPRESSIVE RESTRICTION?

**Needed Reform**

ADVOCATE:    Donald B. Tobin, Professor, Moritz College of Law, Ohio State University

SOURCE:    "Comments on Proposed Rulemaking Notice 2004–5 and Request to Testify," e-mail letter to the Federal Elections Commission, April 5, 2004

## Oppressive Restriction

ADVOCATE:   415 civil rights, environmental, civil liberties, women's rights, public
            health, social welfare, religious, consumer, senior, and social service
            organizations

SOURCE:     "Comments and Request to Testify Concerning Notice of Proposed
            Rulemaking on Political Committee Status," e-mail letter to the
            Federal Elections Commission, April 5, 2004

*Suitable for chapters on Bureaucracy, Civil Liberties, Elections, Interest Groups*

## 24.  BECOMING PRESIDENT

### NATURAL-BORN CITIZENS ONLY *OR* ALL CITIZENS?

### Becoming President: Natural-Born Citizens Only

ADVOCATE:   Forrest McDonald, Distinguished University Research Professor of
            History at the University of Alabama

SOURCE:     Testimony during hearings on "Constitutional Amendment to Allow
            Foreign-Born Citizens to Be President," before the U.S. House of
            Representatives Committee on the Judiciary, Subcommittee on the
            Constitution, July 24, 2000

### Becoming President: All Citizens

ADVOCATE:   John Yinger, Professor of Economics and Public Administration. The
            Maxwell School, Syracuse University

SOURCE:     Testimony during hearings on "Constitutional Amendment to Allow
            Foreign-Born Citizens to Be President," before the U.S. House of
            Representatives Committee on the Judiciary, Subcommittee on the
            Constitution, July 24, 2000

*Suitable for chapters on Civil Liberties, Political Culture, Elections, Presidency*

# PREFACE

## To the Students

This book is founded on two firm convictions. The first is that each of you who read this book is profoundly affected by politics, probably in more ways than you know. The second "truth" is that it is important that everyone be attentive to and active in politics.

### POLITICS AFFECTS YOU

The outcome of many of the 18 debates in this printed volume and the 6 supplemental debates on the Web will impact your life directly. If you play college sports, for example, the controversy over Title IX in **Debate 13** helps determine what teams and athletic scholarship support are available at your school. Similarly, the issue of affirmative action in **Debate 17** may influence your admission to graduate school, if that is the course you take. More generally, **Debate 15** over whether there should be a balanced budget amendment to the U.S. Constitution will play a role in what taxes you pay and what services you receive from the government. Such an amendment might, for example, reduce the availability of Pell Grants and other financial support for college students. It is also college-age students who are most likely to be sent to and to die in wars. There has not been a military draft since the Vietnam War era, and U.S. casualties have been relatively light in wars since then. But in that war, 61% of the more than the 58,000 Americans killed were between the ages of 17 and 21. **Debate 12** addresses who gets to decide if Americans will be sent to war. Under current political and constitutional realities, the answer is, "usually the president." Are you comfortable with that, personally or as a citizen in a democracy? **Debate 22** also address presidential powers and would enhance them if the suggestion of one advocate that the president be giving a line-time veto were to be adopted.

### PAY ATTENTION TO THE POLICY PROCESS

Process may seem less interesting than policy to many people, but you do not have to study politics very long to learn that *who* decides something very often determines *what* the policy will be. Process does not always determine which policy is adopted, but plays a large role. Therefore, there are a number of debates in this volume whose outcome does not directly affect a specific policy, but which could have a profound impact on the policy process. For example, what excites most people about **Debate 2** is the issue of same-sex marriages. But there is also a substantial issue of federalism centering on the division of power between the Washington, D.C. and the state governments in the federal system. **Debate 20** also addresses federalism, and one advocate proposes to strengthen the states by allowing the Constitution to be amended without the involvement of Congress.

Policy is also a reflection, in part, of who serves, and Debates 10, 11, and 21 all focus on that issue. If the Electoral College had been earlier abolished, which is the topic of **Debate 10**, then Al Gore, not George Bush, would have won the presidency in 2000. Both advocates in **Debate 11** argue that they want to give you more choice as to who will represent you in Congress but they disagree about how. One advocate says the way to do it is to limit the term of federal legislators so that there will be regular turnover. The other advocate replies that doing so will limit your ability to be represented for many terms by an effective legislator whom you support. **Debate 21** takes up changing to a proportional representation system of elections. If adopted that would loosen, if not break the seeming strangle-hold that the Republicans and Democrats have on who gets elected. Indeed, such a change might make **Debate 9** on whether the Democrats or Republicans are likely to be the dominant party in the foreseeable future a moot point. Public opinion polls are a relatively new part of the policy process, and **Debate 7** takes up the issue of whether the huge number of polls now taken advance democracy or detract from it by distracting attention from the issues and influencing elections.

## YOU CAN AND SHOULD AFFECT POLITICS

The second thing that this volume preaches is that you can and should take part in politics. You should strive to become involved in the policy process. Anti-terrorist legislation is the subject of **Debate 22**, and many critics think that the freedoms of Americans are threatened by the Patriot Act enacted soon after the 9/11 terror attacks and by Patriot Act II, which the Bush administration has proposed. Others reply that such fears are overblown and that the minor restrictions on civil liberties in the bills help keep Americans safer from terrorism. Whatever your view, your liberties and life are involved, and you can become active in defeating or promoting the necessary renewal of Patriot Act I and the enactment of Patriot Act II.

Other debates may influence your ability to be active. Some people criticize those Americans who feel a strong tie to the land of their heritage and who favor U.S. policies that favor that land. Whether doing so is misplaced allegiance or an all-American tradition is taken up in **Debate 8** on ethnic lobbying. Another line of criticism is leveled at those who dissent from announced policy, especially during time of foreign policy crisis. The advocates in **Debate 6** differ on whether such dissent is un-American or patriotic.

**Debate 23** about campaign finance reform also addresses participation. Those who argue that there should be strict limits on how much people and organizations can give to political candidates claim that the impact of money on politics makes a mockery of the idea that all citizens should have an equal say. Opponents rejoin that the proposed restrictions violate their freedom of speech. This issue is followed by a discussion in **Debate 24** about who can participate in perhaps the ultimate way: seeking the country's highest office, the presidency. Arnold Schwarzenegger may have been able to get elected as governor of California in October 2003, but as a foreign-born citizen he is constitutionally barred from becoming president. Should that barrier be eliminated? Perhaps more than any other issue, **Debate 19** relates to the idea that would most radically change participation in this country. That is instituting direct democracy by allowing the people as a whole to make law directly through processes called initiatives and referendums.

## THERE ARE OFTEN MORE THAN TWO SIDES TO A QUESTION

Often public policy questions are put in terms of "pro and con," "favor or oppose," or some other such stark choice. This approach is sometimes called a Manichean approach, a reference to Manicheanism, a religion founded by the Persian prophet Mani (c. 216–276). It taught "dualism," the idea the universe is divided into opposite, struggling, and equally powerful realities, light (good) and darkness (evil).

The view here is that many policy issues are more a matter of degree, and the opinion of people is better represented as a place along a range of possibilities rather than an up or down Manichean choice. Numerous debates herein are like that. For example, surveys of the American people about abortion, the subject of **Debate 3**, find that only a small minority of people is staunchly pro-choice or pro-life. The majority have a nuanced view that, on the one hand, supports women being able to terminate their pregnancies but that, on the other hand, reflects reservations based on timing and circumstances. Opinion is also something like that about the death penalty, the focus of **Debate 16**. A large majority of Americans favor it, but surveys also show that people are troubled by a range of possible injustices such as the relationship of wealth to the ability to mount a top notch defense, the ability to execute people for crimes committed while a juvenile, and claims of racial injustice. **Debate 18** is also arguably about moral relativism. Torture is an ugly word, but would it be acceptable to extract information by torturing a terrorist to save innocent lives, and if so, are there limits to the torture?

## MANY ISSUES HAVE MULTIPLE ASPECTS

Often political issues are sort of like matryoshkas, the Russian nested dolls in which a doll comes apart revealing a smaller doll inside, inside in which there is another doll, and so on. **Debate 1** is about "the right to bear arms." At its most specific, the issue is whether individuals have such a right. But deciding that involves the larger question of how to decide what those who wrote the Second Amendment meant. That matter, in turn, takes us to an even larger debate about whether we should follow the literal intent of those who wrote constitutional language, most of which is more than two centuries old, or apply the language of the Constitution within the context of the 21st century. In much the same way, **Debate 14**, on qualifications for the bench, has some specific and historical aspects, such what the phrase "advice and consent" of the Senate means. There are also matters of narrow constitutional controversy over whether the Senate parliamentary tactic called a filibuster is permissible as a way for a minority of senators to block the judicial nominees of the president. These smaller, albeit important, matters fall within the larger question of ideology and partisan politics in the selection and confirmation or rejection of judges by the Senate.

The discussion in **Debate 5** over whether immigrants threaten to fragment American cultural identity is also multifaceted. It is just part of a larger question about what being an American means. The idea of the "melting pot" is not attractive to everyone because, to them, melting into the culture means giving up their own and adopting the largely European-based culture that has so far defined Americans.

## SOME CONCLUDING THOUGHTS

The points with which we began are important enough to reiterate. Whether you care about politics or not, it affects you every day in many ways. As the legendary heavyweight boxer Joe Louis put it after knocking out Billy Conn, a more agile but less powerful opponent, in their 1941 championship fight, "You can run, but you can't hide."

Simply paying attention is a good start, but taking action is even better. Everyone should be politically active, at least to the level of voting. Doing so is in your self-interest because decisions made by the federal, state, and local governments in the U.S. political system provide each of us with both tangible benefits (such as roads and schools) and intangible benefits (such as civil liberties and security). Also, for good or ill, the government takes things away from each of us (such as taxes) and restricts our actions (such as speed limits). It is also the case in politics that, as the old saying goes, squeaky wheels get the grease. Those who participate actively are more likely to be influential. Those who do not, and young adults are by far the age group least likely to even vote, are cosigned to grumbling impotently on the sideline.

As an absolute last thought (really!), let me encourage you to contact me with questions or comments. My e-mail address is john.rourke@uconn.edu. Compliments are always great, but if you disagree with anything I have written or my choice of topics or have a suggestion for the next edition, let me know. Thanks!

## To the Faculty

Having plied the podium, so to speak, for three decades, I have some well-formed ideas of what a good reader should do. It is from that perspective that I have organized this reader to work for the students who read it and the faculty members who adopt it for use in their classes. Below are what I look for in a reader and how I have constructed this one to meet those standards.

### PROVOKE CLASS DISCUSSION

The classes I have enjoyed the most over the years have been the ones that have been the liveliest, with students participating enthusiastically in a give and take among themselves and with me. Many of the debates herein have been selected to engender such participation in your classes by focusing on hot-button topics that provoke heated debate even among those who are not heavily involved in politics and who do not have a lot of background on the topic. The very first topic, gun laws, in Debate 1, is just such a subject. More than once I have had students get into spirited exchanges over the "right to bear arms," so I thought it would be a great debate to open the volume. Just a few of the other hot-button topics are abortion (Debate 3), immigration (Debate 5), the impact of Title IX on college athletics (Debate 13), and the death penalty (Debate 16). I hope they rev up your classes as much as they have energized mine.

Another point about class discussion as I point out in the Preface section "To the Students," is that while the debate titles imply two sides, many policy topics are not a Manichean choice between yes and no. Instead, I have tried to include many issues on which opinion ranges along a scale. From that perspective, I often urge students to try to formulate a policy that can gain majority support if not a consensus. You will also find that many of the issues herein are multifaceted, and I try to point that out to the students. For instance, the debate about gun control is more than about weapons, it is also about how we interpret and apply the Constitution.

### PROVIDE A GOOD RANGE OF TOPICS

I always look for a reader that "covers the waterfront," and have tried to put together this reader to do that. There are numerous debates on specific policy issues and others on process. All the major institutions are covered in one or more debates, and there are also debates touching on such "input" elements as parties, campaigns, interest groups, and the media. The primary focus of the reader is on the national government, but federalism also receives attention in Debates 2 and 20. I have also included several debates that are at the intersection of domestic and foreign affairs, including Debate 4 (anti-terrorist legislation), Debate 6 (the acceptability of dissent during foreign crises), Debate 12 (presidential war powers), and Debate 18 (torturing terrorists).

My sense of a good range of topics also means balancing hot-button topics with others that, while they will draw less of an emotional response, are important to debate because they give insight about how the system works and might work differently. Debate 2 on federalism is an example, and hopefully it will get students to think about the federal system, which my experience tells me they mostly take as an unchanging given. Another example is the idea presented in Debate 21 of going from a single-member district, plurality electoral system to a proportional representation system.

## GIVE THE STUDENTS SOME BACKGROUND FOR THE READING

Readers that work well provide the students with some background material that is located just before the reading. This debate volume follows that scheme. There is a two-page introduction to each debate that establishes its context. As part of this set up, each introduction provides the students with several "points to ponder" as they read the debates.

Moreover, the introductions do more than just address the topic per se. Instead they try to connect it to the chapter of the text for which it is designed. For example, the introduction to Debate 14 on the tensions between President Bush and the Senate Democrats over judicial nominations begins with the power of the judiciary in the U.S. political system and how that makes judicial appointments such a high-stakes issue.

## PROVIDE FOLLOW-UP POSSIBILITIES

One of the rewards of our profession is seeing students get excited about a field that intrigues us, and the reader provides a "continuing debate" section after each of the reading pairs. This section has three parts. "What Is New" provides an update of what has occurred since the date(s) of the two articles. "Where to Find More" points students to places to explore the topic further. I have particularly emphasized resources that can be accessed on the Internet on the theory that students are more likely to pursue a topic if they can do so via computer than by walking to the library. Needless to say, I think libraries are great and students should have to use them, so there are also numerous references to books and academic journals. Finally, the continuing debate section has a "What More to Do" part. This segment presents topics for discussion, suggests projects (like finding out how well your school is doing by Title IX standards), and advises how to get active on a topic.

## FIT WITH THE COURSE

I favor readers that fit the course I am teaching. I prefer a book with readings that supplement all or most of the major topics on the syllabus and that also allows me to spread the reading out so that it is evenly distributed throughout the semester. To that end, this book is organized to parallel the outline of the major introduction to American politics texts in use today. For those who favor the foundations-politics-institutions-policy approach, the table of contents of this volume should match almost exactly with their text and syllabus. For those who use a foundations-institutions-politics-policy scheme, a little, but not much, adjustment will synchronize the debates herein with their plans. Moreover to help with that, I have labeled each debate in the Table of Contents with the syllabus topic that fits with the debate. Additionally, for the 18 debates in the printed edition, I have indicated alternative syllabus topic for each. I have also made suggestions about how each of the six debates on the Web might fit with various text chapters and syllabus topics.

## FLEXIBILITY

While there is a fair amount of similarity in the organization of the major introduction to American politics texts, I suspect that the syllabi of faculty members are a good deal more individualistic. With that in mind, I have provided flexibility in the reader. First, there are 18 debates in the printed edition, each which is related to a topic, but each of which has suggestions in the table of contents for alternative assignment. Then there are 6 additional readings on the Longman Web site associated with *You Decide!* Each of these also has multiple uses and my suggestions about how to work them into your syllabus. Thus, you can use all 24 debates or many fewer, you can substitute some on the Web for some in the printed edition, you can follow the order in the book fairly closely with most texts or you can rearrange the order at will. As the Burger King slogan goes, "Have it Your Way!"

As a final note, let me solicit your feedback. The first edition of any text or reader is always a bit of a prototype, and I consider *You Decide!* to be a work in progress. My e-mail address is john.rourke@uconn.edu. Of course I will be pleased to hear about the things you like, but I and the next edition of the reader will surely benefit more from hearing how I could have done better and what topics (and/or readings) would be good in the next edition. Thanks!

# CONSTITUTION

## GUNS, SAFETY, AND THE CONSTITUTION:
### Individual Right *or* Subject to Regulation?

### INDIVIDUAL RIGHT

**ADVOCATE:** Joyce Malcolm, Professor, Department of History, Bentley
College and Senior Fellow, MIT Security Studies Program

**SOURCE:** "Infringement," *Common Place*, July 2002

### SUBJECT TO REGULATION

**ADVOCATE:** Daniel A. Farber, Henry J. Fletcher Professor of Law and
Associate Dean of Faculty and Research, University of Minnesota

**SOURCE:** "Disarmed by Time: The Second Amendment and the Failure of
Originalism," *Chicago-Kent Law Review*, 2000

In the early days of World War II, British Prime Minister Winston S. Churchill
famously described the Soviet Union as a "riddle wrapped in a mystery inside an
enigma." Had he been commenting on the current debate in the United States over
gun control, Churchill might have used the same words to describe it.

The riddle, so to speak, is the meaning of the words of the Second Amendment
to the U.S. Constitution: "A well regulated Militia, being necessary to the security of
a free State, the right of the people to keep and bear Arms, shall not be infringed."
Ask yourself, for example, Does "people" mean individuals, or does it refer to the collective citizenry, as in "We the people"?

The mystery is what, if anything, the framers of the U.S. Constitution and the
Bill of Rights intended the amendment to accomplish. Scholars disagree mightily
about this issue.

The enigma is whether the lawmakers of the late 1700s would argue that 21st
century Americans should be bound by the literal meaning of words written more
than 200 years ago, or should interpret them in the light of modern circumstances.

We might look to the courts to unravel these issues, but they have not been crys-
tal clear. Generally, they have upheld the authority of government to regulate the
ownership of weapons, but the Supreme Court has never ruled directly on the essence
of the Second Amendment. To date, the most important case has been *United States
v. Miller* (1939), in which the Supreme Court upheld a provision of the National
Firearms Act (1934) requiring registration of sawed-off shotguns. The majority opinion held that "in the absence of any evidence…that possession [of a sawed-off] shot-
gun…has some reasonable relationship to…a well-regulated militia, we cannot say
that the Second Amendment guarantees the right to keep and bear such an instrument." Notice that the opinion neither denies nor affirms a right to bear arms. It only
rules that sawed-off shotguns are not protected, leaving it unclear if other weapons
might be.

Most recently, gun control opponents were buoyed by the decision of the Fifth U.S. Circuit Court of Appeals in *United States v. Emerson* (2001). The majority opinion construed the word "people" in the Second Amendment to mean individuals, and said that the clause, "necessary to a well regulated militia," served merely to explain why individuals had the right to keep and bear arms. Still, it was a mixed case, because the judges also upheld the specific federal law that barred Timothy Emerson from owning a firearm based on his history of domestic violence. When the Supreme Court declined to hear Emerson's appeal, as it does in most cases, the major constitutional issues were left largely unresolved. In essence, no Supreme Court decision, including *Miller*, has definitively ruled either that there is an unrestricted right of individuals to keep and bear arms or that government has the unchecked authority to regulate, or even abolish, gun ownership and use.

What would you decide? Considering weapons is one way to start thinking about these policy and constitutional issues. There can be no doubt that weapons have changed. Flintlock pistols and rifles were the personal firearms when the amendment was written in 1789. Today's weapons have much faster firing rates and higher muzzle velocities and, therefore, vastly greater killing power than did their forerunners.

The presence and role of weapons in America is another piece of the puzzle. The latest data indicate that approximately 4.9 million firearms (including 1.7 million handguns) are manufactured or imported for the domestic U.S. market annually. In all, there are about 200 million privately and legally owned firearms in the United States, about 30% of which are handguns. Between 40% and 50% of all households have a legal gun. The uncertain but significant number of illegal weapons adds to these totals.

As for the yearly use of firearms, most are either never fired or are used for target shooting or hunting. But statistics also indicate that 29,477 people died in the United States in 2001 as a result of a gunshot. Most (57%) were suicides. Of the remaining gunshot deaths, 38% were homicides, 3% were accidents, and about 1% each was for unknown causes or by "legal intervention" of law enforcement officers. Left unclear in the government data is what percentage of the "homicides" was committed by individuals exercising their lawful right of self-defense.

## POINTS TO PONDER

➤ The most specific debate is about gun control policy and whether widespread gun ownership provides greater or less safety. Given your views on this issue, would you vote for a bill in Congress to ban the manufacture, importation, sale, and possession of all handguns?

➤ At a second level, the debate is about the specifics of the Second Amendment and the intent of those who drafted and ratified it. What do the two advocates claim that those who wrote the language of the Second Amendment intended it to mean?

➤ The third, most general, and most important dispute is over whether the Constitution is a fixed document whose meaning should be derived by "strict construction" of its words and the original intention of those wrote it, or whether the Constitution is a "living document" that it should be interpreted in light of modern realities. What is your view? Should we be bound in the first decade of the 21st century by what people meant in the last decade of the 19th century when the Second Amendment was added to the Constitution?

# Guns, Safety, and the Constitution:
## Individual Right

JOYCE MALCOLM

In April 1995, I joined three other scholars testifying before the U.S. House Judiciary Committee's Subcommittee on Crime about our research into the meaning of the Second Amendment. As we gave evidence that the Second Amendment guaranteed an individual right to be armed and why the Founders believed it essential, the Republican members of the committee listened politely and with interest. Every Democrat on the committee, however, turned upon us with outrage and disdain. I felt startled and dismayed. The meaning of the amendment, at least for these representatives, seemed less a matter of evidence than of party politics. Sitting opposite us, arguing against an individual right, Dennis Henigan, general counsel for Handgun Control, Inc., presented the committee with a full-page advertisement from the *New York Times* signed by scores of scholars denying that a right to be armed existed. At this juncture one of my co-panelists, Daniel Polsby, then a professor at Northwestern School of Law, pointed out that one signer, a colleague of his, was no expert on constitutional law, let alone the Second Amendment, and that to his knowledge none of the other signers had ever conducted research into the issue. For the scholars who put their names to that testimonial, the conviction that there was no individual right to be armed was an article of faith. The attitudes of both the politicians and the scholars are regrettable. We are all the losers when constitutional interpretation becomes so politicized that otherwise reasonable people are neither willing to accept, nor interested in historical truth.

Political wrangles over the limits of constitutional guarantees are common, proper, and even necessary. The battle over the Second Amendment, however, is being waged at a more basic level, the very meaning of the amendment. This too is understandable where there is doubt about the Framers' intent. But once evidence of that intent is clear, as it now is, further argument, even in the service of a worthy political agenda, is reprehensible. It becomes an attempt to revise the Constitution by misreading, rather than amending it, a precedent that puts all our rights at risk. The argument over the Second Amendment has now reached that stage. But first, some background.

Two important points should be kept in mind as we briefly review this history. First, the debate over the meaning of the Second Amendment is surprisingly recent. Second, many of those who question or disparage the right do so because they believe that guns, in and of themselves, cause crime. Until the end of the nineteenth century, few Americans doubted their right to be armed. The Founders believed privately owned weapons were necessary to protect the three great and primary rights, "personal security, personal liberty, and private property." An armed people could protect themselves and their neighbors against crime and their liberties against tyranny. [James] Madison and his colleagues converted their English right to "have Armes for their defence Suitable to their Condition, and as allowed by Law," into a broader protection that took no account of status and forbade "infringement." "As civil rulers, not having their duty to the people duly before them, may attempt to tyrannize," the *Philadelphia Federal Gazette* explained when the proposed amendment was first publicized, "and as the military forces which must be occasionally raised to defend our country, might pervert their power to the injury of their fellow citizens, the people are confirmed...in their right to keep and bear their private arms." In the 1820s William Rawle, who had been offered the post of attorney general by George Washington, found, "No clause in the constitution could by any rule of construction be conceived to give Congress a power to disarm the people. Such a flagitious attempt could only be made under some general pretense by a state legislature. But if in any blind pursuit of inordinate power, either should attempt it, this amendment may be appealed to as a restraint on both." Supreme Court Justice Joseph Story, writing in 1840, agreed that the right of the people to keep and bear arms had "justly been considered, as the palladium of the liberties of a republic." And after the Civil War, the charge Southern whites were depriving blacks of their right to be armed was instrumental in convincing Congress to pass the Fourteenth Amendment.

Then politics intervened. Early in the twentieth century when American whites, fearful of blacks in the South and the millions of foreign immigrants in the North, wanted to restrict access to firearms, alternative reading of the amendment gained credence. In the absence of serious scholarship, constructions that reduced or eliminated the individual right to be armed seemed plausible, especially in light of the awkward construction of the Second Amendment and the sparse congressional debates during its drafting, both of which relied upon common understandings of the value of a society of armed individuals that had faded over time. These new interpretations emphasized the dependent clause referring to the militia, to the neglect of the main clause's guarantee to the people. The theory developed that the Second Amendment was merely intended to enhance state control over state militia; that it embodied a "collective right" for members of a "well-regulated" militia—today's National Guard—to be armed, not a personal right for members of a militia of the whole people, let alone for any individual. Even when an individual right was conceded, the amendment was proclaimed a useless anachronism. After all, twentieth-century Americans had the police to protect them while armed individuals would be helpless against a government bent on oppression.

Beset by fears and armed with alternative readings of the Second Amendment, restrictive gun legislation followed. In 1911 New York State passed the Sullivan Law that made it a felony to carry a concealed weapon without a license, or to own or purchase a handgun without obtaining a certificate. Discriminatory laws in the South kept blacks disarmed. The first federal gun legislation, the National Firearms Act of 1934, introduced controls on automatic weapons, sawed-off rifles and shotguns, and silencers, weapons popular with gangsters. It was more than thirty years before rising crime-rates, urban riots, and three political assassinations again led to demands for stricter federal firearms legislation. The resulting Gun Control Act of 1968 limited mail-order sales, the purchase of firearms by felons, and the importation of military weapons. Professor Robert Cottrol [historian and legal scholar] finds this statute "something of a watershed" for, since its passage, the debate over gun control and the right to be armed have become "semi-permanent features" of late twentieth century American life. And "semi-permanent" the debate remains as we enter the twenty-first century.

The argument over the Second Amendment became and remains intense and highly political because the stakes are so great. Americans suffer from a high rate of armed crime that many insist is caused, or made worse, by easy access to firearms. Eliminate these, the thinking goes, and streets will be safer. Thousands of federal, state, and local firearms regulations adorn statute books, but a Second Amendment guarantee of the right to be armed blocks the dramatic reduction or banning of firearms that gun-control groups seek. There is a deep desire on their part to believe no individual right exists. On the other side, the traditional belief that guns protect the innocent and deter offenders is even more widely accepted. Studies show the majority of Americans have always believed the Constitution guarantees them a right to be armed. Approximately half of America's households have at least one gun, an estimated arsenal of some 200–240 million weapons, kept for sport and, more crucially, for personal protection. Every new threat to regulate weapons provokes thousands of additional purchases.

Both sides seek a safer nation. But whether one believes guns cause crime or prevent it, the Second Amendment figures in political solution at every level. National elections turn on a candidate's position on the right to be armed. A small Illinois town bans handguns completely; a small Georgia town requires a gun in every home. The state of Vermont, with no gun restrictions at all, boasts the lowest crime rate in the nation. In the name of public safety, the cities of New York, Chicago, Boston, and Washington, D.C., impose ever tighter gun restrictions. In the name of public safety, thirty-three states—some two thirds—now allow every law-abiding citizen to carry a concealed weapon. Is an

individual right to be armed an anachronism? Not in their opinion. Other states are considering this option.

In this clash of strategies, political gestures and competing claims abound. The Clinton administration allocated millions of dollars for gun buy-back programs, knowing a Justice Department study found this approach ineffective. Flushed with the success of lawsuits against tobacco companies, public officials in thirty-one municipalities sued gun manufacturers claiming millions in damages for gun crimes. In response, twenty-six states passed legislation forbidding such suits. Philanthropic foundations finance research that favors gun control, some even establishing whole institutes for "the prevention of violence." Notwithstanding plummeting rates of gun homicides, leading medical journals publish articles that proclaim guns a health emergency. They print seriously flawed research that purports to demonstrate that the presence of a firearm transforms peaceful citizens into killers, although studies of police records show the great majority of murderers are individuals with a long history of violence.

Nor has the popular press been shy in broadcasting its preferences. For seventy-seven consecutive days in the fall of 1989, the *Washington Post* published editorials calling for stricter gun controls. This was something of a record, but it is indicative of a national media in which three-quarters of the newspapers and most of the periodical press have advocated severe curbs on gun ownership and have denied a right to be armed exists. The press is entitled to its opinions, but unfortunately this bias has often affected and distorted news coverage. Every gun accident or shooting, every study that supports gun restrictions, is intensively reported, while defensive uses of firearms are downplayed along with scholarly investigations that tabulate these or that call into question the notion that legally owned firearms increase violent crime.

As a result, much conventional wisdom about the use and abuse of guns is simply wrong. Such reporting, for example, gives the impression that gun accidents involving young children are common and increasing when, in fact, they are happily rare and declining. The same is true of gun violence in schools. Do guns cause violence? In the thirty-year period from 1968 through 1997 as the stock of civilian firearms rose by 262%, fatal gun accidents dropped by 68.9%. Numerous surveys have shown that far more lives are saved than lost by privately owned guns. And John Lott's meticulous study of the impact of statutes permitting citizens to carry concealed weapons found them of value in reducing armed crime. Yet, convinced advocates are unwilling to examine the evidence of the constitutional protection or studies that contradict their view of the danger of private gun use.

All this has taken its toll. Alone among the articles comprising the Bill of Rights, the Second Amendment has, in recent years, come very near to being eliminated from the Constitution, not through the prescribed process of amendment, but through interpretations that reduced it to a meaningless anachronism. The low point came in 1975 when a committee of the American Bar Association was so befuddled by competing interpretations that members concluded, "It is doubtful that the Founding Fathers had any intent in mind with regard to the meaning of this Amendment." Leading textbooks on constitutional law, such as that by Lawrence Tribe, had literally relegated the Second Amendment to a footnote. Yet the American people remained convinced of their right to be armed despite textbooks and newspaper advertisements to the contrary.

Now scholarship has come to the rescue. The past twenty-five years have witnessed a growing number of studies of the Second Amendment, and these have found overwhelming evidence that it was meant to guarantee an individual right to be armed. In 1997, Supreme Court Justice Clarence Thomas in *Printz v. United States,* noting that the Court "has not had recent occasion to consider the nature of the substantive right safeguarded by the Second Amendment," hoped, "Perhaps, at some future date, this Court will have the opportunity to determine whether Justice Story was correct when he wrote that the right to bear arms 'has justly been considered, as the palladium of the liberties of a republic.'" Thomas added, "[A]n impressive array of historical evidence, a growing body of scholarly commentary indicates that the 'right to keep and bear arms' is, as the Amendment's text suggests, a personal right." Such evidence includes the individual right to be armed inherited from England; Madison's intent to list the right to be armed with other individual rights, rather than in the article dealing with the militia; his reference to his proposed rights as "guards for private rights"; the Senate's rejection of an amendment to tack the phrase "for the common defense" to the "right of the people to keep and bear arms"; and numerous contemporary comments. By contrast, no contemporary evidence has been found that only a collective right for members of a militia was intended. The evidence has convinced our leading constitutional scholars, among them Lawrence Tribe, Akhil Amar, and Leonard Levy, that the Second Amendment protects an individual right. In March 1999, Judge Sam Cummings of the Fifth Circuit [of the U.S. Court of Appeals], in the case of *United States v. Timothy Joe Emerson*, found a federal statute violated an individual's Second Amendment rights. The Fifth Circuit Court of Appeals, in a meticulously researched opinion, agreed that the Second Amendment protected an individual right to keep arms. As the [state] Court of Appeals in Ohio pointed out when, in April 2002, it found Ohio's prohibition against carrying a concealed weapon unconstitutional, "We are not a country where power is maintained by people with guns over people without guns."

Since the evidence clearly shows an individual right was intended, we should now move on to discuss the prudent limits of that right. Yet that discussion can't take place because denials of that right continue along with ever more tenuous theories to refute it, claims that the phrase "bear arms" was used exclusively in a military context; that the amendment resulted from a conspiracy between Northern and Southern states to control slaves; and that since the phrase "the right of the people to keep and bear arms" is set off by a comma it can be eliminated. But in early American discourse, as today, "bear arms" often meant simply carrying a weapon; there is no direct evidence of any conspiracy; and the elimination of every phrase set off by commas would play havoc with constitutional interpretation. [Historian] Michael Bellesiles claimed to have evidence there were few guns in early America, Americans were uninterested in owning them, and therefore no individual right to be armed could have been intended. However, his results seriously underestimate numbers of weapons and distort the attitudes toward them. Other scholars looking through some of the same evidence have found widespread ownership of guns.

Why does debate over original intent continue? Lawrence Tribe, who concluded there is an individual right after considering the new evidence, points to the "true poignancy," "the inescapable tension, for many people on both sides of this policy divide, between the reading of the Second Amendment that would advance the policies they favor and the reading of the Second Amendment to which intellectual honesty, and their own theories of constitutional interpretation, would drive them if they could bring themselves to set their policy convictions aside." The time has come for those who deny an individual right exists to set policy convictions aside in favor of intellectual honesty—and a more productive discussion.

# Guns, Safety, and the Constitution: Subject to Regulation

## DANIEL A. FARBER

### INTRODUCTION

[The prevailing] wisdom [is that] the Second Amendment is little more than a footnote to Militia Clauses of the Constitution, themselves virtually irrelevant to today's military. But this conventional view has been challenged by revisionist scholars [who] contend that the framers had a far more sweeping vision of the right "to keep and bear Arms." In their view, the Constitution protects the individual's right to own guns for self-defense, hunting, and resistance to tyranny. These scholars find no room for uncertainty about the historical meaning of constitutional language. "The Second Amendment," we are told by one scholar, "is thus not mysterious. Nor is it equivocal. Least of all is it opaque." The meaning of the "right to bear arms," says another, "seems no longer open to dispute," and "an intellectually viable response…has yet to be made."

The revisionists' confidence about the original understanding is the foundation for their reinterpretation of the Second Amendment. Yet, the appropriate role of original intent in constitutional law has been debated for the past two decades. That debate should, if nothing else, caution against this sense of certainty about the implications of historical materials for present-day constitutional issues such as gun control.…

Reading the historical record on the right to bear arms turns out to be a difficult exercise, full of perplexities. And even if we had a definitive answer that turned out to favor the revisionists, the claim that original intent should always trump contemporary legislative decisions is itself problematic.…

Thus, history cannot provide the kind of unshakable foundation for gun rights. that some scholars have sought. Indeed, there is something profoundly amiss about the notion that the Constitution's meaning today should be settled first and foremost by a trip to the archives. The effort to apply this notion to an issue as contemporary and hotly contested as gun control only serves to underline the fundamental peculiarity of the originalist approach to constitutional law.

Given the deep flaws in originalism, its continuing appeal may seem mysterious. For its more sophisticated adherents, it may appeal as a value-neutral method of decision and as a solution to the counter-majoritarian difficulty—perhaps a solution they would admit to be flawed, yet better than the alternatives. These arguments are ultimately unsatisfactory

For less sophisticated adherents, however, originalism may have another, more visceral appeal. It harkens back to an earlier, purer age, when today's petty political concerns and squalid politicians were replaced with great statesmen devoted to high principle. This implicit appeal to a nobler, more heroic past may have particular resonance in the context of the Second Amendment, where it brings to mind visions of minutemen and frontier lawmen valiantly defending justice and freedom with their guns. These mythic versions of the past, however, can only obscure the all-too-real issues facing our society today. Being inspired by myth is healthy; being ruled by it is unsafe.

[There are] doubts [about] whether originalism provides a workable methodology for judges in deciding Second Amendment cases. Originalism requires them to make difficult historical judgments with little training in doing so; it gives no guidance about how concretely or abstractly to define the original understanding or about how to distinguish the framers' understanding of the text from their expectations about its implementation; and it leaves open the difficult problem of when to relinquish original understandings in favor of precedent or tradition. Furthermore, as practiced today, originalism may not even correspond with the methods used by the framers themselves to understand the text. Consequently, the so-called "original understanding" may not reflect the understanding of the original framers of how the provision would be applied under new circumstances. In short, with the best will in the world, judges who practice originalism will find themselves in vast disagreement over the meaning of the Second Amendment. Thus, if originalism is intended to constrain judges, it is a failure.

But even apart from these difficulties of implementation, the question remains whether we would want to implement originalism even if we could. The Second Amendment is a good illustration of why we should not want to be bound by the original understanding. Originalists claim that only originalism can reconcile judicial review with majority rule and make the Supreme Court something other than a super-legislature. But in reality, the Justices do not need to give up their bar memberships and join the American Historical Society in order to do their jobs properly. The conventional methods of constitutional law are completely legitimate and adequate to the task at hand. Originalism's greatest failing—in contrast to the conventional process of Common-law decision—is its inability to confront historical change. We should reject the originalist's invitation to ignore all of the history that has transpired since 1790 when we interpret the Constitution.

The Second Amendment once again provides an apt illustration of the defects of originalism. If the original understanding is to constrain judicial discretion, it must be possible to ascertain that understanding in a reasonably indisputable way. But, it is not even possible to give a clear-cut definition of what constitutes the original "understanding," as opposed to the original "expectation" or the original "applications" associated with a constitutional provision. And having cleared that hurdle, formidable difficulties confront the originalist judge, including a historical record that combines enormous volume with frustrating holes in key places, a complex intellectual and social context, and a host of interpretative disputes. If we do not trust judges to correctly interpret and apply their own precedents—a skill which they were supposedly taught in law school and have practiced throughout their professional lives—it is hard to see why we should trust them to interpret and apply a mass of eighteenth-century archival documents.

## FIDELITY AND CHANGE

Originalism is an effort to fix of the Constitution once and for all at its birth. But there is an opposing view, one most eloquently expressed by Justice [Oliver Wendell] Holmes:

> [W]hen we are dealing with words that also are a constituent act, like the Constitution of the United States, we must realize that they have called into life a being the development of which could not have been foreseen completely by the most gifted of its begetters. It

was enough for them to realize or to hope that they had created an organism; it has taken a century and has cost their successors much sweat and blood to prove that they created a nation. The case before us must be considered in the light of our whole experience and not in that of what was said a hundred years ago.

The Second Amendment is among the provisions of the Constitution that seem most to call out for Holmes's approach—for the historical changes relating to the right to bear arms have been far-reaching indeed.

Some of those changes relate directly to the two subjects of the Second Amendment: firearms and and the militia. There is first of all the disappearance of the kind of militia contemplated by the framers. As [legal scholar] Akhil Amar explains, perhaps with some regret:

> [T]he legal and social structure on which the amendment is built no longer exists. The Founders' juries— grand, petit, and civil—are still around today, but the Founders' militia is not. America is not Switzerland. Voters no longer muster for militia practice in the town square.

Another relevant change is the development of professional police departments, which limit the need for individuals and groups to engage in self-help. Because these changes, unanticipated by the framers, undermined the asserted original purpose of the Second Amendment, its application today becomes problematic.

Apart from these changes relating directly to the Second Amendment's subject matter, broad changes in the constitutional landscape are also relevant. One watershed is the Civil War, which undermines the insurrectionist argument that armed revolt is a constitutionally sanctioned check on federal power....

Perhaps there may be those who reject the validity of the decision at Appomattox even today. What cannot be disputed as a lesson of the Civil War, however, is that insurrection is not an acceptable practical check on the federal government. Quite apart from the question of whether insurgents could defeat a modern army, the Civil War suggests that the costs of exercising this option would simply be unbearable: if a similar percentage of the current population died during such an insurgency today, we would be talking about five million deaths. Brave talk about insurrection is one thing; "paying the butcher's bill" is quite another. Perhaps the framers can be forgiven for failing to appreciate this reality; it is harder to excuse similar romanticism today.

The Civil War also transformed our concept of the relationship between the state and federal government. The Second Amendment, at least if revisionist scholars are to be believed, was based on the threat a powerful national government posed to liberty. But one effect of the Civil War was to cement the federal government's role as a guarantor of liberty. Since the time of the Fourteenth Amendment, rather than state and local communities being seen as bulwarks of freedom against the federal leviathan, the federal government has been pressed into service to defend liberty. The Fourteenth Amendment arose in part out of a sense of the obligation of the federal government to protect the rights of its citizens, by force if necessary, whether the threat came from a foreign nation or a state or local government.

Thus, rather than entrusting liberty to the "locals," the Fourteenth Amendment calls into play federal judicial and legislative power to ensure that the states respect individual rights. This realignment of the federal government as friend rather than threat to liberty underlies much of our modern Supreme Court jurisprudence and a plethora of twentieth-century civil rights legislation. This fundamental reassessment of the relationship between federal power and liberty would make independent state and local militias as much a threat to liberty as a protector.

If the insurrectionist argument is at odds with the lessons of the Civil War, the self-defense argument for constitutional protection clashes with the modern regulatory state. It is a commonplace that the New Deal [beginning in 1933] was a "watershed" in the development of the regulatory state, enough so to lead one prominent theorist to build a whole theory of constitutional interpretation around this shift. But the New Deal was only the beginning. In the 1960s and 1970s came a new wave of legislation covering matters such as consumer protection, discrimination law, and the environment. As a result, we live in a world where citizens routinely rely on the federal government rather than self-help to protect them against a host of threats.

Today, we expect federal protection against everything from potentially dangerous traces of pesticides in our foods to unwanted sexual overtures in the workplace. In this context, the notion that the government cannot protect us from the dangers of firearms seems like an odd relic of an earlier laissez-faire period. Indeed, it seems peculiar at best to say that the government can constitutionally protect us from one kind of hostile environment—coworkers displaying lewd pictures—but not from a more dramatic kind of hostile environment—neighbors carrying Uzis.

The point here is not that the Second Amendment is an anachronistic text that ought to be ignored, or that its interpretation should necessarily be narrowed in light of these later developments. It is not even that these later developments are fun-

damentally correct. What is wrong with originalism is that it seeks to block judges from even considering these later developments, which on their face seem so clearly relevant to the legitimacy of federal gun control efforts. But try as they may, it seems unlikely that judges can avoid being influenced by these realities.

## CONCLUSION

What do we learn about originalism from the Second Amendment debate? What do we learn about the Second Amendment from the originalism debate?

One set of lessons relates to constitutional interpretation. The Second Amendment shows how the standard academic criticisms of originalism are not just academic quibbles: they identify real and troubling flaws. The debate about the Second Amendment vividly illustrates critical problems with originalism:

- The historical record concerning the right to bear arms is difficult for non-historians such as judges to evaluate, requiring a high level of historical expertise to evaluate the credibility and import of the evidence.
- Originalism might not accurately reflect the way in which contemporary readers understood the document; in particular, it may underestimate their willingness to contemplate limiting the "right to bear arms" clause in light of the purpose clause.
- The original understanding of the Second Amendment can be defined at different levels of generality, and the interpretation will depend on the choice of level as well as on how we distinguish the original "understanding" from mere original "expectations."
- Originalism, to be a realistic option, must acknowledge stare decisis, yet it

does not provide us with clear guidance about whether the current Second Amendment case law should stand.

- Although originalism claims simply to be enforcing the will of "We the People," the Second Amendment shows how originalism can undermine majority rule.
- Because of the difficulties judges would face in basing their decisions on purely historical grounds, originalism would not eliminate the role of personal values in judging.
- Originalism forces us to ignore the ways our world has changed since the eighteenth century: the Civil War and its aftermath have cut the ground away from the notion of insurrection as a protection of liberty against federal power; and the New Deal and *its* aftermath have created a world in which we customarily turn to the regulatory state rather than to self-help to protect ourselves from threats.

It would, in short, be a serious mistake for judges to use originalism as their recipe for interpreting the Second Amendment or other ambiguous constitutional language. The fact that the arguments against this approach are familiar does not make them any less damaging.

At a more fundamental level, however, the lesson is not simply that originalists are wrong about how judges should read the Constitution. More importantly, they are wrong about the nature of the Constitution itself. In general, disputed constitutional provisions cannot simply be applied on the basis of whatever examples were discussed at the time, and so it is natural for originalists to attempt, instead, to reconstruct the theories underlying those provisions. This effort to theorize constitutional provisions is quite evident with the Second Amendment originalists we have discussed, but it is equally clear in the efforts of other originalists to find in the original understanding some unified theory of executive power or of federalism. But to look for an underlying theory is to misconceive the nature of the constitutional enterprise. Unlike physics, law does not lend itself to a "standard model" or a grand unified theory.

While the framers were indeed "concerned with such fundamental questions as the nature of representation and executive power," they were also engaged in "a cumulative process of bargaining and compromise in which a rigid adherence to principle yielded to the pragmatic tests of reaching agreement and building coalitions." In short, they were doing their best to create a viable set of democratic institutions, a task that required the utmost attention to both principle and pragmatism. Their task was not to agree on a theory but to create the basis for a working democracy. We hardly do justice to the spirit of their undertaking if we treat the resulting document as *their* Constitution alone rather than being ours as well. The last thing they would want would be for us to be ruled by false certainties about their intentions. Unfortunately, that is an invitation we have received all too often with respect to the Second Amendment.

## THE CONTINUING DEBATE:
### Guns, Safety, and the Constitution

### What Is New

Advocates and opponents of gun control have both had victories in recent years. Advocates were heartened by several court cases in 2004. The Supreme Court in effect upheld a restrictive California gun law by refusing to hear a challenge to it, and a Federal District Court rejected a suit brought by the National Rifle Association challenging the constitutionality of a Washington, D.C. municipal law limiting gun ownership. But also in 2004, Congress let lapse a 10-year-old ban that barred weapons from having muzzle-flash suppressors, large capacity ammunition magazines, and other characteristics commonly associated with military assault weapons.

### Where to Find More

For data on firearms, see the U.S. Bureau of Alcohol, Tobacco and Firearms report, *Firearms Commerce in the United States—2001/2002,* at http://www.atf.treas.gov/pub/, listed under Firearms Publications. The most recent data on firearms deaths in the United States is available from the U.S. Public Health Service's Centers for Disease Control Web site at: http://www.cdc.gov/nchs/fastats/homicide.htm.

The anti-gun control forces are represented by the National Rifle Association's Web site at http://www.nra.org/. For the opposing view, the URL http://www.bradycampaign.org/ will take you to the Web site of the pro-gun control Brady Campaign to Prevent Violence (named after James Brady, a former White House press secretary, who was shot in the head and disabled during the assassination attempt on President Ronald Reagan on March 30, 1981).

Scholarly legal arguments in favor of a strict constructionist reading of the Second Amendment include Sanford Levinson, "The Embarrassing Second Amendment," *Yale Law Journal* (1989) and Eugene Volokh, "The Amazing Vanishing Second Amendment," *New York University Law Review* (1998). Taking the opposite view is David C. Williams, *The Mythic Meanings of the Second Amendment* (Yale University Press, 2003) and Jack N. Rakove, "The Second Amendment: The Highest Stage of Originalism," *Chicago-Kent Law Review* (2000).

### What More to Do

One constant suggestion for this and every debate in this book is to get involved no matter which side you are on. The issue is important, and you can make a difference if you try. Also keep the larger constitutional questions in your mind as you read other debates in this book. Like this debate, some will involve questions about the meaning of words or phrases, such as "due process of law" in the Fourteenth Amendment. Other debates will also include the ongoing dispute over strict construction versus contemporary interpretation of the Constitution by the courts. Perhaps before any of this, though, think about and discuss with others the policy and constitutional issues presented in this debate. Then, as this book's title urges, You Decide!

# 2
# FEDERALISM

## DECIDING ABOUT GAY MARRIAGE:
### Make It a Federal Issue *or* Leave It to the States?

### MAKE IT A FEDERAL ISSUE

**ADVOCATE:** Orrin Hatch, U.S. Senator (R-UT)

**SOURCE:** *Congressional Record*, July 9, 2004

### LEAVE IT TO THE STATES

**ADVOCATE:** Patrick Leahy, U.S. Senator (D-VT)

**SOURCE:** Statement during hearings on "A Proposed Constitutional Amendment" before the U.S. Senate Judiciary Committee, March 23, 2004

How many Americans are gay or lesbian is controversial, with estimates ranging from 1% to 10%. The figures are speculative because the U.S. Census does not include sexual orientation as a category. However, the 2000 census did inquire whether "coupled households" included "opposite-sex partners" or "same-sex partners." It recorded 594,000 same-sex coupled households, or about 1% of all coupled households, but the social and legal pressures that make many homosexuals unwilling to record themselves as such almost surely mean that their total number exceeds the 1% of openly gay households. In any case, it is clear that there are many gay and lesbian Americans, whether the number is 2.9 million (1%) or 29 million (10%).

It is also certain that federal and state policy has mostly worked against homosexuals since 1610 when Virginia criminalized sexual contact between same-sex individuals. Similar laws and social bias became the norm, and until fairly recently, gay rights was a virtual non-issue in American politics. The seeds of change in that status were sewn in the mid-1900s by the civil rights movement and the slowly growing social tolerance of the American public. The efforts and successes of such African American-led organizations as the Southern Leadership Council, founded in 1957 by Martin Luther King, Jr., served as a model for other disadvantaged groups, and were part of the genesis of organizations such as the National Organization of Women (1966), the American Indian Movement (1968), the National Council of La Raza (1968), and the Asian American Legal Defense and Education Fund (1974). Also established during this era were several gay advocacy organizations, including the National Gay and Lesbian Task Force (1973) and the Human Rights Campaign (1980).

Beginning in 1961, when Illinois decriminalized sexual acts between same-sex adults, laws relating to homosexuality began to change slowly. Also, courts began to rule occasionally that discrimination against homosexuals was unconstitutional. In perhaps the first such case, a male student in Providence, Rhode Island, successfully sued his school in 1980 to force it to allow him to bring a male date to the senior prom. Social attitudes against homosexuals also moderated, and in 1967 Massachusetts elected the first country's openly gay state legislator.

The drive to permit gay marriages gained national attention in 1996 when a judge in Hawaii ruled that barriers to same-sex marriages violated the state constitution. Even though Hawaii soon amended its constitution to reinstitute the ban, an alarmed Congress passed, and President Bill Clinton signed, the Defense of Marriage Act (DOMA, 1996) barring U.S. recognition of same-sex marriages and allowing states not to recognize same-sex marriages licensed by other states. Then in 1999, Vermont's Supreme Court ruled that under the state constitution entitled same-sex couples to the same benefits and protections as married heterosexual couples. The following year, Vermont's legislature enacted a civil union bill granting legal status to gay couples.

In response, many state legislatures and, in a few cases, their citizens through referendums passed laws and even constitutional amendments barring gay marriages. But some courts moved in the opposite direction. Of particular note, Massachusetts' highest court ruled in 2004 that no "constitutionally adequate reason" existed to deny gays the ability to marry and ordered the state legislature to rewrite marriage laws to include same-sex couples. Within days, President George W. Bush called for a constitutional amendment limiting marriage to heterosexual couples. He argued that if states were forced by their courts to allow gay marriages, then those might be valid in all states under Article IV of the U.S. Constitution, which declares, "Full faith and credit shall be given in each state to the public acts...of every other state." Bush also expressed concern that the federal courts might rule that all state laws against same-sex marriages to be a violation of the U.S. Constitution. Soon, Congress took up an amendment that read:

> Marriage in the United States shall consist only of the union of a man and a woman. Neither this [the U.S.] Constitution or the constitution of any State, nor state or federal law, shall be construed to require that marital status or the legal incidents thereof be conferred upon unmarried couples or groups.

The debate over gay marriages has two aspects. One is whether or not they should be permitted. Then there is the question of whether the states or the federal government should decide the matter within the U.S. federal system. That is the focus of the debate here between Senators Orrin Hatch and Patrick Leahy.

## POINTS TO PONDER

➤ Senator Hatch notes repeatedly that Senator John Kerry (D-MA) opposes gay marriages, but Kerry also opposed the constitutional amendment being debated here. Is that a consistent position?

➤ It is somewhat ironic in this debate that supporters of gay marriage argue for states' rights because throughout most of U.S. history that position has been taken to support slavery and to oppose the extension of rights.

➤ An underlying and broader issue in this debate is the power of the judiciary. Do you agree with Senator Hatch's view that decisions by courts which negate policies that have been passed by elected officials in Congress and most state legislatures violate the principles of democracy?

# Deciding About Gay Marriage:
## Make It a Federal Issue

ORRIN HATCH

I...support of an amendment to our Constitution that would maintain the institution of marriage between a man and a woman, an institutional arrangement that is to this date supported by all of our state legislatures, every state legislature in the country. The bedrock of American success is the family, and it is traditional marriage that undergirds the American family.

The disintegration of the family in this country correlates to the many serious social problems, including crime and poverty. We are seeing soaring divorce rates. We are seeing soaring out-of-wedlock birth rates that have resulted in far too many fatherless families. Weakening the legal status of marriage at this point will only exacerbate these problems, and we simply must act to strengthen the family. It is one of the most important things that we can consider and that we should do.

To me, the question comes down to whether we amend the Constitution or we let the Supreme Court do it for us. I know which is the more democratic option, and that is for us, as elected officials, to amend the Constitution. Questions that are as fundamental as the family should simply not be left to the courts to decide. If we permit ourselves to be ruled by judges, we further erode the citizenly responsibility that is central to our republican form of government.

Many in this body [the U.S. Senate], in the ivory tower, often fret that Americans do not take politics seriously enough. Perhaps that is because we, through our inaction, routinely suggest to the electorate that the most important questions facing us as a political community should be decided by a handful of Harvard-educated lawyers, rather than by the people themselves. A free citizenry should not accept such a goal, and should not accept such thin gruel.

Our hope for this amendment is that it will maintain the traditional right of American people to set marriage policy for themselves.

We do not take this proposal lightly. The Constitution has functioned to secure and extend the rights of citizens in this nation, and it serves as a beacon of hope for the world. Aside from the Bill of Rights, it has rarely been amended, but when it is, we have done so to expand the rights of democratic self-government and to resecure the Constitution's original meaning.

That is precisely what we are intending here. Marriage policy has traditionally been set by the states. The states have made their opinion on this subject clear. They have overwhelmingly acted in recent years to preserve traditional marriage.

Still, absent an amendment, we should have no faith that the courts will uphold these state decisions. Believe me, there are other ways we would rather spend our time. We did not choose this schedule—the courts did. But as public representatives, bound by the oath to defend the Constitution, we will not hide from our obligations.

Our case is simple. Last fall, in its *Goodridge v. Department of Public Health* [2003] decision, the Supreme Judicial Court of Massachusetts declared same-sex marriage to be the policy of the Commonwealth of Massachusetts. Today, same-sex marriage couples live in 46 states, and activists are implementing a well-funded, multifaceted, and highly coordinated legal assault on traditional marriage.

Look at this. Not one legislature has voted to recognize same-sex unions. But in 1996, states with same-sex marriage couples, zero; in 2004, states with same-sex marriage couples, 46. That is what has happened as a result of this particular decision by the Massachusetts Supreme Judicial Court.

The inescapable conclusion is that absent an amendment to the Constitution, same-sex marriage is coming whether you like it or not. Regardless of what the people think, regardless of what elected representatives think, it is going to be imposed on America because of one 4-to-3 version of an activist Massachusetts Supreme Court.

The opponents of this amendment urge us to remain patient. Our actions are premature, they tell us. Those opposed to protecting traditional marriage keep moving the goal line, and to ignore this strategy is to guarantee defeat.

Marriage first became a national issue in 1996. Then, as now, a state court threatened to impose same-sex marriage on citizens of their own state, and in so doing they jeopardized the traditional marriage laws of the entire nation.

Given this scenario, it would have been flatly irresponsible for us not to act. So when faced with the potential of the Supreme Court of Hawaii dictating marriage policy for all 50 states, we passed the Defense of Marriage Act [1996], or DOMA.

Then, as now, our opponents accused us of playing election year politics—the same phony argument they are accusing us of today, or in this particular matter. The opposition insisted there was no need for DOMA, the Defense of Marriage Act. In fact, Senator John Kerry argued, and others with him, that it was not necessary

since no state has adopted same-sex marriage. That was their argument. Eight years later, a bare majority of [Senator] John Kerry's [D-MA] own state's supreme court has brought same-sex marriage to the state and to the citizens of Massachusetts.

What is his position now? Sounding much as he did 8 years ago, he said, and I quote: "I oppose this election-year effort to amend the Constitution in an area that each State can adequately address, and I will vote against such an amendment if it comes to the Senate floor."

Keep in mind, the only thing that would permit each state to decide this issue on its own is DOMA, the Defense of Marriage Act. What was Senator Kerry's opinion on DOMA? I don't mean to just single him out; there are others on the other side who have taken the same position. What was their opinion on DOMA? Senator Kerry called it "fundamentally unconstitutional." In fact, that was the opinion of much of the Democratic Party and our academic legal establishment at the time.…

That is what Senator Kerry said against DOMA when he argued against it back then. But now that Massachusetts has had its courts legalize same-sex marriage, Senator Kerry argues we do not need an amendment because we fortunately have DOMA. How convenient. Except for the fact they are all arguing that DOMA is unconstitutional. It just doesn't seem to fit.

I have seen these ads on Senator Kerry flip-flopping. We all know that around here. That is what he does. But this is the grand flip-flop, one of the grandest of all times. A person's head starts to spin just trying to undo this logical mess.

But in the end, that is the point. They hope to confuse and to obfuscate and cast aspersions, and, by so doing, maybe succeed in lulling citizens into apathy on this subject.

Fortunately, this issue is actually rather simple for those who approach it with any sincerity. There are, in fact, only two questions that senators must answer before voting on this amendment; that is, if the filibuster will be ended and we are able to proceed to the constitutional amendment and debate it.

The first thing is whether they support traditional marriage. Bulletproof majorities in this body do. No question about that. The American people do, as well.

The second is whether the majority's desire to protect traditional marriage can be guaranteed without a constitutional amendment.

The assertion this was a state issue, that the states can protect marriage, neglects the likelihood that the courts will overturn the well-considered opinion of citizens in every state. Skeptics and opponents of this constitutional amendment claim, sometimes relying on traditional Republican and conservative principles of federalism and limited government, that this is not the time nor the place for the national government to act.

We must be clear. The states have already acted. Since marriage first became an issue in 1996, over 40 states—look at this—over 40 states have acted explicitly to shore up their traditional marriage laws—40 states. What a national consensus? States where legislatures have approved same-sex marriage, zero; not one state legislature, that is. The people's representatives, the ones who have to stand for reelection, not one state. States where legislators and citizens have recently acted to protect traditional marriage, 40 states.

But all of this legislation has been in danger by the Massachusetts court's actions this past fall and by recent decisions by the U.S. Supreme Court. The courts, in an elite legal culture out of

touch with average Americans, have made this a national issue. It can no longer be adequately resolved by the states. More and more coordinated lawsuits are being filed every day, and the question of same-sex marriage will terminate in federal courts at which point same-sex marriage will become the law of the land, in spite of the desires of the elected representatives throughout at least 40 states, and I believe other states would follow suit in time to preserve traditional marriage.

Let me say this slowly so it can sink in. Absent a constitutional amendment that protects the rights of the states to maintain their traditional understanding of marriage, the Supreme Court will decide this issue for them.

The Massachusetts Supreme Judicial Court commanded, in a fit of hubris, that the state must extend marriage to same-sex couples. Never mind that the Massachusetts Constitution created by the hand of John Adams himself clearly did not contemplate this conclusion.

Never mind there is an obvious national basis for the states' traditional marriage laws and never mind the people in the Bay State were adamantly opposed to this judicial usurpation of policy development best left to legislative judgment. No, they went right ahead and issued a decision that certainly made them the toast of the town on the cocktail party and academic lecture circuit, but they put their personal self-satisfaction ahead of their judicial responsibilities. By doing so, they knowingly threatened the marriage laws in every state in our country.

The people of Massachusetts acted quickly to amend their constitution and overturn this egregious abuse of judicial authority. The problem is that amendment will not be ratified for at least 2 years—a fact, by the way, of which the Massachusetts Supreme Court was keenly aware. In the meantime, people will be married in Massachusetts and they will move to other states. What will become of these same-sex marriages? Will they be recognized? Will they be dissolved? Can these people get divorces in other states? Who will have custody of the children in the event of disillusion? Already, as a result of the lawless issuing of marriage licenses to same-sex couples by the mayor of San Francisco, same-sex marriage couples live in 46 states now. Together, these actions have stirred up a hornet's nest of litigation.

When allowed to choose, legislatures protect marriage rather than dismantle it; therefore, advocates of same-sex marriage resort to strategies involving the executive or judicial branches. In states such as California, Oregon, New York, and New Mexico, rogue local officials have simply defied their own state marriage laws and married thousands of same-sex couples. While saying that New York law does not allow same-sex marriages, State attorney general Elliot Spitzer will nonetheless recognize such marriages performed in other states. That is his opinion. These actions have an impact on the legal landscape for sure, but in most cases advocates turn to the courts to impose their preferred policies on fellow citizens. Their legal war against traditional marriage has at least five fronts.

Remember Article IV of the Constitution, full faith and credit clause. Most authorities believe the Massachusetts Supreme Court will be binding on every other state in the union, not that they will have to allow same-sex marriages themselves in defiance of traditional marriage beliefs, but they will have to recognize the marriages that are performed in Massachusetts that come to their states under the full faith and credit clause. Most constitutional authorities agree with that, and it is believed that

the U.S. Supreme Court will uphold that and thus rule DOMA, or the Defense of Marriage Act, unconstitutional.

There are five legal fronts of attack on the Defense of Marriage Act or traditional marriage. First, as in Massachusetts, gay citizens who wish to marry allege that state laws protecting traditional marriage are violations of their own state constitutions. So far, there are 11 states facing these challenges to their marriage laws.

This week, the ACLU [American Civil Liberties Union] filed suit in Maryland arguing that the state's failure to recognize same-sex unions violates the state's constitution. In California, even though more than 60 percent of the voters recently approved a statewide ballot initiative to maintain traditional marriage, the California Supreme Court is now considering the constitutionality of that democratic action.

In Nebraska, the ACLU has actually challenged a duly passed state constitutional amendment that defines marriage as being between a man and a woman. Similar challenges are pending in Florida, Indiana, Washington, and West Virginia, all of which have passed laws to secure traditional marriage just in the last 10 years as a result of this focused consideration of the subject by citizens of those States.

The legislatures in Delaware, Illinois, Michigan, North Carolina, and Vermont are considering actual amendments to protect traditional marriage. Montana, North Dakota, Ohio, and Oregon have signature-gathering campaigns underway. Amendments are already on the ballot in Arkansas, Georgia, Kentucky, Michigan, Mississippi, Missouri, Oklahoma, and my own home state of Utah.

One would expect and hope that given this public concentration on the subject, a proper respect would be given to a popular resolution of this issue. We can be sure, though, that the legal advocates of same-sex marriage will not display any such reservations.

The second case against traditional marriage will emerge once two citizens legally married in Massachusetts move to Ohio, Louisiana, or some other state and seek to have their marriage recognized. It is simply implausible to deny that this scenario will unfold. Already a suit has been filed in Washington State requesting that Washington recognize same-sex marriages performed in Oregon under a now halted order issued by a rogue county chairman even though Washington law expressly precludes such unions.

The third and fourth cases also specifically involve challenges to the Defense of Marriage Act now passed by 40 states and I believe will ultimately be passed by all 50 states.

One of the standard crutches of those opposed to an amendment is that DOMA, the Defensive of Marriage Act, remains the law of the land. In the hearing before the Judiciary Committee several weeks ago, Senator [Richard] Durbin [D-IL] said that DOMA has "never been challenged in court." This is simply untrue. DOMA has been challenged for violating the U.S. Constitution. It is being challenged right now.

The Defense of Marriage Act did two things. For the purposes of federal benefits, such as social security, it reserved the definition of marriage to traditional unions, and, most importantly, it gave a blanket exception to the full faith and credit laws for marriage policy.

As it is now, the Constitution requires that, barring a rational public policy to the contrary, my marriage in Utah must be recognized in Virginia. DOMA ensures that states would not be compelled under the Constitution to recognize same-sex marriages performed in other states. The

first prong of DOMA is being challenged in a federal court. There is no doubt that a suit will eventually be filed challenging the constitutionality of DOMA's exception to the full faith and credit clause.

Fifth, state laws protecting traditional marriage will be challenged as violating the federal constitution. That the U.S. Constitution protects no such right will hardly be an obstacle to these suits. The death penalty is explicitly provided for in the Fifth Amendment, but that does not stop liberal interest groups from attempting to undo this through judicial action. They cannot get these matters through the elected representatives, so they always try to get these activist court judges to do their bidding for them and to enact legislation from the bench that they could never get through the elected representatives of the people. This is a perfect illustration.

The First Amendment was obviously intended to guarantee political speech, but that does not stop the ACLU from getting nude dancing declared a constitutional right. Nothing in the Constitution guarantees a right to an abortion, but, through a creative analysis of the text, the [Supreme] Court was persuaded to create a right to privacy extended in recent years to include "the right to define one's own concept of existence of the universe, and of the mystery of human life."

These cases will inevitably wind up in federal court. We cannot wash our hands of the implications of this issue's likely judicial resolution. As a senator, my oath obligated me to protect the Constitution. That includes protecting it from corruption at the hands of the judiciary. These corruptions have become commonplace, and they are extremely difficult to undo once secured.

We have tried in the past, when constitutional meaning was violated in the moment-of-silence cases, in abortion rights cases, in religious liberty cases, in flag burning cases—all judicial activists' decisions—we attempted to undo these decisions and to restore the original Constitution. We have never been successful in succeeding along those lines. If this becomes the law of the land by judicial fiat of 4-to-3 verdict in the Massachusetts Supreme Court and because the full faith and credit clause will impose it on every other state in the union, then we will have had the judges legislate for all of America against every state's law that we now must do away with traditional marriage or at least allow this new form of marriage.

Now, there is a constitutional responsibility, I would suggest to my colleagues in the Senate. In fact, once these decisions are in place, the very people who tell us to wait for the courts to decide abdicate their stewardship of the Constitution. It is a phony argument to say wait until the courts decide. I think it is all too clear that if we rely on that, we are going to have the courts tell Americans what they must believe on this matter, and that is in contradiction to all of the elected representatives' rights to determine these types of issues....

Well, I think the Supreme Court has gotten it wrong on a number of occasions. But on this particular issue, when the Supreme Court rules that DOMA is unconstitutional, that will be one of the most monumentally wrongful decisions in the history of this country....

We cannot just sit by and let the courts rule our country. That is not their job. Their job is to interpret the laws that we make as people who have to stand for reelection. We passed a law that is now approved by 40 states, and I believe will be approved by the other 10 states given time....

The members of this body have a sacred trust as constitutional officials, and we must take seriously the results of our inaction. If we fail to pass an amendment, and we delegate our authority over this matter to the Supreme Court of the United States, the decision will come as no surprise. On this point, the justices have made themselves amply clear. There is no reason to believe that state marriage laws protecting traditional marriage will be allowed to stand.

In the *Lawrence* decision [*Lawrence v. Texas* (2003)] handed down just last year, the Supreme Court announced its intentions by effectively overturning *Bowers v. Hardwick*. [In the *Bowers* (1986) case, the U.S. Supreme Court had upheld the constitutionality of a Georgia sodomy law criminalizing sexual contact between consenting adults. The Court reversed itself in *Lawrence* case and declared a Texas law, and by extension all state laws making gay sexual contact between consenting adults illegal, to be unconstitutional.] *Bowers* was hardly an antique. It was decided only in 1986, and it basically put the brakes on 20 years of judicially created privacy rights. That decision concluded that the states remained able to regulate certain sexual practices in order to protect the health, safety, and morals within its political community. But in *Lawrence* the Court reversed course. There, the Court concluded that:

> Liberty presumes an autonomy of self that includes freedom of thought, belief, expression, and certain intimate conduct, and therefore, our laws and tradition afford constitutional protection to personal decisions relating to marriage, procreation, contraception, family relationships, child rearing, and education.

Now, according to the Court, in *Lawrence*, these are fundamental rights, and the states must, therefore, advance a compelling reason for any legislation that denies them. Unfortunately, in *Romer v. Evans* [1996], the Court has previously held that any such legislation could only be based on an "irrational animus" [ill-will] toward homosexuals. [In the *Romer* the Supreme Court struck down an amendment to Colorado's constitution adopted by the state's voters in a 1992 referendum that prohibited the government in Colorado from passing legislation or adopting policies that barred discrimination against lesbians and gay men based on their sexual orientation.]

So what, then, of same-sex marriage, which denies to homosexuals the privilege of marrying? In his dissent in *Lawrence*, Justice [Antonin] Scalia understood that:

> State laws against…same-sex marriage…are likewise sustainable only in light of Bowers' validation of laws based on moral choices. Every single one of these laws is called into question by today's decision; the Court makes no effort to cabin the scope of its decision to exclude them from its holding.

Those who favored the decision at the time said it did no such thing. Privately, however, they understood exactly what it meant. And the judges in the *Goodridge* case were quick studies. In the decision to rewrite the Massachusetts Constitution to compel same-sex marriage, the *Goodridge* court relied heavily on these rulings. Their conclusions that marriage is a fundamental right and that the decision to restrict that right is patently irrational were taken straight out of the U.S. Supreme Court playbook. *Goodridge* has shown us the way. DOMA, the Defense of Marriage Act, will not stand, and absent DOMA, the states will have to defend their marriage laws on their own. Their success, of course, is in serious doubt.

I do not subscribe to the conclusions of the courts. There is an obviously rational basis for legislation that protects traditional marriage. Only a discriminatory animus against people who hold any religious beliefs at all could lead someone to conclude otherwise. For a simple and compelling reason, traditional marriage has been a civilizational anchor for thousands of years. Society has an interest in the future generations created by men and women.

Decoupling procreation from marriage in order to make some people feel more accepted denies the very purpose of marriage itself. Marriages between men and women are the essential institutions to which future generations are produced and reared. Political communities are only as solid as their foundation, and these families and homes, the first schoolyards of citizenship, are essential for the future of republican government.

The fact that so many in the Democratic Party are openly opposed to same-sex marriage should undercut the conclusion that the desire to maintain traditional marriage is grounded simply in rank bigotry.…

There are leading Democrats who have spoken out on same-sex marriage.…[O]ne is Senator Kerry: "I believe marriage is between a man and a woman. I oppose gay marriage and disagree with the Massachusetts Court's decision." I don't think it could be any more clear.

I have to say that I think John Kerry was right in making that statement at the time. [He and other Democrats who agree]…are merely responding to a certain common sense articulated by the American people, and that common sense has expressed itself in legislative actions in nearly every state.

The Supreme Court of the United States, in order to defend itself against the accusation that it is determining constitutional meaning from their morning reading of the *New York Times*, has taken to defending only those rights supported by a developing national consensus. In this case, there is a developing national consensus on the issue of same-sex marriage, but it is developing in the other direction.

State after state has acted to protect this vital institution of traditional marriage. Still it would be a fool's wager to rely on the Supreme Court to affirm this consensus of all the people out there. When California acted through the superdemocratic process of a statewide referendum to protect traditional marriage, that did not stop the liberal mayor of San Francisco from defying this law and instituting his own preferred policy preference instead. When it comes to a liberal agenda at odds with the beliefs of average Americans, legal impediments or even simple respect for these popular decisions do not long stand in the way....

Gays and lesbians have a right to live as they choose. I would be the first to say that. But I am sorry, they do not have the right to define marriage and to redefine it away from the concepts of traditional marriage that have been in existence for over 5,000 years. I have been a leader in advocating hate crimes legislation against gays and lesbians. I know prejudice remains against gay and lesbian citizens. I reject each and every substantiation of it. But this amendment is not about discrimination. It is not about prejudice. It is about safeguarding the best environment for our children.

African-American and Hispanic leaders, Catholics and Jews, Democrats and Republicans, people from every state, religion, and every walk of life support traditional marriage as the ideal for this very same reason. I do not doubt alternative families can lovingly raise children, but decades of study show children do best when raised by a father and a mother....

The Netherlands has recognized same-sex unions since 2001 and registered partnerships since 1998. Since those reforms began, there has been a marked decline in marriage culture. Just yesterday, in a letter published in a Dutch newspaper, a group of respected academics from the fields of social science, philosophy and law made a modest assertion. The decision to recognize same-sex marriage depended on the creation of a social and legal separation between the ideas of marriage and parenting. And in that time, there has been, in their words, a spectacular rise in the number of illegitimate births. These scholars do not argue that this rise is solely attributable to the decision to recognize same-sex partnerships. But the correlation is undeniable. They conclude that further research is needed to establish the relative importance of all the factors.

Precisely! The jury is out on what the effects on children and society will be and only legislatures are institutionally equipped to make these decisions. If nothing else, given the uncertainty of a radical change in a fundamental institution like marriage, popular representatives should be given deference on this issue. However, recent actions by courts prove that no such deference is being given.

This is why we need an amendment. Without an amendment to the Constitution, same-sex marriage will be imposed by judges on an American people who would not choose this institution for themselves....

The amendment does nothing more than preserve perhaps the most fundamental relationship in society. The amendment does not violate the principles of federalism and limited government.

Among other things the Constitution guaranteed to the people a right to govern themselves; in most instances, through their state governments. The Constitution protected traditional state prerogatives over subjects such as marriage and family policy. And should those be in danger, the Constitution guaranteed to the people a right to resecure these prerogatives through the amendment process. This is precisely the situation we face here.

The states have acted on this issue time and time again. They have rejected same-sex marriage. Yet we face legal advocates and a judicial system that care little for these judgments and that are ready and willing to substitute their own judgments for the common sense of the American citizenry.

In the end, the only argument against this amendment is that the Supreme Court is the sole institution that determines the meaning of our Constitution. I reject that conclusion. It grossly misstates the history of this nation....

The popular branches of Government, not the courts, are the primary guarantors of our rights. As senators, we are obligated to interpret the Constitution, and in this case we are not denying rights to same-sex couples, but protecting and extending the right of citizens to govern themselves and to determine marriage policy on their own, and to preserve traditional marriage.

To delay action on the marriage amendment now is like agreeing to repair a cracked dam only after it has burst and forever changed the landscape. We know what the legal situation is on this issue and we know what we have to do to repair it. A Constitutional amendment is the only viable alternative to protect this most

foundational relationship in society. We must act, and we must act now.

We need to send a message to our children about marriage and traditional life and values. The American people must have a voice. The people, through their elected representatives—not judges— should decide the future of marriage.

Montana, Louisiana, West Virginia, Colorado, Washington, Maine, North Dakota, Ohio, New Hampshire, Nebraska, South Carolina, Arkansas, Alaska, Pennsylvania. All of these states and many others have made independent determinations to protect against same-sex marriage. Without an amendment to the Constitution, all that work will be for naught. They have made those independent determinations to protect traditional marriage, not same-sex marriage. I respectfully ask my colleagues to do the right thing here and to guarantee that the right to self-government on important issues such as this remains with the people rather than in the courts.

This is an important issue. Anybody who argues this issue isn't as important as anything that can possibly come before this body fails to recognize that traditional marriage and the rights of families and children are the most important elements of our societal function and we need to protect them. We need to do it now and not wait until 2 or 3 years from now when all this becomes mush and nothing will be able to be done, such as on other bills that have occurred through the years.

# Deciding About Gay Marriage:
## Leave It to the States

PATRICK LEAHY

Today's hearing is merely the latest in what has become a series of hearings on amending the Constitution in one manner or another. It would seem that members of the majority are obsessed with rewriting the Constitution. This is the fourth constitutional amendment to which this [the Senate Judiciary] Committee has devoted significant time for debate in the 108th Congress [2003–2004], and this is the third hearing this month to debate a constitutional amendment seeking to limit rather than expand the rights of the American people. This proposal is one of 61 constitutional amendments introduced so far this session. Sixty-one amendments to the Constitution introduced in this Congress alone, and more than 11,000 since the 1st Congress was convened [on March 4, 1789]. We can only imagine what the Constitution would look like if we had adopted amendments at the wholesale rate seemingly favored by many in the 108th Congress.

I have stated my opposition to the Federal Marriage Amendment at our two previous hearings on this topic, and I state it again today. I oppose the Federal Marriage Amendment because it interferes in a fundamental state matter, and, worse yet, it does so for the purpose of disfavoring a group of Americans. We have never amended our Constitution for that purpose, and we should not start now. The proposed amendment we consider today creates division among the American people. In addition, the timing of these hearings raises concerns that the Constitution is being misused for partisan purposes. Of course, the Republicans who are in the majority in the Senate control the agenda, and this hearing and their concentration on this divisive issue is their choice.

It is all the more disturbing that this hearing takes place less than 24 hours after the sponsors of this amendment have unveiled a new version of it. Proposals to amend the Constitution of the United States that seemingly change as moodily as the latest focus group should give us all the more pause in this rush to amend our national charter.

Neither our witnesses nor the members of this committee have had sufficient opportunity to review the new language and the consequences of the multiple changes Senator [Wayne] Allard [R-CO] has proposed. Our witnesses already had prepared their testimony to the committee before they had even had the opportunity to see this latest version. It is clear, however, that questions raised by the new amendment differ somewhat from the questions raised by the old amendment. As a result, our approach to this hearing would have differed as well. Despite this "bait and switch," the majority rejected our request to postpone this hearing so that we would have an opportunity to review the language and hold this hearing with the respect that is due to our Constitution. At the very least, fundamental fairness requires that the committee hold a second hearing on this amendment before moving forward on it.

The pace of these hearings, the majority's [the Republican's] refusal to postpone today's hearing, and the rhetoric of amendment supporters, including a President of the United States in the midst of a political year, suggests a crisis. Since our last hearing, however, the Massachusetts state legislature and the California Supreme Court have each taken actions that have served to undercut the recognition of same-sex marriage in their own states. Developments in the states have been away from recognition of same-sex marriage and toward recognition of civil unions, in line with the views of the American people. In addition, legal experts have made the case that no states will be made to recognize same-sex marriages from other states against their strong public policy.

Thus, this preemptive attack on the Constitution can no longer be validated by scary allusions to "activist judges." Do Republicans really contend that the United States Supreme Court is staffed by activist liberal judges intent on recognizing same-sex marriages? There is no indication that we are on the verge of such a ruling. There is no case on the Supreme Court docket—or on any federal appellate court docket—that would even raise that issue. We should not alter the Bill of Rights and our Constitution to avert judicial decisions that have not yet even been considered, let alone made, when such a constitutional amendment would hamstring our states in an unprecedented way.

In spite of recent developments, this committee finds it necessary to return, again, to this divisive issue just days after our last discussion. This hearing has been billed as one focusing on the language of the Federal Marriage Amendment, which Senator Allard and Representative [Marilyn] Musgrave [R-CO] have introduced....

Of course, we have yet to see the promised alternative constitutional amendment that Senator Hatch has suggested on this topic. Once that language is introduced, if

Republicans are serious about actually proceeding to amend the Constitution, the committee will need to hold hearings on its wording, meaning, and possible effects....

## AN AMENDMENT THAT DISRESPECTS STATES

Senator Allard's Federal Marriage Amendment is breathtaking both in the scope of its intrusion upon the traditional powers of the states and in the lack of clarity in its drafting. There have been press accounts that its wording was the result of conference calls among activists who themselves could not agree on language. I have written the Bush administration and asked its representatives what language they endorse now that George W. Bush has changed his position and decided to endorse a constitutional amendment on this matter. Although it has been some time and I have provided numerous opportunities for the Bush administration to respond, I have yet to receive an answer. The Bush administration has not told me what words they endorse adding to the Constitution on the United States. Perhaps the President supports the old Allard amendment. Perhaps he supports the new Allard amendment, as some news reports suggest, and his administration was involved in the "bait and switch" that was perpetrated on this committee yesterday afternoon. Perhaps he supports a third version entirely that has yet to be introduced in this Congress. He has informed neither this committee nor the American people. [The "new" Allard amendment, which was the one subsequently debated in the Senate, is as shown above in the introduction to this debate. It differed from the "old" Allard amendment by dropping language that would have prohibited the federal and state governments from allowing civil unions equivalent to marriages in their protections and benefits.]

President Bush has called upon Congress to alter our fundamental charter. We in Congress deal in written proposals and not just convenient political slogans for re-election campaigns. The words of our Constitution are particularly important. The President has still not responded to my February 25 [2004] letter or to my questions of his Assistant Attorney General two weeks ago. For the third hearing on this topic, the Bush administration has chosen not to send a representative to testify. Given the apparent emergency that the President indicated inspired his change of position, I would have thought he would know what he wanted Congress to consider when he so dramatically called upon Congress to act. What is it President Bush is for, what proposal does he endorse, where is the language that he endorses be added to the Constitution? How strident does he wish the language to be in restricting people's rights? How restrictive is the language he endorses to constrict the ability of our states to extend rights and benefits to their citizens as they see fit? I know how much this White House is driven by poll numbers. I want to be sure they have seen the Washington Post-ABC News poll earlier this month [March 2004] which found that 53 percent of Americans believe that states should make their own decisions about marriage.

Of course, without a thoroughgoing response from the White House about what it is the president is endorsing, and without an administration witness, we are left with little more than a political posture without substance. The Constitution should not be used for partisan political purposes. Proposing an amendment to our basic charter of rights is a serious matter and needs to be approached seriously. Otherwise, we risk diminishing respect for the Constitution and for all our basic institutions. The administration's refusal to answer such basic questions and to send a witness to testify suggests a lack of seriousness and a surplus of political motivation about this drive to amend the Constitution that is highly regrettable.

I now turn to the proposal before the committee. The first sentence of Senator Allard's amendment would create a federal constitutional definition of marriage. Congress has already adopted a definition of marriage for the purposes of federal law, in the Defense of Marriage Act ("DOMA"). No court has questioned DOMA, and even the advocates of this amendment have not seriously argued that provision of DOMA is at risk in the courts or that it will be thrown out by the United States Supreme Court. As such, the proponents of this amendment are seeking to define marriage for the states, whether they like it or not. While the political and judicial processes in Massachusetts, California, and elsewhere continue their review of marriage laws, the proponents of this proposed constitutional amendment rush to take those decisions out of the hands of the people and the states for all time. As Professor Lea Brilmayer [Yale University Law School] put it in *The Wall Street Journal* earlier this month [March 9, 2004], "In our 200-year constitutional history, there has never yet been a federal constitutional amendment designed specifically to reverse a state's interpretation of its own laws."

To the extent that this amendment's proponents argue that we need a national definition of marriage to prevent states from being forced to recognize same-sex marriages entered into in other states, they ignore the thoughtful testimony offered by Professor Brilmayer at our last hearing on this topic. The Full Faith and Credit Clause has not been interpreted to require states to recognize other states' marriage licenses that violate their own public policies. States have refused to recognize marriages between cousins, between uncles and nieces, and even marriages entered into within a year of the divorce of one of the parties. In other words, states have always had an inherent right to follow their own policies about marriage, regardless of what other states do. Federal law in the form of DOMA enhances that right by giving specific congressional approval to states that decline to recognize same-sex marriages....

I think Georgetown law professor Michael Seidman was correct when he stated in written testimony to the Constitution Subcommittee [of the Senate Judiciary Committee] earlier this month that "[t]he first obligation we should impose on people who want to amend our Constitution is that they think clearly about what they are doing and be careful with the words they use." Professor Seidman predicted that the amendment would "produce endless litigation about its meaning," and would "give judges total freedom to do virtually anything they want." I do not think that the changes Senator Allard and Representative Musgrave announced yesterday afternoon have changed this analysis. For those who purport to be concerned about so-called activist judges, this vague language about the "legal incidents" associated with marriage provides a vast playground of possibilities at the expense of state government and our citizens. Will it affect laws like the Mychal Judge Act, by which we allowed public servants to designate recipients of benefits? Will it prohibit state law developments allowing same-sex partners additional rights traditionally associated with marriage? Will it federalize divorce, alimony, child custody and other laws that our states have traditionally provided?

We must not forget that this is a constitutional amendment we are considering. Every word counts.

## BIPARTISAN OPPOSITION

I hope that Republicans will speak out against this effort. No less an authority than Vice President [Richard] Cheney said during the 2000 Vice Presidential debate: "I don't think there should necessarily be a federal policy in this area." I suspect we will not hear from him, again, on this issue. When the president abandoned his State of the Union caution to, a month later, endorse this constitutional amendment, the administration put its political interests above the Constitution.

Our former colleague on this committee, Senator Alan Simpson [R-WY], wrote last year: "Like most Americans, and most Republicans, I think it's important to do all we can to defend and strengthen the institution of marriage. And I also believe it is critically important to defend the integrity of the Constitution. But a federal amendment to define marriage would do nothing to strengthen families—just the opposite. And it would unnecessarily undermine one of the core principles I have always believed the GOP stood for: federalism." I thank Senator Simpson for speaking out on this matter. I look forward to hearing the views of Republican Senators currently serving who oppose this effort and will rise to the defense of the Constitution.

I understand that Governor [Arnold] Schwarzenegger of California and a few other Republican Governors, along with former New York City Mayor Rudy Guiliani, have likewise noted that they support "legal incidents" associated with marriage being accorded same-sex couples. I hope they will speak out forcefully on this effort to amend the Constitution that would straightjacket all levels of representative government on these matters.

## CONCLUSION

This proposed constitutional amendment is seriously flawed not only in its words but also in its design. We have amended the Constitution to limit the rights of our citizens only once, with the 18th Amendment, which imposed Prohibition. And that amendment is the only constitutional amendment subsequently repealed. We have never amended the Constitution to limit the rights of a minority group of Americans. If we pass the Allard amendment, we will permanently define millions of Americans today and millions more tomorrow as second-class citizens.

There is an alternative to writing discrimination into our Constitution, and it is as old as our system of government. We can tolerate differences among our states on this issue. Two centuries of law and DOMA protect the right of each state to decide for itself. Some states may allow civil unions or even civil marriage for same-sex couples. Yet others will choose to maintain the status quo. We leave the definition of marriage to religious interpretation and implementation by our great and multiple religious traditions. Americans are free to choose whatever religion they wish. Likewise, our national government has tolerated differences among the states for our entire history. This is no justification for preemptively declaring war on gay and lesbian Americans or tacking a statement of intolerance onto the Constitution of the United states. We need not—and we must not—allow tinkering with the Constitution to become merely the latest election year tool. We should reject this amendment, and we should reject wedge politics.

# THE CONTINUING DEBATE:
## Deciding About Gay Marriage

### What Is New

The amendment to bar gay marriages was defeated in the Senate in July 2004 by 48 to 50 vote, getting far fewer than the 67 vote, two-thirds margin needed to submit it to the states for ratification. Neither Senators John Kerry nor John Edwards voted, but both had said they opposed the amendment. President Bush warned, "Activist judges and local officials in some parts of the country are not letting up in their efforts to redefine marriage for the rest of America, and neither should defenders of traditional marriage flag in their efforts." Judges in several states negated same sex marriage licenses issued by local officials, and other states added constitutional bans. In Louisiana, for example, 78% of voters in a September 2004 referendum approved such a state constitutional amendment. But new challenges to bans on gay marriages have been filed in state and federal courts, and overturning those barriers will set off another effort to amend the U.S. Constitution, a move supported by 58% of Americans who said, in an August 2004 survey, that a constitutional amendment to "ban gay marriages" was a "good idea," while 37% thought it a "bad idea," and 5% were unsure.

### Where to Find More

For the gay and lesbian perspective, access the Web sites of the Human Rights Campaign at http://www.hrc.org/ and the National Gay and Lesbian Taskforce at http://www.thetaskforce.org/. Among those organization opposing gay marriages are the American Family Association at http://www.afa.net/ and the Center for Reclaiming America at http://www.reclaimamerica.org/. More on the battle in the states over gay marriage and current state laws is available at the Stateline.org site at http://www.stateline.org. Enter "gay marriage" in to the search window. The legality of gay marriages and other forms of union in countries around the world is available at http://usmarriagelaws.com/. Click "Alternative Lifestyles" on the left.

### What More to Do

Consider how an amendment might be worded to meet the concerns of both sides. Would you favor an amendment that, instead of saying marriages can only exist between men and women, directed that the decision be left entirely up to the states? Also, look further into the practical implications of gay marriages. The distinction between marriage and civil union is important legally as well as symbolically. Under DOMA and general legal precedent, states without civil union laws do not have to recognize civil unions created in other states. Moreover, under DOMA the federal government denies many benefits to civil union couples that are granted to married couples. The U.S. General Accounting Office found more than 1,000 such differences in treatment related to such benefits as reduced taxes, pension and Social Security benefits, inheritance rights, and loans. Would you favor nationally recognized civil unions carrying the same protections and benefits as heterosexual marriages as an alternative to gay marriages?

# CIVIL RIGHTS

## BANNING D&X (PARTIAL-BIRTH) ABORTIONS:
### Violating Women's Rights *or* Protecting Fetal Rights?

### VIOLATING WOMEN'S RIGHTS

**ADVOCATE:** Center for Reproductive Rights

**SOURCE:** Position paper, "Unconstitutional Assault on the Right to Choose: 'Partial-Birth Abortion' Ban Is an Affront to Women and to the U.S. Supreme Court," February 2003

### PROTECTING FETAL RIGHTS

**ADVOCATE:** Kathi A. Aultman, MD, board certified obstetrician gynecologist, and Fellow, American College of Obstetricians and Gynecologists

**SOURCE:** Testimony during hearings on "Partial-Birth Abortion Ban Act of 2002" before the U.S. Senate Committee on the Judiciary, Subcommittee on the Constitution, July 9, 2002

January 22, 1973, was a pivotal day in one of the most contentious legal and social debates in U.S. history. On that date the U.S. Supreme Court handed down its decision in *Roe v. Wade*. By a 7–2 vote, the justices, in effect, invalidated state restrictions on the ability of women to medically abort their pregnancies. At that time, four states permitted abortion "on demand" (for any reason), 15 allowed abortions if continuing the pregnancy endangered a woman's health, and 31 banned abortions unless the woman's life was endangered.

The court based its decision on a "right to privacy." In the majority opinion, Justice Harry Blackmun conceded, "the Constitution does not explicitly mention any right of privacy." Nevertheless, he continued, "The Constitution recognizes that rights exist beyond those specified in that document…this right of privacy…is broad enough to encompass a woman's decision whether or not to terminate her pregnancy."

Supporters of *Roe v. Wade* often claim it secured the right of women to have to an abortion and to control their bodies. However, Blackmun said otherwise. In his words, "Some argue that the woman's right is absolute and that she is entitled to terminate her pregnancy at whatever time, in whatever way, and for whatever reason she alone chooses. With this we [justices] do not agree." Blackmun continued, "The privacy right…cannot be said to be absolute," and he indicated, "It is not clear to us [the justices] that the claim…that one has an unlimited right to do with one's body as one pleases bears a close relationship to the right of privacy."

Thus, instead of unrestricted right, the court outlined a limited right with different standards for each trimester of a normal pregnancy. In Blackmun's words, during the first trimester, "the abortion decision…must be left to the medical judgment of the pregnant woman's attending physician." Abortion could only be regulated during the second trimester in "ways that are reasonably related to maternal health." And during the third trimester, a state "may, if it chooses, regulate, and even proscribe, abortion except where it is necessary…for the preservation of the life or health of the mother."

The Court's decision changed the law, but the debate continues. Indeed, it is hard for many of those who differ on abortion to discuss the subject calmly. They do not even agree on what the fundamental issue is. Abortion rights advocates view the issue as about a woman's right to choose and thus label themselves "pro-choice." Foes of abortion say they are "pro-life" based on their view that human life begins at conception—or at least much sooner than the beginning of the third trimester.

Since *Roe v. Wade*, those oppose abortions altogether or who want to limit them have made numerous attempts to overturn the decision by amending the Constitution. They have also sought to pass state or federal laws that regulate abortion within the parameters set down by the Supreme Court in *Roe v. Wade* and subsequent court decisions.

This debate, for example, centers on efforts in Congress to ban an abortion procedure termed "intact dilation and extraction" (D&X), the term favored by pro-choice advocates, and also commonly called "partial-birth abortion," the term favored by anti-abortion advocates. However termed, its implications are far-reaching.

From a narrow perspective, the debate in Congress over whether to ban the D&X procedure addresses far less than 1% of the approximately 1.2 million abortions performed annually in the United States. Opponents of banning the procedure make many arguments about its necessity and safety, but from a wider perspective, they also worry that it is a step down the "slippery slope" to even further restrictions. Most proponents of the ban hope that, indeed, the slope does prove slippery.

## POINTS TO PONDER

➤ This debate exists at multiple levels. One involves the D&X procedure and the specifics of the legislation. On a broader level, the debate is about abortion as such. Do you think the Center for Reproductive Rights would accept any restrictions on the D&X procedure, no matter what the law specified? Do you think Kathi Aultman and other abortion opponents would agree to narrowly define the D&X procedure and provide exemptions from the ban?

➤ Watch for terminology differences. They can be critical. For example, what does "maternal health" mean? Aultman argues that physicians often find health problems where none really exist. How should mental and physical health be defined?

➤ This debate primarily focuses on the second trimester, particularly the later stage as a fetus achieves reasonable odds of viability outside the womb. Are "viability" and "life" synonymous? Think about how, if at all, you would regulate abortions during the second trimester.

# Banning D&X (Partial-Birth) Abortions: Violating Women's Rights

## CENTER FOR REPRODUCTIVE RIGHTS

### I. THE HISTORY OF SO-CALLED "PARTIAL-BIRTH ABORTION" BANS

Since 1995, anti-choice fringe groups have waged a campaign to eliminate the right to abortion, as established in the landmark Supreme Court case, *Roe v. Wade* [1973]. As part of their campaign, these organizations have worked to enact so-called "partial-birth abortion" bans throughout the country on both the state and federal level. These bans are unconstitutional, deceptive and extreme measures aimed at making abortion virtually unattainable for women. Falsely touted as a ban on one particular method of post-viability abortion used late in pregnancy, these laws actually represent an attempt to criminalize numerous abortion procedures including the safest and most commonly used pre-viability abortion methods—even early in pregnancy.

In June 2000 in *Stenberg v. Carhart*, a case brought by Center for Reproductive Rights, the U.S. Supreme Court struck down Nebraska's abortion ban, which was similar to laws that had been enacted in 30 other states. The Court ruled that Nebraska's ban was unconstitutional because it failed to contain a health exception and posed an "undue burden" on a woman's right to choose. The Court's ruling had the effect of rendering invalid similar laws throughout the country and exposed these bans for what they are: deceptive and extreme attempts to outlaw the safest and most common methods of pre-viability abortion.

[In] 2002, however, anti-choice forces ignored this crucial Supreme Court ruling and introduced a new federal abortion ban in Congress. [It passed in] the House of Representatives…but was not considered in the Senate. Undeterred,…anti-choice forces reintroduced this bill…, known as the so-called "Partial-Birth Abortion Ban Act of 2003." This new ban suffers from the same fatal flaws and constitutional defects as the earlier versions. Nevertheless, the anti-choice congressional leadership and President Bush are determined to enact this legislation criminalizing numerous pre-viability abortion methods. It is now more important than ever to fight against this unconstitutional bill and protect women's right to choose.

### The Mounting Campaign to Pass a Federal Abortion Ban

1996—The U.S. Congress passed the first nationwide ban on abortion, which was vetoed by President Clinton. Although abortion foes were able to override the President's veto in the House, the Senate sustained the President's action and prevented the act from becoming law.

1997—Congress passed a slightly amended version of the law, which was immediately vetoed by President Clinton.

1998—Once again, the House overrode the President's veto and the Senate sustained the President's action.

1999–2000—The Senate and House passed the 1997 version of the ban. However, the bill died with the end of the congressional session.

June 2000—In *Stenberg v. Carhart*, a case brought by Center for Reproductive Rights, the U.S. Supreme Court struck down a Nebraska abortion ban, which had been modeled on the federal ban.

July 2002—The House passed a new abortion ban that failed to remedy the flaws in the statute found unconstitutional in *Stenberg v. Carhart*. With the end of the congressional session, the bill died.

February 2003—The new federal abortion ban was reintroduced in both the House and Senate.

## II. THE ABORTION BANS ARE UNCONSTITUTIONAL

A woman's right to terminate her pregnancy is firmly rooted in the Constitution, as recognized by *Roe v. Wade* and its progeny [subsequent cases based on that precedent]. *Roe's* essential holding that a woman may terminate her pregnancy prior to viability, and that her health must prevail throughout pregnancy, even after the point of viability, has been repeatedly reaffirmed by the Supreme Court. For example, in *Planned Parenthood v. Casey* [1992], the Supreme Court held that "[t]he woman's right to terminate her pregnancy before viability is the most central principle of *Roe v. Wade*. It is a rule of law and a component of liberty we cannot renounce." So-called "partial-birth abortion" statutes are a direct attack on this firmly established right.

### A. Two Grounds for Unconstitutionality: Undue Burden and Lack of Health Exception

Like the new federal abortion ban, the statute under consideration in *Stenberg v. Carhart* was a broadly worded abortion ban that would have criminalized numerous abortion procedures, including the most common method of abortion used early in the second trimester. In striking down the law, the Court's majority relied on "established principles" of Supreme Court jurisprudence affirming a woman's right to choose, finding that the law violated the U.S. Constitution "for at least two independent reasons":

- The abortion ban posed an undue burden on the right to choose an abortion in the second trimester because it banned several procedures including the safest and most common method; and

- The abortion ban failed to contain a health exception.

### 1. The Nebraska Law Posed an Undue Burden on the Right to Choose Pre-viability Abortion in the Second Trimester

The Court found that the Nebraska law would criminalize more than one abortion procedure, including the safest and most commonly used method of second-trimester abortion, and therefore constituted an undue burden on women's right to obtain an abortion. The proponents of the Nebraska law claimed that it banned a particular second trimester abortion procedure known as dilation and extraction (D & X). However, the Court found that Nebraska's law outlawed not only the D & X technique, it also prohibited the commonly used pre-viability second-trimester abortion method, dilation and evacuation (D & E), of which D & X is a variant. The Court found that "even if the statute's basic aim is to ban D & X, its language makes clear that it also covers a much broader category of procedures."

Under *Casey*, states are free to regulate a woman's decision to terminate a pregnancy unless the regulation poses an "undue burden" on her right to choose. The Court held that the Nebraska law would impose "'an undue burden on a woman's ability' to choose a D & E abortion, thereby unduly burdening the right to choose itself." The Court concluded by stating the following:

In sum, using this law some present prosecutors and future Attorneys General may choose to pursue physicians who use D & E procedures, the most commonly used method for performing pre-viability second trimester abortions. All those who perform abortion procedures using that method must fear prosecution, conviction, and imprisonment. The result is an undue burden upon a woman's right to make an abortion decision. We must consequently find the statute unconstitutional.

Because the abortion ban would criminalize not just one limited abortion procedure, but also covers a much broader category of procedures, the U.S. Supreme Court struck down the ban as unconstitutional.

As Justice [Stephen] Breyer states in the majority opinion [in *Stenberg v. Carhart*], "Even if the statute's basic aim is to ban D & X, its language makes clear that it also covers a much broader category of procedures." As Justice [Ruth Bader] Ginsburg states in her concurrence, "A state regulation that 'has the purpose or effect of placing a substantial obstacle in the path of a woman seeking an abortion of a nonviable fetus' violates the Constitution. Such an obstacle exists if the State stops a woman from choosing the procedure her doctor 'reasonably believes will best protect the woman in [the] exercise of [her] constitutional liberty.'"

### 2. Any Abortion Method Ban Must Contain a Health Exception

The Court also struck down Nebraska's law because it failed to contain a health exception. In Carhart, the Court reaffirmed the importance of the health exception in abortion jurisprudence, emphasizing that the government "may promote but not endanger a woman's health when it regulates the methods of abortion." The Court noted that both *Roe* and *Casey* "make clear that a risk to a woman's health is the same

whether it happens to arise from regulating a particular method of abortion, or from barring abortion entirely," and that "the absence of a health exception will place women at an unnecessary risk of tragic health consequences." The Court noted that earlier decisions "have repeatedly invalidated statutes that in the process of regulating the methods of abortion, imposed significant health risks," and found that "where substantial medical authority supports the proposition that banning a particular abortion procedure could endanger women's health, *Casey* requires the statute to include a health exception." It therefore struck the law down on the basis of this constitutional defect.

For any abortion ban to be constitutional, it must contain a health exception. For example, the Court found that because D & X may be the safest abortion method available to some women, even a ban that was limited to the D & X procedure must contain an exception when the procedure is "necessary, in appropriate medical judgment, for the preservation of the life or health of the mother." The Court stated "a statute that altogether forbids D & X creates a significant health risk. The statute consequently must contain a health exception." Consequently, since the Nebraska ban contained no health exception for the abortion methods it prohibited, it was stuck down as unconstitutional.

As Justice Breyer stated in his majority opinion [in *Stenberg v. Carhart*], "where substantial medical authority supports the proposition that banning a particular abortion procedure could endanger women's health, *Casey* requires the statute to include a health exception."

### B. The New Federal Abortion Ban Has the Same Old Flaws

Any restriction on abortion must satisfy these two requirements set forth by the Supreme Court. Yet the new federal abortion ban flagrantly defies the Court's ruling.

## 1. The Federal Bill Is Similar to the Nebraska Law

The new federal bill is similar to the Nebraska law struck down in *Carhart*. The federal bill states in part:

### Partial-birth abortions prohibited

(a) Any physician who, in or affecting interstate or foreign commerce, knowingly performs a partial-birth abortion and thereby kills a human fetus shall be fined under this title or imprisoned not more than 2 years, or both. This subsection does not apply to a partial-birth abortion that is necessary to save the life of a mother whose life is endangered by a physical disorder, physical illness, or physical injury, including a life-endangering physical condition caused by or arising from the pregnancy itself....

(b) As used in this section—

(1) the term 'partial-birth abortion' means an abortion in which—

(A) the person performing the abortion deliberately and intentionally vaginally delivers a living fetus until, in the case of a head-first presentation, the entire fetal head is outside the body of the mother, or, in the case of breech presentation, any part of the fetal trunk past the navel is outside the body of the mother for the purpose of performing an overt act that the person knows will kill the partially delivered living fetus; and

(B) performs the overt act, other than completion of delivery, that kills the partially delivered living fetus;

Like the Nebraska law, the federal bill fails to limit the stage of pregnancy to which the bill's provisions apply, so the ban could criminalize abortions throughout pregnancy (not just post-viability or "late term" abortions, as the bill's sponsors often claim). Like the Nebraska law, the federal bill fails to limit its prohibitions to abortions involving an "intact" fetus, fails to explicitly exclude the D & E technique or the suction curettage abortion method from the law's prohibitions, and fails to include definitions of key terms such as "living" or "completion of delivery"; therefore it is broad enough to criminalize numerous safe abortion procedures (not just one abortion procedure, as the bill's sponsors misleadingly imply). Like the Nebraska law, the federal bill also fails to include the constitutionally mandated health exception. For these reasons, as discussed in greater detail below, the federal bill must be struck down as unconstitutional for the same reasons as the Nebraska law in *Carhart*.

## 2. The Federal Bill Poses an Undue Burden

In addition to banning the D & X method of abortion, the definition of "partial-birth abortion" in the federal bill, like that contained in the Nebraska bill, is broad enough also to encompass, at the very least, the D & E procedure, which is the safest and most common method of abortion used in the second trimester. Indeed, the language used in the federal bill is substantially similar to the language that was struck down in *Carhart* for posing an undue burden. As the Court held in *Carhart*, "we can find no difference, in terms of this statute, between the D & X procedure as described and the D & E procedure as it might be performed." Furthermore, under the revised wording of the new federal bill, other safe methods of abortion may also be banned.

Moreover, the sponsors of the federal bill ignored clear instructions from the Supreme Court showing how a statute could be written to exclude the D & E from its reach. They neither provided a clear exception for

D & E, nor "tracked the medical differences between D & E and D & X," as suggested by the Court. One of the witnesses supporting the 2002 federal bill confirmed in her testimony at the House Judiciary Subcommittee on the Constitution hearing that the legislation is not limited to a ban on only one procedure, but is intended to cover others as well.

Like the Nebraska bill, the federal bill imposes severe criminal penalties on doctors for performing D & E's, including fines and imprisonment. Enactment of a federal abortion ban could effectively result in a national ban on D & E's due to doctors' justifiable fears of prosecution and imprisonment. Moreover, the statute's broad reach as well as the vagueness of key statutory terms could also have a significant chilling effect even beyond the reach of the statute. Therefore, in addition to creating an unprecedented intrusion into medical practice, the federal bill imposes an undue burden on a woman's right to choose to terminate her pregnancy.

### 3. The Federal Bill Lacks a Constitutionally Mandated Health Exception

As explained above, the Supreme Court has consistently held that any ban on abortion methods must contain an exception to preserve women's health. Even Attorney General John Ashcroft recently conceded in a brief filed by the Justice Department that some type of health exception is required for legislation banning abortions. The new federal bill, in a direct challenge to this most fundamental principle of abortion jurisprudence, fails to provide any health exception.

Substituting the political will of Congress in place of the medical judgment of doctors, the sponsors acknowledge in the text of the federal bill that it does not include a health exception, claiming that the abor-

tion methods banned by the legislation are "never necessary to preserve the health of a woman." Furthermore, in the 2002 markup of the bill, the committee rejected two amendments that would have permitted women whose health was at risk to undergo the banned procedures. Instead, the bill contains only a limited life exception, allowing an abortion when it is necessary to save a woman's life, but even then only when the woman's life is endangered by a physical condition (which also calls into question the constitutionality of the life exception as written in the bill):

> This subsection does not apply to a partial-birth abortion that is necessary to save the life of a mother whose life is endangered by a physical disorder, physical illness, or physical injury, including a life-endangering physical condition caused by or arising from the pregnancy itself.

In refusing to include a health exception, the sponsors of the federal abortion ban inaccurately argue that Congress is not bound to follow the Supreme Court's ruling in *Carhart*. They claim that the *Carhart* decision was based on "very questionable findings," asserting that Congress is better equipped to assess the evidence since it held "extensive" hearings on the subject. Claiming that congressional findings demonstrate that a health exception is unnecessary, they argue that the Supreme Court should accord "great deference" to these findings. However, as demonstrated in the next section, Congress does not have the power to overturn decisions of the Supreme Court by passing a bill that contains contrary Congressional findings.

### 4. A Renegade Congress Flouts the U.S. Supreme Court

The sponsors claim that the Supreme Court must defer to Congress's legal conclusion that a health exception is unnecessary in the proposed bill. Not only is this untrue, but such a rule would violate the principle of separation of powers underlying our tripartite system of government. As the Supreme Court noted recently in *United States v. Morrison* [2000]:

> Many decisions of this Court, however, have unequivocally reaffirmed the holding of *Marbury* [*v. Madison*, 1803], that 'It is emphatically the province and duty of the judicial department to say what the law is.'

In *Morrison*, the Court held that Congress's legal conclusions—based on substantial congressional findings—were unsupportable, and struck down portions of the law at issue as a result. Similarly, Congress is now attempting to hide behind legislative "findings" to support a law that is clearly contrary to Supreme Court precedent. Congress cannot simply ignore a legal ruling it dislikes by adopting conflicting legislative "findings."

*a. Federal Courts Do Not Blindly Defer to Congressional Fact Findings, But Must Conduct an Independent Review of Facts Bearing on an Issue of Constitutional Law*

The Court has repeatedly held…that whatever deference is accorded legislative findings does not "insulate [those findings] from judicial review," nor does it "'foreclose [the judiciary's] independent judgment of the facts bearing on an issue of constitutional law.'" Rather, "[i]t is…a 'permanent and indispensable feature of our constitutional system' that 'the federal judiciary is supreme in the exposition of the law of the Constitution.'" As Chief Justice [Warren] Burger [1969–1986] has explained:

> A legislature appropriately inquires into and may declare the reasons impelling legislative action but the judicial function commands analysis of whether the specific conduct charged

falls within the reach of the statute and if so whether the legislation is consonant with the Constitution.

*b. The Supreme Court Has Rejected Congressional Fact Findings*

The Supreme Court has rejected congressional findings or found them inadequate to inform a constitutional inquiry in many cases. For example, in…*Morrison*, the Court rejected congressional findings outright. The Violence Against Women Act (VAWA) was enacted after Congress held hearings over a four-year period on the impact of domestic violence on interstate commerce. Despite the "numerous" Congressional findings that domestic violence impacted interstate commerce, the Court struck down the civil remedy provision of VAWA, noting that "'[s]imply because Congress may conclude that a particular activity substantially affects interstate commerce does not necessarily make it so.'"

As these cases demonstrate, the courts have the power and the duty to independently assess evidence and have no obligation to defer to congressional findings. As Justice Clarence Thomas has noted,

> We know of no support…for the proposition that if the constitutionality of a statute depends in part on the existence of certain facts, a court may not review Congress's judgment that the facts exist. If [Congress] could make a statute constitutional simply by 'finding' that black is white or freedom, slavery, judicial review would be an elaborate farce. At least since *Marbury v. Madison*, that has not been the law.

Thus, the sponsors of the federal abortion ban are clearly wrong in their assertion that the courts will adjudicate the bill differently because it contains congressional findings.

*c. Similar Attempts by Congress to Overturn Supreme Court Precedents Have Failed*

There have been several instances in the past where congressional attempts to overturn Supreme Court precedents have failed. For example, Congress passed the Religious Freedom Restoration Act (RFRA) [1993] in response to an earlier Supreme Court decision. As in the case with the new federal abortion ban, Congress held separate hearings to assess the issues and made independent findings prior to enacting the law. In striking down RFRA, the Supreme Court [in *Boerne v. Flores*, 1997] held that Congress "has been given the power 'to enforce,' not the power to determine what constitutes a constitutional violation." The Court further held that "The power to interpret the Constitution in a case or controversy remains in the Judiciary" and "RFRA contradicts vital principles necessary to maintain separation of powers and the federal balance."

Similarly, Congress attempted to overturn the requirements set out by the Supreme Court in *Miranda v. Arizona* [1966] by enacting a new "voluntariness" standard in their place. In *Dickerson v. United States* [2000], the Supreme Court reviewed the law, and in striking it down held that "Miranda, being a constitutional decision of this Court, may not be in effect overruled by an Act of Congress," and "Congress may not legislatively supersede our decisions interpreting and applying the Constitution."

Here, again, Congress is attempting to overturn Supreme Court precedent on a matter of constitutional law by enacting a law that clearly violates the Supreme Court's ruling. As in those cases, Congress has overstepped its bounds—the federal abortion ban does not pass constitutional muster.

## III. THE ABORTION BANS ARE DECEPTIVE

Anti-choice extremists have propagated numerous myths about the abortion bans. The new federal statute is part of a deceptive nationwide campaign to eviscerate the key protections guaranteed to American women by *Roe, Casey*, and *Carhart*. Contrary to the way its proponents characterize the legislation, its prohibitions are limited neither to one medical procedure nor to post-viability abortions late in pregnancy.

### A. The Abortion Bans Are Not Limited to Only One Procedure

First, despite a deceptive public strategy that has propagated the myth that these bans target a single, specific abortion procedure, the federal bill is not limited to one specific procedure. "Partial-birth abortion" is a fabricated term that anti-choice activists concocted in an attempt to make almost all abortions illegal. There is no medical procedure known as a "partial-birth abortion." Anti-choice extremists created the term as a smoke screen to divert the public's attention away from the true scope of the bill, which would make most current second trimester abortions illegal.

In the case of Nebraska, proponents of the statute attempted to convince the Supreme Court that the ban was limited to D & X. But the Court noted in *Carhart* "there is no language in the statute that supports it." In fact, the Nebraska legislature rejected an amendment that would have limited the law to only one narrowly defined procedure. As discussed above, the federal bill similarly fails to limit the ban to the D & X procedure and exacerbates the vagueness of the bill's proscriptions by including no less than two different descriptions of what is banned.

### B. The Abortion Bans Are Not Limited to Post-Viability Abortions Late in Pregnancy

Another myth is that these laws ban post-viability abortions late in pregnancy. However, neither the state laws nor the federal bill contain any reference to the stage of pregnancy to which they apply. The vast majority of states already have laws prohibiting most post-viability abortions, and most of them have been in place since the early 1970s. These laws generally adhere to fundamental constitutional principles establishing that women have the right to chose abortion pre-viability, but that states may more strictly regulate and even forbid abortions after viability, except where necessary to preserve the woman's health or life. Therefore, the new federal abortion ban primarily impacts the legality of pre-viability abortions—although proponents of the bill deliberately confuse this issue.

## IV. THE ABORTION BANS ARE EXTREME

The abortion bans are extreme measures promoted by anti-choice politicians and advocacy groups to eliminate a woman's access to the safest methods of abortion. Because the bans are so extreme, medical organizations and the American public oppose them.

### A. The Abortion Bans Would Prohibit the Safest Methods for Many Women

The nationwide legalization of abortions after *Roe* lead to dramatic health advances for women and substantial decreases in the total number of abortion-related deaths and complications. Between 1973 (the year that *Roe* was decided) and 1985, the number of abortion-related deaths dropped eight-fold: from 3.3 deaths per 100,000 in 1973 to 0.4 deaths per 100,000 in 1985. Similarly, abortion-related complications resulting in hospitalization fell sharply during the 1970s, with the steepest drop following *Roe* in 1973. The federal bill, if enacted, would produce a significant rollback of these health gains.

As noted earlier, the federal bill would ban D & E—the safest second-trimester abortion method for many women that accounts for nearly all abortions performed

from 12 to 20 weeks. The D & X technique, which would also be prohibited under the federal bill, is the safest abortion method for some women, and the U.S. Supreme Court has recognized the body of medical opinion supporting this fact. In fact, in *Carhart*, the only expert witness testifying in favor of Nebraska's law and deemed credible by the District Court, conceded that D & X could well be safer than other D & E variants.

Furthermore, lower courts throughout the country have reviewed a wide range of medical evidence and concluded that D & X is safe. The factual records in Carhart and many other cases demonstrate that D & X is in fact the safest and best abortion technique in some cases. Though acknowledging the lack of statistical studies comparing the safety of the D & X technique with other abortion methods, every federal court in the country, with the exception of one, has agreed that D & X is a safe procedure that may well be safer for women in certain situations.

A ban on D & E abortions, including the D & X variant, would force women to undergo riskier and unnecessary medical procedures and deprive many women of access to the method of abortion that would be safest in their own individual circumstances. The federal ban would harm women's health, render abortions more dangerous, and infringe upon women's right to privacy.

### B. The Proposed Federal Abortion Ban Reflects the Sponsors' Extremism

In addition to drafting the extreme language contained within the federal bill that disregards women's safety, the sponsors also pushed the bill through the U.S. House of Representatives in an extreme fashion.... The House Judiciary Committee considered and rejected numerous amendments that would have made the legislation less severe, including proposals that would:

- provide an exception for abortions "performed before fetal viability, or ...performed after fetal viability where necessary, in appropriate medical judgment, for the preservation of the life or health of the mother";

- provide an exception for abortions "performed before viability where necessary, in appropriate medical judgment, for the preservation of the life or health of the mother, or to such a procedure performed after fetal viability if it is to protect the mother from serious, adverse physical health consequences";

- strike the civil cause of action against physicians and women undergoing an abortion that falls within the bill's definition;

- strike the congressional findings of fact as unsubstantiated;

- ban all post-viability abortions except those abortions that in the medical judgment of the attending physician were necessary to preserve the life of the woman or to avert serious adverse health consequences to the woman; and

- strike the penalties for performing an abortion that falls within the bill's definition.

By rejecting these amendments, the bill's proponents demonstrated a complete disregard for women's health, as well as a desire to supplant the sound medical judgment of doctors with the will of politicians in Congress.

The bill's legislative history demonstrates that its sponsors are intent on adopting a broad ban on pre-viability abortion methods with little, if any, regard for the health of pregnant women. Representative Steve Chabot (R-OH), a primary sponsor of the bill, acknowledged the bill's impact on pre-viability abortions during the markup when he claimed that "limiting the prohibition to only viable fetuses would exempt the vast majority" of abortions that would be criminalized under this legislation.

Furthermore, proponents of the bill maintained that once a woman has decided to have an abortion, politicians in Congress can dictate to a woman what medical procedures she can and cannot undergo, regardless of the medical judgment of her doctor. Representative Randy Forbes (R-VA) acknowledged that the bill would not prevent any abortions from occurring, but instead that its intent is to limit the types of abortion methods that are available to women and their physicians: "This bill is not about having an abortion. It's about whether or not you can have a partial-birth abortion"—a fictitious term invented by anti-choice forces. Moreover, Representative Mike Pence (R-IN) suggested that abortions should be performed by caesarean section instead less invasive techniques. These statements clearly indicate that the intent of the bill is to force women to have more risky procedures by criminalizing the safest abortion methods for many women, and demonstrates the sponsors' contempt for women who have abortions.

## C. Medical Organizations Oppose the Abortion Bans

Abortion bans interfere with doctors' medical discretion, create severe health risks for women and impose strict penalties on doctors, including imprisonment and fines. For these reasons, major U.S. medical organizations have publicly opposed these bills.

The American College of Obstetricians and Gynecologists (ACOG), representing over 90 percent of all ob-gyn specialists, has rejected the abortion bans as "an inappropriate, ill-advised and dangerous intervention into medical decision making."

...The American Medical Women's Association (AMWA) also opposes the abortion bans, stating that it is "gravely concerned with governmental attempts to legislate medical decision-making through measures that do not protect a woman's physical and mental health, including future fertility, or fail to consider other pertinent issues, such as fetal abnormalities."

...The American Medical Association (AMA) initially lent support to a 1997 federal bill that was defeated; however, an internal audit indicated that the organization "blundered" and that this support was politically, not medically, motivated. The AMA has declined to support subsequent abortion bans.

Finally, five medical groups, the American College of Obstetricians and Gynecologists, the American Nurses Association, the American Medical Women's Association, Physicians for Reproductive Choice and Health, and the National Abortion Federation, signed onto an amicus curie [friend of the court] brief in *Carhart* arguing against the Nebraska ban. The Supreme Court relied on their medical expertise when rendering the *Carhart* decision....

## V. CONCLUSION

The U.S. Supreme Court has already struck down legislation containing the exact same constitutional flaws contained in the federal version of the abortion ban. It is a violation of the public trust for elected officials to pass laws that are known to be unconstitutional. Through this bill, Congress is also violating fundamental principals of separation of powers upon which this nation was founded, in unabashedly contravening direct U.S. Supreme Court precedent. The federal abortion ban legislation is the latest attempt to attack a woman's basic right to choose, and would force women to undergo abortion procedures that are more dangerous. This ploy must be recognized as an unconstitutional, deceptive and extreme attempt to violate women's constitutional rights.

Members of Congress should heed the Supreme Court's clear message in *Carhart*: sweeping abortion bans that attempt to prohibit numerous pre-viability abortion methods and fail to protect women's health are unconstitutional.

# Banning D&X (Partial-Birth) Abortions:
## Protecting Fetal Rights

### Kathi A. Aultman

I have spent my entire career as a women's advocate and have a keen interest in issues that impact women's health. I was the co-founder and co-director of the first Rape Treatment Center of Jacksonville, Florida and performed sexual assault exams as a medical examiner for Duval and Clay Counties. I also served as the Medical Director for Planned Parenthood of Jacksonville from 1981 to 1983.

After mastering first trimester and early second trimester dilation and curettage with suction (D&C with suction) procedures I was able to "moonlight" at an abortion clinic in Gainesville, FL. I sought out special training with a local abortionist in order to learn mid second trimester dilation and evacuation (D&E) procedures. Although I do not currently perform abortions, I have continued to dialogue with abortion providers regarding current practices and have studied the medical literature on abortion. I continue to perform D&C with suction and rarely D&E and inductions in cases of incomplete abortion and fetal demise.

I see and treat women with medical and psychological complications from abortion and have managed and delivered women with pregnancies complicated by fetal anomalies, and medical, obstetrical, and psychological problems. I have personally had an abortion and I have a delightful adopted cousin who survived after her mother aborted her.

I have first hand knowledge and familiarity with the partial-birth abortion issue, having testified before legislative bodies in Florida and Vermont. I also testified in court as an expert witness in Arkansas and Virginia and assisted Florida and several other states in designing and/or defending their bans.

I support HR4965 [a U.S. House of Representatives bill number], the "Partial-Birth Abortion Ban Act of 2002," for the following reasons:

1) This bill clearly distinguishes Partial-Birth Abortion from other abortion procedures.
2) This bill will not endanger women's health.
3) It protects women from being subjected to a dangerous unproven experimental procedure.
4) Partial-Birth Abortion has blurred the line between abortion and infanticide.
5) It bans a procedure that is abhorrent to the vast majority of Americans.

## 1) HR 4965 clearly distinguishes Partial-Birth Abortion from other abortion procedures.

Partial-Birth Abortion is a legal term that covers a set of circumstances that culminate in the physician intentionally killing the fetus after it has been partially born.

As defined in the act:

> "the term 'partial-birth abortion' means an abortion in which (A) the person performing the abortion deliberately and intentional vaginally delivers a living fetus until, in the case of a head-first presentation, the entire fetal head is outside the body of the mother, or, in the case of breech presentation, any part of the fetal trunk past

the navel is outside the body of the mother for the purpose of performing an overt act that the person knows will kill the partially delivered living fetus: and (B) performs the overt act, other than completion of delivery, that kills the partially delivered living fetus;"

*(In the rest of the text the term "partially born" will be defined as the position of the fetus as described in HR 4965.)*

Partial-Birth Abortion includes but is not limited to D&X performed on live fetuses. It would also include a procedure used in China where formaldehyde is injected into the baby's brain through its fontanel (soft spot), after the head has been delivered, in order to kill it prior to completing the delivery. It does not prohibit medical abortions, D&C with suction, or D&E procedures. It would not cover Induction unless the physician intentionally intervened during the delivery portion of the procedure and killed the fetus after it had been "partially born." It would not cover a D&X on a dead fetus nor would it cover the accidental death of baby during the normal birth process. Under HR 4965 a Partial-Birth Abortion is allowed if it is "necessary to save the life of a mother whose life is endangered by a physical disorder, illness, or injury."

The "Partial-Birth Abortion Ban Act of 2002" eliminates the concern that D&E is prohibited under the act by more precisely defining what is meant by a Partial-Birth Abortion.

According to the Supreme Court in *Stenberg v. Carhart*, the Nebraska statute banning Partial-Birth Abortion was unconstitutional because it applied to **dilation and evacuation (D&E)** as well as to **dilation and extraction (D&X)**. The court held that the statute was unconstitutional because it imposed an undue burden on a woman's ability to choose

D&E (the most common 2nd trimester abortion procedure), thereby unduly burdening her right to choose abortion itself. The Court commented, however, that if the definition were more narrowly defined to clearly differentiate D&E, a ban might be constitutional.

**Despite assertions to the contrary by some abortionists, both the American Medical Association (AMA) and the American College of Obstetricians and Gynecologists (ACOG) clearly distinguish between D&X and D&E.**

D&X (dilation and extraction or intact dilation and evacuation) is generally performed from about 20–22 weeks gestation and beyond and has been done as late as 40 weeks (full term). It is prohibited by HR 4965 if it is performed on a live fetus. In D&X the fetus is delivered intact except for the decompressed head. In order to accomplish this, Laminaria (dried seaweed) or a synthetic substitute, is inserted into the cervix over the course of several days. The goal is to dilate the cervix just enough to allow the body, but not the head, to be pulled through the cervix. The membranes are ruptured and the lower extremities are grasped under ultrasound guidance. If the fetus is not already breech (feet or bottom first) the baby is converted to that position using forceps. The fetus is then delivered except for its head by a method called breech extraction. The abortionist then thrusts a scissors into the base of the skull, suctions out the brains, and then completes the delivery. The placenta is then extracted using forceps and the cavity is curetted to remove any additional tissue. Prostaglandins and/or oxytocin may be used to help "ripen" the cervix and/or help the uterus contract. (There are times when the head may be pulled through the cervix as the abortionist is extracting the body. In that circumstance, if the abortionist isn't careful to hold the fetus in the vagina prior to killing it, he will be faced with the complication of an unwanted live baby.)

**D&E (dilation and evacuation) is generally used from about 13–15 weeks up until 20–22 weeks and occasionally 24 weeks gestation (early to mid second trimester) and is not prohibited under HR 4965 because the fetus is removed in pieces.**

In D&E the cervix is dilated usually using Laminaria over the course of 1–2 days. It is dilated just enough to allow the forceps to be inserted into the uterine cavity and for body parts to be removed. The membranes are ruptured and the fluid is generally suctioned. The forceps are inserted into the uterine cavity with or without ultrasound guidance. Usually an extremity is grasped first and brought down into the vagina. The rest of the body cannot pass through the cervix so the abortionist is able to detach it by continuing to pull on it. After the smaller parts have been removed, the thorax and head would be crushed and removed from the uterine cavity. The ability to dismember the fetus is based on not over-dilating the cervix. Prostaglandins and/or oxytocin may be used to help "ripen" the cervix and/or help the uterus contract. D&E is not prohibited under the act because fetus dies as a result of being dismembered or crushed while the majority of the body is still within the uterus and not after it has been "partially born."

**D&C with Suction (dilation and curettage with suction) is generally used from 6 weeks up until 14–16 weeks gestation (first and early second trimester). It is not prohibited by HR 4965.**

In this procedure the cervix is generally dilated with metal or plastic rods at the time of the procedure, but occasionally Laminaria are inserted the night before for the later gestations. A suction curette is then inserted and the contents of the uterus are suctioned into a bottle. The cavity is then usually checked with a sharp curette to make sure all the tissue has been removed. At times forceps are needed to remove some of the fetal parts in the later gestations. Prostaglandins and/or oxytocin may be used to help "ripen" the cervix and/or help the uterus contract. It would not be prohibited under this act because the fetus or fetal parts pass from the uterus through the suction tubing directly into a suction bottle. The fetus is therefore not intentionally killed while it is "partially born." The fetus is usually killed as it is pulled through the tip of the suction curette or on impact in the suction bottle.

**Medical Induction is generally performed from 16 weeks gestation to term. This method induces labor and subsequent delivery of an intact fetus and would not be prohibited by HR 4965.**

Labor may be induced in several ways. The older methods are termed "Instillation Methods" because they involve injecting something into the uterus. Saline (a salt solution) injected into the amniotic cavity generally kills the fetus and then causes the woman to go into labor but is associated with significant risk. Urea may also be instilled and appears safer than saline but there is a higher incidence of delivering a live baby. It may also need to be augmented with prostaglandins. In another method a prostaglandin called carboprost (Hemabate) is injected into the amniotic cavity or given IM to stimulate labor but may not always kill the fetus. An intra-fetal injection of KCL or Digoxin may be necessary to prevent a live birth.

Newer methods employ the use of prostaglandins. PGE1 (misoprostol) and PGE2 are generally used vaginally, often in conjunction with oxytocin. These methods generally result in the delivery of a live baby so if an abortion is intended an intra-fetal injection of KCL or Digoxin is generally utilized. PGE2 and oxytocin may be used in cases of previous C-section or uterine surgery. HR 4965 would not prohibit a Medical Induction unless the abortionist purposely halted the birth process in order to intentionally kill a still living "partially born" fetus.

Some of the concerns expressed about Inductions, as opposed to surgical methods (D&E and D&X), include 1) the psychological and physical pain of labor, 2) the time involved, and 3) the fact that they are often done in a hospital and are therefore more costly.

Especially if an abortion is the goal, the pain and even the memory of labor can be eliminated with medication. All three procedures generally require more than one day except perhaps in the case of an early D&E. The mean Induction time with vaginal prostaglandins is 13.4 hours and 90% are delivered by 24 hours. All of these methods have been performed in both inpatient and outpatient settings, however, as the gestational age and therefore the risk increases, the inpatient setting generally becomes safer.

Cephalocentesis is a medical procedure during which a needle is inserted into the head of a fetus with hydrocephalus (water on the brain) in order to drain the fluid. It would not be prohibited by HR4965.

This procedure can be lifesaving for the fetus and may prevent brain damage by taking pressure off the brain. The needle is usually inserted through the abdomen but may also be inserted vaginally if the fetus is in the head first position. This is done while the fetus is still inside the womb. This would not be prohibited even if the fetus had been delivered breech if were done to draw off fluid (not brain tissue) in order to shrink the head to allow delivery of an entrapped hydrocephalic head.

Death during the birth process would not be prosecuted under HR 4965, whether or not labor was induced, as long as the fetus was not intentionally killed while it was partially born.

Passage of RH 4965 will not create an undue burden on a woman seeking an abortion because its narrow definition of Partial-Birth Abortion excludes the commonly used methods of abortion which provide alternatives at every gestational level.

Some abortionists have begun to use parts of the D&X technique on earlier gestations. The mere fact that it is possible to use this procedure on pre-viable fetuses should not prevent it from being banned.

## 2) HR 4965 would not endanger woman's health.

Obstetricians regularly handle medical complications of pregnancy that may threaten a woman's health or life without having to resort to using a Partial-birth Abortion.

When the baby is wanted and the pregnancy must be terminated after or near viability, Induction and C-section are commonly used in an attempt to save both the mother and the baby. Destructive procedures are only considered pre-viability or if the pregnancy is unwanted. Standard procedures such as D&C with suction, D&E, and Induction may be used to terminate an unwanted pregnancy. In an emergency situation, when immediate delivery is necessary D&X would not be used because of the length of time required to dilate the cervix. In it's report on Late Term Pregnancy Termination Techniques, the AMA stated, "Except in extraordinary circumstances, maternal health factors which demand termination of the pregnancy can be accommodated without sacrifice of the fetus, and the near certainty of the independent viability of the fetus argues for ending the pregnancy by appropriate delivery.

**Although a Partial-Birth Abortion is never necessary to safeguard the health of the mother, HR 4965 provides an exception just in case "it is necessary to save the life of a mother whose life is endangered by a physical disorder, illness or injury."**

The AMA report on Late Term Pregnancy Termination Techniques states that, "According to the scientific literature, there does not appear to be any identified situation in which intact D&X is the only appropriate procedure to induce abortion and ethical concerns have been raised about intact D&X." Even if there were such a situation, however, the fetus could be injected with Digoxin or KCL, or the cord could be cut at the start of the procedure, in order to kill the fetus so that the procedure could be performed without risking prosecution.

In my opinion the health exception required under current case law is so broad that it basically allows elective abortion through term.

### 3) It protects women from being subjected to a dangerous unproven experimental procedure.

D&X is an experimental procedure that has not been adequately evaluated. There have been no peer reviewed controlled studies that have looked at the benefits and risks of D&X as compared to D&E, Induction, Delivery, or C-Section. We do not have adequate data on its mortality or morbidity. The complications of D&X include hemorrhage, infection, DIC, embolus, retained tissue, injury to the pelvic organs including the bowel and bladder, as well as an increased risk of cervical incompetence. These risks are the similar to those associated with D&E, however, these risks increase with increasing gestational age and D&X may be done at much later gestational ages. There was some suggestion in earlier studies that greater artificial cervical dilation increases the risk of cervical incompetence. With D&X the cervix must be dilated significantly more than with D&E.

One of the problems in determining both the frequency and mortality and morbidity of the various abortion procedures is that the reporting of the numbers and types of abortion procedures at various gestational ages is grossly inadequate. Four states including California don't report their statistics to the CDC and many don't record the necessary details. D&X is not reported separately nor is it clear which category it should be reported under. There is also inadequate reporting of the complications of abortion.

At times I am called to see women in the ER with complications of abortions. I had always assumed that when I wrote the diagnosis on the hospital face sheet that those cases would be reported to the state. I was shocked when I found out that they aren't reported to anyone and that there is no requirement to report them. In light of that, how can we determine what the true complication rate is for any of these procedures since many never return to their abortion provider?

D&X is often done in outpatient settings. The abortionist may not have hospital privileges or know how to handle the complications of the procedure especially if he is not an OB/GYN.

Although previous C-section has been cited as a reason why D&X might be preferred over Induction, Dr. Haskell, the originator of the procedure, excluded those cases. It is now accepted practice to use prostaglandin E2 and/or oxytocin for Induction after previous C-section.

### 4) Partial-Birth Abortion has blurred the line between abortion and infanticide.

When I first heard the term I thought it strange that it would called Partial-Birth

Abortion and not Partial-Birth Infanticide. I didn't understand why Drs. Haskell and McMahon weren't charged with murder, or at least lose their license to practice medicine, once they revealed what they were doing in a D&X. The fact that the babies weren't 100% born when they were killed seemed to me like an awfully flimsy technicality.

**Who decided that just because a fetus was within the birth canal, the abortionist could still kill it?**

Does this mean that the abortionist may kill a baby that has just one foot still in the vagina? Can a woman request, even demand, that the physician attending her delivery, kill her child once it's head has been delivered if she finds it is the wrong race or has a cleft lip? Currently, her claim would be valid if she stated that the birth would damage her psychologically and might actually place her life at risk if her abusive husband found out.

We already have had cases where an infant was not treated with the same care because the mother had intended to abort it. We had several cases where teens killed their babies after delivery and we were horrified. What hypocrites we are. Had they been smart enough to leave a foot in the vagina prior to killing the baby they could only have been charged with practicing medicine without a license.

When my daughter was working on a paper on the Holocaust for school, I became particularly interested in one of her sources. It discussed the mindset of the medical community in Germany right before the holocaust. I was saddened and concerned when I considered where we are as well. Not only are we killing babies during the process of birth, but there are also those in the medical community who are advocating euthanizing babies up to 3 months at the request of the parent. In Nazi Germany defective babies were the first to be eliminated.

In light of current case law, the passage of HR 4965 is necessary in order to re-establish a bright line between abortion and infanticide.

5) **HR 4965 bans a procedure that is abhorrent to the vast majority of Americans.**

Even though I had done mid 2nd trimester D&Es, I was appalled when I heard about D&X and really didn't believe it was being done. The majority of Americans also [has] found Partial Birth Abortion abhorrent and have supported legislation in numerous states banning its use.

When Nebraska's Partial-birth Abortion Ban was ruled unconstitutional several things happened:

(1)  The line between abortion and infanticide was blurred,
(2)  The State's ability to regulate abortion at any gestation even in the case of a procedure as repugnant as PBA was effectively blocked and
(3)  The State's ability to promote any interest in the potentiality of human life, even post viability, was lost.

For these reasons I feel that this committee is justified in sponsoring legislation to once again attempt ban partial-birth abortion.

**Both *Roe* and *Casey* stated that the State has an interest in potential life and could even proscribe certain techniques as long as it did not create an undue burden for women obtaining abortions.**

The court emphasizes that "By no means must a State grant physicians unfettered discretion in their selection of abortion methods," and yet with this decision they have done just that. The fact that a D&X can be done on a nonviable fetus does not mean that it cannot be banned as long as the prohibition does not unduly burden a woman's ability to obtain an abortion. Since there are other more acceptable procedures available this is not an issue.

As a former abortionist I can tell you that the worst complication for an abortionist is a live baby at the end of the procedure. The goal is a dead baby.

At our hospital a fetal death before 20 weeks it is considered a spontaneous abortion or miscarriage. After that time it is considered a stillbirth and a death certificate must be filled out and the baby must be sent to the funeral home. If a baby of any gestation is born alive and exhibits definite signs of life, it is considered a birth and a birth certificate is filled out.

**Unlike D&E, which is limited to about 20–22 weeks by the toughness of the tissue, D&X allows a surgical delivery of the fetus through term. Unlike induction and C-section, however, the fetus has no possibility of survival with D&X.**

Even ACOG, a staunch supporter of abortion rights states in its *Abortion Statement of Policy*, "The College continues to affirm the legal right of a woman to obtain an abortion prior to fetal viability. ACOG is opposed to abortion of the healthy fetus that has attained viability in a healthy woman."

When I reviewed Dr. McMahon's testimony given to the House Subcommittee on the Constitution June 23,1995 I found that the maternal indications he listed for D&Xs he had performed were generally not serious and the vast majority were actually done for fetal indications, many of which were minor. Depression accounted for 39, Induction failure 14, Sexual Assault 19, Down's Syndrome 175, and cleft lip 9.

Dr. Haskell admitted that he did the vast majority of his D&Xs on normal fetuses and pregnancies. During the course of this debate I received a letter from an abortionist in Orlando offering termination of pregnancy up to 28 weeks

for fetal indications. He went on to say that, "To obtain a pregnancy termination beyond 24 weeks gestation, Florida State Law requires that a patient receive a written statement from her personal physician indicating it would be a threat to her health to continue her pregnancy." As the court currently defines health, even continuing a normal pregnancy threatens a woman's health.

I am concerned that some of the effort to preserve this technique is being fueled by the fetal organ trade in addition to the abortion industries desire to have no restrictions on abortion.

**As a moral people there are some things that just should not be allowed and the killing of an infant in the process of birth is one of them.**

Although the courts have given a woman the right to empty her womb they have not given her the right to a dead child. As technology and Induction techniques improve we will hopefully be able to give a woman the right to terminate her pregnancy without the necessity of terminating her child.

When Dr. McMahon first testified regarding D&X he claimed that the fetus was killed by the anesthetic given the mother. That was soundly refuted by several prominent anesthesiologists. We also now know that the fetus feels pain, which makes this procedure even more ghastly.

**I have been accused of being anti-abortion because of my religious beliefs but actually I stopped doing abortions while I was an atheist.**

When I started my OB/GYN Residency I was very pro-abortion. I felt no woman should have go through a pregnancy she didn't want. I felt abortion was a necessary evil and I was determined to provide women with the best abortion care possible. I perfected my D&C with suction technique and then convinced one of our local abortionists to teach me to do D&Es. I moonlighted at an abortion clinic in Gainesville as much as I could. The only time I felt uneasy was when I was on my neonatal rotation and I realized that the babies I was trying to save were the same size as the babies I had been aborting.

I continued to do abortions almost the entire time I was pregnant (with my eldest daughter) without it bothering me. It wasn't until I delivered my daughter and made the connection between fetus and baby that I stopped doing abortions. I found out later that few doctors are able to do abortions for very long. OB/GYNs especially, often experience a conflict of interest because they normally are concerned about the welfare of both their patients but in an abortion they are killing one of them. It's hard for most doctors to deliver babies and do abortions. It also has to do with the fact that to almost everyone else the pregnancy is just a blob of tissue, but the abortionist knows exactly what he is doing because he has to count all the parts after each abortion. I never had any doubt that I was killing little people but somehow I was able to justify and compartmentalize that.

Even though I later became a Christian, I continued to be a staunch supporter of abortion rights. I just couldn't stomach doing them myself anymore....I had dehumanized the fetus and therefore felt no moral responsibility towards it.

I joined the fight to ban this procedure only because I felt we were no longer really dealing with abortion but rather a form of infanticide. This bill safeguards women and does not unduly interfere with their ability to obtain an abortion. It clearly does not cover D&E or other commonly performed abortion techniques. It reestablishes a bright line between abortion and infanticide and it bars a procedure that is abhorrent to most Americans.

I urge you to pass "The Partial-Birth Abortion Act of 2002."

# THE CONTINUING DEBATE:
## Banning D&X (Partial-Birth) Abortions

### What Is New

Congress enacted a ban on D&X/partial birth abortions in 2003 by votes of 281 to 142 in the House and 64 to 34 in the Senate, and President Bush signed it into law. Opponents of the law soon challenged its constitutionality in court. In 2004, three U.S. District Courts ruled against the ban, but is supporters have appealed.

Public opinion has been very divided on abortion since *Roe v. Wade* in 1973. Soon after that decision, one poll found 47% in favor of the ruling, 44% opposed, and 9% unsure. A series of 2004 polls revealed similar opinion, with, on average, 47% of respondents saying they were "pro-choice," 45% being "pro-life," and 8% unsure. As for banning D&X/partial birth abortion, a 2004 poll found that 48% supported doing so, 36% opposed a ban, and 16% were unsure.

### Where to Find More

For a review of the abortion debate, which dates back even beyond Connecticut's enactment of the first anti-abortion law in 1821, see Rosemary Nossiff, *Before Roe: Abortion Policy in the States* (Temple University Press, 2002). A study of more contemporary policy is Donald T. Critchlow, *Intended Consequences: Birth Control, Abortion, and the Federal Government in Modern America* (Oxford University Press, 2001).

Current information on the abortion debate and its politics can be found on the Web sites of those representing both points of view. That of the Center for Reproductive Rights, author of the first reading is at: http://www.crlp.org/. Representing the pro-life point of view is the National Right to Life Committee at http://www.nrlc.org/. A site that claims to be balanced and seems to strive for that can be found at: http://www.religioustolerance.org/abortion1.htm.

### What More to Do

The greatest challenge is to try to reach an agreement on this emotionally charged issue. Certainly it will not be possible to reconcile everyone. There are ardent voices that see no middle ground between the right to choose and the right to life. But polls show that most Americans are less doctrinaire. A 2004 poll recorded 18% of its respondents thinking abortion should be legal in all cases, 35% saying legal in most cases, 27% arguing it should be illegal in most cases, 14% wanting abortion to be illegal in all cases, and 6% uncertain. Somewhere in that majority of 68% Americans who are in the "most cases" or "uncertain" middle there may be a place that takes into account fetal/infant viability, maternal health, and other factors and creates a policy that most Americans can accept. Can your class craft a statement of standards that would receive a majority vote in the class?

# CIVIL LIBERTIES

## REQUIRING REGISTRATION TO ACCESS INTERNET PORNOGRAPHY:
### Abridging Free Speech *or* Safeguarding Children?

### ABRIDGING FREE SPEECH

**ADVOCATE:** Anthony M. Kennedy, Associate Justice, U.S. Supreme Court

**SOURCE:** Opinion in *Ashcroft v. American Civil Liberties Union*, June 29, 2004

### SAFEGUARDING CHILDREN

**ADVOCATE:** Stephen G. Breyer, Associate Justice, U.S. Supreme Court

**SOURCE:** Opinion in *Ashcroft v. American Civil Liberties Union*, June 29, 2004

It is hard to dispute former Vice President Hubert H. Humphrey's view that, "The moral test of government is how it treats those who are in the dawn of life, the children." Equally laudatory is President Andrew Shepherd's declaration in the film *American President* (1995):

> America isn't easy. America is advanced citizenship. You've gotta want it bad, cause it's gonna put up a fight. It's gonna say, "You want free speech? Let's see you acknowledge a man whose words make your blood boil, who's standing center stage and advocating at the top of his lungs that which you would spend a lifetime opposing at the top of yours."…Then you can stand up and sing about the land of the free.

But what if protecting children and defending free conflict? Would President Shepherd, who was speaking about burning the American flag, been so resolute about defending the First Amendment if doing so permitted is his 12-year old daughter, Lucy, to access pornography?

Indisputably, children have more access to sexually explicit material than ever before. The Internet is a particular channel to view such content. Ninety-two percent of Americans worry about this issue, compared to only 8% who do not. But does pornography harm children? The limited research that exists leaves the answer unclear. As one study notes, "Perhaps the most vexing dimension of dealing with children's exposure to sexually explicit material on the Internet is the lack of a clear scientific consensus regarding the impact of such exposure."

Whatever empirical reality may be, 73% of Americans think "the government should do something about" children's access to pornography, with only 26% disagreeing and 1% unsure. Another poll recorded 94% of respondents agreeing "it should be illegal for adults to use the Internet to make pornographic material available to children under the age of 18."

Congress has tried to do that, The latest of these, the Child Online Protection Act (COPA) of 1998, is the subject of this debate. Before reviewing the legislation, it is important to note the difference between what is pornography and what is obscene. Pornography is the broader term and in current usage includes all graphic representations of individuals engaged in sexual activity alone, in pairs, or in groups. Obscene is a legal category and includes, according to the Supreme Court in *Miller v. California* (1973), the subset of pornographic material that is not protected by the First Amendment because it includes representations of sexual acts in a work that (1) "taken as a whole, lacks serious artistic, literary, political, or scientific value," *and* (2) is offensive to the "average person" using "contemporary community" standards.

The Supreme Court in *Miller* and other cases has, on the one hand, given the government the right to regulate, even prohibit, the creation, transmission, and consumption of obscene material, and, on the other hand, has extended First Amendment protection to adults accessing non-obscene pornography. Children, however, are another matter. In *Ginsburg v. New York* (1968), the Supreme Court upheld the conviction of a man convicted of violating a New York State law that prohibited the distribution of pornography to persons less than age 17. However, in *Sable Communications v. FCC* (1989) the court struck down a federal regulation barring "dial-a-porn" telephone messages. Although the regulation was portrayed as protecting children who could call the sites, the court reasoned that most callers were adults and that other steps might be taken to prevent access by children. Then in *Reno v. American Civil Liberties Union* (1997), the court found the Communications Decency Act (1996) which banned all "patently offensive" sexually explicit communications that could be easily accessed by anyone under age 18, to be unconstitutional because it also violated the protection under the First Amendment of adults to access that material.

In response, Congress soon enacted COPA. It made it a crime for commercial Web sites to post material "harmful to minors" unless the site has made a good faith effort to screen out those under age 17. The act suggest such appropriate efforts, as explained in the first reading below. Opponents mounted a legal challenge on First Amendment groups, and the case was taken up by the Supreme Court as *Ashcroft v. American Civil Liberties Union* (2004).

## POINTS TO PONDER

➤ Which do you think would create more harm: limiting First Amendment protection to adults to access pornography or the current access that children have to this material?

➤ In the second reading, Justice Breyer argues that COPA does not prevent adults from accessing pornography, it only imposes a "modest burden" to do so by registering with the site. Do you agree with the justice's depiction of this requirement as "modest?"

➤ This issue relates to others in this volume, such as Debate 2 on the meaning of the Second Amendment on the right to bear arms, in that some argue that those who wrote the First Amendment would have been aghast at the idea that it would someday be construed to protect pornography. Should original intent be applied here?

# Requiring Registration to Access Internet Pornography: Abridging Free Speech

## Anthony M. Kennedy

This case presents a challenge to a statute enacted by Congress to protect minors from exposure to sexually explicit materials on the Internet, the Child Online Protection Act (COPA). We must decide whether the Court of Appeals was correct to affirm a ruling by the District Court that enforcement of COPA should be enjoined because the statute likely violates the First Amendment.

In enacting COPA, Congress gave consideration to our [the Supreme Court's] earlier decisions on this subject. The imperative of according respect to the Congress, however, does not permit us to depart from well-established First Amendment principles. Instead, we must hold the government to its constitutional burden of proof.

Content-based prohibitions, enforced by severe criminal penalties, have the constant potential to be a repressive force in the lives and thoughts of a free people. To guard against that threat the Constitution demands that content-based restrictions on speech be presumed invalid and that the government bear the burden of showing their constitutionality. This is true even when Congress twice has attempted to find a constitutional means to restrict, and punish, the speech in question.

COPA is the second attempt by Congress to make the Internet safe for minors by criminalizing certain Internet speech. The first attempt was the Communications Decency Act of 1996. The Court held the CDA unconstitutional because it was not narrowly tailored to serve a compelling governmental interest and because less restrictive alternatives were available.

In response to the Court's decision in *Reno*, Congress passed COPA. COPA imposes criminal penalties of a $50,000 fine and six months in prison for the knowing posting, for "commercial purposes," of World Wide Web content that is "harmful to minors." Material that is "harmful to minors" is defined as:

> "any communication, picture, image, graphic image file, article, recording, writing, or other matter of any kind that is obscene or that—
>
> "(A) the average person, applying contemporary community standards, would find, taking the material as a whole and with respect to minors, is designed to appeal to, or is designed to pander to, the prurient interest;
>
> "(B) depicts, describes, or represents, in a manner patently offensive with respect to minors, an actual or simulated sexual act or sexual contact, an actual or simulated normal or perverted sexual act, or a lewd exhibition of the genitals or post-pubescent female breast; and
>
> "(C) taken as a whole, lacks serious literary, artistic, political, or scientific value for minors."

"Minors" are defined as "any person under 17 years of age." A person acts for "commercial purposes only if such person is engaged in the business of making such communications." "Engaged in the business," in turn:

"means that the person who makes a communication, or offers to make a communication, by means of the World Wide Web, that includes any material that is harmful to minors, devotes time, attention, or labor to such activities, as a regular course of such person's trade or business, with the objective of earning a profit as a result of such activities (although it is not necessary that the person make a profit or that the making or offering to make such communications be the person's sole or principal business or source of income)."

While the statute labels all speech that falls within these definitions as criminal speech, it also provides an affirmative defense to those who employ specified means to prevent minors from gaining access to the prohibited materials on their Web site. A person may escape conviction under the statute by demonstrating that he:

"has restricted access by minors to material that is harmful to minors—

"(A) by requiring use of a credit card, debit account, adult access code, or adult personal identification number;

"(B) by accepting a digital certificate that verifies age, or

"(C) by any other reasonable measures that are feasible under available technology."

Since the passage of COPA, Congress has enacted additional laws regulating the Internet in an attempt to protect minors. For example, it has enacted a prohibition on misleading Internet domain names, in order to prevent Web site owners from disguising pornographic Web sites in a way likely to cause uninterested persons to visit them. It has also passed a statute cre-

ating a "Dot Kids" second-level Internet domain, the content of which is restricted to that which is fit for minors under the age of 13.

Respondents, Internet content providers and others concerned with protecting the freedom of speech, filed suit in the United States District Court for the Eastern District of Pennsylvania. They sought a preliminary injunction against enforcement of the statute. After considering testimony from witnesses presented by both respondents and the government, the District Court issued an order granting the preliminary injunction. The court first noted that the statute would place a burden on some protected speech. The court then concluded that respondents were likely to prevail on their argument that there were less restrictive alternatives to the statute: "On the record to date, it is not apparent…that [petitioner] can meet its burden to prove that COPA is the least restrictive means available to achieve the goal of restricting the access of minors" to harmful material. In particular, it noted that "[t]he record before the Court reveals that blocking or filtering technology may be at least as successful as COPA would be in restricting minors' access to harmful material online without imposing the burden on constitutionally protected speech that COPA imposes on adult users or Web site operators."

The government appealed the District Court's decision to the United States Court of Appeals for the Third Circuit. The Court of Appeals affirmed the preliminary injunction, but on a different ground. The court concluded that the "community standards" language in COPA by itself rendered the statute unconstitutionally overbroad. We [the Supreme Court justices granted certiorari [agreed to hear the case] and reversed, holding that the community-standards language did not, standing alone, make the statute unconstitutionally overbroad. We emphasized, however, that our decision was limited to that narrow issue. We remanded the case to the Court of Appeals to reconsider whether the District Court had been correct to grant the preliminary injunction. On remand, the Court of Appeals again affirmed the District Court. The Court of Appeals concluded that the statute was not narrowly tailored to serve a compelling government interest, was overbroad, and was not the least restrictive means available for the government to serve the interest of preventing minors from using the Internet to gain access to materials that are harmful to them. The government once again sought review from this Court, and we again granted certiorari.

…The District Court, in deciding to grant the preliminary injunction, concentrated primarily on the argument that there are plausible, less restrictive alternatives to COPA. A statute that "effectively suppresses a large amount of speech that adults have a constitutional right to receive and to address to one another…is unacceptable if less restrictive alternatives would be at least as effective in achieving the legitimate purpose that the statute was enacted to serve." When plaintiffs challenge a content-based speech restriction, the burden is on the government to prove that the proposed alternatives will not be as effective as the challenged statute.

In considering this question, a court assumes that certain protected speech may be regulated, and then asks what is the least restrictive alternative that can be used to achieve that goal. The purpose of the test is not to consider whether the challenged restriction has some effect in achieving Congress' goal, regardless of the restriction it imposes. The purpose of the test is to ensure that speech is restricted no further than necessary to achieve the goal,

for it is important to assure that legitimate speech is not chilled or punished. For that reason, the test does not begin with the status quo of existing regulations, then ask whether the challenged restriction has some additional ability to achieve Congress' legitimate interest. Any restriction on speech could be justified under that analysis. Instead, the court should ask whether the challenged regulation is the least restrictive means among available, effective alternatives.

In deciding whether to grant a preliminary injunction stage, a district court must consider whether the plaintiffs have demonstrated that they are likely to prevail on the merits. (The court also considers whether the plaintiff has shown irreparable injury, but the parties in this case do not contest the correctness of the District Court's conclusion that a likelihood of irreparable injury had been established.) As the government bears the burden of proof on the ultimate question of COPA's constitutionality, respondents must be deemed likely to prevail unless the government has shown that respondents' proposed less restrictive alternatives are less effective than COPA. Applying that analysis, the District Court concluded that respondents were likely to prevail. That conclusion was not an abuse of discretion, because on this record there are a number of plausible, less restrictive alternatives to the statute.

The primary alternative considered by the District Court was blocking and filtering software. Blocking and filtering software is an alternative that is less restrictive than COPA, and, in addition, likely more effective as a means of restricting children's access to materials harmful to them. The District Court, in granting the preliminary injunction, did so primarily because the plaintiffs had proposed that filters are a less restrictive alternative to COPA and the government had not shown it would be likely to disprove the plaintiffs' contention at trial.

Filters are less restrictive than COPA. They impose selective restrictions on speech at the receiving end, not universal restrictions at the source. Under a filtering regime, adults without children may gain access to speech they have a right to see without having to identify themselves or provide their credit card information. Even adults with children may obtain access to the same speech on the same terms simply by turning off the filter on their home computers. Above all, promoting the use of filters does not condemn as criminal any category of speech, and so the potential chilling effect is eliminated, or at least much diminished. All of these things are true, moreover, regardless of how broadly or narrowly the definitions in COPA are construed.

Filters also may well be more effective than COPA. First, a filter can prevent minors from seeing all pornography, not just pornography posted to the Web from America. The District Court noted in its factfindings that one witness estimated that 40% of harmful-to-minors content comes from overseas. COPA does not prevent minors from having access to those foreign harmful materials. That alone makes it possible that filtering software might be more effective in serving Congress' goals. Effectiveness is likely to diminish even further if COPA is upheld, because the providers of the materials that would be covered by the statute simply can move their operations overseas. It is not an answer to say that COPA reaches some amount of materials that are harmful to minors; the question is whether it would reach more of them than less restrictive alternatives. In addition, the District Court found that verification systems may be subject to evasion and cir-

cumvention, for example by minors who have their own credit cards. Finally, filters also may be more effective because they can be applied to all forms of Internet communication, including e-mail, not just communications available via the World Wide Web.

That filtering software may well be more effective than COPA is confirmed by the findings of the Commission on Child Online Protection, a blue-ribbon commission created by Congress in COPA itself. Congress directed the Commission to evaluate the relative merits of different means of restricting minors' ability to gain access to harmful materials on the Internet. It unambiguously found that filters are more effective than age-verification requirements (assigning a score for "Effectiveness" of 7.4 for server-based filters and 6.5 for client-based filters, as compared to 5.9 for independent adult-ID verification, and 5.5 for credit card verification). Thus, not only has the government failed to carry its burden of showing the District Court that the proposed alternative is less effective, but also a government commission appointed to consider the question has concluded just the opposite. That finding supports our conclusion that the District Court did not abuse its discretion in enjoining the statute.

Filtering software, of course, is not a perfect solution to the problem of children gaining access to harmful-to-minors materials. It may block some materials that are not harmful to minors and fail to catch some that are. Whatever the deficiencies of filters, however, the government failed to introduce specific evidence proving that existing technologies are less effective than the restrictions in COPA. The District Court made a specific factfinding that "[n]o evidence was presented to the Court as to the percentage of time that blocking and filtering technology is over- or underinclusive." In the absence of a showing as to the relative effectiveness of COPA and the alternatives proposed by respondents, it was not an abuse of discretion for the District Court to grant the preliminary injunction. The government's burden is not merely to show that a proposed less restrictive alternative has some flaws; its burden is to show that it is less effective. It is not enough for the government to show that COPA has some effect. Nor do respondents bear a burden to introduce, or offer to introduce, evidence that their proposed alternatives are more effective. The government has the burden to show they are less so. The government having failed to carry its burden, it was not an abuse of discretion for the District Court to grant the preliminary injunction.

One argument to the contrary is worth mentioning—the argument that filtering software is not an available alternative because Congress may not require it to be used. That argument carries little weight, because Congress undoubtedly may act to encourage the use of filters. We have held that Congress can give strong incentives to schools and libraries to use them. It could also take steps to promote their development by industry, and their use by parents. It is incorrect, for that reason, to say that filters are part of the current regulatory status quo. The need for parental cooperation does not automatically disqualify a proposed less restrictive alternative, [ruling in another case that] "A court should not assume a plausible, less restrictive alternative would be ineffective; and a court should not presume parents, given full information, will fail to act." In enacting COPA, Congress said its goal was to prevent the "widespread availability of the Internet" from providing "opportunities for minors to access materials through the World Wide Web in a manner that can frustrate parental supervision or control." COPA presumes that parents lack the abil-

ity, not the will, to monitor what their children see. By enacting programs to promote use of filtering software, Congress could give parents that ability without subjecting protected speech to severe penalties....

There are also important practical reasons to let the injunction stand pending a full trial on the merits. First, the potential harms from reversing the injunction outweigh those of leaving it in place by mistake. Where a prosecution is a likely possibility, yet only an affirmative defense is available, speakers may self-censor rather than risk the perils of trial. There is a potential for extraordinary harm and a serious chill upon protected speech. The harm done from letting the injunction stand pending a trial on the merits, in contrast, will not be extensive. No prosecutions have yet been undertaken under the law, so none will be disrupted if the injunction stands. Further, if the injunction is upheld, the government in the interim can enforce obscenity laws already on the books.

Second, there are substantial factual disputes remaining in the case. As mentioned above, there is a serious gap in the evidence as to the effectiveness of filtering software. For us to assume, without proof, that filters are less effective than COPA would usurp the District Court's factfinding role. By allowing the preliminary injunction to stand and remanding for trial, we require the government to shoulder its full constitutional burden of proof respecting the less restrictive alternative argument, rather than excuse it from doing so.

Third, and on a related point, the factual record does not reflect current technological reality—a serious flaw in any case involving the Internet. The technology of the Internet evolves at a rapid pace. Yet the factfindings of the District Court were entered in February 1999, over five years ago. Since then, certain facts about the Internet are known to have changed....It is reasonable to assume that other technological developments important to the First Amendment analysis have also occurred during that time. More and better filtering alternatives may exist than when the District Court entered its findings. Indeed, we know that after the District Court entered its factfindings, a congressionally appointed commission issued a report that found that filters are more effective than verification screens....

On a final point, it is important to note that this opinion does not hold that Congress is incapable of enacting any regulation of the Internet designed to prevent minors from gaining access to harmful materials. The parties, because of the conclusion of the Court of Appeals that the statute's definitions rendered it unconsti-

tutional, did not devote their attention to the question whether further evidence might be introduced on the relative restrictiveness and effectiveness of alternatives to the statute. On remand, however, the parties will be able to introduce further evidence on this point. This opinion does not foreclose the District Court from concluding, upon a proper showing by the government that meets the government's constitutional burden as defined in this opinion, that COPA is the least restrictive alternative available to accomplish Congress' goal.

On this record, the government has not shown that the less restrictive alternatives proposed by respondents should be disregarded. Those alternatives, indeed, may be more effective than the provisions of COPA.

# Requiring Registration to Access Internet Pornography: Safeguarding Children

## STEPHEN G. BREYER

The Child Online Protection Act, seeks to protect children from exposure to commercial pornography placed on the Internet. It does so by requiring commercial providers to place pornographic material behind Internet "screens" readily accessible to adults who produce age verification. [Justice Kennedy's opinion] recognizes that we should "'proceed...with care before invalidating the act,'" while pointing out that the "imperative of according respect to the Congress...does not permit us to depart from well-established First Amendment principles." I agree with these generalities. Like [Justice Kennedy], I would subject the act to "the most exacting scrutiny," requiring the government to show that any restriction of nonobscene expression is "narrowly drawn" to further a "compelling interest" and that the restriction amounts to the "least restrictive means" available to further that interest.

Nonetheless, my examination of (1) the burdens the act imposes on protected expression, (2) the act's ability to further a compelling interest, and (3) the proposed "less restrictive alternatives" convinces me that the [Justice Kennedy] is wrong. I cannot accept hiss conclusion that Congress could have accomplished its statutory objective—protecting children from commercial pornography on the Internet—in other, less restrictive ways.

Although the [Justice Kennedy] rests [his] conclusion upon the existence of less restrictive alternatives, I must first examine the burdens that the act imposes upon protected speech. That is because the term "less restrictive alternative" is a comparative term. An "alternative" is "less restrictive" only if it will work less First Amendment harm than the statute itself, while at the same time similarly furthering the "compelling" interest that prompted Congress to enact the statute. Unlike [Justice Kennedy], I do not see how it is possible to make this comparative determination without examining both the extent to which the act regulates protected expression and the nature of the burdens it imposes on that expression. That examination suggests that the act, properly interpreted, imposes a burden on protected speech that is no more than modest.

The act's definitions limit the material it regulates to material that does not enjoy First Amendment protection, namely legally obscene material, and very little more. A comparison of this Court's definition of unprotected, "legally obscene," material with the act's definitions makes this clear.

Material is legally obscene if

"(a)...the average person, applying contemporary community standards' would find that the work, taken as a whole, appeals to the prurient interest...; (b)...the work depicts or describes, in a patently offensive way, sexual conduct specifically defined by the applicable state law; and (c)...the work, taken as a whole, lacks serious literary, artistic, political, or scientific value."

The present statute defines the material that it regulates as material that meets all of the following criteria:

"(A) the average person, applying contemporary community standards, would find, taking the material as a whole *and with respect to minors*, [that the material] is designed to appeal to, or is designed to pander to, the prurient interest;

"(B) [the material] depicts, describes, or represents, in a manner patently offensive *with respect to minors*, an actual or simulated sexual act or sexual contact, an actual or simulated normal or perverted sexual act, or a lewd exhibition of the genitals or post-pubescent female breast; and

"(C) [the material] taken as a whole, lacks serious literary, artistic, political, or scientific value *for minors*."

Both definitions define the relevant material through use of the critical terms "prurient interest" and "lacks serious literary, artistic, political, or scientific value." Insofar as material appeals to, or panders to, "the prurient interest," it simply seeks a sexual response. Insofar as "patently offensive" material with "no serious value" simply seeks that response, it does not seek to educate, it does not seek to elucidate views about sex, it is not artistic, and it is not literary. That is why this Court…[has] held that the First Amendment did not protect material that fit its definition.

The only significant difference between the present statute and [what Justice Kennedy finds is an acceptable] definition [of pornography] consists of the addition [in COPA] of the words "with respect to minors" and "for minors." But the addition of these words to a definition that would otherwise cover only obscenity expands the statute's scope only slightly. That is because the material in question (while potentially harmful to young children) must, first, appeal to the "prurient interest" of, *i.e.,* seek a sexual response from, some group of adolescents or post-adolescents (since young children normally do not so respond). And material that appeals to the "prurient interest[s]" of some group of adolescents or postadolescents will almost inevitably appeal to the "prurient interest[s]" of some group of adults as well.

The "lack of serious value" requirement narrows the statute yet further—despite the presence of the qualification "for minors." That is because one cannot easily imagine material that has serious literary, artistic, political, or scientific value for a significant group of adults, but lacks such value for any significant group of minors. Thus, the statute, read literally, insofar as it extends beyond the legally obscene, could reach only borderline cases. And to take the words of the statute literally is consistent with Congress' avowed objective in enacting this law; namely, putting material produced by professional pornographers behind screens that will verify the age of the viewer.

These limitations on the statute's scope answer many of the concerns raised by those who attack its constitutionality. Respondents fear prosecution for the Internet posting of material that does not fall within the statute's ambit as limited by the "prurient interest" and "no serious value" requirements; for example:

an essay about a young man's experience with masturbation and sexual shame; 'a serious discussion about birth control practices, homosexuality,…or the consequences of prison rape"; an account by a 15-year-old, written for therapeutic purposes, of being raped when she was 13; a guide to self-examination for testicular cancer; a graphic illustration of how to use a condom; or any of the other postings of modern literary or artistic works or discussions of sexual identity, homosexuality, sexually transmitted diseases, sex education, or safe sex, let alone Aldous Huxley's *Brave New World*, J. D. Salinger's *Catcher in the Rye*, or, as the complaint would have it, "Ken Starr's report on the Clinton-Lewinsky scandal." [Kenneth Starr was the independent prosecutor investigating matters related to President Bill Clinton's sexual contact with White House intern Monica Lewinsky.]

These materials are *not* both (1) "designed to appeal to, or…pander to, the prurient interest" of significant groups of minors *and* (2) lacking in "serious literary, artistic, political, or scientific value" for significant groups of minors. Thus, they fall outside the statute's definition of the material that it restricts, a fact the government acknowledged at oral argument.

I have found nothing elsewhere in the statute's language that broadens its scope. Other qualifying phrases, such as "taking the material as a whole" and "for commercial purposes," limit the statute's scope still more, requiring, for example, that individual images be considered in context. In sum, the act's definitions limit the statute's scope to commercial pornography. It affects unprotected obscene material. Given the inevitable uncertainty about how to characterize close-to-obscene material, it could apply to (or chill the production of) a limited class of border-

line material that courts might ultimately find is protected. But the examples I have just given fall outside that class.

The act [COPA] does not censor the material it covers. Rather, it requires providers of the "harmful to minors" material to restrict minors' access to it by verifying age. They can do so by inserting screens that verify age using a credit card, adult personal identification number, or other similar technology. In this way, the act requires creation of an Internet screen that minors, but not adults, will find difficult to bypass.

I recognize that the screening requirement imposes some burden on adults who seek access to the regulated material, as well as on its providers. The cost is, in part, monetary. The parties agreed that a Web site could store card numbers or passwords at between 15 and 20 cents per number. And verification services provide free verification to Web site operators, while charging users less than $20 per year. According to the trade association for the commercial pornographers who are the statute's target, use of such verification procedures is "standard practice" in their online operations.

In addition to the monetary cost, and despite strict requirements that identifying information be kept confidential, the identification requirements inherent in age-screening may lead some users to fear embarrassment. Both monetary costs and potential embarrassment can deter potential viewers and, in that sense, the statute's requirements may restrict access to a site. But this Court has held that in the context of congressional efforts to protect children, restrictions of this kind do not automatically violate the Constitution. And the Court has approved their use.

In sum, the act at most imposes a modest additional burden on adult access to legally obscene material, perhaps imposing a similar burden on access to some protected borderline obscene material as well.

I turn next to the question of "compelling interest," that of protecting minors from exposure to commercial pornography. No one denies that such an interest is "compelling." Rather, the question here is whether the act, given its restrictions on adult access, significantly advances that interest. In other words, is the game worth the candle?

[Justice Kennedy] argues that it is not, because of the existence of "blocking and filtering software." [He] refers to the presence of that software as a "less restrictive alternative." But that is a misnomer—a misnomer that may lead the reader to believe that all we need do is look to see if the blocking and filtering software is less restrictive; and to believe that, because in one sense it is (one can turn off the software), that is the end of the constitutional matter.

But such reasoning has no place here. Conceptually speaking, the presence of filtering software is not an *alternative* legislative approach to the problem of protecting children from exposure to commercial pornography. Rather, it is part of the status quo, *i.e.,* the backdrop against which Congress enacted the present statute. It is always true, by definition, that the status quo is less restrictive than a new regulatory law. It is always less restrictive to do *nothing* than to do *something*. But "doing nothing" does not address the problem Congress sought to address—namely that, despite the availability of filtering software, children were still being exposed to harmful material on the Internet.

Thus, the relevant constitutional question is not the question [Justice Kennedy] asks: Would it be less restrictive to do nothing? Of course it would be. Rather, the relevant question posits a comparison of (a) a status quo that includes filtering software with (b) a change in that status

quo that adds to it an age-verification screen requirement. Given the existence of filtering software, does the problem Congress identified remain significant? Does the act help to address it? These are questions about the relation of the act to the compelling interest. Does the act, compared to the status quo, significantly advance the ball?

The answers to these intermediate questions are clear: Filtering software, as presently available, does not solve the "child protection" problem. It suffers from four serious inadequacies that prompted Congress to pass legislation instead of relying on its voluntary use. First, its filtering is faulty, allowing some pornographic material to pass through without hindrance. Because the software relies on key words or phrases to block undesirable sites, it does not have the capacity to exclude a precisely defined category of images. That is to say, in the absence of words, the software alone cannot distinguish between the most obscene pictorial image and the Venus de Milo.

Second, filtering software costs money. Not every family has the $40 or so necessary to install it. By way of contrast, age screening costs less.

Third, filtering software depends upon parents willing to decide where their children will surf the Web and able to enforce that decision. As to millions of American families, that is not a reasonable possibility. More than 28 million school age children have both parents or their sole parent in the work force, at least 5 million children are left alone at home without supervision each week, and many of those children will spend afternoons and evenings with friends who may well have access to computers and more lenient parents.

Fourth, software blocking lacks precision, with the result that those who wish to use it to screen out pornography find that it blocks a great deal of material that is valuable....The software's reliance on words to identify undesirable sites necessarily results in the. Indeed, the American Civil Liberties Union (ACLU), one of the respondents here, told Congress that filtering software "block[s] out valuable and protected information, such as information about the Quaker religion, and web sites including those of the American Association of University Women, the AIDS Quilt, [and] the Town Hall Political Site (run by the Family Resource Center, Christian Coalition and other conservative groups).

Nothing in the District Court record suggests the contrary. No respondent has offered to produce evidence at trial to the contrary. No party has suggested, for example, that technology allowing filters to interpret and discern among images has suddenly become, or is about to become, widely available. Indeed, [Justice Kennedy] concedes that "[f]iltering software, of course, is not a perfect solution to the problem."

In sum, a "filtering software status quo" means filtering that underblocks, imposes a cost upon each family that uses it, fails to screen outside the home, and lacks precision. Thus, Congress could reasonably conclude that a system that relies entirely upon the use of such software is not an effective system. And a law that adds to that system an age-verification screen requirement significantly increases the system's efficacy. That is to say, at a modest additional cost to those adults who wish to obtain access to a screened program, that law will bring about better, more precise blocking, both inside and outside the home.

[Justice Kennedy's] response—that 40% of all pornographic material may be of foreign origin—is beside the point. Even assuming (I believe unrealistically) that *all* foreign originators will refuse to

use screening, the act would make a difference in respect to 60% of the Internet's commercial pornography. I cannot call that difference insignificant.

The upshot is that Congress could reasonably conclude that, despite the current availability of filtering software, a child protection problem exists. It also could conclude that a precisely targeted regulatory statute, adding an age-verification requirement for a narrow range of material, would more effectively shield children from commercial pornography.

Is this justification sufficient? The lower courts thought not. But that is because those courts interpreted the act as imposing far more than a modest burden. They assumed an interpretation of the statute in which it reached far beyond legally obscene and borderline-obscene material, affecting material that, given the interpretation set forth above, would fall well outside the act's scope. But we must interpret the act to save it, not to destroy it. The act imposes a far lesser burden on access to protected material. Given the modest nature of that burden and the likelihood that the act will significantly further Congress' compelling objective, the act may well satisfy the First Amendment's stringent tests. Indeed, it does satisfy the First Amendment unless, of course, there is a genuine alternative, "less restrictive" way similarly to further that objective.

I turn, then, to the actual "less restrictive alternatives" that [Justice Kennedy] proposes. [He] proposes two real alternatives, *i.e.,* two potentially less restrictive ways in which Congress might alter the status quo in order to achieve its "compelling" objective.

First, the government might "act to encourage" the use of blocking and filtering software. The problem is that any argument that rests upon this alternative proves too much. If one imagines enough government resources devoted to the problem and perhaps additional scientific advances, then, of course, the use of software might become as effective and less restrictive. Obviously, the government could give all parents, schools, and Internet cafes free computers with filtering programs already installed, hire federal employees to train parents and teachers on their use, and devote millions of dollars to the development of better software. The result might be an alternative that is extremely effective.

But the Constitution does not, because it cannot, require the government to disprove the existence of magic solutions, *i.e.,* solutions that, put in general terms, will solve any problem less restrictively but with equal effectiveness....Perhaps that is why no party has argued seriously that additional expenditure of government funds to encourage the use of screening is a "less restrictive alternative."

Second, [Justice Kennedy] suggests decriminalizing the statute, noting the "chilling effect" of criminalizing a category of speech. To remove a major sanction, however, would make the statute less effective, virtually by definition.

My conclusion is that [COPA], as properly interpreted, risks imposition of minor burdens on some protected material—burdens that adults wishing to view the material may overcome at modest cost. At the same time, it significantly helps to achieve a compelling congressional goal, protecting children from exposure to commercial pornography. There is no serious, practically available "less restrictive" way similarly to further this compelling interest. Hence the act is constitutional.

# THE CONTINUING DEBATE:
## Requiring Registration to Access Internet Pornography

### What Is New

The Supreme Court stuck down the COPA Act by a 5 to 4 vote. Justice Kennedy wrote the majority opinion. Justice Breyer's opinion was a dissent. Congress did not take up the issue again in 2004 as members turned to the national elections. However, legislators will surely again try to write protective legislation. The door is open because of a fragmented majority in this case. Justice John Paul Stevens, joined by Justice Ruth Bader Ginsberg, wrote a separate concurrence with the majority opinion indicating that their concern that COPA's criminal penalties were overly "strong medicine for the ill that the statute seeks to remedy." Stevens conceded that a "compelling interest in protecting minors from exposure to sexually explicit materials" exists and added, "As a parent, grandparent, and great-grandparent, I endorse that goal without reservation." But, he continued, "As a judge,...I [have]...unease when the interest in protecting children from prurient materials is invoked as a justification for using criminal regulation of speech as a substitute for, or a simple backup to, adult oversight of children's viewing habits." This view left him open to "protecting children from harmful materials by other, less drastic means." Thus, a new law with less draconian penalties than contained in COPA might turn a 5 to 4 vote against protection to a 6 to 3 vote in favor.

### Where to Find More

Read the study on children and the Internet quoted in the introduction to this debate: Dick Thornburgh and Herbert S. Lin, eds., *Youth, Pornography, and the Internet*, a report of the Computer Science and Telecommunications Board and the National Research Council (National Academy Press, 2002). The report is available online at http://nationalacademies.org/nrc/. Also good on the topic is chapter 13 of Dorothy G. Singer and Jerome L. Singer, *Handbook of Children and the Media* (Sage Publications, 2001). One perspective on the issue can be gained from the Web site of the Free Speech Coalition, which represents the adult entertainment industry, at http://www.freespeechcoalition.com. An opposing view is on the Web site of Morality in Media, Inc., at http://www.moralityinmedia.org/.

### What More to Do

Have a class exercise in which you consider writing a successor law to COPA. You could take the position that none is necessary for one reason, or another inherently violates the First Amendment and then defend your view. But if you believe that there are valid grounds for trying to restrict children's access to pornography, how can you effectively regulate access, while avoiding unreasonably restricting adult access (and thereby violating the First Amendment) and the harsh penalties that concerned Justice Stevens?

# AMERICAN PEOPLE/
# POLITICAL CULTURE

## IMMIGRATION AS A THREAT TO "WHO WE ARE":
### Valid Concern *or* Unfounded Fear?

### VALID CONCERN

**ADVOCATE:** John O'Sulllivan, Editor-in-chief of the *National Interest*
**SOURCE:** "Who We Are," *The American Conservative*, July 19, 2004

### UNFOUNDED FEAR

**ADVOCATE:** Jim Sleeper, Lecturer in Political Science, Yale University
**SOURCE:** Review of Samuel Huntington's *Who Are We?: The Challenges to America's National Identity*, History News Network, May 3, 2004

The face of America is changing. A nation that was once overwhelmingly composed of European heritage whites is becoming more diverse ethnically and racially. Of the 4.6 million people in the United States in 1790, whites made up two-thirds of the population. The other third was divided about equally between black slaves, and American Indians, none of whom were citizens. Of the whites, 92% were Anglo Saxons, tracing their heritage to the British Isles.

The American population grew rapidly, reaching 281 million in 2000. Immigration has been a key factor. More than 60 million individuals have come to the United States since 1790. The greatest influx of came between 1870 and 1920. During that period, an average of 14% of the U.S. population was foreign born, and in some decades the inflow of immigrants equaled 10% of the U.S. population. Then immigration plunged, with only 500,000 newcomers admitted during the 1930s. It slowly recovered, but through the 1960s both the number of immigrants and their percentage of the population remained well below the rate during the late 1800s and early 1900s. Most immigrants came from Europe, and as late as the 1960s, more than 70% of immigrants were coming from Europe or European-heritage countries (primarily Canada). Reflecting that, the 1960 U.S. population was approximately 82% white, 11% black, 6% Hispanic, 0.5% Asian American, and 0.5% Native American. By 2000, according to the 2000 census, the U.S. population was 69% white, 12% African American, 13% Latino, 4% Asian American, and 1% Native American. This shift is expected to continue, with the Census Bureau estimating that in 2050, the U.S. population will be 52% white, 24% Latino, 15% African American, 9% Asian American, and 1% Native American. One reason for the change is different fertility rates, which is the average number of children a woman in her childbearing years will have. In 2000 the fertility rate was 2.0 for whites, 2.1 for African Americans, 2.5 for Native Americans, 2.3 for Asian Americans, and 2.9 for Hispanics.

Changes in immigration are a second factor accounting for growing diversity. First, immigration increased, nearly tripling for an annual 330,000 in the 1960s to 950,000 annually in the late 1990s. This number seems huge, but during the 1990s, total immigrants equaled only 3.5% of the population, a proportion much lower than some early decades, such as the 10.4% rate between 1900 and 1909. The recent growth of immigration has increased the percentage of the U.S. population that is foreign born to 10.4% in 2000, but that percentage is lower than it was at any time between 1860 and 1940.

A second change is that the flow of immigration now brings in a much greater percentage of people from Asia, Latin American, and Africa. In the late 1990s, Europeans were only 16% of newcomers, compared to 32% from Asia and 48% from Latin America and the Caribbean, and 4% from Africa. The significant shift in the geographic origin of immigrants occurred after Congress amended the immigration laws in 1965 to eliminate the quota system that favored immigration from Europe and replace it with a qualifications system based on job skills and other criteria. Another important factor relates to illegal immigration from Latin America, especially Mexico. Millions have arrived without documentation, and federal legislation in 1986 gave permanent residency to about 4 million of these individuals.

The increased rate of immigration and its increasingly non-European complexion have raised concerns in some quarters. One expression of that view is a book, *Who We Are: The Challenges to America's National Identity* (Simon & Schuster, 2004) written by political scientist Samuel P. Huntington, the Albert J. Weatherhead III University Professor at Harvard University and chairman of the Harvard Academy for International and Area Studies. An introductory review of the book in the *Washington Post* noted that, "Huntington has written a book that poses some of the most critical questions facing our nation" including, "How can a people already preoccupied with ethnic identity absorb and acculturate the millions of immigrants being driven to our shores by global economics?" and "How in the long run will America cohere if everyone feels they belong to a minority?" and the book "tackles these questions with passionate intensity." That effort has engendered other passionate commentary, some of it praising and some of it condemning Huntington, as the following two reviews of his book reveal.

## POINTS TO PONDER

➤ John O'Sulllivan in the first article disparages critics who dismiss Huntington as a bigot and argue his work should have not been published. Do you agree that Huntington should be ignored or do you think his views should be read, analyzed, and debated?

➤ The traditional goal has been a cultural melting pot in which immigrants merged into existing American culture. Some people now advocate multiculturalism, the coexistence of more than one culture. What are the benefits and drawbacks of the melting pot and multicultural images?

# Immigration as a Threat to "Who We Are": Valid Concern

## JOHN O'SULLLIVAN

Samuel Huntington's book was notorious even before the page proofs were sent out to magazine editors for the pre-publication of extracts. Rumors had circulated for at least a year beforehand that the author of *The Clash of Civilizations* [1998] and other distinguished works of political theory was about to produce a book on immigration that was not wholly in favor of it. In fact, while *Who Are We?* deals in detail with current immigration to the U.S., the book as a whole is about the wider and more important topic of national identity. As we shall see, that is making it more controversial rather than less. Still, the first intimations of controversy were inspired by the astounding prospect of an anti-immigration book from one of the nation's most respected political scientists and a fully paid-up member of the American establishment. If Sam Huntington broke ranks, then elite support for high levels of immigration might fracture at the very moment that the Bush administration was proposing an open-borders policy. And that would be high politics as well as intellectual controversy.

Excitement rose higher when the first extract of *Who Are We?* was published [in an article "The Hispanic Challenge"] in *Foreign Policy* magazine [March/April, 2004]. This turned out, as suspected, to be devoted to immigration—and to a particularly contentious aspect of it.

In his book, Huntington argues that post-1965 immigration is very different from previous waves in two significant ways. In the first place, it consists of continuously high levels of immigration.

Previous immigration was either low but continuous (e.g., from the Revolution to the 1840s) or a series of high peaks followed by low troughs (e.g., the second great wave of 1880–1920 followed by 40 years of low immigration under the restrictive quotas of the 1920s). Continuous high immigration tends to retard the assimilation of immigrants into the host community and to foster ethnic ghettoes that then accommodate semipermanent ethnic diasporas. All of these trends will be maximized if the immigration occurs in conditions of official bilingualism and multiculturalism rather than of Americanization. Immigrants will then be less likely to assimilate and more likely to retain ethnic identities and links with home.

The second difference is that the new immigration intake is much less diverse than the immigrants in earlier periods. In brief, one half of new legal immigrants come from Latin America—and 25 percent of them from a single national source, namely Mexico. Even in the absence of other factors, this would hinder assimilation. If immigrants speak several languages, they have a clear incentive to master the *lingua franca* that will help them to communicate both with each other and with the native-born. If they speak one language, however, they are more easily able to continue living in a linguistic enclave that is an overseas version of home, such as Miami, where it is the native-born who feel foreign.

That central difficulty in the case of Latinos in general is aggravated in the case of Mexicans by several other characteristics. Again in brief, Mexican Americans are especially numerous—25 percent and rising of the total of legal immigrants. Their numbers are further supplemented because they are the overwhelming majority of illegal immigrants. They come from a nation contiguous to the U.S. with a long and porous border. They are regionally concentrated in the Southwest (as were Cubans in Florida) so that they are more likely to concentrate themselves in linguistic enclaves. They seem likely to keep coming indefinitely—i.e., in the absence of strong official discouragement, the supply of Mexican arrivals is for practical purposes infinite. And finally Mexicans have a historical presence in the region—there are even some who cherish irredentist claims [to reincorporate the U.S. southwest Mexico] on what they call "Aztlan."

Making these and other points, Huntington concluded that there is a real possibility that the American Southwest might become in time another Quebec [a culturally and linguistically French dominant province of Canada]—namely, a region of the U.S. where the dominant language and culture would be Hispanic —in a Nuevo United States that would be a bilingual and bicultural society. And as Quebec and Belgium [divided between French-speaking Flemings and Dutch-speaking Waloons] demonstrate in different ways, bilingualism distorts and obstructs democratic governance.

It was, of course, this second "inflammatory" theme that *Foreign Policy* magazine made its front-page lead article. The editors of *Foreign Policy* cannot be wholly acquitted of coat-trailing here. They know that controversy sells and set out to have the maximum impact. Still, even they were probably surprised by all the results that followed—namely, an article that everyone talked about, superb advance

publicity for the book, and a string of insulting and threatening remarks about Huntington—"racist," "nativist," "xenophobe," and the rest—in newspaper columns and *FP*'s own letters section.

Three points emerge in retrospect from these early criticisms. First, almost all the replies simply ignored the vast wealth of social science, census, and polling data that the author laid out in support of his thesis. Huntington has been reproved by otherwise respectful critics for the sheer volume of survey evidence he deploys since it inevitably slows down the book's readability. But these spluttering and indignant responses justify its presence. They show that the weight of prejudice against his argument is such that he would have been destroyed if he had not armored himself in advance against it.

Some of the critics however, promptly dealt with the difficulty that they could not refute what he *had* said by refuting things he *had not* said but would have said if he had been the unreconstructed bigot they desperately wanted to wallop. Several denounced him for relying on the "lazy Mexican stereotype." In fact, he had pointed out that Mexicans' propensity for hard work led *inter alia* [among other things] to the displacement and reduced incomes of low-paid native-born American workers. True, he had also quoted Mexican and Hispanic writers to the effect that Mexicans and Mexican-Americans were less inclined than Americans to believe that hard work was likely to lead to success—and that they were held back by that. Yet this argument is so different from the "lazy Mexican stereotype" that they could be confused only by minds already disabled by ideological fanaticism. It is worth noting, though, that falsely accusing others of relying on stereotypes is fast becoming stereotypical in itself.

Second, when his critics did seek to refute his array of evidence, they mostly got it wrong. Sometimes they got it wrong in respectably complicated ways. Writing in *Time* magazine, Michael Elliot produced polling data that showed Mexicans expressing admiration for the U.S. and sharply criticized Huntington for not taking this into account. But Huntington had not denied that many Mexicans were grateful for the opportunities given to them by the U.S. In a subtle examination of the full range of evidence, he had merely pointed out that such feelings were likely to be offset by a range of other influences over time—notably, that under multiculturalism they might assimilate not into Americanism but into a subordinate ethnic identity that was ambivalent at best towards the U.S. He also cited evidence to suggest that this was happening—indeed that the longer Mexicans lived in the U.S., the less they identified with America and American values, very unlike earlier generations of immigrants. Above all, as John Fonte has pointed out (both reviewing Huntington and responding to Elliot in *National Review*), on the key question of patriotic assimilation—i.e., do immigrants identify themselves primarily as Americans or prefer some other identity?—Huntington has the better of the argument. According to a Pew Hispanic Center study taken after Sept. 11—a date and event that had demonstrated the emptiness of Huntington's nativist anxieties according to Louis Menand in the *New Yorker*—55 percent of Americans of Mexican descent said that they considered themselves Mexican "first," 25 percent chose "Latino" or "Hispanic" as their primary identity, and only 18 percent chose "American." That is not conclusive proof of national disintegration, but it is worrying—not least because reluctance to embrace an American identity is not confined to Hispanic- or Mexican-Americans.

Fonte quotes a study of Muslims in Los Angeles showing that only 10 percent of such immigrants felt more allegiance to America than to a Muslim country. Elliot's citation of more optimistic statistics is not false, but it is partial and complacent.

Other critics got it wrong in simple and straightforward ways. Tamar Jacoby of the Manhattan Institute, who seems to have set herself up as a One-Woman Anti-Huntington Truth Squad, sending media organizations an offer to be interviewed in order to correct his errors, declares, "Huntington also mistakes what it means to assimilate. We as a nation have never asked immigrants to buy into the particulars of our culture, Anglo or otherwise." This confident assertion will astonish (in addition to the world) Norman Podhoretz who, in his autobiographical writings, has written powerfully of "the brutal bargain" whereby immigrants and their children surrendered their cultural identities and transformed themselves into imitation WASPs. It also overlooks the "Americanization" campaigns of both government and private industry, the English language proficiency test in citizenship examinations, and even the Battle of the Bulge, when G.I.s tested each other on such cultural particulars as the name of Betty Grable's husband in order to separate the Americans out from Otto Skorzeny's infiltrators.

The final resort of critics when faced with evidence they don't like—especially statements by irredentists claiming that the American Southwest is destined to return to Mexico—was either "well, they don't represent anyone" (even when the speaker was the spokesman for an irredentist organization) or "well, they don't really mean it." There is no answer to that. Nor is any answer needed.

But the third point is more worrying. An alarming number of critics, some apparently academics, denounced Huntington's arguments as "poisonous," "incendiary," "unabashed racism," and so forth in a highly intemperate fashion, while misquoting and misunderstanding his actual arguments. Professor Bruce E. Wright of California State at Fullerton remarked that the article was an affront not only to Hispanics and Catholics (a Catholic myself, I had failed to be affronted) but also to "those of us"—such *sang froid* [imperturbability]!—"whose identity is not so shallow as to be threatened by a massive invasion of others." The Rev. Edward Lopez of New York thought that Huntington was "threatened by diversity" and "frightened by the world around him." Patricia Seed of Rice University lamented "the arrogance of an East Coast Brahmin." There was the usual irrelevant blather about how earlier Huntingtons had measured skulls and dismissed the potential of now successful immigrant groups. And there was a theme running through almost all of these critiques—the America of Huntington's youth was being replaced by a better, more vibrant, and more just America, one of diversity and multiculturalism. To resist this evolution in defense of a past America was a sign of nostalgia at best, of wicked nativist racism at worst.

It is tempting to dismiss these denunciations as a cry for help. But they must be taken more seriously. After all, several letter-writers went to the lengths of arguing that Huntington's article should not have been published and that *Foreign Policy* should apologize for printing it. It seems reasonable to infer that people holding such views would not willingly allow such arguments to be expressed in their churches, schools, and colleges or treat fairly any student who submitted an essay advancing them. The later anonymous *Economist* reviewer, who was not uncritical of the book, was nonetheless upset by these outbursts that sought, in effect, to censor the rational expression of reasonable fears. They reflect a disturbing willingness to enforce an orthodoxy on dissenters and indicate a moral atmosphere that might best be described as "soft totalitarianism"—even when, or particularly when, the orthodoxy is a minority opinion and the majority has invariably rejected any clear expression of it.

The first effect of these attacks—and the controversy they generated—was to make people want to read the book. (At the National Airport [Washington, D.C.] bookshop where I bought it, I got their last copy a day after publication.) But the book they bought was very different from the article that had prompted them to buy it. It is about much more than immigration. It is a comprehensive analysis of the threats that are undermining America's common culture and sense of itself. As such, it analyses virtually every major skirmish in the cultural wars of the last 40 years. And it analyzes them from a distinctly conservative standpoint.

Huntington is, of course, very far from being a "movement conservative," or even a neoconservative, let alone a paleoconservative. He is a Democrat for starters, and he gave the *New York Times* interviewer a bad fit of cognitive dissonance by telling her that he opposed the war in Iraq and intended to vote for John Kerry. Yet almost 50 years ago, in an article in the *American Political Science Review*, he advanced what still remains the single best definition of conservatism: namely, that it is the set of ideas that men adopt in defense of their social and political institutions when they come under fundamental attack. Huntington believes that America's national identity and the social and political institutions and traditions that sustain it are under fundamental attack. His book is a conservative defense of them.

His starting point is that the American nation, as it developed from the colonial period to the 1960s, was built around certain core institutions, customs, and practices. To oversimplify brutally, these were the English language, dissenting Protestant Christianity, individualism and work ethic, and the political culture of the Founding Fathers with its emphasis on individual rights. Over time, later immigrants groups assimilated to the cultural core of "Anglo-Protestant Christianity" that evolved from these origins and assented to the American Creed that was its self-conscious political expression. They added spicy cultural contributions of their own, of course, but these did not fundamentally alter the national character. And by the late '50s, "Americans were one nation of individuals with equal political rights, who shared a primarily Anglo-Protestant core culture, and were dedicated to the liberal-democratic principles of the American creed."

In the course of outlining this national development, Huntington punctures several comforting national myths dear to both liberals and conservatives but false and sometimes destructive in their current implications. He points out, for instance, that the U.S. is not "a nation of immigrants." It is a nation that was founded by settlers—who are very different from immigrants in that they establish a new polity rather than arrive in an existing one—and that has been occupied since by the descendants of those settlers and of immigrants who came later but who assimilated into the American nation. Americans therefore are under no moral obligation to accept anyone who wishes to immigrate on the spurious grounds that everyone is essentially an immigrant. Americans own America, so to speak, and may admit or refuse entry to outsiders on whatever grounds they think fit.

Huntington similarly demolishes the notion that America is a "proposition nation" and that its national identity consists of adherence to the liberal principles of the American Creed of liberty and individual rights. The American Creed is certainly part of America's national identity—it is the distilled essence of America's culture—but it is too abstract and theoretical to provide a fulfilling patriotism on its own. Men sacrifice themselves for home and beauty, for the comradeship of battle, for loyalty to the flag, to ensure that experience of a free life is not lost to their children—they are very unlikely to sacrifice themselves for political ideas unless they also convey this range of loyalties.

Nor does the Creed sufficiently distinguish Americans from people in other countries. If belief in liberty and individual rights were sufficient to make one an American, half the people in the world could claim citizenship. And if the Creed is seriously taken to be the totality of American identity, then the way is open for a multiculturalism that treats the English language, U.S. history, and American cultural practices from baseball to hard work as simply one set of options in a cultural and ethnic smorgasbord—a smorgasbord, moreover, in which preference for traditional American beliefs and customs counts as discrimination. Of course, words and ideas take a goodly portion of their meaning from the surrounding culture—so that our current understanding of such concepts as liberty would be significantly altered if we were to interpret them in the light not of "Anglo-Protestantism" but of Hispanic, Confucian, or Islamic culture or even of continental Roman Law. Are such anxieties alarmist? Judge Robert Bork has recently pointed out that U.S. Supreme Court justices have been advocating that American courts take account of legal precedents from courts as remote as European Court and the Zimbabwe Supreme Court. It would be a curious irony if the Zimbabwe Supreme Court ended up exercising more legal influence in the U.S. than it does in [authoritarian President] Robert Mugabe's Zimbabwe. But if this is alarmism, it may perhaps be early-warning alarmism.

What has aroused most disquiet among otherwise receptive readers, however, is Huntington's claim that America's common culture to which later immigrants assimilated is one of "Anglo-Protestant conformity." Interestingly, this is one of his less controversial arguments among cultural historians, who have long acknowledged the role of dissenting British religious groups in the shaping of America. Recent major social and cultural histories, such as *Albion's Seed* by David Hackett Fischer, suggest that, if anything, this influence was even stronger than traditionally understood. It may soothe affronted Catholics to learn that this influence was not, strictly speaking, a matter of religious belief, but rather a set of social practices that encouraged freedom of belief in the first instance, and following on from that other sorts of freedom under a dispersed social and economic leadership. As the Anglo-American religious sociologist David Martin has observed of the modern revival of evangelical Protestantism in Latin America in *Tongues of Fire*, dissenting sects brought to the fore a hitherto "buried intelligentsia" that in turn took the leadership of their communities in non-religious roles. Plainly this had effects in strictly religious terms—*inter alia,* the establishment of a still flourishing "marketplace of religions" in the U.S., the conversion of the Catholic Church in America to Protestant notions of liberty, and the gradual adoption by Rome of these "Americanist" heresies. Most devout American Catholics today are Protestants in political theory. But the main effect in the

colonial period and the early years of the Republic was to instill in Americans the habits of self-reliance and voluntary co-operation that so impressed [Alexis de] Tocqueville on his visit [in the 1830s, leading to his famous book, *Democracy in America*]. And the vital, successful political culture built on these foundations—Anglo-Protestantism, the American Creed, and the rest—was still clearly traceable to its early origins in the 1960s.

It was at this point, circa 1965—or just after the Civil Rights Act had finally brought black America fully within the ambit of the American political nation—that influential Americans set about systematically demolishing this impressive structure. Huntington lists the accomplishments of "the deconstructionists" in the following paragraph:

The deconstructionists promoted programs to enhance the status and influence of subnational, racial, ethnic and cultural groups. They encouraged immigrants to maintain their birth country cultures, granted them legal privileges denied to native-born Americans, and denounced the idea of Americanization as un-American. They pushed the re-writing of history syllabi and textbooks so as to refer to the "peoples" of the United States in place of the single people of the Constitution. They urged supplementing or substituting for national history the history of subnational groups. They downgraded the centrality of English in American life and pushed bilingual education and linguistic diversity. They advocated legal recognition of group rights and racial preferences over the individual rights central to the American Creed. They justified their actions by theories of multiculturalism and the idea that diversity rather than unity or community should be America's overriding value. The combined effect of these efforts was to promote the deconstruction of the American identity that had been gradually created over three centuries and the ascendance of subnational identities.

On every point listed here, Huntington examines in detail how these changes occurred and what their significance is to America's future. He pulls not a single punch. To take just one example, he makes clear that the replacement of individual rights by group rights amounts to a "counter-revolution" that reintroduced racial discrimination into American law and practice, implied that individuals are defined by blood, undermined equal justice and equal citizenship, and ultimately denied the existence of a common good. And by the time he has performed the same surgery on the challenge to the English language, the undermining of the common culture, the discrediting of assimilation, the erosion of American citizenship, and much else, he has in effect mounted a comprehensive attack on the main social policies of the last 40 years.

The scale and boldness of Huntington's assault appears to have unmanned reviewers of his book. It seems at times as if they can hardly believe that one author is taking on so many social pieties simultaneously. *Who Are We?* is a veritable abattoir [slaughterhouse] of sacred cows. And the reviewers reacted by looking nervously away, by failing to grasp the main point, and by taking refuge in minor and trivial critiques.

Thus, writing in *Foreign Affairs*, Alan Wolfe disputed Huntington's historical account thus:

> It is…incorrect to claim that American identity was shaped by dissenting Anglo-Protestantism.

Two of the churches prominent at the United States's founding were established rather than dissenting: the Church of England became the established church of Virginia under the Episcopal name, and Presbyterianism had been established in Scotland.

Really, this is the kind of thing that gives nit-picking a bad name.

Or here is Louis Menand in the *New Yorker*:

> …it is absurd to say that [multiculturalism] is anti-Western. Its roots, as Charles Taylor and many other writers have shown, are in the classic texts of Western literature and philosophy.

Has Menand never heard of [Karl] Marx? The German social philosopher is undoubtedly a major figure in the Western tradition of literature and philosophy— few more so. Yet there is no doubt either that his major works are anti-Western. They seek to undermine Western society and to replace it with something fundamentally different—and from all the evidence of experiments in Marxism, something a great deal worse. If it finally succeeds in replacing America's traditional national identity, multiculturalism seems likely to be a great deal worse too.

Menand is nearer the mark when he observes that *Who Are We?* is a work of identity politics and that for Huntington "the chief reason—it could even be the only reason—for Americans to embrace their culture is that it is the culture that happens to be theirs." That is not strictly true. Both Huntington and Americans in general can give other good reasons for thinking their culture admirable—and Huntington does so at intervals throughout the book. Given that American culture, like Western culture in general, is a self-conscious culture of critique, it could hardly be otherwise. But to love something because it is familiar and one's own is, in fact, a perfectly respectable reason for loving it. Many good daughters love fathers who are thoroughly dislikeable by any objective standard—and the world is a better and more stable place for it. Huntington even quotes the Copenhagen School to the effect that people want "societal security" almost as much as they want "national security." In other words, they want a society "to persist in its essential character" and to sustain "within acceptable conditions for evolution, of traditional patterns of language, culture, association, and religious and national identity and custom." If these are all removed or destroyed, then anomie, despair, and disintegration tend to be among the consequences. Why should Americans not be protected against them?

The answer, as it emerges in this controversy, is twofold. The first reason is consequential: there are trade-offs. If some people are contented living in a society made in their own image, then others—namely, minorities of one kind or another—are likely to feel out of place. A sentimental reluctance to make minorities feel like outsiders, even if that means discomfiting the American majority, is one of the major factors driving the critical hostility to Huntington. Huntington himself has the courage to say straightforwardly that if people have minority opinions or minority tastes, then they will to that extent be outsiders—and cannot reasonably expect the majority to conceal or suppress its loyalties in order to make them feel at home. He makes this argument both in relation to atheists who want American Christians to surrender all public expression of their religion and in relation to immigrants who want society to be re-ordered to make the

English language and American institutions merely one set of cultural options. And he does so because, in the end, he thinks that solidarity—or "societal security"—is essential to the well-being of American society as a whole, including in time the well-being of the minorities.

If Huntington's argument is designed to prefer the interests of the American majority, however, why is it at bay rather than triumphant? Here the second sociological reason comes into play: America's elites—both the corporate elites of the Right and the academic elites of the Left—do not share the opinions and tastes of the American people. Both elites have been, in effect, "de-nationalized" by the processes of economic and cultural globalization. They are more likely to share the tastes and opinions of their counterparts in other countries than those of their own countrymen in provincial and small-town America. They regard patriotism and national feeling as atavistic emotions that retard both economic rationality (in the case of the Right) and cosmopolitan ideologies of "democratic humanism" (in the case of the Left). And they see America not as a nation like other nations, if more powerful, but as the embryo either of the global market or of a new "universal nation" without boundaries or restrictive citizenship. As a result, on a whole range of policy issues—racial preferences, bilingual education, military intervention abroad, open borders—the American people are firmly on one side and the American elites are on the other. This tends to produce cynicism about government and electoral abstention, punctuated by rebellious referendum initiatives such as Propositions 187 and 209 in which the voters briefly impose their will on the elites. Even then elitists in the courts frequently declare the people's victories to be unconstitutional.

This is an unstable situation, and the elites are well aware of the fact. Hence their usual reluctance to join debate on the kind of issues raised by Huntington's book. But the extremes of both elites—libertarians on the Right and multiculturalists on the Left—cannot restrain themselves. Their solution, as illustrated in the early reactions to Huntington's *Foreign Policy* piece, is to treat anyone who departs from the official orthodoxies on these matters as a heretic to be shamed, scarred, and effectively silenced. Huntington, fortunately, is too eminent to be crushed in that way.

So *Who Are We?* is worth ten divisions in the new American culture war about patriotism. It demystifies every radical argument employed to deconstruct the American nation and the customs, habits, and traditions that sustain it. Even more usefully, it demonstrates that some conservatives and neoconservatives are unwitting accomplices in this demolition. They are misled in this direction either because of their attachment to outworn ideological definitions of America—formulae that once served a useful role in smoothing assimilation but that now act as carriers for multiculturalism—or because they have the false patriotic belief that America is not a nation with its own character but the entire world in embryo and so capable of indefinite expansion. Above all, perhaps, by attracting the kind of denunciations that reveal a deep animus towards the United States in the attackers, Huntington's book has revealed that there is a substantial anti-American intelligentsia (and lumpen [mentally sluggish] intelligentsia) within the American nation committed to a sort of "counter-tribalism." These are the patriots of an America that does not exist—the America of multiculturalism, bilingualism, and diversity that, in President Clinton's words, "can live without a dominant European culture." They therefore hate the America that does exist as an obstacle to their dreams. And they tend to sympathize with attacks upon it—and to react against anyone who defends it.

In acting as a sort of lure to draw the various tribes of "counter-tribalists" from their academic and corporate lairs into the open, Huntington has performed an important intellectual service. After *…Who Are We?* perhaps his next book should be *The Anatomy of Counter-Tribalism.*

# Immigration as a Threat to "Who We Are": Unfounded Fear

## Jim Sleeper

With the publication of this, his thirteen book, the magisterial, sometimes dyspeptic Harvard political scientist Samuel P. Huntington has once again indulged—nay, has stage managed—his inclination to administer jolts of counterintuitive, debate-changing Truth to distracted American elites. Once again, establishment players of many stripes are swooning in dismay at his dark revelations or girding up their loins to join him in another long, twilight battle for Western civilization. Once again, Huntington is arrestingly right about challenges facing liberal democracy that many liberals have been loath to acknowledge.

But never before has so big a part of his argument been so thunderously wrong and so cheaply sustained. Those who value his chastening realism about liberalism's dicey prospects will have to work hard to follow his most important insight in *Who We Are?*: that American cosmopolitans who would like to dispense with nations and multiculturalist zealots who would like to dismantle them have converged with American multinational profiteers to fray the fabric of liberal democracy, which only a renewed civic patriotism here at home can sustain. This argument, eminently worth arguing about, has already been overshadowed by another: about Huntington's ill-conceived, crotchety and (pardon the word) undocumented jeremiad against Latino immigration.

The distraction is the fault of Huntington the stage manager as much as of Huntington the thinker. In 1993, to prompt a national debate about themes

that would figure in his 1996 book, "The Clash of Civilizations and the Remaking of World Order," he published a *Foreign Affairs* essay of virtually the same title highlighting his most important warning: The economic, ideological and nationalist rivalries that most global analysts and activists presumed were driving world affairs would soon be eclipsed by deep cultural and religious differences among civilizations. He foresaw the ferocity of our conflict with Islamicist terrorists and warned against the American unilateralism and moralism that have been brought to bear on it, widening the civilizational divide.

Huntington didn't clearly define these civilizations; he seemed unsure whether Latin America is a distinct civilization or is part of the West. Two months ago [in March 2004] he seemed to answer the latter question by heralding *Who We Are?* with an essay in *Foreign Policy*, this one called "The Hispanic Challenge." It has made the book a lightning rod for the least credible of his warnings: America's Latino immigration deluge, he claims, is so little like any earlier wave, so hostile or resistant to sharing the common American language, civic rites and virtues upon which our republican self-governance depends, that it constitutes "a major potential threat to the cultural and possibly political integrity of the United States." If this clash isn't civilizational, what is?

The problem is that, most likely, it isn't, and *Who We Are?* doesn't persuade this reader that most Latino immigration is a threat to liberal democracy. Two months ago, Huntington also published (in the conservative journal *National Interest*) a less-noted essay, "Dead Souls: The Denationalization of the American Elite," whose title and contents come from another, smaller section toward the end of the book. Contradicting his own claims that the Latino tidal wave is shifting the balance of American political culture against patriotism, he announces, "A major gap is growing in America between its increasingly denationalized [academic, corporate and cultural] elites and its 'Thank God for America' public." The latter, he reports, has remained consistently patriotic over time, even as the former "reject expressions of patriotism and explicitly define themselves as multinational....The CIA...can no longer count on the cooperation of American corporations...[which] view themselves as multinational and may think it not in their interests to help the U.S. government." And we're supposed to wring our hands instead about Mexican immigrants?

He opens *Who Are We?* by admitting he's too close to our crisis of American identity to address it only as a scholar; he's writing also as a patriot to defend a distinctive "Anglo-Protestant" political culture, which he believes is indispensable to republican self-governance here. Anyone of any race or ethnic background can join this "nonracial society composed of multiracial individuals," but only after having absorbed and adapted—or been absorbed into—the enduringly Anglo-Protestant idiom and ethos that most Americans of all colors and ethnicities do share but which, he says, most Latino immigrants resist.

But Huntington is disappointingly dull in evoking the Anglo-Protestant civic nationalism he wants to defend. These sections are as potted and derivative as an undistinguished term paper. "Eighty-five percent of Americans...cited their 'governmental, political institutions' as that aspect of their country of which they were the most proud, compared with 46 percent of Britons, 30 percent of Mexicans, 7 percent of Germans, and 3 percent of Italians. For Americans, ideology trumps territory." Endless recitations like this trump reader engagement.

Sometimes his flinty realism yields observations as arresting as they may be uncongenial: "America was created as a Protestant society just as and for some of the same reasons Pakistan and Israel were created as Muslim and Jewish societies in the twentieth century." This is classic Huntington—an understatement so true it makes us realize how much we have forgotten. (It also makes me wonder if he understands how much we have changed.) He chooses interestingly among familiar culinary metaphors for American civic identity, rejecting "melting pot" (too monolithic and suppressive of legitimate differences) and "tossed salad" (too diffuse) for a sturdy Anglo-Protestant "tomato soup," to which new arrivals contribute croutons and distinctive spices without changing its basic constitution.

Most new Americans have been glad to do this, but Huntington turns the holdouts' own words against them with a trademark sang-froid: Writers such as the black nationalist Harold Cruse declared that "America is a nation that lies to itself about who and what it is. It is a nation of minorities ruled by a minority of one—it thinks and acts as if it were a nation of white Anglo-Saxon Protestants." To which Huntington responds, Kabuki-like: "These critics are right." Then he says that Anglo-Protestant conformity, which absorbed people of many colors and faiths into a common identity that made possible the New Deal, the war against fascism and the rise of a new middle class, has "benefited them and the country."

Why doesn't it do so now? Here he sounds diversionary and at times testy. Pondering widespread adoption of the name "African American" over "black" in the 1980s, he writes, "Given the pervasive penchant of Americans to prefer single-syllable over multi-syllable names for almost everything, this high and growing popularity of a seven syllable, two-word name over a one-syllable, one-word name is intriguing and perhaps significant." As is Huntington's own preference for the eight-syllable "white Anglo-Saxon Protestant" over "WASP" to denote his own ethno-religious group.

He doesn't take black Americans seriously in this book, by whatever name. It was the black civil rights movement that made Huntington's Anglo conformism even possible for millions of nonwhites, and yet he takes no cues from that breakthrough and its subsequent breakdowns: The fabric of American civic trust has been nowhere more severely tried than in blacks' cultural, electoral, legal and public psycho-dramatic renderings of disaffection with white America.

Nor does Huntington examine such Latino responses to black disaffection as a 1992 editorial in San Diego's Mexican American newspaper *La Prensa* that declared Latinos the new "bridge between blacks, whites, Asians, and Latinos." Latinos, the editorial said, "will have to bring an end to class, color, and ethnic warfare. To succeed, they will have to do what the blacks failed to do: incorporate all into the human race and exclude no one."

If Huntington wants "a non-racial society composed of multiracial individuals," shouldn't he reach for those Latino immigrants whose notions of race are more fluid and ecumenical than those of most blacks and whites, locked together for so long in a brutal embrace? Mightn't they lead in renewing the quasi-ethnic bondings of an

American civic culture that, shorn of racist exclusions, could ask more of citizens than does the current ethnic pandering in commercialism and demagoguery?

There's no denying Huntington's observations about the uniqueness of the 2,000-mile-long border that (barely) separates Mexico's northern states from its former provinces in the United States, or that Mexican and other Latino immigrants' sheer numbers and concentration bring them linguistic and political hegemony, not only in southern Texas and California but also in Miami and parts of New York.

But he conflates demographic and political developments through intuition, stray anecdotes, newspaper stories and poll after vapid poll, whose findings are often contradictory: At times the gaps between Latinos and the rest of us in patriotism and perception are growing; at other times the American public—already 12.5 percent Latino, thanks to immigration that is 50 percent Latino—is maintaining its patriotism, defying cosmopolitan and capitalist elites. He can't have this both ways and describe a Latino "reconquista" of former Spanish territories in California, Texas and Florida that is "well underway."

Although he gives no evidence of having left a metaphorical armchair, Huntington sometimes writes as if he's just returned from a visit like the ones Henry James made to Eastern European Jewish immigrants on Manhattan's Lower East Side, where he concluded that the Yiddish-speaking "hard glitter of Israel" could never be truly American [see James' book, *American Scene*, 1907]. And Huntington glosses the tortuous reception of peasant, supposedly anti-republican, "papist" waves of Irish Catholics, and of Germans in the Midwest who long resisted efforts to impose English.

Not surprisingly, the public and private bureaucrats in our vast, national race industry are lambasting Huntington's claims. Some have noted quite rightly that American forces in Iraq are commanded by Army Lt. Gen. Ricardo Sanchez, who grew up in one of the dirt-poor, 98 percent-Latino counties in Texas that prompted Huntington's quasi-civilizational despair. But they and Huntington's Latino "nationalist" critics ignore his condemnation of American interventions abroad, such as the very war Sanchez is fighting. That skews debate about who we are as a nation. (It also misses the possibility that Huntington would be relieved if his pessimism about Latinos' becoming full Americans provoked enough of them to prove him wrong.) Keeping him busy answering charges of racism only spares him the trouble of having to own up to his book's anti-corporate arguments and implications.

For example, even as he angers multiculturalist activists by condemning the Ford Foundation's national "diversity" crusades—on the grounds that a country as diverse as ours should work overtime to deepen some common bonds—he also condemns Ford Motor Co., one of the corporations he tells us no longer describes itself as American and has non-Americans as top executives. The company, even more than the foundation, drives what he bemoans as the "deconstruction" of civic patriotism. That's a point worth developing, as are his criticisms of such enemies of civic trust as these companies' intrusive culture of consumer marketing and what he considers our government's faux-patriotic interventions abroad.

Huntington's condemnation of the latter, in which some honorable conservatives are now joining, is squarely in the tradition of his Harvard predecessors William James and Charles Eliot Norton, and of Andrew Carnegie and Carl Schurz, who opposed the Spanish-American War on republican grounds. And since he's writing about clashes between Mexican and American identities, why not examine Woodrow Wilson's disastrous, humiliating efforts to impose "democracy," Iraq-like, in Mexico in 1917?

Why doesn't he ponder the irony that George W. Bush and Jeb Bush, two of this country's most prominent "Anglo-Protestant" political leaders, accept the corporate defections from America and, in the former Spanish territories, including Texas, Florida and California, bear responsibility for immigration policies that Huntington would tighten and enrich with stronger civic socialization?

When the venerable black former U.S. Rep. Barbara Jordan of Texas chaired the U.S. Commission on Immigration Reform in 1995, she called for just such programs to induct immigrants more fully into American civic life. She noted that the word "Americanization" had "earned a bad reputation when it was stolen by racists and xenophobes in the 1920s....But it is our word and we are taking it back." Shouldn't Huntington join Jordan's successors against both facile multiculturalists and caste-forming, low-wage employers, instead of sniping at blacks and uttering dire prophecies about Latinos? This book and the way he has promoted it suggest he isn't up to the challenge.

## THE CONTINUING DEBATE:
## Immigration as a Threat to "Who We Are"

### What Is New

The debate about Huntington's book and its off-shoot articles in such journals as *Foreign Policy* has remained torrid in intellectual and ideological circles and among those, such as Latinos, who were offended by his assertions. Although much of the general public may not have heard of Huntington's book, immigration, multiculturalism, and the other topics that it addresses are very much part of the national policy debate. For example, President Bush and congressional Democrats have proposed competing plans to allow illegal immigrants who have been in the country and working for an extended time to remain and, in the Democratic plan, gain resident status. There are also many related debates, such a periodic attempts in Congress to enact legislation designating English as the official U.S. language and a current debate in California about whether illegal aliens should be able to apply for driver's licenses. The general level of immigration is also at issue, with 49% of Americans wanting it decreased according to a 2004 poll, 33% thinking the current levels are about right, 14% wanting to increase them, and 4% unsure. As far as the "melting pot" versus the multicultural visions of American society, most Americans favor the melting pot. A 2003 poll found 60% of respondents saying immigrants should "blend in" to American culture, compared to 31% who thought newcomers should retain their own culture, 6% who favored doing both equally, and 3% who were unsure.

### Where to Find More

Read Huntington's two articles derived from his book, "The Hispanic Challenge," *Foreign Policy* (March/April 2004) and "Dead Souls," *National Interest* (Spring 2004). For other reviews of Huntington's work, read Francis Fukuyama, "Identity Crisis," June 4, 2004, on the ezine *Slate* at http://slate.msn.com and John Fonte, "How to Make an American," American Enterprise Online, September 2004, at http://www.taemag.com/. An important source of information about matters such as the attitudes and language capabilities of Latinos, the largest group of immigrants, is the Pew Hispanic Center at http://www.pewhispanic.org/. Yet more data can be accessed by consulting "Race and Ethnicity in 2001: Attitudes, Perceptions and Experiences," a Washington Post/Kaiser/Harvard Survey Project report, September 2001, at http://www.kff.org/kaiserpolls/3143-index.cfm.

### What More to Do

One thought is for your class to analyze Huntington's evidence for itself. Take the book and divide it up, looking for key arguments and the evidence that Huntington cites to support it. Then investigate the evidence using, but not limiting yourself to, the sources noted above in Where to Find More. Give each assertion a 1 if it proves right, 0.5 if the evidence is contradictory, and a zero if it proves wrong. A score of 0.5 or above favors Huntington's thesis; a score of below 0.5 means the professor may have flunked his analysis.

#  PUBLIC OPINION/PARTICIPATION

## POST-9/11 CRITICISM OF U.S. FOREIGN POLICY:
### Un-American *or* Patriotic?

### UN-AMERICAN

**ADVOCATE:** Victor Davis Hanson, Shifrin Visiting Professor of Military History, U.S. Naval Academy, Annapolis

**SOURCE:** "I Love Iraq, Bomb Texas," *Commentary*, December 2002

### PATRIOTIC

**ADVOCATE:** Gore Vidal, novelist, playwright, and essayist

**SOURCE:** "We Are the Patriots," *The Nation*, June 2003

Americans like to think of themselves as living in the "land of the free," as the national anthem goes. Part of what makes the United States a land of the free is the First Amendment's guarantee of free speech. Polls show that Americans strongly support free speech in the abstract. For example, when a survey asked in 2002 whether people should be allowed to express "unpopular opinions," fully 94% of respondents said they should be; just 6% disagreed.

Americans are less supportive of First Amendments rights when they are applied to specific situations. This is especially apt to occur during times of foreign conflict and other crises. A poll during the war with Iraq in March 2003 found that 57% of its respondents thought it was "okay" for war opponents to hold public protests, while 41% thought protesting was not okay, and 2% were unsure. Certainly it is the case that a majority of the public supported the protestor's constitutional rights, but it is also true that the majority willing to do so was far smaller than the 94% who supported the First Amendment in theory.

Such attitudes often engender the sort of dismay voiced by Victor Davis Hanson in the first reading and also create social and economic pressures on dissenters. For example, the Dixie Chicks paid the price in 2003 when singer Natalie Maines spoke against the war with Iraq and added, "We're ashamed the president of the United States is from Texas." Facing an uproar, she argued, "One of the privileges of being an American is you are free to voice your own point of view." However other people agreed with the Reverend Jerry Fallwell's rebuke, "You don't talk about your own country, especially during war," and the group's sales and concert bookings dropped off, and some radio stations refused to play their songs.

The increased disapproval of dissenters during foreign crises has two causes. One is the "rally effect." Feelings of patriotism, the urge to rally 'round the flag,' usually increase during foreign crises. This emotional response increases the propensity of people to think patriotism demands that everyone agree with the famous toast given in 1816 by Commodore Stephen Decatur, "Our country! In her intercourse with foreign nations, may she always be in the right; but our country, right or wrong." The second reason that disapproval of protesters increases is the belief that they undermine the U.S. position or its war effort. Polls found that this attitude was held by 38% of the public during the Iraq War of 2003 and 43% during the Persian Gulf War in 1991.

Do protesters undermine a country's war effort? Undeniably, such activity is watched closely by leaders of countries confronting the United States, and those leaders sometimes factor American domestic dissent into their decisions. Years after the Vietnam War ended, Bui Tin, a former high-ranking North Vietnamese officer, told a *Wall Street Journal* reporter that North Vietnam's leaders had "follow[ed] the growth of the American antiwar movement," and that it "gave us confidence that we should hold on in the face of battlefield reverses."

It is also true, though, that U.S. leaders try to manipulate opinion by warning that foreign policy divisions create national danger. "The way to do that," former U.S. Secretary of State Dean Acheson once admitted, "is to say politics stops at the seaboard—and anyone who denies that postulate is a son-of-a-bitch or a crook and not a true patriot. Now, if the people will swallow that, then you're off to the races."

Before turning to the two advocates, it is important to note that this issue is a long-standing one. At times, the United States has moved to legally curb dissenters. As early as 1798 amid fears of war with France, Congress passed the Sedition Act specifying fines and imprisonment for "any person [who] shall write, print, utter or publish" anything that would "excite...the hatred of the good people of the United States" against the government. Similarly, in 1917, Congress passed the Espionage Act that, among other things, made it illegal to oppose purchasing war bonds or to interfere with military recruiting.

The courts have validated some such actions. In *Schenck v. United States* (1919), the Supreme Court upheld a conviction under the Espionage Act of 1917 for urging resistance to the military draft. Speaking for the court, Justice Oliver Wendell Holmes held that the legality of curbing free speech rests, "in every case [on] whether the words used are used in such circumstances and are of such a nature as to create a clear and present danger that they will bring about the substantive evils that Congress has a right to prevent. It is a question of...degree."

## POINTS TO PONDER

➢ This debate is about boundaries. Think about Justice Holmes's comments as you read the following articles. As for his standard of "degree," do you agree with Vidal that he and other critics are the true patriots or would you characterize them, as Hanson does, as unpatriotic "anti-Americans" whose "creed is really a malady [that] cries out to be confronted and exposed"? Or do you see "a clear and present danger" that should be legally restrained?

➢ Think about the argument that protests in time of crisis weaken the country and encourage its enemies. Do you agree or disagree? And, whichever view you hold, do you think it is acceptable for protestors to demonstrate and take other actions during times of crisis?

➢ Which comes closer to your belief: Commodore Decatur's toast, "Our country, right or wrong" or Albert Einstein's comment, "Heroism on command, senseless violence, and all the loathsome nonsense that goes by the name of patriotism—how passionately I hate them!"?

89

# Post-9/11 Criticism of U.S. Foreign Policy:
## Un-American

### Victor Davis Hanson

With [the] discussion in Washington over what to do about Iraq there arrived also the season of protests. They were everywhere. In the national newspapers, Common Cause published a full-page letter, backed by "7,000 signatories," demanding (as if it had been outlawed) a "full and open debate" before any American action against Iraq. More radical cries emanated from Not in Our Name, a nationwide "project," spearheaded by [MIT professor] Noam Chomsky and affiliates, which likewise ran full-page advertisements in the major papers decrying America's "war without limit," organized "Days of Resistance" in New York and elsewhere, and in general made known its feeling that the United States rather than Iraq poses the real threat to world peace; at one late-October march in Washington, there were signs proclaiming "I Love Iraq, Bomb Texas," or depicting President Bush wearing a Hitler mustache and giving the Nazi salute. In the dock with America was, of course, Israel: on university campuses, demands circulated to disinvest from companies doing business with that "apartheid state"—on the premise, one supposes, that a democratic society with an elected government and a civilian-controlled military is demonic in a way that an autocratic cabal sponsoring the suicide-murder of civilians is not.

Writers, actors, and athletes revealed their habitual self-absorption. The novelist Philip Roth complained that the United States since September 11 had been indulging itself in "an orgy of national narcissism," although he also conceded, re-claiming his title as the reigning emperor of aesthetic narcissism, that immediately after the fall of the Twin Towers New York "had become interesting again because it was a town in crisis"—a fleeting, final benefit to connoisseurs of literature from the death of thousands. Barbra Streisand, identifying Saddam Hussein as the dictator of Iran, faxed a misspelled and incoherent but characteristically perfervid memos to Congressmen, while Ed Asner, of sit-com fame, threatened publicly to "lose his soul" if we went into Iraq. The Hollywood bad boy Sean Penn, not previously known for harboring a pacifistic streak, demanded that the President cease his bellicosity for the sake of Penn's children. Traveling abroad, the actress Jessica Lange pertly announced: "It makes me feel ashamed to come from the United States—it is humiliating." And the jet-setting tennis celebrity Martina Navratilova, who fled here to escape Communist repression and has earned millions from corporate sponsors, castigated the repressive atmosphere of her adopted homeland, a country whose behavior is based "solely on how much money will come out of it."

And so forth. Harbingers of this sort of derision were, of course, on view a year ago, in the period right after September 11 and well into the campaign against the Taliban in Afghanistan. Thus, Michael Moore, currently making the rounds plugging his movie *Bowling for Columbine* and a sympathizer of Not in Our Name, bemoaned the 9/11 terrorists' lack of discrimination in their choice of target: "If someone did this to get back at Bush, then they did so by killing thousands of people who did not vote for him!" Norman Mailer, engagingly comparing the Twin Towers to "two huge buck teeth," pronounced their ruins "more beautiful" than the buildings themselves. In the *London Times,* the novelist Alice Walker speculated whether Osama bin Laden's "cool armor" might not be pierced by reminding him of "all the good, nonviolent things he had done." There was the well-known poet who forbade her teenage daughter to fly the American flag from their living-room window, the well-known professor who said he was more frightened by the speech of American officials than by the suicide-hijackers of 9/11, and the well known columnist who decried our "belligerently militaristic" reaction to the devastation of that day.

Not all the criticism of the American response to terrorist cells and rogue governments has partaken of this order of irrationality; serious differences, responsibly aired, are also to be found, including in newspaper ads. But in the year since the slaughter of September 11 there has emerged an unpleasant body of sentiment that has little or nothing to do with the issues at hand but instead reflects a profound and blanket dislike of anything the United States does at any time. For a while, the *New Republic* kept track of this growing nonsense by Western intellectuals, professors, media celebrities, and artists under the rubric of "Idiocy Watch," and the talk-show host Bill O'Reilly is still eager to subject exemplars of it to his drill-bit method of interrogation. The phenomenon they represent has been tracked daily by Andrew Sullivan on his weblog, [www.andrewsullivan.com/], and analyzed at greater length by, among others, William J. Bennett (in *Why We Fight*), Norman Podhoretz (in "The Return of the 'Jackal Bins,'" *Commentary*, April 2002), and Keith Windschuttle (in "The Cultural

War on Western Civilization," the *New Criterion,* January 2002), the last-named of whom offers a complete taxonomy of schools and doctrines. And yet the sheer strangeness of the overall enterprise, not to mention its recent proliferation and intensification, would seem to merit another look.

A number of general truths emerge from any survey of anti-American invective in the context of the present world conflict. First, in each major event since September 11, proponents of the idea of American iniquity and/or Cassandras of a richly deserved American doom have proved consistently wrong. Warnings in late September 2001 about the perils of Afghanistan—the peaks, the ice, the warring factions, Ramadan, jihad, and our fated rendezvous with the graveyard of mighty armies gone before us—faded by early November in the face of rapid and overwhelming American victory. Subsequent predictions of "millions" of Afghan children left naked and starving in the snow turned out to be equally fanciful, as did the threat of atomic annihilation from across the border in Kashmir.

No sooner had that theater cooled, however, than we were being hectored with the supposed criminality of our ally [Israeli Prime Minister] Ariel Sharon. Cries of "Jeningrad" followed, to die down only with the publication of Palestinian Authority archives exposing systematic thievery, corruption, and PA-sanctioned slaughter. During the occasional hiatus from gloomy prognostications about the Arab-Israeli conflict, we were kept informed of the new cold war that was slated to erupt on account of our cancellation of the anti-ballistic-missile treaty with the defunct Soviet Union; of catastrophic global warming, caused by us and triggering floods in Germany; and always of the folly of our proposed intervention in Iraq.

That effort to remove a fascist dictator, we are now assured (most tediously by Anthony Lewis in the *New York Review of Books*), is destined to fail, proving instead to be a precursor to nuclear war and/or a permanently inflamed Arab "street." On the other hand, a *successful* campaign in Iraq, it is predicted, will serve only to promote America's worst instincts; its imperial ambition, its cultural chauvinism (a/k/a hatred of Muslims and Arabs), and its drive for economic hegemonism (a synonym for oil). Those who oppose preemption warn on Monday that the Iraqi dictator is too dangerous to attack and shrug on Tuesday that he is not dangerous enough to warrant invasion. Take your pick: easy containment or sure Armageddon.

The striking characteristic of such judgments is that they, too, are wholly at odds with the known facts. Confident forecasts of American defeat take no notice of what is the largest and best-trained military in history, and fly in the face of recent American victories in the Gulf war (where, at the time, Anthony Lewis likewise predicted quagmire and disaster) and Kosovo, both achieved at the cost of scarcely any American casualties. Alleged American hatred of Muslims hardly comports with our record of saving Kuwaitis from fascist Iraqis, Kosovars and Bosnians from Christian Serbs, or Afghans from Russian Communists and then from their own Islamist overlords, all the while providing billions of dollars in aid to Egypt, Jordan, and the Palestinian Authority. It was Jordanians and Kuwaitis, not we and not Israelis, who ethnically cleansed Palestinians; Iraqis and Egyptians, not we, who have gassed Muslim populations. And it is to our shores that Muslims weary of Middle Eastern despotism are desperate to emigrate.

Is there a consistent theme here? We are talking, largely though not exclusively, about a phenomenon of the aging Left of the Vietnam era and of its various progeny and heirs; and once upon a time, indeed, the anti-American reflex could be linked with some rigor to the influence of Marxism. True, that particular religion, at least in its pristine form, is just about gone from the picture these days. Some of its fumes, though, still linger in the doctrines of radical egalitarianism espoused by postmodern relativists and multiculturalists and by now instilled, in suitably diluted and presentable form, in several generations of college and high-school students. Hence, for example, the regular put-down of George W. Bush as a "Manichean" [after the Persian philosopher Mani (A.D. 216–A.D. 276) who saw the cosmos as a dualistic struggle between good and evil]—for could anything be more self-evidently retrograde than a view of our present conflict as a war of good versus evil, or anything more simplistic than relying on such "universal" arbiters of human behavior as freedom, pluralism, and religious tolerance?

Eschewing any reference to truths of this kind, adherents of postmodernist relativism assess morality instead by the sole criterion of power: those without it deserve the ethical high ground by virtue of their very status as underdogs; those with it, at least if they are Westerners, and especially if they are Americans, are ipso facto oppressors. Israel could give over the entire West Bank, suffer 10,000 dead from suicide bombers, and apologize formally for its existence, and it would still be despised by American and European intellectuals for being what it is—Western, prosperous, confident, and successful amid a sea of abject self-induced failure.

One is bound to point out that, as a way of organizing reality, this deterministic view of the world suffers from certain fatal defects, primarily an easy susceptibility to self-contradiction. Thus, a roguish [Chilean dictator Augusto] Pinochet, who executed thousands in the name of "law and order" in Chile, is regarded as an incarnation of the devil purely by dint of his purportedly close association with the United States, while a roguish and anti-American [Fidel] Castro, who butchered tens of thousands in the name of "social justice" in Cuba, is courted by Congressmen and ex-Presidents even as Hollywood celebrities festooned with AIDS ribbons sedulously ignore the thousands of HIV-positive Cubans languishing in his camps. [U.N. Secretary General] Kofi Annan gushes of Saddam Hussein, "He's a man I can do business with," while the ghosts of thousands slain by the Iraqi tyrant, many of them at his own hand, flutter nearby; for this, the soft-spoken internationalist is lionized.

Few have exploited the contradictions of this amoral morality as deftly as Jimmy Carter, who can parlay with some of the world's most odious dictators and still garner praise for "reaching out" to the disadvantaged and the oppressed. As President, Carter evidently was incapable of doing much of anything at all when tens of thousands of Ethiopians were being butchered; but as chief executive emeritus, he has managed to abet the criminal regime of North Korea in its determination to fabricate nuclear bombs and lately, having been rewarded with the Nobel Prize for peace, has brazenly attempted to thwart a sitting President's efforts to save the world from the Iraqi madman.

But all such contradictions are lightly borne. Since, for our postmodern relativists and multiculturalists, there can be no real superiority of Western civilization over the available alternatives, democracy and freedom are themselves to be understood as mere "constructs," to be defined only by shifting criteria that reflect local prejudices and tastes. Like Soviet commissars labeling their closed societies "re-

publics" and their enslaved peoples "democratic," Saudi officials assert that their authoritarian desert monarchy is an "Islamic democracy"—and who are we to say them nay? ("To my ear," the *New York Times* columnist Nicholas Kristof helpfully explains, "the harsh [American] denunciations of Saudi Arabia as a terrorist state sound as unbalanced as the conspiratorial ravings of Saudi fundamentalists themselves.") In Afghanistan, the avatars of multiculturalism and utopian pacifism struggled with the facts of a homophobic, repressive, and icon-destroying Taliban, but emerged triumphant: according to their reigning dialectic, the Taliban still had to be understood on their own terms; only the United States could be judged, and condemned, absolutely.

As for the roots of elite unhappiness with America, this is a subject unto itself. It would hardly do to reduce everything to a matter of psychology: a whole class of unhappy individuals motivated by resentment over the failure of their society to fulfill their own considerable aspirations. Nor does it quite satisfy to say more globally, and theoretically, that they suffer at several removes from the paradoxes of the radical Enlightenment: the unquestioned belief that sweet reason alone, in the hands of its proper acolytes, and yoked to commensurate powers of coercion, can remake the world. But we need not discount other and much simpler factors—like the law of the pack.

As in the medieval church or among Soviet apparatchiks, the pull of groupspeak is always strong among compliant and opportunistic elites. For today's intellectuals, professors, and artists, being on the team pays real dividends when it comes to tenure, promotion, publication, reviews, lecture invitations, social acceptance, and psychic reassurance. And the dividends are compound: one is a lockstep member of one's crowd *and* one enjoys the frisson of dissidence, of being at variance, but always so comfortably at variance, with one's benighted fellow citizens.

Our unprecedented affluence also explains much, although its role as a facilitator has been relatively scanted in most discussions of anti-Americanism that I have seen. The plain fact is that civilization has never witnessed the level of wealth enjoyed by so many contemporary Americans and Europeans. Vast groups are now able to insulate themselves from the age-old struggle to obtain food, shelter, and physical security from enemies both natural and human. Obesity, not starvation, is our chief health problem; we are more worried about our 401(k) [retirement] portfolios than about hostile tribes across the border.

What does this have to do with the spread of anti-Americanism? Home-grown hostility to American society and the American experiment is hardly a new phenomenon, but in the 19th century it tended to be limited to tiny and insulated elite circles (see the writings of Henry Adams). Now, it is a calling card for tens of thousands who share a once rare material splendor. That brilliant trio of Roman imperial writers, Petronius, Suetonius, and Juvenal, warned about such Luxus and its effects upon the elite of their era, among them cynicism, nihilism, and a smug and crippling contempt for one's own.

An ancillary sort of unreality has emerged in modern Western life alongside the reduced need to use our muscles or face physical threats. In a protected world, Saddam Hussein comes to seem little different from a familiar angry dean or a predictably moody editor, someone who can be either reasoned with or, if necessary, censured or sued. In this connection, it is not surprising that those most critical of America are not the purported victims of its supposedly rapacious capitalist system—farm workers, car mechanics, or welders—but more often those in the arts, universities, media, and government who have the time and leisure to contemplate utopian perfection without first-hand and daily exposure to back-breaking physical labor, unrepentant bullies, or unapologetically violent criminals. For such people, the new prosperity does not bring a greater appreciation of the culture that has produced it but rather enables a fanciful shift from thinking in the immediate and concrete to idle musings of the distant and abstract.

For many, today's affluence is also accompanied by an unprecendented sense of security. Tenure has ensured that tens of thousands of professors who work nine months a year cannot be fired for being unproductive or mediocre scholars, much less for being abject failures in the classroom. In government at every level, job security is the norm. The combination of guarantees and affluence, the joint creation of an enormous upper-middle class, breeds a dangerous unfamiliarity with how human nature really works elsewhere, outside the protected realm.

Such naiveté engenders its own array of contradictory attitudes and emotions, including guilt, hypocrisy, and envy. Among some of our new aristocrats, the realization has dawned that their own good fortune is not shared worldwide, and must therefore exist at the expense of others, if not of the planet itself.

This hurts terribly, at least in theory. It sends some of them to their fax machines, from where they dispatch anguished letters to the *New York Times* about the plight of distant populations. It prompts others, more principled and more honorable, to work in soup kitchens, give money to impoverished school districts, and help out less fortunate friends and family. But local charity is unheralded and also expensive, in terms of both time and money. Far easier for most to exhibit concern by signing an ostentatious petition against Israel or to assemble in Central Park: public demonstrations that cost nothing but seemingly meet the need to show to peers that one is generous, fair, caring, and compassionate.

As if that were not hypocrisy enough, those who protest against global warming, against shedding blood for oil, or against the logging of the world's forests are no less likely than the rest of us to drive SUV's, walk on hardwood floors, and lounge on redwood decks. Try asking someone awash in a sea of materialism to match word with deed and actually disconnect from the opulence that is purportedly killing the world and its inhabitants. Celebrity critics of corporate capitalism neither redistribute their wealth nor separate themselves from their multinational recording companies, film studios, and publication houses—or even insist on lower fees so that the oppressed might enjoy cheaper tickets at the multiplex. Jessica Lange and Alec Baldwin so hate George W. Bush that they threaten to leave our shores—promises, promises.

An even less appetizing quality of the new privileged is their palpable and apparently unassuageable envy. Intellectuals and people in the arts are perennially surprised—no, outraged—to find that corporate managers and Rotary Club businessmen, with far less education and infinitely less taste than they, make even more money. To the guilt they feel over what they have is therefore added fury at those who not only have more but seem to enjoy it without a necessary and concomitant sense of shame. Worse yet, because America is still a plutocracy where riches and not education, ancestral pedigree, or accent bring status, it can be galling for a sensitive professor of Renaissance literature to find himself snubbed at dinner

parties by his own university's president in favor of the generous but (shall we say) less subtle owner of a chain of Taco Bells. From there it is but a step to seeing the face of that same smiling and unapologetic plutocrat before him whenever he gazes upon the likeness of George W. Bush or Richard Cheney.

This brings us to another element of the new anti-Americanism. All of us seek status in accordance with what we feel we have accomplished or think we know. This naturally selfish drive is especially problematic for radical egalitarians, who must suppress their own desire for privilege only to see it pop out in all sorts of strange ways. I do not mean the superficially incongruous manifestations: Hollywood actors in jeans and sneakers piling into limousines, Marxist professors signing their mass mailings with the pompous titles of their chairs, endowed through capitalist largesse, or the posh Volvos that dot the faculty parking lot. Rather, I have in mind the pillorying by National Public Radio of those who say "nucular" for "nuclear," the loud laments in faculty clubs over threats posed to rural France by McDonald's, and all the other increasingly desperate assertions of moral and cultural superiority in a world where meaningful titles like earl, duke, and marquis are long gone and in theory repugnant. "Axis of evil? Totally banal," scoffed Felipe Gonzalez, the former prime minister of Spain, not long before his own country swaggeringly recaptured an uninhabited and rather banal piece of rock that had been briefly snatched by Morocco.

The superciliousness of the educated knows no end, and may even betray a final anxiety. One million bachelor's degrees are awarded in this country each year, but under the new therapeutic curriculum there is little to guarantee that any of the holders of these certificates can spell a moderately difficult English word or knows which dictator belongs to which enslaved state. And what is true of students is too often true as well of their pretentious professors, as can be seen whenever Noam Chomsky pontificates about war ("Let me repeat: the U.S. has demanded that Pakistan kill possibly millions of people...") and in place of references to historical examples or citations from the literature raves on with "as I have written elsewhere," "there are many other illustrations," "as would be expected," "it would be instructive to seek historical precedents," "as leading experts on the Middle East attest," and all the other loopholes and escape clauses that are the mark not of a learned intellectual but of a calcified demagogue.

But who has time to acquire expertise or exhibit patience with human frailty? The innate limitations of mortals matter little tour irritated utopians, nor can moral progress ever be rapid enough to keep up with a definition of perfection that evolves as quickly as the technology of cell phones. That Afghanistan a mere year after the fall of the Taliban is not yet as tranquil and secure as New England proves that our postbellum efforts there are not much better than the Taliban. "No one," asserts [Columbia University professor] Edward Said, "could argue today that Afghanistan, even after the rout of the Taliban, is a much better and more secure place for its citizens." No one? That we once *aided* Saddam Hussein is a supposedly crippling fact of which we are reminded ad nauseam, as if, not before but after the Gulf war, France, Russia, and Germany did not proceed to sell him the components for weapons of mass destruction, or as if we ourselves did not once give the Soviets a third of a million GMC trucks to thwart Hitler, only to see them used in the Gulag. But in the perfect world of America's critics, if Barbra

Streisand can fly to Paris in four hours and fax her scrambled thoughts in seconds, and if Gore Vidal from his Italian villa can parse sentences better than the President of the United States, then surely we are terminally culpable for not having solved the globe's problems right now.

Is it because these elite Americans are so insulated and so well off, and yet feel so troubled by it, that they are prone to embrace with religious fervor ideas that have little connection with reality but that promise a sense of meaning, solidarity with a select and sophisticated group, moral accomplishment, and importance? Is it because of its very freedom and wealth that America has become both the incubator and the target of these most privileged, resentful, and unhappy people? And are their perceptions susceptible of change?

If the answer to the first two questions is yes, as I believe it is, then the reply to the third must be: I doubt it. The necessary correctives, after all, would have to be brutal: an economic depression, a religious revolution, a military catastrophe, or, God forbid, an end to tenure. At least in the near term, and whether we like it or not, the religion of anti-Americanism is as likely to grow as to fade.

But it can also be challenged. The anti-Americans often invoke Rome as a warning and as a model, both of our imperialism and of our foreordained collapse. But the threats to Rome's predominance were more dreadful in 220 B.C.E. than in 400 C.E. The difference over six centuries, the dissimilarity that led to the end, was a result not of imperial overstretch on the outside but of something happening within that was not unlike what we ourselves are now witnessing. Earlier Romans knew what it was to be Roman, why it was at least better than the alternative, and why their culture had to be defended.

Later in ignorance they forgot what they knew, in pride mocked who they were, and in consequence disappeared.

The example of Rome, in short, is an apt one, but in a way unintended by critics who use passing contemporary events as occasions for venting a permanent, irrational, and often visceral distrust of their own society. Their creed is really a malady, and it cries out to be confronted and exposed.

# Post-9/11 Criticism of U.S. Foreign Policy: Patriotic

## GORE VIDAL

I belong to a minority that is now one of the smallest in the country and, with every day, grows smaller. I am a veteran of World War II. And I can recall thinking, when I got out of the Army in 1946, Well, that's that. We won. And those who come after us will never need to do this again. Then came the two mad wars of imperial vanity—Korea and Vietnam. They were bitter for us, not to mention for the so-called enemy. Next we were enrolled in a perpetual war against what seemed to be the enemy-of-the-month club. This war kept major revenues going to military procurement and secret police, while withholding money from us, the taxpayers, with our petty concerns for life, liberty and the pursuit of happiness.

But no matter how corrupt our system became over the last century—and I lived through three-quarters of it—we still held on to the Constitution and, above all, to the Bill of Rights. No matter how bad things got, I never once believed that I would see a great part of the nation—of we the people, unconsulted and unrepresented in a matter of war and peace—demonstrating in such numbers against an arbitrary and secret government, preparing and conducting wars for us, or at least for an army recruited from the unemployed to fight in. Sensibly, they now leave much of the fighting to the uneducated, to the excluded.

During Vietnam, [President George W.] Bush fled to the Texas Air National Guard. [Vice President Richard] Cheney, when asked why he avoided service in Vietnam, replied, "I had other priorities." Well, so did 12 million of us sixty years

ago. Priorities that 290,000 were never able to fulfill.

So who's to blame? Us? Them? Well, we can safely blame certain oil and gas hustlers who have effectively hijacked the government from presidency to Congress to, most ominously, the judiciary. How did they do it? Curiously, the means have always been there. It took the higher greed and other interests to make this coup d'état work.

It was Benjamin Franklin, of all people, who saw our future most clearly back in 1787, when, as a delegate to the Constitutional Convention at Philadelphia, he read for the first time the proposed Constitution. He was old; he was dying; he was not well enough to speak but he had prepared a text that a friend read. It is so dark a statement that most school history books omit his key words.

Franklin urged the convention to accept the Constitution despite what he took to be its great faults, because it might, he said, provide good government in the short term. "There is no form of government but what may be a blessing to the people if well administered, and I believe farther that this is likely to be well administered for a course of years, and can only end in Despotism, as other forms have done before it, when the people shall become so corrupted as to need despotic Government, being incapable of any other." Think of Enron, Merrill Lynch, etc., of chads and butterfly ballots, of [Supreme Court Justice Anthony] Scalia's son arguing before his unrecused father at the Supreme Court while unrecused Thomas sits silently by, his wife already at work for the approaching Bush Administration. Think, finally, of the electoral college, a piece of dubious, antidemocratic machinery that Franklin doubtless saw as a source of deepest corruption and subsequent mischief for the Republic, as happened not only in 1876 but in 2000.

Franklin's prophecy came true in December 2000, when the Supreme Court bulldozed its way through the Constitution in order to select as its President the loser in the election of that year. Despotism is now securely in the saddle. The old Republic is a shadow of itself, and we now stand in the glare of a nuclear world empire with a government that sees as its true enemy "we the people," *deprived* of our electoral franchise. War is the usual aim of despots, and serial warfare is what we are going to get unless—with help from wellwishers in new old Europe and from ourselves, awake at last—we can persuade this peculiar Administration that they are acting entirely on their vicious own, and against all *our* history.

The other night on CNN I brought the admirable Aaron Brown to a full stop, not, this time, with Franklin but with John Quincy Adams, who said in 1821, on the subject of our fighting to liberate Greece from Turkey, the United States, "goes not abroad, in search of monsters, to destroy." If the United States took up all foreign affairs, "she might become the dictatress of the world. She would no longer be the ruler of her own spirit," her own soul.

Should we be allowed in 2004 to hold a presidential election here in the homeland, I suspect we shall realize that the only regime change that need concern our regained spirit—or soul—is in Washington.

President Adams is long since dead. And we have now been in the empire business since [the Spanish-American War in] 1898: We had promised to give the Filipinos their independence from Spain.

Then we changed our mind, killing some 200,000 of them in the process of Americanizing them.

A few years ago there was a significant exchange between then-General Colin Powell [Chairman, Joint Chiefs of Staff] and then-statesperson [Secretary of State] Madeleine Albright. Like so many civilians, she was eager to use our troops against our enemies: What's the point of having all this military and not using it? He said, They are not toy soldiers. But in the interest of fighting Communism for so long, we did spend trillions of dollars, until we are now in danger of sinking beneath the weight of so much weaponry.

Therefore, I suppose it was inevitable that, sooner or later, a new generation would get the bright idea, Why not stop fooling around with diplomacy and treaties and coalitions and just use our military power to give orders to the rest of the world? A year or two ago, a pair of neoconservatives put forward this exact notion. I responded—in print—that if we did so, we would have perpetual war for perpetual peace. Which is not good for business. Then the Cheney-Bush junta seized power. Although primarily interested in oil reserves, they liked the idea of playing soldiers too.

Last September Congress received from the Administration a document called the National Security Strategy of the United States [aka the Bush Doctrine]. As the historian Joseph Stromberg observed, "It must be read to be believed." The doctrine preaches the desirability of the United States becoming—to use Adam's words—dictatress of the world. It also assumes that the President and his lieutenants are morally entitled to govern the planet. It declares that our "best defense is a good offense." The doctrine of pre-emption is next declared: "As a matter of common sense and self-defense, America will act against such emerging threats *before* they are fully formed." (Emphasis added.) Doubtless, [Attorney] General [John] Ashcroft is now in Utah arresting every Mormon male before he can kidnap eight young girls for potential wives.

Article 1, Section 8 of the Constitution says that only Congress can declare war. But Congress surrendered that great power to the President in 1950 and has never taken it back.

As former [Wyoming] Senator Alan Simpson said so cheerily on TV the other evening, "The Commander in Chief of the military will decide what the cause is. It won't be the American people." So in great matters we are not guided by law but by faith in the President, whose powerful Christian beliefs preach that "faith is the substance of things hoped for, the evidence of things not seen."

In response to things not seen, the USA Patriot Act was rushed through Congress and signed forty-five days after 9/11. We are expected to believe that its carefully crafted 342 pages were written in that short time. Actually, it reads like a continuation of Clinton's post–Oklahoma City antiterrorist act. The Patriot Act makes it possible for government agents to break into anyone's home when they are away, conduct a search and keep the citizen indefinitely from finding out that a warrant was issued. They can oblige librarians to tell them what books anyone has withdrawn. If the librarian refuses, he or she can be criminally charged. They can also collect your credit reports and other sensitive information without judicial approval or the citizen's consent.

Finally, all this unconstitutional activity need not have the slightest connection with terrorism. Early in February, the Justice Department leaked Patriot Act II, known as the Domestic Security Enhancement Act, dated January 9, 2003. A Con-

gress that did not properly debate the first act will doubtless be steamrolled by this lawless expansion.

Some provisions: If an American citizen has been accused of supporting an organization labeled as terrorist by the government, he can be deprived of his citizenship even if he had no idea the organization had a link to terrorists. Provision in Act II is also made for more searches and wiretaps without warrant as well as secret arrests (Section 201). In case a citizen tries to fight back in order to retain the citizenship he or she was born with, those federal agents who conduct illegal surveillance with the blessing of high Administration officials are immune from legal action. A native-born American deprived of citizenship would, presumably, be deported, just as, today, a foreign-born person can be deported. Also, according to a recent ruling of a federal court, this new power of the Attorney General is not susceptible to judicial review. Since the American who has had his citizenship taken away cannot, of course, get a passport, the thoughtful devisers of Domestic Security Enhancement authorize the Attorney General to deport him "to any country or region regardless of whether the country or region has a government." Difficult cases with no possible place to go can be held indefinitely.

Where under Patriot Act I only foreigners were denied due process of law as well as subject to arbitrary deportation, Patriot Act II now includes American citizens in the same category, thus eliminating in one great erasure the Bill of Rights.

Our greatest historian, Charles Beard, wrote in 1939:

> The destiny of Europe and Asia has not been committed, under God, to the keeping of the United States; and only conceit, dreams of grandeur, vain imaginings, lust for power, or a desire to escape from our

domestic perils and obligations could possibly make us suppose that Providence has appointed us his chosen people for the pacification of the earth.

Those Americans who refuse to plunge blindly into the maelstrom of European and Asiatic politics are not defeatist or neurotic. They are giving evidence of sanity, not cowardice, of adult thinking as distinguished from infantilism. *They* intend to preserve and defend the Republic. America is not to be Rome or Britain. It is to be America.

# THE CONTINUING DEBATE:
## Post-9/11 Criticism of U.S. Foreign Policy

### What Is New

The American victory over and occupation of Iraq set off a new round of criticism that the United States was attempting to become a new Rome, imperially dominating the world. The inability to uncover any weapons of mass destruction (WMDs) furthered the suspicions of critics that the war had been one of aggression rather than defensive preemption. The continued resistance within Iraq furthered dissent even more. By late October 2003, more American troops had been killed after the fall of Baghdad than had been killed during the war itself, and by October 2004, U.S. battle deaths in Iraq were over 900. There were early signs that the public was becoming restive with the occupation and it became a major issue in the 2004 presidential election. At the end of the war, 70% of Americans thought it had been "worth fighting." Four months later, only 57% held that view.

### Where to Find More

For a volume that contains a range of views on patriotism, read Martha C. Nussbaum, *For Love of Country?* (Beacon Press, 2002). A review of the origins and nature of patriotism can be found in Daniel Bar-Tal and Ervin Staub, *Patriotism* (Wadsworth, 1999). Insights into earlier anti-war protests can be gained from Melvin Small's, *Antiwarriors: The Vietnam War and the Battle for America's Hearts and Minds* (Scholarly Resources, 2002). A book that argues that freedom of political speech can be carried too far is Walter Berns, *Making Patriots* (University of Chicago Press, 2001).

### What More to Do

Discuss the concepts of "degree" of dissent and "clear and present danger" enunciated in *Schenck v. United States*. A one end of a continuum of dissent, opposition to American policy, including foreign policy, is a both healthy for a democracy and a core right of Americans. At the other ends of the continuum lies treason, which the Constitution defines as not only "levying war against" the United States but also "adhering to [its] enemies, giving them aid and comfort." Somewhere in the many degrees of activity between those extremes is the "clear and present danger" point that separates legitimate protest from actions that can lawfully be suppressed.

One way to shape your discussion is to consider the case of Jane Fonda and her opposition to U.S. involvement in Vietnam. In 1972, Fonda travelled to North Vietnam. There she made anti-war speeches over Radio Hanoi, had her picture taken wearing a North Vietnamese helmet while crewing an anti-aircraft gun used to shoot down U.S. planes, and said that American prisoners of war were "U.S. aggressor pilots" who were "healthy and repentant" in captivity. Some anti-war activists hailed her as a heroine of democratic dissent; others labeled her Hanoi Jane. What is your view? Should she have been lauded, chided for bad judgment, or tired for treason?

# MEDIA

## USE OF POLLS BY THE MEDIA:
### Out of Control *or* Valid Reporting?

### OUT OF CONTROL

ADVOCATE: Lori Robertson, Managing Editor, *American Journalism Review*

SOURCE: "Poll Crazy," *American Journalism Review,* January/February 2003

### VALID REPORTING

ADVOCATE: Bill McInturff and Lori Weigel, partners, Public Opinion
Strategies, a national survey research firm

SOURCE: "Servants of the People: Political Leadership and the Public Voice,"
*Public Perspective*, July/August 2001

Sometimes it seems hard to tell the difference between a presidential campaign and
a horse race. Certainly the news media broadcast and print stories about policy,
but there is also a great deal of attention to public opinion polls about who is ahead,
by how much, with which groups, where, and how all that is changing. You almost
expect to hear newscasters to breathlessly intone:

> And, racing fans, at the three-quarters poll it's George Bush in the lead.
> John Kerry is a quarter length behind and gaining with two furlongs to
> go, and Ralph Nader trails by ten lengths and is fading.

Moreover, polls do not always get it right. During the 2004 presidential election,
they often gave out such mixed messages that *Washington Post* journalist asked rhetor-
ically in an article who was winning then had to confess, "I have no idea." But, he
added hopefully, "check this out: The latest national survey...finds that the president's...[lead among] likely voters...[is only] 47%–46%,...down from the huge
54%–39% [earlier] advantage." The information was short lived, however. Within
hours, the reporter recorded himself as thinking, "Uh-oh. Looks like the Kerry surge
has faded. Here's a *new* poll—new in the sense that I got the results 12 hours after
[the first poll]—that has Bush...surging to a 13-point lead...among likely voters."
"Now I'm all confused!" the writer lamented understandably. Even worse, he wondered, "What if the polls are wrong, and we aren't surveying the real likely electorate?"
Critics of what they argue is an overuse of polling by the media might also add,
"So what?" Their view is that the focus during a campaign should be the candidates'
qualifications and positions and that who is ahead is only important when the final
vote is tallied on election day. Critics also claim that "who's ahead" polls are worse than
meaningless, that excessive "temperature taking" of the electorate distracts it from what

is important, can sway some to vote for the seeming winner, can persuade some supporters of the seeming loser to stay home, and can be wrong. Surely at least one of the two simultaneous polls cited in the *Post* was way off base.

Those who worry about the glut of polls aim their fire at more than election polling. They contend that Americans are hooked on polls and that the media supplies that addiction by conducting and reporting on opinion surveys on everything from serious policy matters to beliefs on whether Elvis Presley is really dead.

Supporters of polls do not contend that survey techniques are perfect or that all polling organizations are equally skilled. Still, they contend that polls advance democracy by making the views of the people known to policymakers. It cannot be doubted that public opinion is inherently linked to democracy, but the relationship is complex and not necessarily positive. For example, there is a long-standing debate about to what, if any, degree public opinion should influence which policies officials support. On the one hand, democracies are supposed to be "of, by, and for the people," but then the U.S. Constitution was explicitly written in 1787 to insulate the policy process from too much public pressure.

Whatever the specific answer, public opinion has been the subject of considerable attention during the history of the United States. Indeed, the *Federalist Papers* mentioned in the second reading were an attempt to sway public opinion in favor of ratifying the new constitution. The rub, of course, was that throughout most of U.S. history and that of other democracies, there was little way to know what public opinion was, except perhaps at election times. As early as the 1880s, there were attempts to conduct opinion polls, but they remained highly inaccurate until George Gallup began to use more sophisticated methods of sample selection in the mid-1930s. From that point, taking surveys has expanded to the point where it has become a constant on the political landscape and has also spread to marketing and other endeavors. There is a host of private national and regional survey firms, and there are even many academic-based polling organizations, such as the University of Connecticut's Center for Survey Research and Analysis. One count of 700 survey research organizations is probably far from a complete list. They generate many thousands of polls large and small in the United States each year, and many of these with questions profound or trivial are reported in the media. The questions in this debate are When is enough, enough? and Have we reached that stage? Have Americans gone "poll crazy," as Lori Robertson suggests in the first reading, or are polls truly the "servants of the people," as Bill McInturff and Lori Weigel claim in the second reading?

## POINTS TO PONDER

➢ The question of polling relates to many other aspects of story selection by the media, such as whether to emphasize lurid news and how graphically. If the public wants such stories and the media supplies them, then who is to blame: the users or dealers?

➢ Poll results almost surely sometimes impact the policy stands taken by elected officials. Does this represent officials democratically abiding by the voice of the people or a lack of leadership?

➢ Have you or anyone you know ever been polled?

# Use of Polls by the Media:
# Out of Control

## Lori Robertson

Freelancer Dana D. Kelley wrote a column in the October 18 [2002] *Arkansas Democrat-Gazette* about drug laws. In it, the writer opined: "They don't take polls on such things, but my guess is that 95 percent of Americans would support a 'shoot on sight' policy toward the sniper."

As far as a Lexis-Nexis search can tell, they haven't taken a poll on such a thing. But it's a wonder.

Americans—or those who don't have caller ID and haven't mistaken the pollster for yet another telemarketer—have been asked everything from the standard "Whom will you vote for?" to "Do you think Elvis is alive?" A mere day after the September 11 attacks, the poll machine was up and running, featuring questions ranging from whether people would change their travel plans to how long it would take the United States to find those responsible. NBC News asked if the terrorist attacks were worse than Pearl Harbor.

In June, a Fox News Channel poll asked, "While it is a highly unlikely situation, if you had the opportunity, would you personally kill Osama bin Laden?" *TV Guide*, in what it called a "fun" survey, inquired whether respondents would rather have Barbara Walters or Diane Sawyer interview bin Laden. (He's popular in poll questions.) Other polls have asked Americans what they think about things they can't possibly know, such as when the war in Afghanistan will end or if Iraq has nuclear weapons. A Time/CNN poll queried, "Just your best guess, do you think Osama bin Laden is alive or dead?"

And then there are the Internet polls— sorry, "surveys," "questions" and "live votes," because everyone (we think) knows that these are not real polls and the results mean nothing. There's more license in what you can ask when the results mean nothing. Hence, a nearly endless range of topics. From CNN.com (and read and touted on air): "Do you think authorities will ever catch the sniper?" [who was killing people in the Washington, D.C. metropolitan area] and the incredibly [un]balanced question, "Should the feds learn to leave California's medical marijuana growers alone?" MSNBC TV's Question of the Day (which can be e-mailed to your inbox every day) was "Do you think this latest terror arrest will lead us to Osama?" after news broke of the capture of the al Qaeda operative who allegedly planned the USS *Cole* attack. The day before was more pop-culture— "Should Michael Jackson's kids be taken away from him?"

"We've become poll crazy as a society," says Ken Dautrich, director of the Center for Survey Research and Analysis at the University of Connecticut. "When you look at a few decades ago, there were a handful of polls that had a code of ethics and kind of a code of science and a methodology that was applied to what they do. Given that polls are so popular, there are hundreds of organizations…that have gotten into the polling business." And, says Dautrich, there are polls "on any topic you can imagine."

No one is counting the number of polls out there, so it's hard to say when a dramatic increase occurred. Kathleen A. Frankovic, CBS News' director of surveys, puts the brunt of the upsurge in the '90s. "I think we do see more polls, but I think the number is not hugely larger than it was, say, seven or eight years ago....I think the number of surveys increased in the 1990s—the number of real polls—and then secondly, that's when you started to see all these Internet quick polls out there."

So, with all this picking of people's brains, we have a better idea of what Americans think, right?

Maybe not. Steve Farkas, senior vice president and director of research at Public Agenda, a public opinion research organization, offers the following as a possible lead for this story: "We have more surveys than ever, yet our understanding of the public's mind is impoverished, and why is this so?" Surveys that are meaningless, he says, answering his own question, "add to the random noise, so it's difficult to distinguish quality work from just plain silliness."

Which brings us to the *AJR* [*American Journalism Review*] Question of the Month: Has polling gotten a bit out of control?

A silly question is clearly in the eye of the beholder. Take the would-you-kill-Osama poll. The majority of those interviewed for this story either groaned or laughed when they heard that one, though one person—a media critic—said the issue of whether he would kill bin Laden had crossed his mind.

After hemming and hawing for a few seconds, *National Journal's* William Powers says yes, he'd kill him. (Wait—have you been skimming ahead to find out how many Americans would kill Osama?...Yeah, yeah, guilty pleasure.)

With the large number of polling organizations, and opinions, out there, questions that are silly, ridiculous or just plain bad are bound to pop up. And to be

fair, most of these inquiries are part of lengthy polls that include about 20, often disparate, questions. "There are some things that people will ask and other people won't, and I think everybody draws that line quite differently," Frankovic says, adding that she has seen questions that she wouldn't have asked, and she's sure she has asked things that other people wouldn't. Frankovic readily takes credit for that Elvis inquiry. (Don't worry, only about 7 percent of those polled thought The King was still breathing.)

Other pollsters are more perturbed by the current poll-o-rama, especially when they consider online surveys. "I think one of the things that people in my profession...are quite wary of is that polling has become entertainment, and to us...polling is a very serious business. It's a science requiring very great skills," says Mark A. Schulman, president of the American Association for Public Opinion Research. "And we every day see examples of how our profession, our science is being misused...or being used frivolously."

Regarding that Pearl Harbor question, Farkas says: "People say [these are] public opinion polls. Public opinion polls for what? What is the purpose?" To inform policymakers of the concerns of the American public? he asks. "Some of these questions become a little bit of a stretch....Some of this stuff is a little cheesy."

Iain Murray, director of research at the Statistical Assessment Service, an organization that helps journalists understand scientific and social surveys, says hypothetical questions, in particular, are pretty meaningless. "If the purpose of the poll is to find out information, then obviously a meaningless question doesn't help you in any way."

Frankovic agrees, though she says that doesn't mean she would never ask a hypothetical. She adds questions that could harm someone or frighten people to the list of polling don'ts. Also, "you don't ask things where the respondent can't make a judgment," she says. "I don't like asking the American people to be experts…but other pollsters have no problem with that."

Farkas says he remembers seeing questions that asked the public how long the war in Afghanistan would last. "Asking people questions that they have no clue about and yet they're willing to give you an answer…I think that's very unfortunate." Some of these, he says, "make me chuckle, and I feel guilty about chuckling." Pollsters shouldn't be so high and mighty about what can be asked, Farkas adds, but at the same time, frivolity contributes to an anything-goes attitude. "There were some questions about [the sex scandal between President Bill] Clinton and [Monica] Lewinsky…that I'm happy I don't remember anymore." (Perhaps he means questions that asked the public to predict the outcome of the Clintons' marital crisis and speculate as to why Hillary was putting up with Bill's shenanigans. Or, "How would you rate President Clinton as a husband?")

"Having fun with polls is OK," says Schulman. But, he stresses, using polls as entertainment instead of as a bridge between government or corporate decision makers and the public—the original purpose of polls—"really undermines the credibility of a lot of what we do."

Because so many surveys are commissioned by news organizations, this is not just a question of polling etiquette. It's one of media ethics as well. "There's always the serious question of what is your journalistic purpose," says Al Tompkins, who teaches broadcasting and online journalism at the Poynter Institute. "You don't ever want to do anything that would end up compromising your journalistic integrity."

Of course, where you draw the integrity line is quite subjective.

Some think the media need to stop using polls as much as they do, silly questions or no silly questions. Mike Littwin, a *Rocky Mountain News* columnist, says journalists should rely less on surveys. "It's religion," he says of the media's infatuation with public opinion polls. "We have come to believe in them even when we don't."

When poll results are ambiguous, journalists often find some meaning in them anyway. Tompkins says when a news organization has forked over the money for a survey, it wants an answer. "And it's not much news if a poll turns up inconclusive," he says. "I think news organizations feel some pressure" to get a poll to say something that it might not.

For instance, a CNN/Time magazine poll released September 13, 2001, asked Americans whether Congress should declare war. Sixty-two percent said yes. When they were then asked against whom war should be declared, 61 percent said they didn't know. To some, this would be comical, or at least suggest that it was inappropriate to be asking such questions already. But journalists found some significance in the results. CNN's Garrick Utley surmised, "That uncertainty gives President Bush flexibility and time to determine what kind of a war he intends to wage." (Two percent, by the way, chose "no one/just declare war.")

Littwin wrote a column questioning the validity of another nationwide poll that asked, "Thinking about the recent serial killings by a sniper in the Washington, D.C., area, how worried are you that someone in your family might become a victim of this kind of violence?" Forty-seven percent of the respondents said they were either "very" or "somewhat" worried.

Littwin had a hard time swallowing this one. "I don't think that half the people in

America are afraid that a sniper is going to shoot them," he says. "Some of these [polls] defy reason and that was one of them."

The question, asked in a poll commissioned by *Newsweek*, also took a beating in a scathing column by Powers in *National Journal*, in which he chastised the media for instilling fear in the public. "They may have asked the question at a time when media outlets like *Newsweek* had flogged the story" so much that the poll results were true, he says in an interview. "It's like they were fulfilling their own self-created prophecy."

Powers says he also wondered if the question was designed to get the answer it got. "If you say, no, you're not concerned, it seems like you're irresponsible....Sometimes people are not as stupid as their aggregate poll answers suggest."

The results *are* irrational. *Newsweek's* Marcus Mabry, chief of correspondents and senior editor, says he was surprised, initially, by the response. The magazine included the topic because it had been asking a similar question about fear of a terrorist attack, he says. Once Mabry started thinking about the sniper results, he says, he realized that unlike the terrorist attacks, which to many people still seemed remote, the sniper shootings were occurring at gas stations and a school, places every American knows. "All of those things were part of everyday Americans' intimate experience," he says, "places where they feel safe."

"How logical is it for someone in California to be fearful of [a sniper attack]?" says Mabry, who orders up polls for the magazine. "But it's not about logic....It's greater than that."

A list of percentages may not provide enough information about what Americans are thinking and why. Such is the limitation of a poll. Farkas suggests journalists use common sense in reporting survey results.

"If it doesn't ring true and it doesn't make sense," he says, "then you are probably on to something and you should probably not take any poll finding at face value."

MSNBC.com takes pains to make viewers realize that its live votes and questions of the day are not scientific polls—a fact that should be obvious. The public isn't really in a position to answer meaningfully whether they think Saddam Hussein has "come clean" with his weapons list or which strategy could be the most fruitful in the search for extraterrestrial life.

The results are not meant to be taken seriously. Says MSNBC.com Managing Producer Reed Price, "We offer them because it's an opportunity for interactivity. It's fun....It's an opportunity for the viewer or the reader to interact with the Web site...but it isn't meant to be anything more than that."

MSNBC.com and CNN.com both use the term "vote" or "question" instead of poll and include disclaimers saying that the results are not scientifically accurate and only represent the views of the people who choose to respond. MSNBC.com also provides with every vote a link to a page that explains in detail the difference between online tallies and real polls.

CBS News's Frankovic says news organizations do a good job of making a distinction between these pseudo polls and scientific polls, and she likens the online phenomenon to call-in surveys that were very popular pre-Web. "Internet companies or Web site designers believe that putting a poll on your site keeps people there longer" and that people love to answer these questions, she says. (This, in fact, is the reason a few of those interviewed for this article give for the high number of polls out there in general.)

Since the results are not representative of anything, what information is someone supposed to take away from online surveys? The obvious answer: absolutely none. But it's hard to look at a bar graph with percentages (an *informational* graphic) and not think something.

"Our fear," says AAPOR's Schulman, "is that in the public's mind a poll is a poll is a poll." Many of the Internet "polls" are done by the news media, which, Schulman says, lends them "the aura of this news organization's credibility." As for the disclaimers, he says, "How many people read the small print?...It sort of looks like a poll and sounds like a poll to the uninitiated."

Pollsters like Schulman wish these proliferating online surveys would just go away.

"I think especially with the invention of Internet polls, [the state of polling seems] to be worse now," says Iain Murray of STATS. "People seem to want to find out their opinion instantly...with the Internet." But "they're actually not able to do that."

Schulman calls these votes and surveys "gimmicks" used to drive traffic to a Web site.

*Newsweek's* Mabry says he does get letters from online readers asking why the results have been different between online polls and regular Newsweek polls. Frankovic says she gets fewer such inquiries now than she did five or six years ago. She heard from a lot of people during the Clinton-Lewinsky scandal, she says, when the findings of Web polls were much different than real polls and the feelings about the results were intense. "So I don't know if

we've sort of fallen into a less intense period," she says, "or if people are more likely to recognize the difference now."

It's unclear what the public thinks of these Internet surveys (I couldn't find a poll on this), but in a January/February 2001 *AJR* article, "Polled Enough For Ya?" Gallup Poll's Frank Newport said the average American doesn't understand the mechanics behind scientific polling. People do not think that a poll of 1,500 to 2,000 people can represent how all Americans feel, he said. "They find that hard to believe."

So the responsibility, as usual, rests with journalists. They have to ferret out the statistically sound from the sloppily compiled in their reporting. And news organizations need to ponder what they're polling about and why.

The real question that needs to be asked, says Poynter's Tompkins, is, "What's the news value here? What's the real value of this?"

News outlets seem to be less inclined to report the results of someone else's poll than they are to broadcast their own surveys. (Most of the polls mentioned in this story got little play outside stories by the sponsoring media organizations.) Which suggests that sometimes polls are more about promotion than information.

Ask yourself, "If you're Channel 9 and Channel 7 has a poll, would you report it?" Tompkins says. "Sometimes we overplay them—overhype them—because they're ours."

# Use of Polls by the Media:
## Valid Reporting

BILL MCINTURFF AND LORI WEIGEL

There are reasons John McCain's town hall approach to politics sparked interest and enthusiasm in the presidential primaries over a year ago. For a public weary of the poll-driven policies of the Clinton administration, the [Senator] McCain [R-AZ] style of direct interaction with the voters, campaigning against special interests under the rubric of campaign finance reform, and "straight talk" seemed to catch fire all by itself.

Those reasons are spelled out quite vividly in the new Kaiser/*Public Perspective* survey on polling and democracy. Americans still do not feel they are being heard in Washington and want more direct interaction with government officials. And although the public is distrustful of government and politics, the news media are carrying forward that cynicism to a greater degree than ever previously suspected.

Overall, the poll quantifies a number of seemingly conflicting, yet consistently "American," themes in the public's views of the proper use of polling and the role of polls in conveying Americans' input inside the beltway. These themes include a distrust of special interests, a desire to be heard, and the meaning of democratic leadership; and implicit in them are a number of key lessons for policymakers and politicians in how they should incorporate the will of the people into their decision-making process.

Policymakers need to be aware that Americans feel a sharp disconnection between how much influence they believe they actually have on government officials and how much they think they should have.

Sixty-eight percent of Americans think they should have a great deal of influence on the decisions of elected and government officials in Washington, but fewer than one in ten (9%) believe they do.

A far smaller degree of disconnection exists among policy leaders. One-third said the views of the majority of Americans have a great deal of influence inside the beltway [which surrounds Washington, D.C.], only nine points lower than the level of influence they said the public should have.

Who instead do Americans think bends the ears of the politicians and officials in the Capitol? According to the public, money talks. Nearly six in ten (59%) said that politicians pay a great deal of attention to their campaign contributors when making decisions about important issues—more than any of the eight other groups or factors tested, including policymakers' own knowledge on the issue (35%), their conscience or judgment (24%), and outside experts (28%). In fact, campaign contributors were second only to lobbyists and special interests in the public's perception as the greatest influence on officials' decisions about important issues (45%).

Americans rank their own ability to influence their elected and government officials dead last. Only 14% think that members of the public who contact officials about an issue have a great deal of influence, while a mere 18% think officials would listen to public opinion polls.

The media are even more cynical about the influence of special interests on policymakers. A stunning 70% of the press rated campaign contributors, and 67% rated lobbyists and special interest groups, as having the most influence on decisions in Washington. This contrasts with the 59% of the public and 43% of policy leaders who said campaign contributors have a great deal of influence, and the 45% of both samples who said lobbyists and special interest groups have that level of influence.

The survey adequately demonstrates a wide gap between the press and everyone else on this issue. Sixty-eight percent of policy leaders and 65% of the public said that when officials make a decision that isn't supported by a majority of Americans, it is often because they choose to follow what special interests want instead. However, an amazing 84% of the news media pointed to the influence of special interests—19 points more than the public.

What does this mean? First and most clearly, the news media need to gain some perspective when they are so far out of step with the views of policy leaders and the public. Second, Americans are not willing to chalk up policy mistakes to even benign neglect on the part of public, but instead are more likely to view these decisions as an out-and-out thwarting of their will.

Americans' belief that special interests have a disproportionate influence on government officials is closely linked to a strong yearning for their own voices to be heard, and their opinions understood, above the din of clamoring lobbyists. While "I feel your pain" became a trite joke for late-night television comedians, it was first grounded in one of the foremost measurements of a candidate's voter strength: the belief that the candidate "understands the concerns of people like me."

Currently, many Americans are rating their public officials fairly low on this barometer of understanding, and rightly so, according to the Kaiser/*Public Perspective* survey. Less than half (49%) of the public believes that elected and government officials in Washington understand what the public thinks about the issues facing the nation.

That message hasn't gotten through the beltway, however. Washington arrogance is overflowing when fully 85% of policy leaders and 90% of journalists say they feel they understand what the public thinks.

So, if officials aren't in tune with the voices of the people, how does the public want them to learn what the majority thinks about important issues? Any way they can, according to the survey.

Over three-quarters of the public said that good ways for elected and government officials to learn what people think include holding town hall meetings (88% said it's a good way to learn), conducting public opinion polls (84%), talking to people who call, write or email an official's office (82%), and talking to people at shopping malls and on the street (75%).

However, while the public placed the most faith in the Norman Rockwell setting of a town hall meeting, with 43% saying it's the best way for officials to learn what people think about important issues, 46% of policy leaders and 52% among the media chose public opinion polls as the preferred means of communication.

The upshot is that policymakers faced with the time constraints imposed by their jobs must balance the appeal of direct interaction with the voters with what Americans say is an equally valid means of understanding their thoughts: polling.

In fact, voters embrace their ability to have a say via the medium of opinion polls. They are quite judicious in thinking that officials in Washington should pay more attention to polls on subjects about which they consider most Americans to be adroit, particularly health care and education. Conversely, they want government officials to rely less on popular sentiment on issues where they have less confidence in the public's knowledge, such as foreign policy issues.

The amount of influence the will of the people has on the decisions of policymakers creates a fundamental tension in any government. In the early '90s, when American political consultants were first working in Eastern Europe, a group of political consultants provided counsel to the Hungarians, who were experiencing their first-ever democratic elections for Parliament.

Two years later, the same consultants went back to explore how the Hungarians were faring in their experiment with democracy. The most pointed question Hungarian policymakers posed was whether they were supposed to vote for what they thought was right, or for what the majority of their constituents wanted.

The question was, of course, greeted with self-deprecating laughter from the consultants, who pointed the Hungarians to the *Federalist Papers* [a series of arguments written by Alexander Hamilton, James Madison, and John Jay in favor of ratifying the proposed U.S. Constitution and published in 1787 and 1788] and indicated that this dilemma was still a stumbling block for American elected officials.

In fact, this question is one of the most divisive issues in the Kaiser/*Public Perspective* survey. What is really telling is simply how much the public wants its views taken into account in the decision-making process.

Given two choices on this issue, 54% of Americans expect their officials to follow what the majority wants, even if it goes against the officials' knowledge and judgment. Fewer (42%) want officials to use their own judgment if it goes against the wishes of the majority.

Even when given the caveat that past majority positions have later been judged to be wrong (e.g., racial segregation), only a bare majority (51%) expressed a desire to have officials rely on their knowledge when they think the majority is wrong, while 40% continued to prefer they do what the majority wants "because the majority is usually right."

Some major implications emerge for policymakers from the Kaiser/*Public Perspective* survey as they navigate the shoals of public opinion.

The [George W.] Bush administration and countless other politicians remain caught in the wake of the Clinton scandal wave, a particularly treacherous situation whenever suggestions of improper influence arise. Policymakers need to be aware that the media, as well as opposing campaigns, are going to keep trying to tie votes and policy decisions to campaign contributions. Therefore, an issue like the environment, which is not a top priority for voters at all, could be used as the basis for a negative campaign message because the potency of the message lies not in the issue itself, but in attaching it to campaign contributions or special interest money.

Related to this, media cynicism about campaign contributions and special interests is so far out in left field compared to the views of the public and policy leaders that it is clear a thorough internal examination of these problems is long overdue.

While many people who go to Washington today aren't exactly the Capraesque icon of Mr. Smith, they certainly consider themselves to be well-intentioned individuals. [The reference is to the 1939 film, *Mr. Smith Goes to Washington*, directed by Frank Capra and starring James Stewart as Jefferson Smith, a "common" man who is appointed to fill a vacancy in the U.S. Senate and who stands firm when his plans collide with political corruption]. The survey clearly demonstrates the high level at which Americans want their opinions considered in the decisions made by these policymakers. In addition, it stresses the extent to which the American people think policymakers "just don't get it," despite whatever good intentions they might have. A majority (51%) thinks policymakers don't understand what the public wants when they make decisions contrary to the majority sentiment. Therefore, it is doubly important for policymakers not to succumb to the chatter inside the "echo chamber" of the beltway and lose perspective on the opinions of average Americans.

Despite the bashing that public opinion polls took in the 2000 presidential campaign, it is clear that Americans still value polls as a means of having their voices heard, curbing the influence of special interests, and injecting a democratic style of leadership in which the voices of many are considered in the formulation of public policy.

If we all lived in small New England states, then perhaps town hall meetings would be a realistic means of injecting public opinion into the national debate. However, when it takes one western senator a whole year to travel to every single county in his or her home state, it is clear that the limits imposed by geography and time necessitate a continuing place for polling in public policy.

Moreover, that's just fine with most Americans. Consider the following:

- 84% or more of general public respondents to the Kaiser/*Public Perspective* survey said officials in Washington should pay a great deal or a fair amount of attention to what opinion polls say on various domestic issues.

- 84% agreed that polling is one of the best means we have for communicating what the public is thinking.

- 84% said a poll is a good way for government officials to learn what the majority of people in our country thinks about issues.

- 81% said that when people are interviewed for an opinion poll they usually answer honestly.

- 78% said that polls on social and political issues serve a useful purpose.

- 86% of policy leaders and 94% of the media said that polls are useful in understanding how the public feels about issues.

These attitudes—combined with the proclivity of the press to report opinion polls—mean that polling is, should be, and will continue to be a major player in framing the public debate.

# THE CONTINUING DEBATE:
## Use of Polls by the Media

### What Is New

The closeness of the race between George Bush and John Kerry made polling a major focus during the 2004 presidential race. Within minutes of the conclusion of the first presidential debate on September 20, one national network was airing the results of an "instant poll" about who had "won" (Kerry, 48%; Bush, 14%; a draw, 38%). The survey had such a small sample (200) that even the network's commentators seemed embarrassed to report it. However, the final pre-election polls proved generally accurate. Of 10 national polls, seven found Bush narrowly ahead, two had Kerry with a slim lead, and one was tied at 49% each.

American attitudes toward political polling remained consistent with those detailed in the reading by McInturff and Weigel. For instance, when asked in 2004, "Do you think...opinion polls have too much or too little power and influence in Washington?" 47% of respondents said "too little," but 36% said "too much," with 8% volunteering the answer "about right" and another 8% being unsure. In a poll that applied to a specific policy issue, the issue of whether to go to war with Iraq in 2003, 47% of the public wanted President Bush to pay "a lot" of attention to public sentiment, and 44% wanted him to pay "some" attention. Only 9% thought he should pay "not much" attention, 6% replied "none at all," and 4% were unsure.

### Where to Find More

For the impact of opinion surveys on the political process, read James A. Stimson, *Tides of Consent: How Public Opinion Shapes American Politics* (Cambridge University Press, 2004). A study that looks at public opinion and polling techniques in a comparative perspective is Willem E. Saris and Paul M. Sniderman, eds., *Studies in Public Opinion: Attitudes, Nonattitudes, Measurement Error, and Change* (Princeton University Press, 2004). To explore the role of opinion on a specific policy issue, see Douglas C. Foyle, "Leading the Public to War? The Influence of American Public Opinion on the Bush Administration's Decision to Go to War in Iraq," *International Journal of Public Opinion Research*, Fall 2004. More on the conduct and use of polls is available through polling associations including the American Association for Public Opinion Research at http://www.aapor.org/ and the National Council on Public Polls http://www.ncpp.org/. A list of sites with current and past polls is on the Californian Institute of Technology site at http://survey.caltech.edu/links.html.

### What More to Do

Review the polling in the closing days of the presidential race of 2004. To what degree did the polls agree or disagree with one another and with the final results? Also discuss the proposition that if public opinion polls are as important to democracy as the second reading argues they are, then logically governance should have improved since the advent of scientific, widespread polling about a half century ago. Has government become more responsive to the people in that time?

## ETHNIC FOREIGN POLICY LOBBYING:
### Misplaced Allegiance *or* All-American Tradition?

### MISPLACED ALLEGIANCE

**ADVOCATE:** Geoffrey Wheatcroft, a British journalist

**SOURCE:** "Hyphenated Americans," *Guardian Unlimited* online, April 25, 2000

### ALL-AMERICAN TRADITION

**ADVOCATE:** Yossi Shain, Aaron and Cecile Goldman Visiting Professor, Georgetown University; Professor of Political Science, Tel Aviv University

**SOURCE:** "For Ethnic Americans, The Old Country Calls," *Foreign Service Journal*, October 2000

*E pluribus unum* (out of many, one) reads the banner the eagle holds in its beak on the Great Seal of the United States. These words on the seal, which was adopted by the Congress in 1782, refer to the union of 13 former colonies into one United States. Whatever its initial meaning, *e pluribus unum* has come to symbolize what is sometimes called the "American melting pot." This is the idea that one nation, the American people, have been created by the assimilation of people of diverse national origins. More accurately, it might be said that the blending of foreign immigrants in the melting pot into one puree in which the original makings cannot be distinguished, has never been realized. Instead, Americans are something of a demographic stew, one in which carrots, potatoes, celery, and other ingredients often maintain their identity.

Scholars disagree about why this imperfect amalgamation has occurred. Whatever the cause, though, many Americans tend to think of themselves as not just Americans, but as Irish Americans, Italian Americans, Mexican Americans, African Americans, Jewish Americans, and many other kinds of Americans. The hyphen to denote these groups (as in Irish-American) has gone out of style, but its earlier use has left the term "hyphenated American" to designate the lingering identification of many Americans with the heritage of their immigrant ancestors. Identification with a specific country is the most common link, but there are others. Religion is one, with, for example, many Jewish Americans having a strong sense of community with Israel. Other groups have regional cultural connection. For example, because the history of slavery wiped out the ability of most blacks to trace their heritage to a specific location, what sense of identification that group does have is linked more to sub-Saharan Africa than a single country. Similarly, many Arab Americans identify with that broader cultural identity instead of, or along with, a specific country.

For many the foreign connection is quite recent. Some 12% of all U.S. residents were born elsewhere, and many others are second and third generation Americans. When the U.S. Census Bureau asked people to identify their cultural heritage, 80% did so. The most frequent answers were German (15%), Irish (11%), English (9%), Italian

(6%), Mexican (7%), Chinese (4%), Polish (3%) and French (3%). Another 7% of U.S. residents chose "American" as their ethnic heritage.

Throughout American history, hyphenated American groups have often acted as interest groups dedicated to influencing U.S. foreign policy to be favorable to their homeland and ancestral culture. For one, Jewish Americans who support Israel are represented by such organizations as the American-Israel Public Affairs Committee (AIPAC, http://www.aipac.org/), which declares itself, "America's Pro-Israel Lobby." Among the groups trying in part to counterbalance the efforts of AIPAC is the Arab American Institute (http://www.aaiusa.org/), which lists among its missions, "represent[ing] Arab American interests in government and politics" on such issues as "U.S. Middle East policy." To this list of ethnic lobbies could be added the Cuban American National Foundation, American Latvian Association, the TransAfrica Forum, the Armenian National Committee of America, the American Hellenic Institute (Greek Americans), the Irish National Caucus, the Polish American Congress, and myriad others.

The issue that the activity of these groups raises is the propriety of ethnic foreign policy lobbying. There can be little doubt that the language of the First Amendment guaranteeing the right "to petition the government for a redress of grievances," gives ethnic interests groups, as all interest groups, the right to lobby the U.S. government. Equally certain is that lobbying by groups of every ideological and policy persuasion is a key, and perhaps a necessary, element of the American democratic tradition and process. Some people, however, believe that lobbying for a policy to benefit a foreign government falls outside the boundaries of what is, or should be, acceptable. They charge that such pressures distort U.S. foreign policy in ways that can actually contravene U.S. national interests.

Such concerns are not new. For example former President Theodore Roosevelt was outraged at the opposition of German American groups, Irish American groups, and others to U.S. entry into World War I against Germany and as a British ally. In a 1915 speech, Roosevelt declared, "There is no room in this country for hyphenated Americanism." He asserted that "Our allegiance must be purely to the United States" and he condemned the "tangle of squabbling nationalities,…each at heart feeling more sympathy with Europeans of that nationality, than with the other citizens of the American Republic." Roosevelt even termed it "treason" for "an American citizen to vote as a German-American, an Irish-American, or an English-American."

## POINTS TO PONDER

➤ Advocate Yossi Shain writes of a "flexible world of multiple loyalties." Think about this idea. Is it possible to simultaneously be a loyal American and loyal to another country? What if those two countries disagree?

➤ To argue that ethnic lobby groups sometimes advocate policies counter to the national interest necessarily assumes that there is an objective national interest. Is that so, or is the national interest subjective—that is, whatever the American policy process eventually decides it is?

➤ There are foreign policy lobby groups based on economic interests, ideological views, gender, and many other bases, as well as ethnicity. Are your views on the legitimacy of foreign policy lobbying the same for all these groups? If you differentiate, why?

# Ethnic Foreign Policy Lobbying:
# Misplaced Allegiance

### GEOFFREY WHEATCROFT

Although the old saying that hard cases make bad law might seem to apply to the case of Elian Gonzalez, it wasn't really so hard. The law held that he should be reunited with his father, that is what most Americans thought should be done and that is what has now happened. But the case leaves ugly scars, and it raises once again the question of what should be the rights—and responsibilities—of "hyphenated Americans." The boy would have joined his father in Cuba weeks ago if he hadn't become an emblem, or a pawn, for one of the most noisiest and most feared of such groups, the Cuban Americans.

The United States is a land of immigrants, with complicated feelings towards their ancestral lands. It is also a free country where interest-group politics have always flourished, which does not mean that the effects of these groups or lobbies have been benign. To the contrary, the pressure exerted by the "hyphenates" has been almost unfailingly malign, for the American republic and for American people as a whole.

It is made worse by the cravenness of American politicians. In *Of Thee I Sing*, the Gershwin brothers' very funny 1931 musical satire on American politics, the campaign song goes, "He's the man the people choose,/Loves the Irish, loves the Jews." Real-life American polls have all too often taken this jest as a true word.

The US's emergence as a great power dates from the first world war, which the country entered belatedly, and despite the wishes of many Americans. Tens of millions of German Americans obviously didn't want to fight against their fathers' fatherland. Millions of Irish Americans were scarcely keener to fight for the king of England, or millions of Jewish Americans for the tsar of all the Russians whose oppression most of them had fled. And indeed the US did not enter the war until after the 1917 February revolution and the fall of tsardom.

Then the fun began. Irish-American pressure led towards the creation of an Irish Free State. Whatever else may be said of this, it was by no means in the American national interest. During the second world war, the most important war the Americans ever fought, once they, again belatedly, entered it, that Irish state was sullenly neutral.

There has recently been much bitter criticism in America of Swiss neutrality during the war. Apart from the fact that Switzerland was surrounded by the Axis and had no choice between neutrality and annihilation, Swiss neutrality did no military harm to the Allied cause. By contrast, Irish neutrality delayed victory in the battle of the Atlantic and thus the defeat of Hitler, with all that implies.

After the Irish came the Czech Americans' turn. Largely thanks to them President Woodrow Wilson's 14 points included the 10th point: "The peoples of Austria-Hungary...should be accorded the freest opportunity of autonomous development." From this light-hearted undertaking came the destruction of the Habsburg monarchy.

The rights and wrongs of that aren't simple, but it is worth noting that the allegedly national "successor state" of Czechoslovakia thereby called into being no longer exists. Nor does Yugoslavia, the other state invented after the great war.

No other hyphenated group has been as politically powerful as the Jewish-American lobby. Although Washington politicians may tremble at the phrase "the 40m[illion] Irish Americans," they tremble more before the numerically fewer Jewish Americans. The American-Israeli Public Affairs Committee has won a reputation as the most formidable, and often the most ruthless, of all such pressure groups. Having spent some little time looking into this subject, I would merely say that the activities of that lobby will one day come to be seen as not having served the true interests of the United States, of Jewish America, or even, in the end, of Israel.

The behavior of Cuban America over Elian speaks for itself, and the lobby has anyway prevented a necessary rapprochement between the US and Cuba. What has been more shocking than the hysteria of Little Havana in Miami has been the fawning on the Cuban Americans by politicians, including both presidential candidates?

Yet even that is trivial compared with what may prove to be the true "legacy" (in the president's favorite word) of the Clinton administration. The eastward expansion of NATO [North Atlantic Treaty Organization by adding many new countries in Eastern Europe to the alliance] must rank, in a hotly contested field, as the craziest single piece of American statecraft since the invasion of Cambodia 30 years ago this week. After the end of the cold war, it has no good strategic or political justification but can only justifiably inflame Russian suspicions and means, strictly speaking, that we must go to war on behalf of Hungary in a border dispute with Slovakia.

Why has it happened? It was inspired partly by the president's desire to enrich what his wiser predecessor Eisenhower called the military-industrial complex, but more importantly by his ingratiating himself with ethnic lobbies. Historians will date NATO expansion [to include many new countries in Eastern Europe in the alliance] to Clinton's groveling to a Polish-American audience in Chicago.

Even if the politics of hyphenated-America didn't produce such sorry practical consequences, it would be an affront to the "American idea." In direct contrast to European nationalism, the concept of "the American nation" is not based on ethnicity. Unlike European nation states, the American republic is founded not on a people, but on a proposition. This ideal has often been neglected, to put it mildly, and it may not say much to many black Americans, but it is noble in inspiration. If only American politicians remembered that more often.

In between sucking up to Cuban Americans and claiming to have invented the Internet, Vice-President Gore not long ago produced an exquisite howler. The country's motto is *E pluribus unum*, which means, he told his audience, "out of one, many." It was a true Freudian slip. He made a mistake, but in his ludicrous way he expressed a truth, about the fragmentation of America into all too many fractious and competitive components.

What the 18th-century creators of the American republic believed in was "out of many, one." One people would emerge from many different origins, sharing common creeds (that all men are created equal, entitled to life, liberty and the pursuit of happiness), rather than common gene pools. What the 20th century has seen is a regression to the primitive atavistic group loyalties which the new country was meant to avoid.

More than a hundred years ago, a federal judge told an Irish-American agitator that any American was entitled to sentimental sympathies for another country, but that every American's first political duty must be to the United States.

# Ethnic Foreign Policy Lobbying: All-American Tradition

## Yossi Shain

American ethnics don't just lobby for their ancestral homelands—they also export American values.

Last March, when Marie Jana Korbelova returned to her birth city, Prague, this time as Madeleine Albright, U.S. secretary of State, Czech President Vaclav Havel declared, "I would personally consider it excellent [if Madeleine Albright could succeed me as President of the Czech Republic] because into this rather staid provincial environment this would bring an international spirit, someone who knows the world well, understands it, and would be able to act." In the Czech Republic, the president must be a Czech citizen over 40 years of age. Albright, a naturalized U.S. citizen, qualifies for Czech citizenship under the law that enables those who fled the communist regime after 1948 to reclaim citizenship. Albright smiled and said "I am not a candidate and will not be a candidate....My heart is in two places, and America is where I belong."

Havel's vision, that transnational allegiance to both an ancestral homeland and to the U.S. can exist without conflict, is quite remarkable. It represents not only his own liberal-humanistic vision of world affairs—where boundaries of state and culture are no longer so rigid—but also the perception that Americans are the best conveyers of this mentality. As members of an open liberal society where multiple ethnic identities are no longer suspect and where, in fact, ancestral identities are welcomed as the cornerstone of multiculturalism, Americans in the post-Cold War world are often perceived as the best rep-

resentatives of a more flexible concept of citizenship and loyalty.

Havel's extraordinary invitation is just one sign of a changing configuration of national and ethnic loyalties. For the United States, a nation of immigrants, the meaning of ethnic identity is being transformed. Old nativist fears—that Americans with emotional ties to their ancestral homelands cannot be fully loyal to the United States—are rapidly disappearing. Those people once disparagingly called "hyphenated Americans" feel increasingly free to organize and lobby on behalf of the "old country." Even within America's foreign policy establishment, one finds increasing acceptance of the legitimacy of ethnic lobbies and full participation by ethnically identifiable players such as Jews and Cuban-Americans.

But what is arguably the most interesting new development is that the flow of political influence is becoming more of a two-way street. American diasporas—of Arabs, Jews, Armenians, Chinese—are playing significant roles in their ancestral homelands. They bring American ideologies and influence into the politics of the mother country. At times—taking up the challenge that Secretary Albright declined—U.S. citizens have even returned to their countries of origin to play leading political roles.

## DIVERSITY AND DIASPORAS

The signs of this more flexible world of multiple loyalties are easy to find. For example, The *Washington Post* reported this year a sharp increase in the number of young Americans who are spending summers in their parents' homeland. These parents apparently no longer fear that their children will be stigmatized; in fact, many now consider their children's bilingual abilities and familiarity with ancestral culture an asset in a globalized world order. Indeed, as America recognizes the value of diversity, homeland countries that previously restricted their kin abroad to single citizenship now permit them dual nationality. These countries have also enabled their kin diasporas to retain broad economic and political rights in their kin states, including absentee voting, even though the individuals have clearly established themselves as loyal citizens in the U.S.

The December 1996 passage of Mexican legislation permitting dual nationality is but one example. That law affects the lives of millions of Mexican-Americans—the fastest-growing voting bloc in American politics. With Mexican politicians now routinely courting support of the Mexican community in the United States, Mexico has laid to rest the image of the "pocho"—a derogatory term that questions the loyalty of diasporic Mexicans seen as having abandoned their roots in order to assimilate into American society.

There are many reasons that Mexico and other countries have reversed course and now encourage rather than prohibit dual nationality. Most importantly, they see numerous advantages in cultivating the continued loyalty of their kin diasporas. For countries such as Colombia, Nicaragua, the Dominican Republic and El Salvador, remittances and investments from kin communities in the United States play an important economic role. Diaspora money also now influences national politics and political campaigns in many countries, so politicians may want to win the approval of their financial backers abroad. More generally, they want to keep their diaspora's loyalty intact, and thus they use citizenship as an incentive for ethnic or national pride.

Many states [countries] also want to use the lobbying power of their kin, especially in the United States. Armenia, for example—which is involved in a bitter territorial struggle with a neighboring state—works hard to maintain the intensity of diasporic involvement in the motherland's cause.

During the past decade, Eastern European countries have evoked kinship ties even more dramatically by inviting expatriates in the U.S. to take leading roles in their countries of origin. Consider Milan Panic, a California pharmaceutical industrialist who became the prime minister of Yugoslavia in 1992; Alexander Eiseln, an American Army colonel who became the defense minister of Estonia in 1993; and Valdas Adamkus, a Lithuanian-American who moved to Lithuania in 1997 and was elected Lithuania's president in 1998. In the words of one Lithuanian voter, "He lived in America for a long time....He knows how the system works there. I think he will bring democracy from America to us." Also, in Armenia, former foreign minister Raffi Hovannisian and energy minister Sebuth Tashjian are both from California. These are of course rather rare cases of ethnically identified Americans taking posts in their countries of origin at a time when American political and business expertise is sought in nascent states or in new democracies emerging from the shadow of communism. Because of their American experience, these individuals with dual attachments are in a special position to help their ancestral homelands.

Leaders in other countries, realizing that ethnic Americans can be a powerful lobbying force, have at times encouraged their kin to become involved in U.S. foreign policy. However, they fail to recognize that in the process of empowerment, these ethnic Americans may become even more American, and in turn bring back unexpected messages and ideas, such as democratic reforms, much to the chagrin of the kin state. Take, for example, Arab-American relations with Saudi Arabia.

In April 1999, Jeddah's conservative newspaper Al-Madina ran an editorial entitled "A Clinton Victory and Arab Americans." Noting that the peace accord in Ulster showed the great political clout of Irish-Americans, the editorial stated, "The Arab minority in the United States must move toward influential centers in a society where domestic politics [is so crucial]." However, when Arab-American lobbyists like Jim Zogby and Khalil Jashan were welcomed by the Clinton administration as harbingers of peace in the Middle East and subsequently began to contemplate advocating greater openness in the Arab world, they were immediately rebuffed by Arab states, including Saudi Arabia.

## FEAR OF HYPHENATED AMERICANS

The question of expatriate loyalty has evolved over the years. In the 19th and early 20th centuries, the idea of hyphenated Americans was used by nativists to question the allegiance of immigrants, despite the newcomers' claims that their ancestral identities were not incompatible with their loyalty to America. Even cultural assimilation in America did not shield many immigrants from feeling threatened because of a perceived affinity to their homelands. This was especially the experience of diasporas whose homelands were enemy states at war with the U.S. American fear of transnational allegiance was also behind the exclusionary laws of the late 1910s and the early 1920s. During World War I, the issue of dual loyalties became particularly prominent with the growing suspicion of pan-German organizations, which prompted America's demand for total assimilation and unqualified renunciation of German-American past loyalties. President Woodrow Wilson feared

that American involvement against Germany might unleash "serious domestic clashes inside the U.S."

The most vivid example of misguided fear manifested itself during World War II after the attack on Pearl Harbor. The belief that Japanese-Americans might still be loyal to the ancestral homeland resulted in the relocation and internment of 120,000 Japanese-Americans. As recently as 1991, this animosity surfaced again (albeit in a much milder form), as Arab-Americans became vulnerable to attack during the Gulf War with Iraq.

During the Cold War years, ethnic Americans who sought a voice in foreign policy matters regarding a country of origin could gain access to decision-makers mostly when their views coincided with America's hostility to communism. Richard Allen, Ronald Reagan's first national security adviser, encouraged Cuban-Americans to build up an ethnic lobby that would serve as a tool furthering the administration's effort to delegitimize the Castro regime. Over time, Jorge Mas Canosa and the Cuban-American National Foundation became a major power broker in American foreign policy.

With the changing nature of America's ethnic mix—i.e., with the proliferation of non-European immigrants arriving mostly from Latin America and Asia, and with the growing advancement of minority groups, especially African-Americans—ethnic Americans began to consider a voice in foreign policy an additional form of empowerment. In America today, there are many new ethnic voices making themselves heard. Even groups which are satisfied with their accomplishments in the American economic arena no longer shy away from foreign policy. Thus, in contrast to their historical timidity in American public affairs, the 1.4 million Indian-Americans have found a political voice and are raising the stature of India in Washington.

## ETHNIC LOBBIES' GROWING POWER

At a time when global foreign relations are no longer defined in strictly East-West terms [the cold war rivalry between the U.S-led bloc and the Soviet-led bloc] and [when] U.S. foreign policy is characterized by a diminished cohesiveness, ethnic lobbies are becoming more important in influencing foreign policy makers. The fact that American society and politics permit, or even welcome, expressions of ethnic solidarity and no longer discourage preoccupation with motherlands lends itself to special diasporic influences on the U.S. foreign policy agenda. This reality has raised concerns about the ability of the U.S. to develop foreign policy in the "American national interest." Will its foreign policy be tainted and confused by partisan and divisive ethnic voices? On this point, Samuel Huntington says that by accepting the validity of multiculturalism and by heeding ethnic voices, American decision-makers are at risk of compromising American national interests.

Such concerns are usually exaggerated. In my book, *Marketing the American Creed Abroad: Diasporas in the U.S. and Their Homeland*, I document that ethnic Americans who engage in U.S. foreign policy are frequently carriers of American foreign policy messages and values, rather than being agents or fifth columns for their countries of origin.

For example, Iranian radicalism is said to be waning as reformist politicians win elections in Teheran. Even Iranian-Americans now see the possibility of building an ethnic lobby without compromising their American loyalties or without being suspected of treason by their kin in Iran. Especially when a homeland is at odds with America, first-generation exiles may feel compelled to remain silent, lest they be accused of being traitors at home or spies abroad. Over time, however, their offspring become sufficiently comfortable to organize as ethnic Americans, and eventually to act as a liaison between the U.S. and their homeland. In the case of the million-strong and economically thriving Iranian-American community, Negar Akhvi has recently noted that after the revolution of 1979, first-generation immigrants were too timid either to speak against Ayatollah Khomeini or to organize as diasporic Americans. Describing the younger generation of Iranian-Americans in Los Angeles, Akhvi maintains, "the fatigue and the stress that enveloped the generation that fled Iran has not been passed on to my own. My generation is less scared by the Revolution and at greater ease in democratic forums. In short, we are American enough to form a lobby, yet Iran an enough to care about what happens in our homeland."

Other American ethnic communities, both newcomers and those of long standing, have discovered they can unify and mobilize their particular community by pursuing goals related to the homeland as well as domestic issues in the U.S. That was certainly true of African-Americans as they effectively protested apartheid in South Africa in the mid-1980s. When in 1988 a number of American black leaders announced their preference for the appellation "African-American" over "black," the Rev. Jesse Jackson declared, "Every ethnic group in this country has a reference to some land base, some historical cultural base. African-Americans have hit that level of maturity." Indeed, in recent years African-American activists inside and outside Congress have gained high visibility and importance in the foreign policy arena. When in 1994 President Clinton was hesitant about restoring deposed President Jean-Bertrand Aristide in Haiti, it was the Congressional Black Caucus and the hunger strike of Randall Robinson, director of the

African-American lobby TransAfrica, which forced him to act.

The recent case of Elian Gonzalez [a Cuban boy who survived the sinking of the boat in which his mother and others fleeing to the United States died. The father, still in Cuba, and the Cuban government demanded the boy's return. The Cuban-American community strongly opposed his return, but he was eventually taken by U.S. Marshals and sent back to Cuba] is a fascinating example of how diaspora community leaders try to safeguard the exile mentality against the atrophy that would be quite natural for a community of immigrants after 40 years in the United States. It appeared that the Cuban-American community found itself at a critical juncture: Was its identity that of exiles and refugees nurturing their old rhetoric and the hope of return—or were they to become ethnic Americans plain and simple? For Cuban-Americans, the Gonzalez case served as the impetus for reassessing the question of their loyalty, and the community found itself in a precarious dilemma. The difficulty is that if Cuban-Americans are perceived as acting outside the laws of America regarding child custody, or in opposition to congressional tendencies to relax the economic sanctions against Cuba, they endanger the sympathy they enjoy as adherents of American interests and values and opponents of the Castro regime. That struggle over the loyalty and identity of Cuban-Americans is certain to continue.

In today's America it becomes more and more difficult to distinguish between domestic and foreign politics. America's divided government, which empowers single members of Congress and even local municipal leaders in foreign policy, enhances the stature and the clout of well-organized ethnic lobbies. These lobbies also benefit from the declining power of traditional foreign policy elites—the old "Eastern establishment." For example, the highly mobilized and well-funded Armenian-American community has gained its reputation over the past decade as the most important element in shaping U.S. foreign policy posture toward the newly independent states in the Caucasus and especially toward the conflict in Nagorno-Karabakh, a territory claimed by both Armenia and Azerbaijan. While Congress continues to support the lobby's position and prohibits direct U.S. assistance to Azerbaijan under Section 907, the Clinton administration strongly opposes Section 907 and has testified in favor of repeal of these sanctions. In his inaugural address in 1998, Armenian President Robert Kocherian emphasized the importance of "the unification of efforts of all Armenians, and ensuring the Armenian diaspora's active participation in the social, political and economic life of our republic. …Armenia should be a holy motherland for all Armenians, and its victory should be their victory."

## JEWISH AMERICANS AND MIDDLE EAST POLICY

When U.S. foreign policy was determined by traditional professional elites, there was a tendency to perceive Jewish-American affinity with Israel as a liability, especially since the Foreign Service held that America's close ties to Israel could jeopardize its interest in the Arab world or the oil-rich countries. In the 1950s, U.S. foreign policy-makers under Eisenhower viewed Israel as, at best, a benign presence in the Middle East and, more commonly, as an irritant in America's strategic planning in the region. At the height of the Cold War, Jewish Americans were leery about breaking with the American official line. For instance, during the Suez Crisis of 1956, the Jewish-American lobby emphasized its allegiance to American interests and was reluctant to push Israel's case for fear of being labeled disloyal....

The emphasis on American allegiance by Jewish Americans could also be seen in Secretary of State Henry Kissinger's handling of the Middle East conflict. During the Nixon and Ford administrations, Kissinger downplayed his Jewish origin in his work on this policy area. Kissinger was attacked vehemently by the American-Israel Political Action Committee when he attempted to push Israel into a deal with the Arabs. In light of Israel's reluctance to accept an American dictate, AIPAC mobilized the Congress against President Ford's decision to reassess U.S. policy in the Middle East and U.S. relations with Israel. When 76 senators wrote to the president urging him to declare that "the U.S. acting in its own national interest stands firmly with Israel," Kissinger responded angrily. He berated Israeli Ambassador Simcha Dinitz and told him that the letter "will increase anti-Semitism, it will cause people to charge that Jews control Congress." As a result, Kissinger was accused of betrayal and hounded by demonstrators in Israel. His insistent loyalty to the United States thus resulted in his being pulled from both sides of the ethnic bridge.

The allegation that Jews cannot always be both good Americans and good Jews surfaced on various occasions when there was a contest between the White House and the Israel lobby. Today, however, as foreign policy-making in Washington is becoming more dispersed and influenced by, among other things, think tanks, public opinion and the media, ethnic lobbyists are no longer perceived as an inherent threat to the national interest, and the dreaded charge of "divided loyalties" is less and less persuasive. In fact, the end of the Cold War and deep splits within Israel regarding the direction of the Palestinian peace process and the character of the Jewish state have tended to divide the U.S. Jewish community. Thus, when President Clinton wanted to demonstrate his frustration with former Israeli Prime Minister Benjamin Netanyahu, he could call upon certain Jewish-American community leaders to mobilize their constituencies to reprimand the Israeli government for its behavior.

At times, individuals associated with ethnic lobbies have even established themselves as leading experts in their respective kin states and, as such, are mobilized by the American government as more effective messengers in the United States or in their ancestral homelands. When persons of Jewish origins, such as Aaron Miller, Dennis Ross, or Martin Indyk (who was a member of the pro-Israel lobby before he established the Washington Institute for Near East Policy) are situated at the forefront of American foreign policy in the Middle East, the idea that committed Jews cannot be trusted as brokers in the Arab-Israeli peace process is no longer viable. Even Arab leaders and Arab-Americans have grudgingly accepted this as a fact of life, despite ongoing Arab-Israeli conflicts. Take, for example, Daniel Kurzer, America's current ambassador to Egypt, who is a deeply committed and publicly identified Jew. The prominence of these individuals in Middle East policy-making is a clear indication that in America at least, Jewish identity does not provoke serious suspicions of divided loyalties.

Finally, we should not forget that America's generally benign attitude toward questions of ethnic loyalty does have its limits. After Jonathan Pollard, an Israeli-American, was convicted of spying for Israel, it was not surprising that the Jewish-American community was much less merciful toward Pollard than was the Israeli government, which has been trying for years to secure his release from prison. More recently, Wen Ho Lee, the physicist formerly at Los Alamos National Laboratory who is alleged to have passed nuclear secrets to China, has reportedly caused a cloud of suspicion to be cast over other Chinese-American scientists. Despite these rare cases, the overall trend in the United States has clearly moved in recent decades in a more positive direction. There is an ever greater acceptance of the legitimacy of ethnic Americans in national policy-making, as well as a growing appreciation that in the present period of globalization, America's ethnic groups can strengthen and expand U.S. influence around the world.

## THE CONTINUING DEBATE:
## Ethnic Foreign Policy Lobbying

### What Is New

Ethnic lobbying continues to exert influence on foreign policy. For example, recent studies have shown that foreign aid is connected to ethnic lobbies, not only in the United States, but also in other aid-giving countries. Other recent research has shown that ethnic lobbying groups influence U.S. economic sanctions policy.

In 1915, Theodore Roosevelt condemned lobbying by various European American groups. The changing demographic characteristics of Americans and the rising political activity and strength of non-European heritage groups has diversified ethnic lobbying. The TransAfrica Forum, for one, is a relatively new organization, which, its mission statement says, "focuses on U.S. policy as it affects Africa and the Diaspora in the Caribbean and Latin America" on behalf of "African-American community." Cuban Americans have for decades influenced U.S. foreign policy, and now they are being joined by such other Latino groups, such as the National Council of La Raza, which includes among its missions presenting "an Hispanic perspective on trade, assistance, and other international issues."

### Where to Find More

A good place to begin would be Thomas Ambrosio's edited study, *Ethnic Identify Groups and U.S. Foreign Policy* (Praeger, 2002). Additionally, a recent book that frets about ethnic lobbying while also supporting its validity is Tony Smith, *Foreign Attachments: The Power of Ethnic Groups in the Making of American Foreign Policy* (Harvard University Press, 2000). A study that worries that strong multiculturalism, including on foreign policy, is endangering American national unity is Arthur M. Schlesinger Jr., *The Disuniting of America: Reflections on a Multicultural Society* (W. W. Norton, 1998). For an optimistic view of competing identities, read Peter J. Sprio, *Embracing Dual Nationality* (Carnegie Endowment for International Peace, 1998). Also positive toward ethnic lobbying is James M. Lindsay, "Getting Uncle Sam's Ear: Will Ethnic Lobbies Cramp America's Foreign Policy Style?," *Brookings Review*, Winter 2002. It is available on the Web at: http://www.brook.edu/. Also worthwhile and available on the Web is a summary of a conference on ethnic foreign policy lobbying. See David J. Vidal, "Defining the National Interest Minorities and U.S. Foreign Policy in the 21st Century: Project for Diversity in International Affairs" at: http://www.ciaonet.org/conf/vid01/.

### What More to Do

The view of many people may be that ethnic foreign policy lobbying is neither always good nor always bad. Given that, one thing to do in class is to work with others to come up with a "do's and don'ts" list of such activities.

You will also find it enlightening to analyze the 2004 U.S. presidential race for evidence of influence by various foreign policy lobby groups on that contest. The Middle East, U.S.-Cuba relations, immigration, and numerous other foreign policy or mixed *inter*national/dom*estic* (intermestic) issues of interest to one or another ethnic groups played a role in who takes the oath of office on January 20, 2005 and who just watches the swearing-in ceremony.

# 9

# POLITICAL PARTIES

## THE ODDS-ON FAVORITE IN THE FUTURE:
### Democrats *or* Republicans?

### DEMOCRATS

**ADVOCATES:** John B. Judis, Senior Editor, *The New Republic*, and Ruy
   Teixeira, Senior Fellow, the Century Foundation

**SOURCE:** "America's Changing Political Geography: Where Democrats Can
   Build a Majority," *Blueprint: Ideas for a New Century*,
   September/October 2002

### REPUBLICANS

**ADVOCATE:** Daniel Casse, Senior Director, White House Writers Group

**SOURCE:** "An Emerging Republican Majority?" *Commentary*, January 2003

This debate brings to mind the classic tune, "The Party's Over," originally made
famous by Judy Holliday in the 1956 Broadway musical *Bells Are Ringing*. The
theme of the lyrics is captured in two lines:

> The party's over, it's time to call it a day,
> They've burst your pretty balloon and taken the moon away.

Judy Holliday was singing about lost love, but the advocates in this debate might
use her words to back up their theme that one of the major parties is destined to fade in
the affections of a majority of American voters. What the advocates disagree about is
which party is destined for loneliness and which is destined for love. John Judis and Ruy
Teixeira contend that the country is entering an age of "a new Democratic majority"
because demographic "growth trends within states favor the Democrats, not the
Republicans." To the contrary, Daniel Casse argues in his essay that the Republican Party
has a good chance of building on the string of successes it had in the presidential and
congressional elections of 2000 and 2002 and turning those victories "into something
more permanent and more meaningful."

There can be little doubt that the immediate picture was looking bright for
Republicans when Casse published his article in early 2003. Not only was a Republican
in the Oval Office, but President George W. Bush's poll number were exceptional. A CBS
poll taken during the first week of January 2003 found 64% of its respondents indicating
they approved of "the way…Bush is handling his job as President," compared to just
28% who disapproved, and 8% who were unsure. Additionally, the GOP (Grand Old
Party) was in control of Congress with majorities in both the House and the Senate.

Recent history clearly shows, however, that current success does not necessarily
translate into positive long-term prospects. Just three decades ago, the Watergate scandal that forced President Richard M. Nixon to resign in August 1974 also tainted his
Republican Party, which lost 48 House seats in that November's elections. When the
new Congress convened in 1975, the Democrats held 291 seats in the House, more

than two-thirds of the total, against only 144 Republicans. The GOP also lost five Senate seats, leaving it was almost nearly as lop-sided, with 60 Democrats, 38 Republicans, and 2 independents. The Democrats made even further gains in both houses in 1976 when their presidential nominee, Jimmy Carter, captured the White House, and the opinion columns and talk-show airwaves around the country were full of predictions about the imminent demise of the Republican Party.

That did not occur. Republicans Ronald Reagan and George H. W. Bush won the presidency in 1980 and 1984 and in 1988 respectively. The GOP also gained in Congress, and even was the majority party in the Senate for six years under Reagan. Then Democrat Bill Clinton won the 1992 presidential election, but the uncertain start his presidency helped cost Democrats 54 House seats in 1994. When the 104th Congress convened in January 1995, the GOP controlled both house of Congress for the first time since 1954. Many pundits touted the so-called "Republican revolution," and opined that new GOP Speaker of the House, Newt Gingrich would be powerful enough to move the center of political gravity in Washington a considerable distance eastward on Constitution Avenue away from the White House and toward the Capitol. Gingrich proved inept as speaker, however, and was soon forced from office. But that GOP setback was overcome when George W. Bush completed the Republican trifecta by edging Al Gore for the presidency in 2000. To make matters even better for the Republicans, they gained seats in Congress in 2002, thereby overcoming the tradition of the president's party losing seats in the off-year elections.

Do these shifts in recent decades mean that one or the other party cannot dominate for a significant period? The answer is no. The Republicans controlled both houses of Congress for all but six years (1913–1919) between 1901 and 1933. During this time, Woodrow Wilson (1913–1921) was the sole Democratic president. Then the Democrats took control with the election of President Franklin Roosevelt. Except for four years (1947–1949, 1953–1955), they then were a majority in the Senate until 1981 and in the House of Representatives until 1995. Furthermore, Democrats served as president for 8 of the 12 presidential terms between 1933 and 1981.

In addition to personalities and issues, another factor that affects the parties' fortunes is the percentage of the electorate that identifies with one of the two parties. Between 1952 and 2000, the percentage of people who either said they were Democrats or "leaned" in that direction declined from 57% to 47%, while Republican partisans or leaners increased marginally from 35% to 37%. True independents increased from 6% to 12% and people describing themselves as apolitical or attached to another party made up the balance.

## POINTS TO PONDER

➤ Think about the concept of "ideopolises" in the essay by Judis and Teixeira and the role they think these focuses of political geography will play. Do you find this a helpful analytical approach?

➤ The country is experiencing demographic shifts in voting activity. Women, African Americans, Asia Americans, and Latinos have become a significant part of the voting electorate. What do these changes augur for the parties?

➤ What are the chances that neither Judis and Teixeira nor Casse are correct? What has the best odds: a Democratic majority, a Republican majority, or a shifting political contest in which neither party dominates during the next decade or two?

# The Odds-On Favorite in the Future:
## Democrats

JOHN B. JUDIS AND RUY TEIXEIRA

After the 2000 election, political commentators began referring to the Democrats as the "blues" and the Republicans as the "reds"—terms corresponding to the colors used on electoral maps to denote which states each party's presidential ticket carried. So the question of America's political future has become: Who will dominate, the blues or the reds?

The Republicans think it'll be the reds. They look at the 2000 electoral map and see good things. For one thing, there's more red than blue, reflecting the fact that Republican states tend to be physically larger. More important, they figure that if they just hold the states they carried in 2000—which basically means the Solid South, the Mountain States, the Border States, and the more conservative Midwestern states—their electoral vote margin of four (271–267) will go up to 18 (278–260), due to reapportionment. Then, for a safety margin, all they have to do is pick off a few of the states they lost by less than 5 percent—Oregon, New Mexico, Iowa, Wisconsin, Washington, Minnesota, Michigan, Pennsylvania, and Maine—and they're home free.

That was Bush political guru Karl Rove's essential message in his now infamous lost-and-accidentally-found PowerPoint presentation to a group of California Republicans [in] June [2001]. Stick with us, allow us to do a little judicious pandering to workers in states like Wisconsin and Pennsylvania, and the GOP's Reagan coalition—albeit a bit slimmed down—will rise again. And, he might have added, we don't even need California, that current bastion of blue America; we can build our red America without it.

Republicans don't just rest their case on reapportionment. They think that below the state level, the trends favor the GOP. They argue that the pattern of growth within states favors the Republicans since formerly rural counties on the fringes of metropolitan areas are growing the fastest and these counties lean strongly Republican. Political analyst Michael Barone called these fringe areas "edge counties" in his influential "49 percent nation" article in *The Almanac of American Politics 2002*. David Brooks referred to these "fast-growing suburbs mostly in the South and West" as "sprinkler cities" in his recent cover article in *The Weekly Standard*, "Patio Man and the Sprawl People," but his argument is basically the same as Barone's: Demographic trends favor the Republicans.

Fortunately for the Democrats, these arguments don't hold up to scrutiny. The Solid South is unlikely to remain solid; some of the mountain and Midwestern states that are red are likely to go blue; and the blue states that Al Gore carried by small margins in 2000 are likely to get harder, not easier, for the Republicans to pick off. Moreover, and crucially, growth trends within states favor the Democrats, not the Republicans.

As we argue in our new book, *The Emerging Democratic Majority*, the reason for these trends is the emergence of a new American political geography—a geography intimately linked to the spread of a postindustrial economy. Rove, Barone, and Brooks are missing the contours of this new geography as they attempt to resuscitate a California-less Reagan coalition. They're living in the past; they don't see that the same changes that have moved California into the Democratic column over the last decade are moving most of the rest of the country in the same direction. Here's how:

Democrats have been gaining strength in areas where the production of ideas and services has either redefined or replaced an economy dependent on manufacturing, agriculture, and resource extraction. Many of these areas are in the North and West, but they are also in states like Florida and Virginia. Republicans are strongest in areas where the transition to postindustrial society has lagged. Many of these are in the Deep South and Prairie States. As Democratic politics has evolved over the last decade, it has increasingly reflected the socially liberal, fiscally moderate priorities of these new areas—what we call a politics of progressive centrism. Republicans have continued to espouse an anti-government credo closely identified with business and the religious right—a politics that plays well in parts of the Deep South but not in a new postindustrial America.

This new postindustrial politics is not defined by states but by metropolitan regions within states. These postindustrial metropolises, which we call "ideopolises," are the breeding ground for the new Democratic majority. Insofar as these areas are not confined to the Northeast, far West, and upper Midwest but are found also in the South and Southwest, the Democrats have a chance to build a large majority and to rewrite today's political map. By 2008, Democrats could enjoy an electoral base of 332 electoral votes, many more than they need for a majority, while holding a competitive position in a number of additional states that might swell that majority.

**The Role of Ideopolises.** The transition to a postindustrial society has transformed the economic geography of the country. After World War II, industrial society was divided into three domains: the cities of offices and manufacturing plants, where white ethnics, minorities, and immigrants lived; suburbs, where many of the white middle class were moving; and rural areas of farms, mines, and forests. Postindustrial society is organized around metropolitan areas that include both suburbs and central cities. The production of goods has moved out of the central city into the suburbs, or even into semi-rural areas. And many ethnics and minorities have migrated from the city to the suburbs. The sharpest contrast now is not between city and suburb, but between the new metropolitan areas, taken as a whole, and the rural countryside. The suburbs themselves have become extensions of the city—demarcated artificially on maps—rather than extensions of the countryside housing city workers.

Some of the new postindustrial metropolitan areas like Silicon Valley [near San Francisco] or the Boulder, Colo., metro area contain significant manufacturing facilities, but it is manufacturing—whether of pharmaceuticals or semiconductors—that consists in the application of complex ideas to physical objects. And some of these metro areas specialize in producing what Joel Kotkin and Ross C. DeVol call "soft technology"—entertainment, media, fashion, design, and advertising—and in providing databases, legal counsel, and other business services. New York City and Los Angeles are both premier postindustrial metropolises that specialize in soft technology.

Most of these postindustrial metropolises also include a major university or several major universities that funnel ideas and, more important, people into the hard or soft technology industries. Boston's Route 128 feeds off Harvard and MIT. Silicon Valley is closely linked to Stanford and the University of California at Berkeley. Dane

County's biomedical research is tied to the University of Wisconsin at Madison. And all of them have a flourishing service sector, with ethnic and vegetarian restaurants, multimedia shopping malls, children's museums, book store-coffee shops, and health clubs.

Professionals and technicians are heavily concentrated in the workforces of these postindustrial metropolises. A quarter or so of the jobs in Austin, Texas, Boston, San Francisco, or North Carolina's Research Triangle are held by professionals and technicians. Plentiful, too, are low-level service and information workers, including waiters, hospital orderlies, sales clerks, janitors, and teachers' aides. Many of these jobs have been filled by Hispanics and African-Americans, just as many of the high-professional jobs have been filled by Asian immigrants. It's one reason that the workforces in these areas we call ideopolises tend to be ethnically diverse and more complex in their stratification (various combinations of employers, employees, contract workers, temps, consultants, and the self-employed) than the workforce of the older industrial city.

The ethos and mores of many of these new metropolitan areas tend to be libertarian and bohemian because of the people they attract. Economists Richard Florida and Gary Gates found a close correlation between the concentration of gays and of the foreign-born and the concentration of high technology and information technology within a metropolitan area. They also found a high percentage of people who identified themselves as artists, musicians, and craftspeople. Concluded Florida, "Diversity is a powerful force in the value systems and choices of the new workforce, whose members want to work for companies and live in communities that reflect their openness and tolerance. The number one factor in choosing a place to live and work, they say, is diversity. Talented people will not move to a place that ostracizes certain groups."

The politics of these ideopolises emphasizes tolerance and openness. It is defined by the professionals, many of whom were deeply shaped by the social movements of the '60s. They worry about clean air and water, and when the market fails to provide them, they call on government. They favor civil rights and liberties and good government. They disdain the intolerance and fundamentalism of the religious right. But they are also leery of the old Democratic politics of "big government" and large-scale social engineering. Some backed Ronald Reagan in 1980 and 1984, but since then, they and the places they have lived have moved steadily into the Democratic column—and in the meantime, they have reshaped the Democratic Party in their own postindustrial image.

Metropolitan areas come in different stages and configurations. In the San Francisco Bay area or the Chicago metro area, the work and culture of the ideopolis pervades the entire metropolitan area. Many of the same people, the same businesses, and the same coffee shops or book stores can be found in the central city and in the suburbs. These are the most advanced and integrated ideopolises. Many of these areas were once Republican but have become extremely Democratic in their politics. Gore won Portland's Multnomah County [in Oregon] 64 percent to 28 percent. Princeton University's Mercer County [New Jersey] went for Gore 61 percent to 34 percent. Seattle's King County was 60 percent to 34 percent for Gore. Other metropolitan areas like Fresno, Calif., or Muncie, Ind., have not yet made the transition to a postindustrial economy. They lag in telecommunications, computers, and high-tech jobs. In some of these areas, which are not yet ideopolises, Republicans continue to have a strong following.

The Democrats' vote in the integrated ideopolises has included three groups that loom large in the emerging Democratic majority: professionals, women (especially single, working, and highly educated women), and minorities. But it has also included relatively strong support from the white working class—white workers who have not graduated from a four-year college and tend not to have credentialed jobs—the very group whose defection from the Democrats allowed conservative Republicans to build a majority. In the most advanced ideopolises, the white working class seems to embrace the same values as professionals and in some of them, white working-class men vote with remarkable similarity to their female counterparts. As a result, Republican appeals to hot-button issues such as race (or resentment against immigrants), guns, and abortion have largely fallen on deaf ears, and these voters have not only rejected Republican social conservatism but also reverted to a preference for Democratic economics. In Seattle's King County, white working-class voters backed Gore 50 percent to 42 percent. In Portland's Multnomah County, it was by 71 percent to 24 percent. By comparison, working-class whites nationwide supported Bush 57 percent to 40 percent.

To gauge the effect of these ideopolises nationally, we looked at 263 counties that are part of metro areas that have the highest concentrations of high-tech economic activity or contain a highly ranked research university. Most of these areas used to be Republican and voted for Republican presidential candidates in 1980 and 1984. In 1984, for instance, they went 55 percent to 44 percent for Reagan. But in 2000, Gore garnered 54.6 percent of the vote in these areas compared to 41.4 percent for Bush. And since Ralph Nader got 3.3 percent in these counties, the total Democratic-leaning vote in America's ideopolises can be reckoned at close to 58 percent.

By contrast, Democrats have continued to lose in rural areas in states like Missouri and Pennsylvania and in many low-tech metropolitan areas like Greenville, S.C., that have not made the postindustrial transition. In all, Gore lost the non-ideopolis counties 52.9 percent to 43.6 percent. Indeed, if you compare 1980, the beginning of the Reagan era, to today, it is clear that almost all of the pro-Democratic change in the country since then has been concentrated in America's ideopolis counties. This is what has happened to the Reagan coalition: It has vanished into the postindustrial economy.

**Ideopolises v. Edge Counties and Sprinkler Cities.** The changes wrought by this new political geography can be readily seen by looking at three states that voted Republican in the six presidential elections from 1968 to 1988—California, Illinois, and New Jersey—but are now solidly Democratic.

*California.* In the Reagan era, the Los Angeles area in Southern California, except for minority and Jewish enclaves, backed Republican conservatives while the Bay area in Northern California was divided between Democratic-leaning San Francisco and the moderate Republicans of San Mateo, Santa Clara, and Contra Costa counties. But in the '90s, the economic and political differences between the Bay area and Los Angeles County suddenly disappeared. The Bay area, of course, became the headquarters for Silicon Valley and one of America's leading ideopolises. But Los Angeles County also changed. In 1983, there had been almost twice as many aerospace workers as workers in the motion picture industry. By 2000, there were almost three times more workers employed in motion pictures than in aerospace. It, too, became an ideopolis and, like the Bay area, began voting about 2-to-1 for Democrats. In the state as a whole, Gore in 2000 won the ideopolis counties but lost the counties that had not yet been transformed by the postindustrial economy. California's 14 ideopolis counties, which made up 69 percent of the overall vote, supported Gore 57 percent to 38 percent, while the 44 non-ideopolis counties supported Bush 49 percent to 46 percent.

*Illinois.* In 1972, Richard Nixon actually won Chicago and Cook County, and Walter Mondale won the county by only 3 percent in 1984. But Chicago and Cook County were making the transition to a postindustrial metropolitan area. Between 1970 and 1997, Chicago lost 60 percent of its manufacturing jobs. While Chicago still manufactured goods, what it made was often high-technology computer equipment like modems or semiconductor chips. According to a Humphrey Institute study, the Chicago metropolitan area now has the highest number of high-tech jobs of any metropolitan area. All in all, the hog butcher of the world now has twice as many professionals and technicians in the metro area as production workers.

At the same time, Chicago and its suburbs began to move Democratic in 1988, but the most dramatic change came in the 1990s. In the 1992, 1996, and 2000 elections, the Republicans never got more than 30 percent of the vote in Cook County, and the Democratic total rose from 58 percent in 1992 to 69 percent in 2000. With Cook County tallying about 40 percent of the votes in the state, Bush in 2000 would have had to win 65 percent outside of Cook County to carry Illinois. That's an insuperable obstacle in a state that, even outside of Chicago and Cook County, is beginning to trend Democratic. For example, Lake County, one of Chicago's "collar counties" and part of the overall Chicago ideopolis, backed George H. W. Bush against Michael Dukakis in 1988 64 percent to 36 percent; in 2000, it supported his son by just 50 percent to 48 percent, with 2 percent going to Nader. In general, Illinois' ideopolis counties have gone from about a 50–50 split in 1988

to a 59–39 Democratic margin in 2000, while the Democratic disadvantage in the rest of the state—a shrinking share of the electorate—has remained steady at about 7 percentage points.

*New Jersey.* In the '80s, Reagan and Bush won the first and third biggest counties, Bergen in the North and Middlesex in the center, by comfortable margins. But in the 1990s, the central and northeastern sections of the state became almost a continuous ideopolis. The state's largest occupational group—and fastest growing—consists of professionals, who make up 23.3 percent of the workforce compared to 15.4 percent nationally. Counties like Bergen and Middlesex moved sharply Democratic. Bill Clinton in 1996 and Gore in 2000 took the two counties by identical margins: 14 points in Bergen and 24 points in Middlesex. In Bergen County, Gore won 65 percent of college-educated white voters, including 77 percent of college-educated white women. In the state, he won voters with postgraduate degrees (usually a good indication of professionalism) by 62 percent to 34 percent. At the same time, he won 88 percent of the black vote and 58 percent of the Hispanic vote (which includes pro-Republican Cubans from Union City.)

But what of the Republican Solid South? The changes that have swept through California, Illinois, and New Jersey are affecting politics there. Take Florida, which the Republicans desperately need to keep in their column. As Florida's high-tech and tourist centers have grown dramatically, they have also moved sharply Democratic. For example, Orlando's Orange County, once the center of Florida agriculture, has become a major entertainment center and a home for computer services. Democrats lost Orange County by 37 percent in 1988; in 2000, Gore won it by 2 points.

But the changes are not just in Orange County. As the table shows, since 1988,

Democratic strength has dramatically increased in all five counties of the state that added the most people during the last decade—Fort Lauderdale's Broward County, Miami-Dade, Palm Beach, and Tampa's Hillsborough County, as well as Orange County. It's not hard to see where Florida's political future lies.

As the postindustrial economy grows, change is coming to the rest of the South as well. As North Carolina has moved away from reliance on textiles and tobacco, it has become more receptive to a progressive centrist politics. All the state's postindustrial areas have become more Democratic since 1988. Dukakis lost Charlotte's Mecklenberg County 59 percent to 40 percent in 1988, but Gore lost it only by 51 percent to 48 percent in 2000, even though he did not campaign in the state (Clinton carried it by 3 points in 1996). The Democrats' edge in Durham County in the Research Triangle increased from 54 percent to 45 percent up to 63 percent to 35 percent over the same time period. In the Raleigh metro area as a whole, Gore edged Bush by a point, up from a 5 point Democratic deficit in 1988.

Virginia's premier postindustrial area, the Northern Virginia suburbs of Washington, D.C., where AOL and many of the nation's telecommunications firms are headquartered, has also been moving Democratic. Fairfax has gone from a 61 percent to 38 percent Republican margin in 1988 to a 49 percent to 47 percent Bush margin in 2000, with 3 percent to Nader. Arlington went from a 53 percent to 45 percent Democratic edge to a 60 percent to 34 percent Democratic advantage, with 5 percent to Nader, over the same time period. If these suburban voters keep increasing their proportion of the Virginia vote, and if they continue to trend Democratic, they could very well tilt Virginia back to the Democrats, even in presidential elections. Certainly, Democratic

Gov. Mark Warner's recent victory suggests this is a very real possibility.

But what about all those fast-growing edge counties and sprinkler cities that Barone and Brooks write about? Won't the increasing weight of these pro-Republican counties tilt these states and others back toward the Republicans? That's not likely for two simple reasons. First, most of these counties aren't very big (the 50 fastest growing average 109,000 in population), so their high growth rates translate into only modest increases in actual Republican voters. These modest increases pale in comparison to the additional Democratic voters provided by populous metropolitan counties (the 50 largest growing average 1.46 million) that had the largest increases in population. Al Gore gained a 2.7 million vote advantage from the 50 largest growth counties; George W. Bush gained only a 500,000 vote advantage from the 50 fastest growing counties.

Second, as these edge counties and sprinkler cities get bigger and become more integrated into a metropolitan area, they typically become more Democratic (call it the 'ideopolis effect"). Combined with their relatively small size, it means that even Brooks' and Barone's best-case counties are unlikely to have the potent political effects they predict.

Take Loudon County in the Northern Virginia suburbs, the sixth-fastest growing county in the country, cited by Brooks in his article. Even after a decade of very fast growth, Loudon still has only about 170,000 inhabitants. And, as Loudon has grown, it has become less Republican, going from a 66 percent to 33 percent Republican margin in 1988 to a much more modest 56 percent to 41 percent Republican advantage in 2000. The county's modest size and its declining Republican edge mean it can't stop an area-wide pro-Democratic trend (much less start a pro-Republican one): Even as Loudon was growing like topsy, the Northern Virginia suburbs as a whole went from a 20 point Democratic disadvantage to almost even over the same time period.

Or take Douglas County, Colo., outside of Denver, the fastest growing county in the country and lovingly cited by both Brooks and Barone. Douglas still has only 176,000 inhabitants. And, while it went for Bush by 34 points in 2000, that's down from 42 points in 1988 and 60 points in 1984. Reflecting these realities, Douglas' fast growth just hasn't been enough to drive its metro area toward the Republicans. Instead, the Denver metro area has gone from a 3 point Republican margin in 1988 to a 1 point Democratic advantage in 2000.

And Loudon and Douglas are two of the larger, fast-growing counties. The smaller ones, of course, have even less chance of impacting political trends. Contrary to Barone and Brooks, edge counties/sprinkler cities are clearly no antidote for trends in the nation's ideopolises—not in states that still lean Republican and certainly not in states that lean or are solid Democratic.

The new political geography has a powerful logic that should lead, over time, to a Democratic, not Republican, electoral majority. Of course, demography is not destiny—Democrats could fall back into the bad habits of their past, while Republicans could move decisively to the center. But barring unforeseen developments, the trends moving America toward a postindustrial economy should favor Democrats in the decade to come.

# The Odds-On Favorite in the Future:
## Republicans

DANIEL CASSE

By the time Al Gore conceded the presidency to George W. Bush in December 2000, there was widespread agreement that the razor-close election they had just fought, and the fractious litigation that followed it, had exposed a disturbingly deep fissure in our national politics. In newspapers and magazines and on television, brightly colored maps showed a country divided almost exactly in half into red (Republican) and blue (Democratic) voting patterns. "There are now two distinct Americas," proclaimed *Business Week* in a typical cover story, "split along geographic, social, religious, and racial lines." So disparate were the tastes and attitudes of the people inhabiting those two different Americas, the story continued, as to "demand entirely different things from government."

Not only was the country said to be fractured, it was also said to be, on that account, ungovernable—and certainly ungovernable by George W. Bush. Wherever the new President turned, averred the political scientist Walter Dean Burnham, he was bound to find himself crippled by severely "limited opportunities" to forge a consensus behind his policies.

It was in this very circumstance, indeed, that some in the still-smarting Democratic party saw a sign of hope. Although the Democrats had lost not only the presidency but, as it then seemed, both houses of Congress, opportunity lurked in Bush's irreparable weaknesses. The new President, after all, was woefully inexperienced, especially in foreign affairs. The Republican coalition that had supported him—an unlikely mix of business groups, social con-

servatives, and libertarians remained as fragile as ever. Only through the tiebreaking vote of the Vice President could the GOP expect to hold its majority in the Senate. And, as if these difficulties were not enough, the new administration was facing the first serious downturn in the national economy after eight years of remarkable prosperity presided over by a Democratic executive.

As the 2000 results were further digested, Democratic strategists took particular comfort in their reading of the red-blue map. The blue metropolitan clusters that had gone for Al Gore were composed disproportionately of educated professionals, women, and minorities—groups that were projected to grow more quickly than the rural and suburban voters who had pulled the lever for Bush. These demographic trends, along with the swooning stock market and other economic woes, suggested that Democrats might be well positioned to mount a fresh challenge to the GOP as early as the mid-term election of 2002. The party's prospects brightened further when, in June 2001, Senator James Jeffords announced that he was bolting the GOP and would henceforth vote as an independent—thus giving Democrats a majority in the Senate. In July, for the first time since Bush's inauguration, a Zogby poll showed a majority of Americans disapproving of his performance. Around Washington, "Re-Elect Gore" bumper stickers began to appear.

But then came September 11, followed by the war in Afghanistan and the budding confrontation with Saddam Hussein—events whose political importance served to boost George W. Bush's popularity to once-unimaginable levels and make the Gore defeat fade into memory. Last year's midterm campaign, on which the Democrats had pinned so much hope, became instead a month's-long exercise in frustration; by November 5, the actual results left in tatters the party's dream of a public backlash against an "accidental" President and of its own quick reemergence in American politics. In fact, its fortunes today are lower than they were in November 2000. Two years after the country seemed split down the middle, it is George W. Bush's Republicans who look to be on the verge of creating a new and wholly unexpected political majority.

To get a sense of the magnitude of the Democratic defeat, it helps to bear in mind that only twice since 1862 has the party not holding the White House failed to gain seats in the House of Representatives in a midterm election, and seldom has it failed to gain in the Senate. As November 5 approached, however, candid Democratic leaders were already admitting they had little hope of winning the House (though none foresaw the loss of fully seven Democratic seats). As for the Senate, eleven races were still deemed to be toss-ups through the final weekend before the balloting. Stunningly, the Republicans went on to win all but one of them. At the end of the balloting, the President enjoyed larger majorities in both houses of Congress than on the day he took office.

The morning after the voting, the line from the Democratic National Committee (DNC) was that the party's losses in Congress were offset by significant gains in gubernatorial races, including in such former Republican strongholds as Michigan, Pennsylvania, Wisconsin, Kansas, and Arizona. But this was spin. Not a single elected Republican governor lost on November 5. Most of the Democratic victories occurred in states where Republicans had held the governor's mansion for twelve years

or more, making it relatively easy for Democratic candidates to call for a change. Moreover, many of the victorious Democrats had campaigned on explicitly conservative platforms, and in Tennessee, Kansas, and Arizona they had vigorously opposed tax increases. The one notable exception was Mark Fernald in New Hampshire, who advocated an increase in state taxes and lost to the Republican candidate by 21 points.

Democratic gubernatorial victories also have to be seen against even more surprising wins by the GOP. Sonny Perdue became the first Republican governor to be elected in Georgia since Reconstruction. Robert Ehrlich, a graduate of [Speaker of the U.S. House of Representative] Newt Gingrich's congressional class of 1994, defeated Kathleen Kennedy Townsend in Maryland, a state widely viewed as the most Democratic in the nation. And [Florida Governor] Jeb Bush, the President's brother, resoundingly upset the prediction of DNC chairman Terry McAuliffe that he would soon be "gone," defeating his challenger by thirteen points.

There were other significant reverses at the state level as well, where Democrats lost control of seven legislatures. Republicans now control 21 state capitols nationwide, compared with only seventeen still in the hands of Democrats. (Another eleven are split.) This marks the first time since 1952 that Republicans have enjoyed such a majority. In Texas, the state House of Representatives is ruled by Republicans for the first time since 1870; in Missouri, for the first time since 1955.

From one perspective, of course, the results of the November election were not so astonishing. Ever since September 11, President Bush's approval rating had stood at historically high levels, and in most polls a majority of Americans were saying that the country was on the right track. In the new era of patriotism and national unity, the deep political chasms that separated Bush voters and Gore voters had become less meaningful.

The mid-term election reflected this changed mood in more ways than one. Although many Senate races were closely contested, and there were many tight gubernatorial races, none was a pitched ideological battle. In no contest did abortion, the death penalty, gun control, race, or class warfare play a major role. With the exception of the late Paul Wellstone [of Minnesota, who died in a plane crash during his 2002 reelection campaign], no candidate for the U.S. Senate actively argued against disarming Saddam Hussein or removing his regime from power. Even on the economy, which remains worrisome to most voters, the campaigns produced no clear party-line disagreements that might have tipped the balance one way or another in the hundreds of local races.

If the country was no longer so bitterly torn, however, Democratic activists failed to notice it or so their campaign strategy would suggest. Many in the party's leadership appeared to believe that Bush's post-September 11 popularity was ephemeral, and that the lingering wounds of the "stolen" election of 2000 would be enough in themselves to excite the Democratic base. "We must never, ever forget what happened" in 2000, intoned Ralph Neas, president of People for the American Way. Donna Brazile, Gore's former campaign manager, advised activists to "go out and say, 'Remember what happened in Florida.'"

It may well have been this mistaken assumption of a generalized desire for payback that lay behind the failure of the party's elites to present a genuine challenge to Bush's Republicans. That failure, at any rate, was the burden of much post-election analysis. The Democrats, lamented Peter Beinart, the editor of the *New Republic*, had "fought this election from the meek and cynical center." Two former Clinton advisers, Tom Freedman and Bill Knapp, sounded a similar note in the *New York Times*, complaining that the Democrats had "ended up arguing over seemingly esoteric differences [and] let bigger national trends, like the war on terrorism, dominate."

But what all such Monday-morning criticisms ignore is that, from the very start of the election year, Democrats in Congress had in fact tried to seize upon every possible issue by which to create a clear distinction between their own priorities and those of the White House. In every instance, however, they found themselves outmaneuvered by a President who seemed determined not to let them get the upper hand on any contentious matter.

Thus, early in 2002, Democrats proposed a reconsideration of the Bush tax cut, only to be waylaid by a White House gleefully reminding reporters of the many Democrats who had initially supported the cut. When, soon thereafter, congressional Democrats joined Senator John McCain's call to rid election campaigns of soft money, they found the President suddenly willing to sign a campaign-finance bill even if it was patently defective and constitutionally suspect. Democrats hoping to tie a cascade of corporate scandals to Republicans and their business donors came up against a White House that welcomed bipartisan legislation to contain corporate fraud. On government financed prescription-drug benefits—a winning Democratic issue according to every poll—the GOP produced a plan that to the casual eye was indistinguishable from the Democrats'. And so it went.

In short, the Democratic problem in 2002 was not just the failure to win a fight but the inability even to pick one. Politically, the war on terror was off-limits—even John Ashcroft, Bush's attorney general and the Democrats' nemesis, was given a relatively free hand to implement his controversial measures for detaining and investigating suspected terrorists. And in the meantime, again and again, domestic issues that had once seemed the exclusive preserve of the Democratic party were being quietly co-opted by a President riding a crest of popularity and a White House enjoying a unique moment of immunity to complaints from the Right that it was pandering to liberals or selling out its own political base.

So what has happened to the red and blue map, with its supposedly hard-line divisions between Democratic and Republican voters? Few analysts of American politics could have been more confounded by the electoral transformation wrought by Bush than John Judis and Ruy Teixeira. Ever since the 2000 election, these two authors had been arguing tirelessly that the demographic facts signified by that famous map augured well for the Democratic party. In a book bearing the now-embarrassing title *The Emerging Democratic Majority*—a play on Kevin Phillips's prescient book of 1969, *The Emerging Republican Majority*, Judis and Teixeira drew a profile of the new, winning coalition. Its members are the educated professionals, working women, minorities, and middle-class Americans who live in large metropolitan areas— "ideopolises," in the authors' coinage— and are affiliated with the technology sector, universities, social-service organizations, and government.

Today it still seems indisputable that these urban clusters will be increasingly important in national elections—and also that, as Judis and Teixeira demonstrated, they are growing faster than the older suburbs and rural areas in the South and West where Republicans have dominated. But

the core of the Judis-Teixeira argument rests less on shared demographics than on shared ideas. What has drawn this particular group of voters together, they give the collective name "progressive centrism."

If the name sounds somewhat oxymoronic, that is for a reason. On the one hand, the authors write, these voters "do not subscribe to the [Republican] gospel of deregulation and privatization. They want to supplement the market's invisible hand with the visible hand of government. ...They want to strengthen social-insurance programs...[and they] reflect the outlook of the social movements that first arose during the 60's....They oppose government interference in people's private lives...[and] support targeted programs to help minorities that trail the rest of the population in education and income."

But, on the other hand, this is not your father's brand of progressivism. Although these voters may indeed "favor government intervention," they do not, "except in very special circumstances," favor the government's supplanting and replacing the operation of the market....They want incremental, careful reforms that will substantially increase health-care coverage....They want aid to minorities, but they oppose the largescale imposition of quotas or the enactment of racial reparations.

And so forth. Judis and Teixeira are quite deliberate in defining what is to their mind this winning combination of fiery Democratic populism with the tempered incrementalism of "New Democrat" politics a la Bill Clinton. This "new synthesis," they believe, accurately reflects the transformation of America into a post-industrial society characterized by large, diverse metropolitan centers; it speaks to the interests and preferences not only of the blue (Democratic) states but of most denizens of "ideopolises" who are hungering for a new political brew. And it is the natural property of the Democratic party, its two components having been clearly if separately at work in, respectively, Clinton's 1992 centrist appeal and Gore's populist defiance of corporate power in 2000. The successful amalgam of these two strategies is what, in their view, will help usher in the new era of Democratic dominance.

After the divisive election of 2000, it was surely not unreasonable to suggest that a new brand of politics would emerge. But Judis and Teixeira's analysis, shaped by hopes as much as by facts, was out of date even as they were writing it, and is at odds with the current disposition of both political parties.

Concerning the Republicans, Judis and Teixeira are stuck in the year 1994, the year of Newt Gingrich's Contract with America. Their straw man is a GOP supposedly rife with racial hatred, disdainful of single mothers and homosexuals, hostile to all government programs, and eager to infiltrate religious orthodoxy into every nook and cranny of American life. This overheated caricature prevents them from recognizing a lesson that in retrospect can be seen emerging out of their own reading of the 2000 election data. Two years later, not only had major parts of the agenda of "progressive centrism" been seized by a Republican president, but the party he led was no longer, if it ever had been, the party of their imagining.

Judis and Teixeira are hardly the only observers who thought the Republicans were heading for the precipice in the mid-1990's. As Christopher Caldwell wrote in the *Atlantic Monthly* in 1998, the party had allowed itself to be captured by a Southern voting bloc that socially and culturally was far to the right of the rest of the country, and as a result it had lost the confidence of the electorate. But if voters once told pollsters that they trusted Democrats more on everything from education to the economy to crime and taxes, that is surely not the case today.

In a Gallup survey conducted a few days after November's mid-term elections, respondents consistently held a much more positive image of Republicans than of Democrats, and regarded them as better equipped to lead the country by a margin of 57 to 47 percent. To be sure, those findings reflected the afterglow of a Republican electoral triumph, and would undergo revision in later surveys. But the fact remains that, thanks largely to Bush, Republicans have become more palatable to a majority of Americans, and they have done so by moving away from some of the defining themes of late 20th-century Republicanism.

I have already mentioned a number of signposts from last year, but the shift really goes back to the fall of 2001. It was then, in the weeks immediately following the attacks of September 11, that Bush sent a signal of things to come by adroitly acquiescing in Democratic demands to federalize airport security workers. The shift could be seen again last spring when he announced the imposition of tariffs on imported steel, a stunning retreat from the free trade principles he himself had advocated during his campaign for the presidency. Since then, he has signed a massive expansion of farm subsidies, reversing a market-driven policy instituted just a few years earlier; agreed to a corporate-accounting law that includes a high level of new regulation and a considerable expansion of federal intrusiveness; and created a $37-billion Department of Homeland Security that may augment and consolidate federal power to a breathtaking degree.

One can defend each of these initiatives on its merits, or at least try to explain why it has been politically necessary. But that is beside the point. Nowhere in this list can one find the themes—limited government, reduced spending, local empowerment—that preoccupied Republican leaders only a few election cycles ago.

As those themes have faded, so, too, have the cultural hot buttons that gave the GOP such strength among social and religious conservatives. As the columnist John Podhoretz has pointed out, it was only three years ago that prominent conservative spokesmen, notably including Lynne Cheney, appeared before Congress to condemn the violence purveyed in rap lyrics by stars like Eminem. But when Eminem's semi-autobiographical movie *8 Mile* opened to large crowds recently, not a syllable of conservative criticism was to be heard. Of course, rap singers in general and Eminem in particular have somewhat moderated the raw brutality of their message in recent months; but it is also true that, in the age of terrorism, the battle against the liberal culture has faded as a key component of Republican politics.

If once high-profile conservative causes are losing their punch, the same can be said of certain high-profile conservative spokesmen. Jerry Falwell may have permanently lost his place in acceptable conservative circles when, on the heels of the September 11 attacks, he appeared to place the blame on America's "tolerant" culture. More recently, the Bush White House has distanced itself from both Falwell and his fellow Christian broadcaster Pat Robertson for antagonistic remarks about the Muslim religion.

Nor are conservative Christian activists the only ones out of favor with the White House. In the lead-up to the mid-term elections, it was widely reported that Karl Rove, the President's top political strategist, was discouraging openly ideological candidacies. In California's GOP primaries, Richard Riordan, the former mayor of Los Angeles, known as a moderate, was said to be favored by the White House over the conservative activist Bill Simon.

In Minnesota, the majority leader of the state House of Representatives was reportedly dissuaded by Vice President Richard Cheney from challenging Democrat-turned-Republican Norm Coleman in the primary. Both stories, if true, reflect an effort to shape the public face of GOP challengers, and in retrospect the political judgment involved is hard to fault: Coleman's victory in Minnesota relied in part on his ability to attract Democratic voters, while Bill Simon, who won the Republican primary in California, went on to be trounced by the incumbent Gray Davis in a race that many thought Riordan would have won.

This is hardly to say that George W. Bush is out to create a Republican party in the mold of a James Jeffords or even a John McCain. After all, he pressed for and signed the largest tax-cut package in more than a decade and is now seeking to make those cuts permanent. He has consistently selected bona-fide conservatives as his nominees to the federal bench. He fought, successfully, to keep the new Homeland Security Department exempt from federal-employee union rules. He is a strong opponent of human cloning, and has severely restricted the use of stem cells in federal medical research. His administration has proposed privatizing thousands of government jobs. In his personal style, and in his religious faith, he appears genuinely conservative. And this is not even to mention his vigorous stance in foreign policy, clearly reminiscent of Ronald Reagan and clearly distinct from the typical Democrat of today.

But there is also no mistaking the fact that Bush is prepared to offer voters something different from Reaganism and Gingrichism, something that goes beyond even the "compassionate conservatism" he introduced in his campaign for the presidency. What he and his advisers—and his party appear to have grasped is that mustering the kind of bipartisan support required by a wartime Republican President depends on the ability to stand in or near the center, and so turn to advantage the same demographic and cultural trends that, a mere two years ago, seemed so threatening to the GOP's future. The question is whether the palpable successes of Bush and the new GOP as measured in the mid-term elections are an artifact of the moment, or whether they can be molded into something more permanent, and more meaningful.

That will depend in large measure on the Democrats, and on how they play the hand they have now been dealt. So far— and here again is where Judis and Teixeira go wrong—there are abundant signs that they will play it not by sticking to "progressive centrism" but by moving left. For all the alleged changes that the Democratic party underwent during the Clinton years, it now appears that its congressional wing is retreating to a familiar form of interest-group populism. Despite all the attempts to create a coalition of the center, the party as a whole remains hostage to public-employee unions, trial lawyers, and organized lobbyists of every kind.

The choice of the unreconstructed liberal Nancy Pelosi to lead the minority caucus in the House, together with the emergence of Senator Hillary Rodham Clinton in a leadership role in the Senate, is a clear indication of the left's determination to claim for its own the shreds of the party's fortunes. Similarly not to be ignored is Al Gore, still the most recognizable presidential aspirant in the Democratic field. In the last year, Gore has almost entirely abandoned the "New Democrat" creed by which he was once defined and moved sharply to the left, criticizing the administration's response to al Qaeda, its handling of the economy, and its alleged neglect of the changing American family.

If this pattern continues, one can safely predict that on the road to the next presidential campaign, even as Republicans continue to downplay their "wedge" issues, Democrats will be more and more likely to emphasize theirs—especially in such areas as environmental protection and guaranteed health insurance, already emerging as favored themes. So far, faced with challenges on these or similar issues—the Patient's Bill of Rights, protection of the domestic steel industry—Bush Republicans have tended to respond with their now-standard "me, too." But a more left-wing, populist Democratic party may render this strategy unworkable by robbing Bush of any chance of compromise.

That will be a testing moment for the GOP and, conceivably, an opportunity to define itself for the foreseeable future. If it is to hold on to its edge, the party may be driven to articulate a more consistent and more truly conservative approach to issues of policy, if not to evolve a true conservative philosophy of governance. This does not mean veering sharply right in a move mirroring the Democrats' turn to the left. It does mean, in the broadest terms, developing a constantly reiterated commitment to the virtues of limited government over expanded entitlements, to market incentives over command-and-control regulation, to competition in place of entrenched bureaucratic monopolies, to economic growth over austerity, to conservation over radical environmentalism.

Such an exercise has much to recommend it, and not just in order to reassure doubting conservatives that Republican politics is about more than winning elections from Democrats. There is, in fact, a real danger in the strategy being pursued by the White House. In the hands of a less gifted, or less convincing, politician than Bush, and in circumstances other than wartime, it may represent less a blueprint for future political dominance than a reversion to an older and thoroughly failed Republican role. I am thinking, of course, of the long decades after the New Deal when the GOP was defined primarily by its efforts to slow the inexorable march of liberal ideas—not by substituting better ones but by accommodating them and sanding down their sharper edges. This is essentially a defensive form of politics, and it is a losing proposition. By contrast, making the case for limited government in a consistent and serious and positive manner could actually increase the appeal of the GOP in the eyes of many centrist and/or traditional Democratic voters who have been drawn to it in the months since September 11.

Over the last three decades, the GOP has gone through a number of minor revolutions in an effort to reinvent itself. Kevin Phillips chronicled the start of the process in *The Emerging Republican Majority*, where he forecast a GOP majority based in the new entrepreneurial communities of the South and West rather than in the old WASP business elites. Ronald Reagan transformed the political face of the party, combining supplyside economics and anti-big-government themes at home with internationalism abroad. Fifteen years later, Gingrich shook up the party once again, demanding the reform of Congress and a shifting of power from Washington to state governments.

Today, Bush's mix of aggressive foreign policy, expanded government in the interest of domestic security, and a willingness to find a middle ground on domestic issues long owned by the Democrats has given him strengths that have defied almost every prediction of how his presidency would evolve. To be sure, he is a beneficiary of extraordinary circumstances. Nor do we yet know whether the brand of politics he has practiced is ultimately driven by expediency or by principle. But it is certain to set the terms of political debate for the balance of his first term, inform his reelection bid two years hence, and just possibly determine whether his party will emerge unexpectedly as a new political majority.

## THE CONTINUING DEBATE:
### The Odds-On Favorite in the Future

### What Is New

Political currents shifted considerably between the time Daniel Casse wrote his essay in early 2003 that this writing in late 2004. President Bush's public approval rating declined, and the 2004 presidential election was closely fought with his challenger, John Kerry. This affected partisan identification somewhat, with a 2004 poll finding 49% of respondents saying they were Democrats or leaned toward the Democrats, 45% being Republicans or Republican leaners, and 6% classifying themselves as true independents. A poll that asked which party had a better vision for the future recorded 42% opting for the Democrats, 35% choosing the Republicans, and 6% saying "both," "neither," or "unsure." However, specific issues made a huge difference in party evaluations. When asked which party would do better dealing with the economy, the Democrats bested the Republicans by 40% to 32%. When respondents were asked about terrorism, 48% favored the Republicans compared to only 37% who thought the Democrats would be more successful. In the end, the slim half-percent popular vote difference between Bush and Kerry show how closely the two parties are matched.

### Where to Find More

A good recent study that emphasizes the recent changes in the Democratic and Republican parties and their support and that makes a strong case for parties as a vital part of the American democratic process is Larry J. Sabato and Bruce Larson, *The Party's Just Begun: Shaping Political Parties for America's Future* (Longman, 2002). The full-scale version of the argument by advocates John B. Judis and Roy Teixeira is their *The Emerging Democratic Majority* (Scribner 2002). As a follow up, to learn how one of these two "pro-Democrat" advocates evaluated the impact of the Republican gains in the 2002 elections, read Roy Teixeira, "Deciphering the Democrats' Debacle," *Washington Monthly Online*, May 2003 at: http://www.washingtonmonthly.com/. Click "print archive" on the left. A view of the future of party politics that is more optimistic about Republican chances is Lee Edwards, *Conservative Revolution: The Movement That Remade America* (Free Press, 2002). Also worthwhile are the Web sites of the two major parties: the Republican National Committee is at http://www.rnc.org/ and the Democratic National Committee at http://www.democrats.org/.

### What More to Do

The most important thing to do is to become a part of the decision. Neither Judis and Teixeira nor Casse argues that the emergence of a Democratic or Republican majority that will dominate politics in the foreseeable future is certain. The party Web sites are a place to start if you identify with one of the two. For a nonpartisan effort aimed especially at young adults, visit the Web site of Rock the Vote at: http://www.rockthevote.com/. Project Vote Smart has a good site to learn about candidates and issues at: http://www.vote-smart.org/.

# 10 VOTING/CAMPAIGNS/ELECTIONS

## THE ELECTORAL COLLEGE:
### Abolish *or* Preserve?

### ABOLISH

**ADVOCATE:** Becky Cain, President, League of Women Voters

**SOURCE:** Testimony during hearings on "Proposals for Electoral College Reform: H.J. Res. 28 and H.J. Res. 43" before the U.S. House of Representatives Committee on the Judiciary, Subcommittee on the Constitution, September 4, 1997

### PRESERVE

**ADVOCATE:** Judith A. Best, Professor of Political Science, State University of New York at Cortland

**SOURCE:** Testimony during hearings on "Proposals for Electoral College Reform: H.J. Res. 28 and H.J. Res. 43" before the U.S. House of Representatives Committee on the Judiciary, Subcommittee on the Constitution, September 4, 1997

Sometimes figuring out your course grade in college can get pretty complicated. Your raw score on tests may not exactly equate to your final "curved" grade. Determining the final score in the Electoral College can be a little like this. The raw score (the popular vote) and the final score (the vote of the electors) never match up. In 1980, for example, Ronald Reagan received 90.1% of the electors' votes, while getting only 51.6% of the popular vote. It is even possible in the Electoral College to have a higher raw score than anyone else yet lose. Al Gore received 51,003,238 popular votes to only 50,459,624 votes for George Bush in the 2000 presidential election. Yet Bush received 50.4% of the electoral vote compared to 49.4% for Gore.

Then, like in some college grading, the Electoral College has other variables. For example, electors selected by the voters in many states can legally vote for someone other than the candidate to whom they are pledged. Such unexpected votes are not common, but they have occurred in 10 elections. For example, a disgruntled elector from Alabama who was supposed to vote for Democratic candidate Adlai Stevenson in 1956 instead cast his ballot for Walter B. Jones, a judge from his hometown who was not even running.

These oddities and other quirks bring up three questions. What is the Electoral College? Where did it come from? Should we keep it? The first two questions are easier. The Electoral College is an indirect process for selecting the U.S. president. Each state selects a number of electors equal to its representation in Congress, and the District of Columbia gets three electors, for a total of 538 electors. The exact process for choosing electors varies by state, but as a general rule each party or candidate selects a slate of electors. It is for one of these slates that the people vote in November. In all states except Maine and Nebraska, there is a "winner-take-all" system in which the slate that receives the most votes wins. Then the individual electors cast their separate ballots for president and vice president in December. The ballots are sent to Congress, where they are counted in early January. It takes a majority of all electoral votes (270) to win. If no individual receives a majority, then the House selects a president from among the candidates with the three highest electoral votes. Each state casts one vote in the House, and it requires a majority of the states (26) to win. The Senate, with each member voting individually, chooses a vice president from among the top two electoral vote recipients. It is not possible to detail here all the possible permutations, but the choice has gone to the House twice (1800 and 1824), and on three occasions (1876, 1888, and 2000) the candidate with the most popular votes has lost the electoral vote.

The Electoral College was established for two reasons. One is that it stressed the role of the states. They can choose electors as they wish and are not even obligated to have popular elections. The second motive for the Electoral College was to insulate the selection of president from the people. As Alexander Hamilton explained in *Federalist* #68 (1788), he and others worried that the "general mass" would not "possess the information and discernment requisite to such complicated investigations," raising the possibility of "tumult and disorder."

The question is whether to abolish or preserve the Electoral College. Throughout its history, the process has been controversial, and it has provoked over 700 proposals in Congress to reform or eliminate it. Yet it survives. The following articles lay out their respective attack on and defense of the Electoral College, but beyond those substantive arguments, the process continues for two additional reasons. One is that changing it would require a constitutional amendment, most probably through a two-thirds vote by each house of Congress and ratification by three-fourths of the state. Obtaining such supermajorities is very difficult. The second procedural reason the Elector College survives is that, for contradictory reasons, it appeals to many states. States with big populations, such as California with its 55 electoral votes (more than 20% of those needed to win), believe they gain political advantage through their hefty share of the electoral votes. States with small populations also see political advantage. Wyoming may have only 55/100ths of one percent of the electoral vote, but that is more than three times the state's 17/100ths of one percent of the U.S. population. States in a middle position come out mathematically about right. For example, New Jersey with 8.1 million people and 15 electoral votes has 2.86% of the population and 2.78% of the electoral votes. Thus the Electoral College seems either politically favorable or neutral to almost every state, making an amendment even more difficult to pass and ratify.

## POINTS TO PONDER

➤ Becky Cain, testifying in 1997, predicts a fiasco if, once again, a candidate were to lose the electoral vote while winning the popular vote. Three years later that occurred, yet there were no widespread protest demonstrations. Why not?

➤ Judith Best contends that abolishing the Electoral College would diminish the influence of minority groups. Why might this occur?

➤ Which is more important, the aspect of federalism that is part of the Electoral College vote calculation or the principle of "one person—one vote"?

# The Electoral College:
## Abolish

BECKY CAIN

Mr. Chairman, members of the subcommittee, I am Becky Cain, president of the League of Women Voters.

I am pleased to be here today to express the support of the League [League of Women Voters of the United States] for a constitutional amendment to abolish the Electoral College and establish the direct election of the President and Vice President of the United States by popular vote of the American people.

The League of Women Voters of the United States is a non-partisan citizen organization with 150,000 members and supporters in all fifty states, the District of Columbia and the Virgin Islands. For over 75 years, Leagues across the country have worked to educate the electorate, register voters and make government at all levels more accessible and responsive to the average citizen.

Since 1970, the League has supported an amendment to the Constitution that would abolish the Electoral College and establish a direct, popular vote for the President and Vice President of the United States. The League arrived at this position through its time-honored study and consensus process. Leagues in over 1,000 communities across the country participated in the study and came to the same conclusion: our method of electing a President must be changed to ensure a more representative government.

Political developments since the 1970s have only underscored the need for the elimination of the Electoral College system. The downward trend in voter participation, coupled with increased cynicism and skepticism amongst the public about the ability of elected leaders to provide meaningful representation are the warning signs of a potential electoral fiasco.

Picture if you will a future national election in which a presidential candidate receives a majority of the popular vote, but is denied the 270 votes necessary for election by the Electoral College. This has already happened once in our nation's history, when, in 1888, Grover Cleveland outpolled Benjamin Harrison in the popular vote but lost the Electoral College vote by 233 to 168. It caused a public furor then, when political office was often gained through back-room deals and closed-door maneuvering. Imagine the public outcry today, after a long primary campaign and a grueling race for the Presidency. Imagine the public's rage at being denied their candidate of choice.

Now go one step further. Consider a close three-way race for President in which no candidate earns the necessary Electoral College votes to win. This has happened twice before in our nation's history, in 1801 and 1825, when the House of Representatives chose Thomas Jefferson and John Quincy Adams, respectively. While the League believes both of these men were great presidents, we are troubled about the potential for a future presidential candidate with the highest number of popular votes to lose the election in a House of Representatives dominated by one or another political party.

In the twentieth century, we have only narrowly avoided a series of constitutional crises in which the Electoral College could have over-ruled the popular vote.

• In the 1916 presidential election, a shift of only 2,000 votes in California would have given Charles Evans Hughes the necessary electoral votes to defeat Woodrow Wilson, despite Wilson's half-million vote nationwide plurality.

• In 1948, a shift of only 30,000 votes in three states would have delivered the White House to Governor [Thomas] Dewey, in spite of the fact that he trailed President Truman by some 2.1 million popular votes.

• In 1960, a shift of only 13,000 votes in five states (5,000 in Illinois, 5,000 in Missouri, 1,200 in New Mexico, 1,300 in Nevada and 200 in Hawaii) would have made Richard Nixon president.

• In 1968, a shift of 42,000 votes in three states (Alaska, Missouri and New Jersey) would have denied Nixon an Electoral College victory and thrown the election into the House of Representatives.

• In 1976, a shift of only 9,300 votes (5,600 from Ohio and 3,700 from Hawaii) would have elected Gerald Ford, even though he trailed Jimmy Carter in the popular vote by 1.6 million ballots.

Apart from the public outcry that would be caused by a circumvention of the popular will, there are a number of other serious flaws in the Electoral College system.

The Electoral College system is fundamentally unfair to voters. In a nation where voting rights are grounded in the one person, one vote principle, the Electoral College is a hopeless anachronism.

The current system is unfair for two reasons.

First, a citizen's individual vote has more weight if he or she lives in a state with a small population than if that citizen lives in a state with a large population. For example, each electoral vote in Alaska is equivalent to approximately 112,000 people. Each electoral vote in New York is equivalent to approximately 404,000 eligible people (based on 1990 census data). And that's if everyone votes!

The system is also unfair because a citizen's individual vote has more weight if the percentage of voter participation in the state is low. For example, if only half of all people in Alaska vote, then each electoral vote is equivalent to roughly 56,000 people.

Moreover, the electoral vote does not reflect the volume of voter participation within a state. If only a few voters go to the polls, all the electoral votes of the state are still cast.

Finally, the Electoral College system is flawed because the constitution does not bind presidential electors to vote for the candidates to whom they have been pledged. For example, in 1948, 1960 and 1976, individual electors pledged to the top two vote getters cast their votes for third place finishers and also-rans. Defecting electors in a close race could cause a crisis of confidence in our electoral system.

For all these reasons, the League believes that the presidential election method should incorporate the one-person, one-vote principle. The President should be directly elected by the people he or she will represent, just as the other federally elected officials are in this country. Direct election is the most representative system. It is the only system that guarantees the President will have received the most popular votes. It also encourages voter participation by giving voters a direct and equal role in the election of the President.

Of course, a direct popular vote does not preclude the possibility of a close three-way race in which no candidate receives a majority, or even a plurality, of the votes. The League believes that if no candidate receives more than 40 percent of the popular vote, then a national run-off election should be held.

Until there is a constitutional amendment to abolish the Electoral College, the League supports the early establishment of clear rules and procedures for the House and Senate to handle their responsibilities in electing the President and Vice President if there is no majority vote in the Electoral College.

Procedures should be established to avoid the last-minute partisan wrangling that would inevitably take place. In addition, we believe any congressional vote for President must take place in full public view, with individual representative's votes entered into the Congressional Record.

When the constitution was first written, our nation was a vastly different kind of democracy than it is today. Only white, male property owners could vote. The 15th Amendment gave black men the right to vote. The 17th Amendment provided for direct popular election of the Senate. The 19th Amendment gave women the vote. The 26th Amendment established the right of citizens 18 years of age and older to vote.

The time has come to take the next step to ensure a broad-based, representative democracy. Fairness argues for it. Retaining the fragile faith of American voters in our representative system demands it. We urge the House and the Senate to pass a constitutional amendment abolishing the Electoral College system and establishing the direct popular election of our President and Vice President.

# The Electoral College:
## Preserve

### JUDITH A. BEST

Critics of the electoral vote system believe that the principle of democratic legitimacy is numbers alone, and therefore they think the system is indefensible. On the contrary, the electoral vote system is a paradigm—the very model—of the American democracy, and thus is quite easy to defend. For all practical purposes it is a direct popular federal election. (The Electors are mere ciphers, and the office of elector, but not the electoral votes, can be abolished.) The critics' principle of democratic legitimacy is inadequate because it is apolitical and antifederal. Logically it boils down to: the majority must win and the minority must lose no matter what they lose. It is a formula for majority tyranny. But majority rule is not the principle of our Constitution. Rather it is majority rule with minority consent. The critics, however, think that because the system does not follow an arithmetical model it may produce the "wrong" winner. In fact, I contend, because it is federal it produces the right winner.

The following passage from my recent book, *The Choice of the People? Debating the Electoral College* explains my point:

Politics and mathematics are two very different disciplines. Mathematics seeks accuracy, politics seeks harmony. In mathematics an incorrect count loses all value once it is shown to be wrong. In politics even though some people are out-voted they still have value and must be respected in defeat. Efforts must be made to be considerate and even generous to those who lost the vote, to make them feel they are part of the community, for if they feel alienated they may riot in the streets. Further, mathematical questions, like those in all the sciences, deal with truth and falsehood. But politics is an art, not a science. Political questions do not deal primarily with truth and falsehood, but with good and bad. We do not ask whether a political decision on war or taxation or welfare or agricultural subsidies is true. We ask, is the policy good for the country? And, will it actually achieve its purpose?

Those who confuse politics and mathematics, the head counters, operate on an unstated assumption that the will of the people is out there like some unsurveyed land, and all we need do is send out the surveyors with accurately calibrated instruments to record what is there. They also assume that our democratic republic is a ship without a specific destination. Whatever most of the people want, most of the people must get, and the minority be damned. Mathematical accuracy being their sole criterion for legitimacy, they make a great fuss about politically imposed devices, intermediary institutions like the electoral vote system with its federal principle and its winner-take-all rule. From their perspective, such majority building and structuring devices complicate their self-assigned task, distort the accuracy of their count and possibly produce the "wrong" result.

If their assumptions were correct they would have a point. But their assumptions are false. Ours is a ship of state bound for a port called Liberty. On such a ship majority rule doesn't suffice without the consent of the minority. Their assumption about the will of the people is particularly false in this vast and varied country, in a continental republic populated by a people who do not share a common religion, race, or ethnic heritage, in a commercial republic populated by people with diverse and competing economic interests. In such a country the will of the people and the will of the majority can be two very different things. Therefore, the will of the people—that one thing which all can share, which is the goal of liberty for all—must be constructed and periodically reconstructed. This requires a political, not a mathematical process.

In this country, it requires a federal political process. The federal principle is one of the two fundamental structural principles of our Constitution (the other being the separation of powers). The proposals to abolish the Electoral College are proposals to abolish the federal principle in presidential elections. All of our national elective offices are based on the federal principle— they are state based elections for we are a nation of states. Thus our national motto: *E Pluribus Unum*.

The federal principle in presidential elections forces presidential candidates to build broad cross-national political coalitions. Thereby it produces presidents who can govern because of their broad cross-national support. In politics as well as in physics there is such a thing as a critical mass. In presidential elections numbers of votes are necessary but not sufficient. To create the critical mass necessary for a president to govern, his votes must be properly distributed. This means he must win states and win states in more than one region of the country.

Under the federal presidential election system, a successful candidate can't simply promise everything to one section of the country and neglect the others. Analogy: Why are professional football teams required to win games in order to get into the playoffs and win the Super Bowl? Why not simply select the teams that scored the most points during the regular season? Any football fan can tell you why. Such a process wouldn't produce the right winner. Teams would run up the score against their weakest opponents, and the best teams in the most competitive divisions would have the least chance to get into the playoffs. Such a system isn't the proper test of the team talent and ability. A nonfederal election is not a proper test of support for the president.

If we abandon the federal principle in presidential elections, we will be abandoning a national consensus building device by allowing candidates to promise everything to the populous Eastern megalopolis, or to promise everything to white Christians, or to suburbanites who are now half of all the voters. These are formulas for inability to govern or even civil war. And a system, like direct popular election, based on raw unstructured numbers alone rather than on the structuring federal principle, would effectively reduce the influence of minorities who often are the swing votes in closely divided states—groups like farmers who are only 2 percent of national population or blacks who are only 12 percent.

We need to remember that when we change the rules, we change the game and the game strategy and the skills needed to win. Under the federal principle successful candidates must have consensus building skills. The goal of politics in this country is harmony—majority rule with minority consent. But when and why would a minority consent to majority rule? The answer is only if the minority can see that on some occasions and on some vital issues it can be part of the majority. It is irrational to consent to a game in which you can never win anything at all. To gain minority consent, the Framers created many devices to allow minorities to be part of the game, devices that give minorities more influence than their raw numbers would warrant including the state equality principle for representation in the Senate and the state distracting principle for the House of Representatives. (The majority party in the House is often "over-represented" if our measure is raw numbers of votes nationally aggregated.) Then, of course, there is the state equality principle in voting on constitutional amendments. And there is the three-fourths requirement for passage of amendments. Such devices are designed to give minorities an influential voice in defining the national interest. The president is a major player in defining the national interest, and therefore it is necessary that the presidency be subjected to the moderating influence of a federal election system.

An equally important outcome of a state based election system is that it serves to balance local and national interests. It is not just racial, religious, ethnic or occupational minorities that must be protected, there are local minorities whose consent must be sought; the people in small states must be protected against misuse of the phrase "the national interest." My favorite example is the problem of nuclear waste which none of us want in our backyards—not in my state. The rest of us can outvote Utah—so let's turn Utah into our national nuclear waste dump. This is majority tyranny in action. Nuclear waste is a national problem and the burden of solving it should not be placed on the people of one state without their consent. Since the president is a major player in making national policy, it is just as important that he be sensitive to balancing

national and local interests, and the federal election system is designed to make it so. The right winner is a presidential candidate who recognizes the necessity and often the justice in balancing national and local interests. As Jefferson said, "the will of the majority to be rightful must be reasonable." The federal principle even and especially in presidential elections is a device for building reasonable majorities.

The opponents of the electoral vote system are head counters who confuse an election with a census. In a census our goal is mere accuracy. We want to know how many people are married or divorced, or have incomes over or under $20,000, or are Catholic or Protestant etc. In short, we want to break down the population into its multiple individual parts. In an election especially a presidential election, we want to bring the people together. We want to build consensus, to build the support necessary and sufficient for our president to govern.

The proponents of direct national election think their system solves problems, but in fact it creates problems that are addressed or avoided by the federal election system. Presidential elections have multiple goals. Obviously we want to fill the office with someone who can govern, but we also want a swift, sure decision, and we want to reduce the premium on fraud and most of us want to support the two party system—a major source of national stability and a consensus, coalition-building system.

From this perspective, the current system has been very successful. Since 1836 with the almost universal adoption of the state unit rule, awarding all of a state's electoral votes to the winner of the popular plurality, we have had never had a contingency election. That's a proven record of 160 years. And we know the reason why: the magnifier effect of the state unit rule, a.k.a. the winner-take-all system. The victor in the popular vote contest for president will have a higher percentage of the electoral vote. The Magnifier effect does not exaggerate the mandate—popular vote percentages are widely reported, not electoral vote percentages. The magnifier effect is not like a fisherman's story in which the size of the fish grows with the telling. Rather it is like the strong fishing line that serves to bring the fish, whatever its size, safely to shore. It supports the moderate two-party system, and balances national and state interests. And it makes the general election the only election.

Of course, there would be no magnifier effect under direct non-federal election, and the result is that contingency elections would become the rule. Under one proposal there would be a national run off if no candidate received 50 percent of the popular vote. This provision would turn the general election into a national primary, proliferate candidacies and weaken or destroy the two-party system. It would also increase the potential for fraud and result in contested general elections with every ballot box in the United States having to be reopened and recounted under court supervision. Even the Left-handed Vegetarians Party could bring a court challenge because 1 percent or less of the popular vote could trigger a runoff election. And there would be a reason to challenge. In a runoff election even candidates who are not in the contest can win something by making a deal with one of the remaining two in return for support in the runoff. Not only would this mean an extended period of uncertainty about who the president will be—a temptation to foreign enemies, but also little time for the orderly transfer of power.

Most proponents of direct election, recognizing that to require a majority of the popular votes would produce these problems, suggest a 40 percent instead of a 50 percent runoff rule. The fact that most supporters of direct election are willing to make this concession indicates the seriousness of the problems attending contingency elections. This is a compromise of their principle—the arithmetical majority principle. Logically, on their principle, whenever no one polls 50 percent plus one vote there should be a runoff election.

And 40 percent is not a magical figure. It could be 42 or 44% with similar result—frequent runoffs. It is true that only one president, Lincoln, (who was not on the ballot in 10 states) failed to reach-the 40 percent plurality figure. However, history under the current system cannot be used to support the 40 percent figure because when you change the rules you change the game. Under the current rules we have had 17 minority presidential terms—presidents who came to the office with less than 50 percent of the popular vote. The last two are Clinton's terms. The list includes some of our best presidents, not only Lincoln, but also Wilson (twice), Polk and Truman. Seventeen minority presidential terms out of 42 presidents! The unit rule magnified their popular pluralities into electoral vote majorities because they won states.

But under direct nonfederal election there would be no magnifier effect. Potential candidates would recognize that multiple entries would be likely to trigger a runoff wherein one losing candidate could win a veto promise, another a Supreme Court nomination and a third a special interest subsidy in return for an endorsement in the runoff. And there is no reason to believe all such deals would be struck in the open. There would be no incentive for coalition building prior to the general election. The two major national parties would lose all control over the presidential nomination process—their lifeblood. Factional candidates, single issue candidates, extremist candidates would serve as spoilers. As one commentator noted, on the day prior to the election, the *New York Times* would have to publish a twenty-page supplement simply to identify all the candidates.

Add to this the second chance psychology that would infect voters, and you have the formula for a national ordeal. Second chance psychology arises from the recognition that a popular vote runoff is a real possibility. Many a voter, thinking he will have another chance to vote in a runoff, will use his general election vote to protest something or other—to send a message.

Recounts would be demanded not only to determine who won, but also whether any candidate actually polled the 40% minimum, and if not which two candidates would be in the runoff—Under the unit rule magnifier effect which discourages multiple candidacies, we have already had five elections in which the popular vote margin was less than one percent. In the 1880 election the margin was one tenth of one percent. If such could happen under the current system where it is unlikely to trigger a runoff, it surely will happen under a 40 percent rule with a hair trigger runoff system. Weeks or months could pass with the outcome in doubt. One candidate could claim victory and start naming his cabinet only to be told some weeks later that he would have to participate in a runoff.

Further, the electorate wearies of prolonged elections. Even in the sports world players as well as teams reach a point where they want an end to it, and so accept sudden death rules. It is so important to fill the office on a timely basis that we have even had one president, Gerald Ford, who was not confirmed by a national election. Ford succeeded to the office on the resignation of his predecessor, Richard Nixon, but unlike vice presidents who had succeeded before him, he had been nominated by Nixon and confirmed by congressional vote under the provisions for filling vice presidential vacancies in the Twenty-fifth Amendment.

No election system is perfect, but the current system has borne the test of time. It has never rejected the winner of a popular vote majority. In every case but one it gave the victory to the winner of the popular plurality. And that one case proves the rule. Cleveland, who lost in the electoral vote, won the popular vote while running a sectional campaign. He did not seek to broaden his support; he focused his message on one section of the country. Unintentionally, he thereby sent a message about the current system to all future presidential candidates: Remember 1883! Don't run a sectional campaign! Further, he won the popular vote by only eight tenths of one percent! This was an election that verged on a tie. Since a timely decision is so important, a reasonable tiebreaker is the win states federal principle.

The proposed amendments would deform not reform the Constitution. It is not just the presidency that is at risk here if the federal principle is illegitimate in presidential elections, why isn't it illegitimate for Senate and House elections? Why should a state with half a million people have the same representation in the Senate as a state with twenty million people? Why should every state have at least one representative in the House? Why shouldn't states with very small populations have to share a representative with folks in another state? And why should each state regardless of its population size have an equal vote on constitutional amendments? The Framers knew the answer to these questions—the federal principle. It is true that the electoral vote system did not work out in precisely the fashion that the Framers anticipated, but it did evolve in conformity to the federal principle and the separation of powers. I have no doubt that they would recognize this if they were here today. It evolved in conformity with the fed-

eral spirit of the constitution, the "great discovery," the Framers themselves made.

For this, let us turn to Alexis de
Tocqueville, who commenting [in
*Democracy in America*, 1835] on the federal principle in the Constitution, called it "a
wholly novel theory, which may be considered as a great discovery in modern political
science." He goes on to explain that combines the best of both worlds. He says that
its advantage is to unite the benefits and
avoid the weaknesses of small and large societies. He learned this not only from obser-
vation, but also from reading James
Madison in *Federalist 39*, who said that our
form of government "is, in strictness, neither a national nor a federal Constitution,
but a combination of both."

Madison's word "combination" is the key.
The federal principle is a "great discovery,"
because it is a combination like an alloy—
my term not his. We create alloys because
we want to combine the advantages and
avoid the weakness of two different things.
We fuse copper and zinc to create brass
because brass is harder, more malleable and
more ductile than copper. We create steel
alloys for the same reason. The federal system is an alloy. It not only makes us strong
as a nation, it also allows us to be diverse
and flexible, to experiment. It thereby
increases our freedom without destroying
our national unity. Tocqueville was right; it
was a "great discovery" of modern political
science. Let us preserve it.

# THE CONTINUINC DEBATE:
## The Electoral College

### What Is New

Generally, the country reacted mildly to the odd ties of the 2000 election. A few proposals to abolish the Electoral College were introduced in Congress, but they died in committee. Nor did the public react strongly. When one poll pointed out the popular vote/electoral vote mismatch and asked Americans about their reaction, 51% said the outcome was "fair," 46% thought it "unfair," and 3% were unsure. Yet, numerous polls also found about 60% of respondents in favor of instituting direct popular election of the president. Thus Americans were willing to abide by the rules but also favored changing those rules. It is unclear, though, if most people understand the implications of such a change. One poll that asked respondents if they understood the Electoral College found that 69% said they did, just 27% said they did not, and 4% were uncertain. Yet when another poll asked people what the Electoral College did (correct answer: elect the president), only 20% gave the right answer, 35% gave an incorrect answer, and 46% confessed they did not know. Whether the oddities of the 2004 election, especially the issues involving Ohio, spark an effort to change the electoral system remains to be seen.

### Where to Find More

An edited book in which contributors discuss various alternatives to the Electoral College and the implications of each is Paul D. Schumaker and, Burdett A. Loomis, *Choosing a President: The Electoral College and Beyond* (Chatham House, 2002). For a defense of the Electoral College, read Gary L. Gregg's edited volume, *Securing Democracy: Why We Have an Electoral College* (Westview, 2001). A valuable Web site for further research is that of the Office of the Federal Register in the National Archives at http://www.archives.gov/federal_register/. The site even has an interactive function that you can use to try to predict the electoral vote count in the next presidential election. Also excellent is the information on the Electoral College on the site of the Federal Election Commission at: http://www.fec.gov/elections.html.

### What More to Do

Calculate your state's percentage of the national population and its percentage of the electoral vote. Based on this equation, would your state gain or lose political advantage if the Electoral College were to be abolished?

In addition to debating the future of the Electoral College, it is important to consider the alternatives. If the Electoral College were abolished, how would you determine who is on the ballot? That is now governed by state law, and the candidates vary from state to state. In 2004, there were 20 candidates on one or more state ballots. Some were one-state candidates, such as the Prohibition Party's Earl Dodge, who received 208 votes in Colorado. A national ballot qualifying procedure that was too difficult would restrict democratic choice. A standard that was too easy might replicate the gubernatorial recall election in California in 2003, with 135 candidates on the ballot. Then there is the question of what to do in races with three or more contenders. Does the candidate with the most votes win, even if that is less than 50.1%, or should there be a run-off system to eventually achieve a majority vote? Just since World War II, no presidential candidate has received a majority in 6 (1948, 1960, 1968, 1992, 1996, 2000) of the 14 presidential elections. So, if not the Electoral College, then what?

# CONGRESS

## CONGRESSIONAL TERM LIMITS:
### Promoting Choice *or* Restricting Choice?

### PROMOTING CHOICE

**ADVOCATE:** Paul Jacob, Executive Director, U.S. Term Limits

**SOURCE:** Testimony during hearings on "Limiting Terms of Office for Members of the U.S. Senate and U.S. House of Representatives," U.S. House of Representatives, Committee on the Judiciary, Subcommittee on the Constitution, January 22, 1997

### RESTRICTING CHOICE

**ADVOCATE:** John R. Hibbing, Professor of Political Science, University of Nebraska

**SOURCE:** Testimony during hearings on "Limiting Terms of Office for Members of the U.S. Senate and U.S. House of Representatives," U.S. House of Representatives, Committee on the Judiciary, Subcommittee on the Constitution, January 22, 1997

One way this debate could have been entitled was with a riddle: "When Does Restricting Voter Choice Improve Democracy?" An alternative riddle/title might have been, "When Does Unrestricted Voter Choice Diminish Democracy?" Those who advocate limiting the number of terms members of Congress may serve argue that incumbents have advantages that make it nearly impossible for challengers to unseat them, thereby limiting the "real" choice of voters. Opponents counter that, among other drawbacks, term limits abridge the voters' democratic right to choose whomever they wish to represent them for as long as they wish.

Statistically, once someone gets elected to Congress they have an extraordinarily good chance of being reelected again. For example, during elections between 1980 and 2002, about 90% of all incumbent members of Congress sought another term, and of those who did, voters returned 93% of the representatives and 89% of the senators. Moreover, incumbents in House races received an average of 71% of the vote in 2002. The senators in office in 2003 had amassed an average 62% of the vote in their previous election. Also indisputable is the fact that the average number of years a person spends in Congress has increased over time. During the 1800s only 3% of representatives and 11% of senators served more than 12 years. Those figures jumped to 27% and 32% during the 1900s, and since 1947 to 35% and 41% respectively.

There are numerous reasons why incumbents have an advantage, which, in sum, create a positive view by most people of their individual members of Congress. One survey found that 62% of respondents approved of the job their members of Congress were doing, only 17% disapproved, and 21% were not sure. This is remarkable given that only 43% of those respondents approved of the job Congress as an institution was doing, with 33% disapproving and 24% unsure.

Term limits have long applied to the tenure of many chief executives. The presidency had a two-term tradition until Franklin Roosevelt sought and won four terms. Soon thereafter, the Twenty-Second Amendment (1951) made the two-term limit mandatory. Additionally, 36 states have term limits for governor. Recently, the idea of also limiting the terms of state and national legislators began to become prominent. California and Oklahoma passed the first such legislation in 1990. It was an idea whose time had come, and soon 20 other states followed suit. Most of these restrictions were enacted by direct democracy techniques, including initiatives and referendums.

Opponents of term limits quickly challenged their constitutionality. In 1995 by a 6 to 3 vote in *U.S. Term Limits, Inc. v. Thornton*, the U.S. Supreme Court struck down the limits that Arkansas (and by implication all other states) had placed on terms in the U.S. Congress. Term limits on state legislatures, by contrast, are matters primarily of state constitutional law, and in this realm, the federal courts and most state courts have upheld term limits.

The Supreme Court decision means that it would be necessary to amend the Constitution in order to limit the number of terms that members of the U.S. Senate and House of Representatives can serve. Part of the "Contract with America" put forth by the successful Republican congressional campaign in 1994 was a pledge to work for such a constitutional amendment, with a limit of two terms (12 years) for senators and 6 terms (12 years) for members of the House. Numerous such proposals were introduced in Congress in 1995, and others have been submitted since then. But none have gathered sufficient support. The "hot topic" of the 1990s faded somewhat in face of the daunting prospect of getting two-thirds of each of the two houses to pass a constitutional amendment and thereby truncate their own political careers. This fate has, among other things, increased the calls to adopt national direct democracy procedures (see Debate 19) and to amend the Constitution so that states can initiate amendments to the U.S. Constitution (see Debate 20). What many see as the problem of entrenched legislators remains, however. The senior senator in the 108th Congress, Robert Byrd, has held his seat since 1959 when Dwight D. Eisenhower was president, and the dean of the House, John Dingle, began his tenure four years before that in 1955 when the current president, George W. Bush was nine years old. As a historical note, the record for the longest combined service in Congress (57 years) is held by Carl Hayden, who served in the House from the time of Arizona's admission to the union in 1912 to 1927, then was in the Senate until 1969. The oldest member ever of Congress was South Carolina Strom Thurmond, who retired at age 100 in 2003 after 43 years in the Senate.

## POINTS TO PONDER

➤ Would term limits enhance or diminish Congress' power compared to the president?

➤ John Hibbing notes that senior members of Congress are often more effective in terms of getting legislation passed. Is this because they gain expertise or because they use the power structure to limit the role of junior members?

➤ What impact do you think term limits would have on the proportion of under-represented groups (such as women and racial and ethnic minorities) in Congress?

# Congressional Term Limits:
# Promoting Choice

## PAUL JACOB

America has one clear and decisive advantage over the rest of the world: Our political system.

Our system is unique a democratic republic with constitutional limits on the federal government. It's a system designed to maximize individual freedom and citizen control of government at all levels. Our forebears not only set up this system of protected freedoms, but also recognized the need for change, for continual reform, and for constitutional amendment in order to preserve and enhance our freedom.

George Washington said in his farewell address, "The basis of our political systems is the right of the people to make and alter their constitutions of government." President [Abraham] Lincoln explained: "The country, with its institutions, belongs to the people who inhabit it. Whenever they shall grow weary of the existing government, they can exercise their Constitutional right of amending it." As Thomas Jefferson said to those who object to amending the Constitution, "We might as well require a man to wear still the coat which fitted him when a boy."

The vast majority of Americans today want to amend their Constitution. They want congressional term limits of three terms for House members and two terms for Senators.

## EXPERIENCE WITH TERM LIMITS

Term limits is not a new idea. Democracy as far back as Aristotle has known term limits, or rotation in office. Certainly our Founders appreciated rotation in office. John Adams, Ben Franklin, Thomas Jefferson all spoke to the need for limited tenure in public office. Today, term limits are the law of the land for the President, 40 state governors, 20 state legislatures and thousands of local elected officials including many large cities most notably New York and Los Angeles. Americans support congressional term limits not only for what they hope it will do to the culture in Congress, but for what it has already done at other levels of government.

According to Jody Newman, former head of the National Women's Political Caucus, "Our political system is tremendously biased in favor of incumbents." While this has slowed the progress of women and minorities into elected office, term limits are helping to bring more women, minorities and people from all walks of life into politics. This has been the case in cities like New Orleans and Kansas City where record numbers of minorities now hold office as well as the legislature in California which, according to the *Los Angeles Times*, now includes "a former U.S. Air Force fighter pilot, a former sheriff-coroner, a paralegal, a retired teacher, a video store owner, a businesswoman-homemaker, a children's advocate, an interior designer…and a number of businessmen."

Term limits are bringing more competition, and arguably fairer competition. A recent study by Kermit Daniel of the University of Pennsylvania and Joan R. Lott of the University of Chicago concluded: "California's legislative term limits have dramatically reduced campaign expenditures, while at the same time that more candidates are running for office and races are becoming more competitive. The changes are so large that more incumbents are being defeated, races are closer, more candidates are running, and there are fewer single candidate races than at any other time in our sample."

In Ohio, state legislative term limits were credited with helping pass serious ethics reform. "Term limits established a kind of public-interest momentum" according to Ohio Common Cause executive director Janet Lewis, whose group had led the fight against term limits. Robert McCord, a columnist with the *Arkansas Times* declared "the Arkansas House of Representatives has been reborn" after the state's voters enacted a six-year House limit and representatives were quick to dismantle the seniority system.

Anecdotal and empirical evidence abounds that term limits have reduced partisanship, gridlock, and special interest influence. At the same time, more people are running for office, additional reforms are following in the term limits wake, and the disastrous predictions of opponents are being quietly forgotten.

Unfortunately, Congress continues to be locked in partisan warfare, ethics problems, and largely uncompetitive elections. Congress needs term limits.

## CONGRESS HAS A CONFLICT OF INTEREST

When the amendment process of the Constitution was originally debated [in 1787], delegate George Byron of Pennsylvania had tremendous vision. He saw the potential of a congressional conflict of interest and warned, "We shall never find two-thirds of a Congress voting for anything which shall derogate from their own authority and importance."

Even with consistent and overwhelming public support, about three out of four Americans believe Congress will refuse to propose a constitutional amendment for term limits. Why? Because Congress has a clear conflict of interest. Term limits is

about limiting your personal power and the power of any individual who takes your place in our system.

Most members of Congress do support the concept of term limits and have for some time. After all, Congress voted by two-thirds of both Houses to propose the Twenty-Second Amendment limiting the President to two terms, eight years, in office. More recently (in the 104th Congress) [1995–1996], 355 members of the House voted to limit committee chairs to three terms. Yet, while supporting and imposing the concept on others, many members do not want limits to apply to them personally.

The congressional conflict of interest results in many members of Congress favoring limits twice as generous as most voters, that is, if they favor any limits at all. Congress has also shown a tremendous ability for political maneuvering on the issue.

Last Congress, the House of Representatives failed to represent their constituents as term limits were defeated by outright opponents and "loved to death" by some questionable friends. The three-term House limit enacted by 15 states and supported by gigantic percentages of voters was opposed by a majority of Republicans, as well as Democrats. Only the freshman Republicans were in sync with the wishes of the American people 72 percent voting for a three-term limit, a constitutional majority itself demonstrating the benefit of regular rotation in office.

This conflict also can be found in some members' demand that Congress, rather than the voters, set the limits. As David Mason of the Heritage Foundation wrote, "At a February 28 [1995] House Judiciary Committee mark-up session on these proposals a coalition of opponents and wavering supporters amended the McCollum bill, so that it...explicitly would preempt state term limit laws (the original bill was silent on state powers)." What Mr. Mason didn't report was Representative McCollum pro-posed this amendment to his own bill that would have specifically struck down the shorter term limit imposed on him by the voters of Florida. That the House GOP's point-man on the issue would seek to pre-empt his own state's term limit law passed by a 77 percent vote is a striking example of his conflict of interest.

The commitment of the House Repub-lican Leadership, especially Speaker Newt Gingrich, has been the subject of much doubt. Television producer Brian Boyer, who spent a great deal of time with Gingrich while filming a 1995 documentary, said, "It was very surprising, and this was, remember, from very long conversations with Gingrich, to learn that he personally is not in favor of term limits." Gingrich's spokesperson Tony Blankley told the *American Spectator* in July of 1994 that term limits was "something con-ceptually [Newt] doesn't like." Columnist Robert Novak wrote in the *Washington Post*, "Republican leaders profess to want 12 years, but it is clear they prefer no limits at all."

A number of Republicans in the leader-ship voted against every term limit bill as did five committee chairs. Only one mem-ber of the leadership, Majority Leader Dick Armey, and only one committee chair voted for the three-term House limit passed by most states. Yet while Mr. Armey said he would have stripped a member of a com-mittee chairmanship had they like Senator Mark Hatfield voted against the Balanced Budget Amendment, there was no such pressure brought to bear for term limits.

Freshman Michael Forbes of New York told the *New York Times* after the failed House vote, "Candidly, this leadership didn't want [term limits] anymore than the old leadership did." But the American people were not fooled—a *Washington Post*/ABC News poll found close to two-thirds believe neither Republicans nor Democrats in Congress really tried to pass term limits.

## THREE TERMS VS. SIX TERMS

The question as to the proper length of the term limits is not merely: What should the limits be? Rather, the essential ques-tion is: Who should set the limits? U.S. Term Limits is dedicated to the proposi-tion that the people, not Congress, should set the limits.

Some observers of the battle in Congress over whether House terms should be limit-ed to three terms or six terms have posited that the term limits movement is split. This is simply not the case. The term limits movement is strongly united behind three terms. Only in Congress (and especially among longtime members whose support for any limit whatsoever is questionable) is there significant approval of six terms and fierce opposition to three terms.

Throughout the rest of America, sup-port for three terms far surpasses support for six terms. The American people, pro-limits scholars and virtually every state term limit group in the country supports a three-term limit in the House and a two-term limit in the Senate. Poll after poll demon-strates public support for three terms over six. A 1996 Fabrizio-McLaughlin poll of 1,000 adults nationally found supporters favored three terms 81 percent to 16 per-cent over six terms.

Not surprisingly, election results bear this out. In every head to head vote three terms has won over six terms. Colorado voters went to the polls in 1994 and vot-ed to lower their limits from six terms to three terms. The arguments in favor of a six-term House limit are so barren, that one such Beltway advocate brazenly and erroneously claims this is "compelling" evidence of support for the longer limit.

## ONLY IN WASHINGTON

South Dakota has voted on both a 12-year House limit and a 6-year House limit in separate elections where one would not replace the other. The 6-year limit received 68 percent of the vote to 63 percent for the 12-year limit. After the Wyoming legislature voted to double its state House limits from three terms to six, voters said keep the three-term limit 54 to 46 percent. This even after the sitting governor and three former governors came out in favor of the longer limits.

In fact, the latest trend for politicians opposed to term limits is to pretend to favor term limits, but only longer ones like 12 Years. In New York City, Peter Vallone, Council President and adamant term-limit opponent, was unsuccessful in his attempt to defeat term limits in 1993. Just this past election, he sought to extend the limits from eight years to twelve years. Even with a purposely slanted and misleading ballot title, the voters saw through the council's scheme and rejected this term extension. The same effort to claim support for the term limits concept in order to extend the limits has been and is being repeated in many cities and states with term limits. The voters continue to oppose these term extensions.

The intellectual support for a shorter House limit is also very substantial. A working group of 31 scholars formed by Empower America in December of 1994 studied the term limits issue and concluded, "We put term limits on our agenda, and would even go so far as to favor the specific proposal to limit terms to 6 years in the House and 12 in the Senate."

Mark Petracca, a professor at the University of California-Irvine and a leading scholar on limits, told Congress "my preference is strongly for a limit less expansive than 12 years or 6 terms in the House....A six-term or 12-year limit in the House...won't do much to deprofessionalize the House. Neither may it do much to remedy the other exigencies driving the term limits movement."

David M. Mason of the Heritage Foundation points to "Senate-envy" as the number one reason House members favor the much longer six-term limit and reminds us, "The incumbents' plea for experience only echoes arguments of term limits opponents."

Senator Fred Thompson of Tennessee pointed out one of the reasons people oppose a six-term limit and support three terms. In his 1995 House and Senate testimony, he stated, "Limiting House Members to six terms, instead of the three terms as I have proposed, would leave the seniority system intact and do little to level a playing field that has huge advantages for incumbents." Missouri Senator John Ashcroft recognizes a three-term limit would reduce the incentive for gerrymandering congressional districts for the benefit of incumbents, stating, "it would be one of several benefits exclusive to the 3/2 term proposal..."

Of the major Republican candidates for president in 1996, Lamar Alexander, Pat Buchanan, Steve Forbes, Phil Gramm, and Alan Keyes all supported a limit of three House terms. As Pat Buchanan told the Senate, "Now, what about this 12-year proposal? Well, let me associate myself with what...Lamar Alexander...said. I am unalterably opposed to 12 years. I am for 6 years and out. I know that folks say let's treat both Houses the same way. But the Founding Fathers did not treat both Houses the same way."

There are a plethora of other important policy reasons for enacting a three-term limit as opposed to six terms. Three-term limits will mean greater turnover, more competitive elections, more and quicker campaign reform, and a larger dose of fiscal sanity.

The "Legislative Backgrounder" attached as an appendix to this testimony details further evidence of the public policy benefits associated with a three-term rather than six-term limit.

In reality, many in Congress supposedly favoring a six-term limit appear to not support term limits at all. Representative Bill Barrett of Nebraska has supported the six-term McCollum bill, but wrote in 1995, "I understand voters are frustrated and dissatisfied with the performance of Congress, but I doubt term limits are the answer." Another cosponsor of the McCollum bill is Representative David Camp of Michigan who like Barrett voted against the three-term limits passed in his state. Camp told the *Michigan Midland Daily News* [May 23, 1995], "Voters understand that if they want to limit a member of Congress' term, they can vote for the opponent." These are not the statements of term limit enthusiasts.

In the face of popular and intellectual reasons that three-term limits are superior, the main argument advanced by the longer limit advocates in Congress is that they will simply refuse to support any limits shorter than 6 terms regardless of any support or rationale evidenced against them. This is presented as realism and practicality, but at its core it's the intellectual integrity of a hijacker. Congress in such a case is saying, "The people may have right on their side, but we have the power to ignore them."

### INFORMED VOTER LAWS

Nobel prize-winning economist Milton Friedman recognizes the congressional conflict, but also appreciates the ingenuity of the American people in declaring, "Congress is never, not in a million years, going to impose term limits on itself unless it has to."

After the vote in the House in 1995, the American people understood they would have to take matters into their own hands, and they did. The result? In 1996, nine states passed Informed Voter Laws sometimes called Term Limits Accountability

Laws. These states are Alaska, Arkansas, Colorado, Idaho, Maine, Missouri, Nebraska, Nevada and South Dakota.

The laws are very simple. First, they instruct members of Congress to support a specific 3/2 term limits amendment written precisely in the initiative. With differing opinions among members of Congress in the past, and the built-in conflict of interest, the voters of these states seek to make the term limits amendment they want explicitly clear.

Secondly, these laws create a procedure for informing the voters if their instructions on term limits are simply disregarded. If members from these states fail to support the 3/2 amendment or attempt to enact watered-down limits longer than 3/2, the Secretary of State will inform the voters by printing "DISREGARDED VOTER INSTRUCTION ON TERM LIMITS" next to the incumbents' names on the ballot.

Candidates who are not incumbents are allowed to sign a pledge to abide by the voters' instructions when they file for the office. If they do not so pledge, the voters will again be informed by the Secretary of State printing "DECLINED TO PLEDGE TO SUPPORT TERM LIMITS" next to their name on the ballot.

Some will argue these laws are unconstitutional. The opponents of term limits have long used the lawsuit as their primary weapon. Already the voters are being sued by special interests and politicians in a number of states trying to overturn the people's vote. But let me suggest the courts will not save politician-kind this time.

Prior to the 1996 election, the Arkansas Supreme Court declared the state's Informed Voter Initiative unconstitutional and removed it from the ballot. The state court argued the measure would cause "potential political deaths" if elected officials did not heed the instructions of an informed public. To this end, I can only say I certainly hope so. But the U.S. Supreme Court did not allow the Arkansas court to deny the people a vote on this measure. In a highly unusual move, the High Court 7 to 2 issued an emergency stay of the state court decision and the voters got their opportunity to cast ballots for or against the Informed Voter Law.

On November 5, more than 60 percent of Arkansans voted to add the Term Limits Informed Voter amendment to their state constitution. Now the U.S. Supreme Court has been petitioned to take the case, and we believe the people of Arkansas will prevail on the merits.

The response to these Informed Voter Laws has been universal shock and horror from the political establishment. What is there to cause such objection? These laws offer congressmen non-binding instructions from the people they work for and are charged with representing. The republican right of instruction is nothing new and surely no elected official could object to his or her constituents making their desires known regarding their government and their very own representative.

The informational aspect of the initiative has been attacked as the Scarlet Letter. Yet term limit enemies do not argue the information is anything but accurate. Their claims that such an "instruct and inform" tactic is coercive are all predicated on their understanding that the public deeply favors term limits and will likely use the accurate information to oppose those not representing their position. Do incumbents have a right to block truthful information harmful to them from the voting public? If citizens are free to make their instructions known, are they to be denied any knowledge as to how their elected representatives have acted? There is no public good in promoting public ignorance on term limits.

Some have argued that the voters will demand similar information on a whole host of issues. They imagine ballot information such as "VOTED TO RAISE TAXES" or "SUPPORTED CONGRESSIONAL PAY RAISE" next to candidates' names. What if it were so? Isn't public education a good thing? If the voters want more information, then they should have it. Yet, similar voter instructions were given and ballot notations used 90 years ago by the Progressives in pursuit of the Seventeenth Amendment for popular election of U.S. Senators and not until now on term limits have citizens returned to this device. The reasons are obvious. Voters understand they must call the tune if they can hope to overcome the political self-interest of members on the issue.

Harry Truman was called "Give 'em Hell Harry." But Truman remarked, "I never did give anybody hell. I just told the truth and they thought it was hell." These Informed Voter Laws likewise only tell the truth, and while they have popular support, term limits opponents will think they're hell. With public knowledge, politicians lose their wiggle-room on an issue that truly matters to voters.

The American people want a constitutional amendment for a three-term limit in the House and a two-term limit in the Senate. The sooner this body proposes such an amendment, the sooner Congress can be reconnected to this great country. For as the great Englishman Edmund Burke said: "In all forms of Government the people [are] the true legislator."

I ask you to put aside all political games and offer a proposal the American people have endorsed. If this Congress chooses to vote it down, so be it. At least the people will have a clean vote on real term limits.

# Congressional Term Limits:
## Restricting Choice

### John R. Hibbing

I urge you to do what you can to keep the terms of members of Congress from being limited to a set number. I will organize my case against term limits around three points: the value of congressional experience, the uncertain consequences of term limits for representation, and the inability of term limits to improve the public's opinion of Congress.

## CONGRESSIONAL EXPERIENCE

The term limit movement believes it is important to have a constant infusion of "new blood" in Congress lest the body become stale and set in its ways. Opponents of term limits worry that too much new blood would lead to a decrease in both legislative quality and institutional memory as inexperienced members wrestle with devilishly complex issues. Which side is correct? What is the optimal level of membership turnover for an institution like Congress? Most of the debate on these questions has proceeded without any firm evidence for the value of congressional experience. I would like to interject some evidence now.

About 10 years ago, I attempted to determine the manner in which members of this house changed as their careers in Congress unfolded. I found that, with a few exceptions of course, most members did not change much ideologically. Liberals stayed liberal and conservatives stayed conservative. Early career roll call patterns were good predictors of late career roll call patterns. Surprisingly, perhaps, early career electoral results were also good predictors of late career electoral results. It is not the case

that many members transform marginal seats into safe seats. The chances of losing office because of an election are nearly as great for senior members as they are for junior members. Attention to the district, as measured by the number of trips home, diminishes with increasing tenure but only by a little. Most senior members work quite hard at maintaining a presence in the district. Finally, the odds of a member being involved in some type of scandalous behavior do not increase with tenure. Junior members are just as likely as senior members to be scandal-ridden. The popular vision of an inert, uncaring, corrupt, and electorally unchallengeable senior member is simply inaccurate. On each of these counts, senior members are almost no different from junior members.

This statement does not apply, however, when attention shifts to legislative activity, that is, actually formulating and passing legislation. Here I found substantial differences between junior and senior members. Senior members, it turns out, are the heart and the soul of the legislative process. They are more active on legislation (giving speeches, offering amendments, and sponsoring bills), they are more specialized (a greater portion of their legislative attention goes to a focused substantive area), and they are more efficient (a greater percentage of their legislation becomes law). These patterns, I might add, persist even when senior members do not become leaders on committees or subcommittees, so it is not just that member activity reflects the positions of power that some senior members hold. The reasons for altered legislative contributions are broader than that and have to do, simply, with increased legislative experience.

Now, I will be the first to admit that many of these indicators of legislative involvement are badly flawed. It is impossible to measure quantitatively a representative's overall legislative contribution. As members know better than anyone, the legislative process is too rich and subtle to be captured by counting speeches or calculating legislative batting averages. But we must try to understand the relative contributions of senior members if we are to know the consequences of statutorily prohibiting the service of senior members, and here it can be said with some confidence that senior members have more active, focused, and successful legislative agendas. Junior members tend to introduce bills on topics about which they know very little. The subject matter of these bills is all over the map and the bills have precious little chance of making it out of committee let alone becoming law. These are empirical facts. We need more senior members; not fewer.

## UNCERTAINTY ABOUT CONSEQUENCES

Many people support the term limit movement because they believe it would make members more responsive to the people. The argument is that Congress has grown out of touch and that if members served only short time periods, along the lines of the citizen legislatures of old, they would be more in touch with the needs and concerns of ordinary people. But there are others who support the term limit movement for exactly the opposite reason. [Columnist] George Will is probably the best-known proponent of the position that term limits should be enacted in order to make Congress less sensitive to the desires of ordinary people. Will and others believe that mandatory term limits would embolden representatives, giving them the nerve to go against public opinion. Only when members know their stint in Congress will soon end, the argument is, will members stop pandering to unrealistic public demands for both lower taxes and more government services. I do not know which side is correct about the consequences of term limits for the proximity of Congress to the people but I do know that the inability of those in the term limit movement to agree amongst themselves on whether Congress is too close or not close enough to the people together with their inability to know whether term limits would in actuality reduce or increase the distance between the people and their Congress should give us pause. Before we enshrine a reform in the Constitution of the United States, should we not at least expect the champions of that reform to know what they want to accomplish?

### Public Opinion of Congress

My current research interests have to do with the reasons the public tends to be displeased with Congress. People believe Congress has been captured by special interests, extremist parties, and professionalized politicians and that ordinary folks have been lost in the shuffle. They want changes that would restore the public's role in the process. The only way we can restore public confidence in Congress, some reformers argue, is to enact measures, like term limits, that are central to the public's populist agenda.

It is my belief that term limits would not improve the public's opinion of Congress in the long run. Much public unrest stems from the belief that Congress creates conflict. The common notion is that agreement exists among the masses but that when special interests, parties, and ambitious politicians come together in Congress they manage to construct disagreement where it need not exist. But the truth of the matter is that, while interest groups, parties, and politicians sometimes create conflict, most of the time they only reflect the people's diverse views. Survey research indicates clearly that people are deeply divided over how to solve almost every major societal problem. This disagreement would exist whether or not term limits were enacted. In fact, I contend the public would be even more disillusioned than they are currently once they saw political conflict continuing unabated long after term limits were enacted.

The real solution is to educate people on the extent of their own disagreements and on the difficulties faced by elected officials in moving from these disagreements to responsible, brokered solutions to problems. People harbor beliefs that reforms such as term limits will be able to reduce conflict and the accompanying deliberation (bickering) and compromise (selling out) that they find so objectionable. Nothing could be further from the truth. Rather than pretending there is a magic solution to political conflict, we need to educate the people on the necessity of having learned, experienced legislators who can work their way through the challenging assignment of coming to agreement in the face of public ignorance and uncertainty.

# THE CONTINUING DEBATE:
## Congressional Term Limits

### What Is New

The 2004 elections demonstrated the relative safety of incumbents. Of the 34 senators whose terms were up, 26 sought new terms, and 25 were reelected. There was also scant turnover in the House, to which voters returned 99% of the 400 incumbents who ran again. For the 108th Congress (2003–2005), the average length of service in the House was 9.2 years and the average senator had been serving 10.9 years. If a term limit using the most often discussed parameters (12 years in either chamber) existed, it would mean 163 of 435 members of the House would be barred from seeking reelection in 2004, as would be 70 of 100 senators in their next election.

Since the late 1990s, term-limit advocates have had more defeats than victories. The "informed voter measures" favored by advocate Paul Jacobs did not withstand the test of constitutionality. Those in Missouri were challenged and ruled unconstitutional by the U.S. Supreme Court in *Cook v. Gralike* (2001). As for term limits as such, the Supreme Courts of Massachusetts, Oregon, and Washington struck them down as violating their respective state constitutions. Idaho's legislature repealed limits in 2002, and Utah's legislature followed suit in 2003. The last states to hold a referendum on term limits were Mississippi in 1999 and Nebraska in 2000. In Mississippi, 55% of the voters rejected term limits, making the state the first to do so by direct democracy. Taking the opposite stand, 55% of Nebraska's voters supported term limits. This leaves 16 states with limits in place. A final note is that the concept remains popular with the public. When a 2003 survey asked about term limits, 67% of the respondents said term limits were a "good idea," 27% thought them a "bad idea," 3% replied "it depends," and 4% were unsure.

### Where to Find More

A good new study that presents a series of empirical studies of the impact of term limits on state legislatures is Rick Farmer, John David Rausch, Jr., and John C. Green (eds.), *The Test of Time: Coping with Legislative Term Limits* (Lexington, 2003). U.S. Term Limits, the group represented by advocate Paul Jacob, has a helpful Web site at: http://www.termlimits.org/. You can also find good information on the site of the National Conference of State Legislators at http://www.ncsl.org/programs/legman/about/termlimit.htm.

### What More to Do

Think about one or more members of Congress whom you admire or who, because of their seniority, are powerful advocates of positions you support but who, at the end of their current term, will have been in their chamber 12 years or longer. Would you want them to be forced to retire because of term limits?

Consider your two senators and one member of the House. How do they stand with the 12-year rule? Also figure out which of the U.S. senators running for the Democratic presidential nomination would have had to retire in 2002 or before if the 12-year rule had been in place and, thus, probably would have faded politically and not been a candidate. Would term limits affect the quality of future presidents?

# PRESIDENCY

## PRESIDENTIAL WAR POWERS AND TERRORISM:
### Unilateral Authority *or* Constitutional Constraints?

### UNILATERAL AUTHORITY

**ADVOCATE:** Douglas Kmiec, Dean of the Columbus School of Law, The Catholic University of America

**SOURCE:** Testimony during hearings on "Applying the War Powers Resolution to the War on Terrorism," before the U.S. Senate Committee on the Judiciary, April 17, 2002

### CONSTITUTIONAL CONSTRAINTS

**ADVOCATE:** Jane Stromseth, Professor of Law, Georgetown University Law Center

**SOURCE:** Testimony during hearings on "Applying the War Powers Resolution to the War on Terrorism," before the U.S. Senate Committee on the Judiciary, April 17, 2002

"We're going to find out who did this, and we're going to kick their asses," President George Bush vowed angrily to Vice President Richard Cheney on September 11, 2001. Soon thereafter, Bush asked Congress for a resolution supporting action against terrorism in Afghanistan and elsewhere. But in doing so he claimed the right to act without legislative support, "pursuant to my constitutional authority to conduct U.S. foreign relations as Commander in Chief and Chief Executive." In other words, the support of Congress would be nice, but was not necessary.

The immediate debate here is whether in this case the president had the unilateral war powers authority he claimed. This question is part of the larger issue about when presidents may use military force without congressional authorization. It is a dispute that begins with two clauses in the Constitution. Article I empowers Congress "to declare war." Article II designates the president as "commander in chief" of the military. It is clear that the framers of the Constitution believed that the president should be able to act unilaterally in some but not all circumstances. As one framer, Roger Sherman put it, the president should "be able to repel and not commence war." The question is where one begins and the other ends.

There is a long history of the use of the president's war powers, but the matter did not become a central concern until after World War II. Two things changed. First, the United States became a superpower, deployed its forces around the world, and used them often. Second, presidents for the first time asserted broad powers as commander in chief. In the Korean War (1950–1953), the Truman administration argued that it could act alone because, "the president, as commander in chief of the armed forces,…has full control over the use thereof."

This self-proclaimed authority prevailed unchallenged until the trauma of the Vietnam War led Congress to try to rein in the president's war powers. Over a presidential veto, Congress in 1973 enacted the War Powers Resolution (WPR). Unfortunately, the terms of WPR are open to dispute. Section 2c specifies that the authority of the president "to introduce [U.S. forces] into hostilities, or into [so-called harm's way] situations where imminent involvement in hostilities is [likely] are properly" exercised only pursuant to (1) a declaration of war, (2) specific statutory authorization, or (3) a national emergency created by attack upon the United States, its territories or possessions, or its armed forces. Note that this language includes the president putting the military in "harm's way," as well as actual combat use. What causes confusion is section 5b's stipulation that when the president has ordered troops into combat or deployed them in harm's way, then "Within sixty…days…the president shall terminate [military action]…unless the Congress (1) has declared war or has enacted a specific authorization…[or], (2) has extended [the] period." Some read this to mean that the president has unilateral authority for 60 days. Others take the language to mean that the 60 days apples only to the three circumstances indicated in section 2c and that, in other cases, the president must get prior authority from Congress to act.

For all the controversy over the meaning of the WPR, it must also be said that its relevancy is limited by the fact that all presidents since its passage have asserted that the measure violates their authority as commander in chief. Moreover, despite several challenges to "presidential war" in recent years, the Supreme Court has refused to hear such cases, leaving the matter in legal limbo. As a result, whatever relevancy the WPR does have comes from the fact that presidents, despite their claims of constitutional authority, have usually found it politically wise to seek support from Congress. As President Bush explained his appeal for support for the war on terrorism, "I am a product of the Vietnam era. I remember presidents trying to wage war that were very unpopular, and the nation split."

It is also a matter of politics that many members of Congress, even if they oppose the president's policy, are reluctant to deny him authority to act because doing so will seem like not supporting the troops. Some members were worried after 9/11 when Congress considered a resolution giving the president broad authority "to use all necessary and appropriate force…to prevent any future acts of international terrorism against the United States." The fear was the president could use the language to justify action against any county in the world that he determined was aiding terrorism. Yet despite the misgivings of many in Congress about the resolution, it passed by votes of 98 to 0 in the Senate and 420 to 1 in the House (the lone dissenter: Barbara Lee, D-CA).

## POINTS TO PONDER

➤ Distinguish between your view about whether a particular military action is wise policy and the constitutional process by which that decision should be made.

➤ Given that President George H. W. Bush acted as commander in chief in 1990 to deploy U.S. forces to protect Saudi Arabia from attack by Iraq even though there was no attack on or threat against the United States nor an alliance with the Saudis, ask your self under what circumstances the president may not unilaterally use force?

➤ Think about what, if any, should be the limits on the authority of the president to deploy military force in harm's way or to order them into combat.

# Presidential War Power and Terrorism: Unilateral Authority

## DOUGLAS KMIEC

The President is constitutionally authorized as Commander in Chief to introduce troops into hostilities without prior congressional enactment. No President has ever conceded otherwise; no Congress has ever disputed this point, as even the highly controverted (and largely admonitory) War Powers Resolution necessarily concedes the President's constitutional assignment. Today, there are unprecedented terrorist dangers aimed directly at the civilian populations of our Nation and its allies. Congress shares this concern, rightly so. However, a shared concern must not become an occasion to undermine the well-settled constitutional responsibility of the President. Rather, with great respect for the important deliberations of this body, Congress should direct its legislative efforts at determining how best the President can be supported with the people's resources; not how cleverly the President's military judgment can be second-guessed or hampered.

The power to declare war is not a condition predicate to the duties of military self-defense imposed by the Constitution upon the President. No President from [George] Washington onward has ever construed it to be so, and it is largely modern academic commentary that has obscured or misstated this crucial aspect of constitutional understanding. Rather, the purpose of a declaration of war is to define the international effect of military actions undertaken by direction of the President.

In the present War, the Congress by joint resolution has confirmed the President's constitutional authority. That resolution, when construed together with the President's Article II power, is ample and plenary, allowing the President, together with his military, national security and homeland defense advisors, to determine the timing, scope, and appropriateness for military intervention.

Congress's role is one of material support, not tactical judgment. As the representative of the people, Congress is obliged to provide this support if it determines that our lives, safety and security justify the actions being taken by the President. Of course, this appropriations-related authority is a well-considered check upon presidential action. Prudentially and practically, both the President and Congress must necessarily collaborate if wartime efforts are to succeed. No Congress should give a blank check to a President, nor is it constitutionally obligated to do so, and no President should expect one. That said, Congress oversteps its constitutionally determined role if it uses monetary conditions to usurp or impede the tactical decisions that only the President can make.

The President has determined that terrorism is worldwide. It exists in networks or cells of individuals driven by religious or political fanaticism and supported by an international network of drug dealers and other shadowy criminal enterprises, not infrequently disguised as NGOs [non-governmental organizations: private group with multinational memberships] and charities. Unfortunately, no credible intelligence suggests that the War is confined to one nefarious leader or a single country. The successful military campaign in Afghanistan is a start, not a finish of this War. Congress, of course, has the formal power—as the holder of the Nation's purse—to refuse to adequately support the further military efforts to confront what the President has properly called an "axis of evil." It can discount the noncompliance of Iraq with UN sanction and its willingness to use biological weapons on its own people; it can turn a blind eye to the terrorist renegades in Somalia and the Philippines. At the farthest extreme, the legislature is constitutionally empowered even to defend our military and intelligence communities. I doubt that few Americans would think the exercise of congressional powers in this peremptory way to be responsible. In doing so, Congress will have indulged a calculus or risk assessment far different from the President, and perhaps, saved money. In the President's judgment, the Congress very likely will not have saved lives.

Ultimately in our democratic republic, it is the people who either affirm or dispute the policy choices made by their President and the Congress. It will then be up to the people to decide which was the better course—that of the sword aimed at those who hate the responsible exercise of freedom or that of the purse aimed at restraining the sword in this mission. Neither the President nor the Congress can avoid making its respective judgments. Certainly, neither can (or should) use the Constitution as a cover plane for its failure to decide.

The actions being taken by President [George H. W.] Bush are well within the parameters of the authority given to him by the Constitution. I am confident that the U.S. Supreme Court would not say otherwise. Congress may decide not to support these actions with the people's money. That is its prerogative, and it is one for which it will be held accountable.

## THE PRESIDENT'S ROLE

The President's power to use military force to respond to terrorist and other attack is clear. Article II, Section 2 provides that the "President shall be Commander in Chief of the Army and Navy of the Unites States, and of the Militia of the several States, when called into actual Service of the United States." Beyond this, the President is fully vested with all executive power and the authority to "take care" that the laws are faithfully executed.

Constitutional practice dating to our first president removes any doubt that wars were, and can be, fought without congressional authorization. During the first five years of his administration, Washington engaged in a prolonged Indian war in the Ohio Valley. This was not a small skirmish, as President Washington himself proclaimed, "We are involved in an actual war"—one, by the way, that went badly initially for the standing army in 1791. Similarly, John Adams fought a naval war with France, known as the Quasi-War that erupted in 1798 out of France's interference with our commercial relations with Britain. Congress provided the funding, and set the rules for naval engagement, but did not declare war, even as the historical record demonstrates that one was being fought.

Many cases affirm the scope of the President's war power, but it is particularly well affirmed in *The Prize Cases* [1863], where the Supreme Court opined that it was for Abraham Lincoln, as Commander in Chief to determine what necessary means could be used to respond to belligerents, for such questions under the Constitution, are "to be decided by [the President]." In this century, Attorney General [1940–1941] (later [Supreme Court] Justice) Robert Jackson put the matter equally forcefully:

> [The President] shall be Commander in Chief....By virtue of this constitutional office he has supreme command over the land and naval forces of the country and may order them to perform such military

duties as, in his opinion, are necessary or appropriate for the defense of the United States. These powers exist in times of peace as well as in time of war....[T]his authority undoubtedly includes the power to dispose of troops and equipment in such manner and on such duties as best to promote the safety of the country.

In writing in these terms, Attorney General Jackson was reflecting an unbroken line of undisturbed federal interpretation that properly places both the burden and authority upon the President to preserve "our territorial integrity and the protection of our foreign interests as a matter of constitutional provision, [and not] the enforcement of specific acts of Congress."

The framers justified this grant of authority to the President by the need for military and executive action to be taken with "secrecy and dispatch." Without the quality of what Hamilton referred to as "energy in the executive," the community would be unable to protect itself "against foreign attacks." These were not merely the sentiments of those who favored a strong national government. Thomas Jefferson, serving as George Washington's Secretary of State, observed that "[t]he transactions of business with foreign nations is executive altogether; it belongs, then, to the head of that department, except as to such portions of it as are specially submitted to the senate. [And what's more] [e]xceptions are to be construed strictly."

This exercise of presidential power has been bi-partisan. For example, on August 20, 1998, President [Bill] Clinton launched an air strike against terrorist activity (the African embassy bombings) traced to Osama bin Laden. The President acted without congressional authorization, and he did so for reasons that are directly applicable and similar to the present War on Terrorism: intelligence information that traced the bombings to terrorist groups that have acted against U.S. interests in the past, and suggested planning for additional attacks in the future. These groups were employing or seeking weapons of mass destruction, including chemical and dangerous weapons.

As scholars have pointed out, President Clinton's actions have much in common with President [Ronald] Reagan's April 14, 1986, air strike against Libya in response to that nation's involvement with the killing of Americans and others in Berlin. Like the Clinton actions, the Reagan strike was necessary not only in retaliation, but also as a defensive and preventative response to a terrorist attack on U.S. military personnel and her citizens.

### The Congress' Power to Declare War

The Congress' power to declare war is not the power to make war, as should be obvious to every American who has lived through both Pearl Harbor and September 11. War can be made upon us. As was noted expressly in the Constitutional convention, the executive must have the power to repel sudden attacks without prior Congressional authorization. The drafters of our Constitution knew how to use precise language, and indeed, as careful scholarship has since pointed out, "[if] the Framers had wanted to require congressional consent before the initiation of military hostilities, they would have used such language."

The power to declare war, rather than the power to initiate one, was a power to confirm—for international and domestic law purposes—the existence of hostilities between two sovereigns. This was how Blackstone understood the phraseology, and in historical context, how it was understood by the framers as well. In the decades leading up to constitutional drafting and ratification, declaring war meant not authorizing a proper executive response to attack, but to defining the relationship between the citizens of warring nations as to, for example, the seizure or expropriation, of assets. Even the use of the word "declare" in the context of the framing suggests not authorization, but recognition of that which pre-exists. This, for example, is the usage in the Declaration of Independence, recognizing rights that are not created by the government, but pre-exist by virtue of human creation. Professor John Yoo (now of the Office of Legal Counsel) has ably canvassed this area writing that the declare war clause was meant largely to bolster the exclusion of the individual states from the question. He summarizes the historical evidence this way: "a declaration of war was understood as what its name suggests: a declaration. Like a declaratory judgment, a declaration of war represented the judgment of Congress, acting in a [quasi-]judicial capacity (as it does in impeachments), that a state of war existed between the United States and another nation. Such a declaration could take place either before or after hostilities had commenced."

If military activity could only occur upon congressional declaration, this proposition would leave most of American history unexplained, such as American intervention in Korea, Vietnam, Iran, Grenada, Libya, and Panama. Congress has declared war only five times: the War of 1812; the Mexican American War of 1848, the Spanish-American War of 1898, and World War I (1914) and World War II (1941).

Some have disputed this account of the declare war clause, arguing in support of a congressional pre-condition by reference to Article I, Section 8, Clause 11 which gives Congress the power to "grant Letters of Marque and Reprisal,..." This somewhat arcane aspect of constitutional text, however, cannot bear the weight of the claim. Letters of Marque and Reprisal are grants of authority from Congress to private citizens, not the President. Their purpose is to expressly authorize seizure and forfeiture of goods by such citizens in the context of undeclared hostilities. Without such authorization, the citizen could be treated under international law as a pirate. Occasions where one's citizens undertake hostile activity can often entangle the larger sovereignty, and therefore, it was sensible for Congress to desire to have a regulatory check upon it. Authorizing Congress to moderate or oversee private action, however, says absolutely nothing about the President's responsibilities under the Constitution.

The drafters of the American Constitution knew how to express themselves. They were familiar with state constitutional provisions, such as that in South Carolina, which directly stated that the "governor and commander-in-chief shall have no power to commence war, or conclude peace" without legislative approval. Article I, Section 10 expressly prohibits states, without the consent of Congress, from keeping troops or ships of war in time of peace, or engaging in war, unless actually invaded, or in such imminent danger that delay would not be warranted. There is no parallel provision reciting that the President as commander in chief shall not, without the Consent of Congress, exercise his military responsibility.

That the power to declare war is not a power of prior authorization does not leave Congress without check upon executive abuse. That check, however, is anchored in Congress' control of the purse, and, of course, impeachment. When challenged by the anti-federalists, most notably Patrick Henry, to explain how tyranny would not result unless the sword and purse were held by different governments, Madison responded that no efficient government could exist without both, but security is to be found in "that the sword and purse are not to be given to the same member." No reference was made to the declare war clause or marque and reprisal letters.

How great a role can Congress play in the funding process? Here, the historical record would suggest that Congress is as free as the people they represent. It may explore and evaluate the military mission as the President has outlined it. Congress can refuse to fund the continuation of tactical decisions that it believes unsound; Congress, however, cannot dictate a particular course of engagement or so fetter the President's judgment as to preclude its exercise.

## THE WAR POWERS ACT

It is facetious to suggest that the War Powers Act or Resolution [WPR] limits constitutional authority, something which it expressly proclaims not to do. (Section 8(d) of the WPR states that "nothing in the Resolution is intended to alter the constitutional authority of either the Congress or the President.") In any event, insofar as the WPR presumes to limit the extent of operations already undertaken by a president, it "makes sense only if the President may introduce troops into hostilities or potential hostilities without prior authorization by the Congress." After surveying comprehensively the large number of occasions where the President has deployed troops without legislative involvement, the Office of Legal Counsel concluded:

> Our history is replete with instances of presidential uses of military force abroad in the absence of prior congressional approval.…Thus, constitutional practice over two centuries, supported by the nature of the functions exercised and by the few legal benchmarks that exist, evidences the existence of broad constitutional power.

Even if the WPR could be construed to statutorily amend constitutional text (which it cannot), by its express terms the WPR acknowledges presidential power to introduce Armed Forces into hostilities as a result of an "attack upon the United States, its ter-

ritories or possessions, or its armed forces." Certainly, that was September 11th. In any event, no president has ever accepted the limiting provisions of the WPR.

No president has ever formally complied with the WPR, even as Presidents have used the vehicle to accomplish consultation with Congress. For example, both the first President Bush and President Clinton sent reports to Congress that were described carefully as "consistent with the Resolution," but not pursuant to, or required by, the WPR. Congress has not sought to use the enforcement mechanism under the WPR, though it has occasionally been referenced or advocated by individual members.

Of course, proponents of the WPR take a different view; a view that posits the need for specific authorization. As mentioned, this view is contrary to constitutional text, history and practice, but in the present circumstance, even this objection is superceded by Congress' own legislative action.

### The Effect of the Joint Resolution

If presidential power apart from congressional authorization was somehow questionable as a general matter, it is not open to doubt in the present War on Terrorism which Congress has specifically authorized (S.J. Res. 25) [hereinafter "force resolution"]. The force resolution recites that "the President has authority under the Constitution to take action to deter and prevent acts of international terrorism." While this recital might be argued to concede that the force resolution, itself, was unnecessary, the better construction is one that the force resolution acknowledges the contending views over the legality of the WPR and removes all doubt in the present instance. The President thus has full legal authority with respect to either responding with "all necessary and appropriate force against those nations, organizations, or persons [the President] determines planned, authorized, committed or aided the terrorist attacks that occurred on September 11, 2001, or harbored such organizations or persons," and with respect to the steps necessary "to prevent any future acts of international terrorism against the United States by such nations, organizations or persons."

In my judgment, the force resolution must be read consistently with the President's authority. Some have commented that it relates only to "individuals, groups or states that [are] determined to have links to the September 11 attacks." Yet, Congress clearly intended to authorize the President to address terrorist threats of the future, and therefore, it is highly reasonable to construe the linkage to "nations, organizations, or persons" broadly, especially as we are practically discovering that the terrorist network has manifold capacity to direct and aid cells in multiple guises and distant parts of the world.

### WHETHER A WAR IS PROPERLY WAGED IS NOT FOR THE COURTS

The Supreme Court has consistently avoided passing upon the legality of particular military engagements, such as Vietnam and Korea. Lower federal courts have also regularly dismissed these matters as political questions and non-justiciable. The Persian Gulf War yielded two variants on this theme in *Dellums v. Bush* and *Ange v. Bush*. Unusually, in Dellums, the trial court decided that Congress possessed sole authority to declare war, and that troop movements authorized without congressional approval by the first President Bush might be challenged if a majority of Congress or the Congress in its entirety joined the litigation. That was not to be, and the suit was dismissed as unripe. By contrast, and far more in keeping with past decision, Judge Lamberth decided in Ange, the parallel case brought by a deployed member of the military, that determining whether the President had exceeded either his constitutional authority or violated the WPR was a nonjusticiable political question.

The judicial branch has consistently found any disagreement between the President and Congress to be a political question, not susceptible to judicial resolution. Common sense and the absence of public measures or standards of judgment readily explains why courts would abstain. Neither the President nor Congress have that luxury. Both must make their constitutionally separate choices. A President who endangers the lives of his military unnecessarily (or for a purpose that is contrary to the first principles in the Declaration of Independence and implemented by the Constitution) or a Congress that obdurately refuses to support those engaged in necessary combat will be accountable to the people.

### CONCLUSION—DOES THE WAR ON TERRORISM CHANGE THE CONSTITUTIONAL ORDER?

The short answer is, no. Yet, as General Joulwan, the former NATO Supreme Allied Commander, reflected before the Senate Foreign Relations Committee (February 7, 2002):

> We are at war. But it is a different war than those we fought in the past. There are no front lines. The enemy is dispersed and operates in small cells. The underpinnings of this threat are in its religious radicalism and its hatred of the United States and the civilization that embraces freedom, tolerance and human dignity. It is an enemy willing to commit suicide of its young to achieve its aims and with little regard for human life. While the enemy may be small in number it would be wrong to underestimate the threat—or the depth of their convictions.

Samuel Berger, former National Security Advisor, echoed the same sentiment at the same hearing:

> We must continue to take down al Qaeda cells, and hunt down al Qaeda operatives elsewhere—in Asia,

Europe, Africa, here and elsewhere in this Hemisphere. Disruption will be an ongoing enterprise—a priority that will require international intelligence, law enforcement and military cooperation for the foreseeable future. These cells of fanatics will reconstitute themselves. We must treat this as a chronic illness that must be aggressively managed, while never assuming it has been completely cured.

A dispersed enemy needing to be constantly addressed and combated is ill-met by a historically mistaken, if mistakenly commonplace, understanding of the declare war clause. Our national interests are equally ill-served by a wooden interpretation of a likely unconstitutional war powers resolution that even when enacted largely accommodated conventional warfare or deployments on the scale of World War II, rather than the needed (and often covert) responses to the smaller, yet more insidious and diffused nature of modern terrorism.

From 1975 through October 2001, Presidents—without conceding the constitutional validity of the WPR—submitted some 92 reports under the Resolution. In the same period, there were no declarations of war. One can argue that the resolution has fostered dialogue between the legislative and executive departments. So long as that dialog did not compromise classified information or strategy and facilitated Congress' appropriations role in war making, constitutional purposes were well served. Yet, the primary infirmity of the resolution lies in its faulty assumption: namely, that the Constitution envisions a "collective judgment" on the introduction of armed forces. It does not. It envisions a President capable of responding with ener-

gy and dispatch to immediate threat, and a Congress that can deliberate on the actions already taken, and through judicious resource choices, influence others. Congress, itself, recognized this in Section 3, when it modified the statutory consultation to "in every possible instance" and in Section 4 when it admits the possibility of presidential deployment without advance reporting and only reporting "within 48 hours, in the absence of a declaration of war or congressional authorization."

Wisely, Congress by its September 2001 force resolution has authorized the President to respond to the terrorist threat, as it exists—dispersed, chronic and global. In my judgment, the force resolution fully satisfies Section 5(b)(1) of the WPR and therefore exempts the President's deployment from termination by Congress under the controversial time clock set-out in the WPR. Section 5(c)'s provision for termination by concurrent resolution is also unconstitutional under Supreme Court precedent [set in] *INS v. Chadha* [1983]. While Congress has attempted to address the gap created by the decision in Chadha which held legislative veto devices to be unconstitutional, other far more serious constitutional questions would be raised if the subsequent 1983 amendment to section 601(b) of the International Security and Arms Control Act of 1976 (P.L. 94–329) fixing the WPR legislative veto failing is construed to empower Congress to countermand the President's military judgment and "direct" the withdrawal of troops. As suggested above, Congress properly speaks in its allocation of funds; the Constitution does not envision that Congress would determine the deployment of troops or related law enforcement and intelligence personnel—that is for the President.

# Presidential War Power and Terrorism:
## Constitutional Constraints

### JANE STROMSETH

The September 11th attacks pose unprecedented challenges for our Nation. We were attacked by a global network that was able to inflict massive casualties upon innocent civilians and would do so again, possibly with greater effect, if given the opportunity. Under such circumstances, we have begun to mobilize a broad range of military, diplomatic, intelligence, law enforcement, economic, and financial tools in order to wage this global war on terrorism. This campaign is likely to be long-term and open-ended, with conflict potentially on multiple fronts; and, in contrast to more conventional operations, it will be much harder to determine when or if the war is over or what constitutes victory.

Despite these complexities, indeed, in fact because of them, I will argue here that the basic principles of our Constitution regarding war powers remain as vital and relevant as ever—indeed even more so—in the fight against global terrorism. I will also argue that Congress's post-September 11th authorization of force correctly recognized that both Congress and the President have a vital constitutional role to play in prosecuting the global war on terrorism; that meaningful high-level consultations are essential as the campaign against terrorists with global reach and their state sponsors unfolds; and that additional congressional authorization may be constitutionally required in some situations in the future.

## THE CONSTITUTION'S
## ALLOCATION OF WAR POWERS

Our Constitution deliberately divided war powers between the Congress and the President. In making this choice, the framers sought to create an effective national government capable of protecting and defending the country while also remaining accountable to the American people. The Constitution's provisions concerning war powers—like those concerning other aspects of governance—reflect a structural system of checks and balances designed to protect liberty by guarding against the concentration of power. In a deliberate break with British precedent, the Constitution gave Congress the power to declare war because the founders believed such a significant decision should be made not by one person, but by the legislature as a whole, to ensure careful deliberation by the people's elected representatives and broad national support before the country embarked on a course so full of risks. Reflecting on this allocation of power, James Madison wrote: "In no part of the constitution is more wisdom to be found, than in the clause which confides the question of war or peace to the legislature, and not to the executive department."

At the same time, the framers wanted a strong Executive who could "repel sudden attacks" and act with efficiency and dispatch in protecting the interests of the United States in a dangerous world. By making the President Commander in Chief, moreover, they sought to ensure effective, unified command over U.S. forces and civilian accountability. The Constitution's division of war powers between the President and the Congress has led inevitably to tension between the branches—and to an enduring tug of war over war powers—even as the participation of both branches clearly is essential in protecting our country and advancing American interests.

There is a huge scholarly literature about the Framers' intentions with respect to constitutional war powers and about whether historical practices in the two centuries since the Constitution was ratified should alter how we should understand these authorities today. It is impractical for me to offer a detailed and comprehensive discussion here, but let me instead highlight four propositions from the historical record that, in my estimation, are central for understanding the constitutional roles of Congress and the President today.

First, the power to "declare war" vested in Congress was intended by the Framers to be a power to decide, to make a choice, about whether the United States should go to war; it was not a formalistic power to simply validate that a legal state of war existed. On the contrary, Congress was given the power to determine whether the United States should initiate war in order to ensure that the decision to expose the country to such risks and sacrifices reflected the deliberation and judgment of the legislature— the branch most directly representative of the American people, whose lives and resources will be placed on the line—and to ensure broad national support for such a course of action. This interpretation is further validated by the Constitution's grant of authority to Congress to authorize reprisals, or acts of limited war, that could lead to a wider war, which clearly indicated a broader understanding of Congress's war-commencing role than simply a formal declaration that a state of war existed.

Second, the Chief Executive's authority to repel sudden attacks by force is incontestable. The founders expected the President, as Chief Executive and Commander in Chief, to protect the United States by repelling actual or imminent attacks against the United States, its vessels,

and its armed forces. Moreover, if another nation effectively placed the United States in a state of war—by declaring or openly making war upon the United States—the President as Commander in Chief was expected to exercise the nation's fundamental right of self-defense. However, if an enemy engaged in limited attacks that did not rise to the level of war, the founders expected the President to repel those attacks but not to go beyond this authority and change the state of the nation from peace to war without congressional authorization.

Third, Congress's power of purse, though critically important, is not a substitute for congressional authorization of war before it is commenced. The founders understood that the British monarch's power to go to war was qualified to a substantial degree by the Parliament's power of the purse and its control over military supplies. In giving Congress the power of the purse, including the power of appropriating money to "raise and support Armies" and to "provide and maintain a navy," the Constitution continued this important legislative check. But the Constitution did not stop here. The Constitution also gave Congress the power to declare war and authorize reprisals, so that congressional deliberation would occur before war was commenced. Reliance on the power of the purse alone as a check on executive war powers, moreover, can be an overly blunt and sometimes ineffective tool for expressing the will of Congress. Limiting or cutting off funds after forces have already been committed is problematic because it undercuts both troops in the field and America's credibility with her allies. Restricting funds in advance is often undesirable as well because it can harm the President's ability to carry out effective diplomacy. In short, as important as Congress's power of the purse is, it is not a substitute for Congress's power to authorize war.

Fourth, historical practice has not fundamentally altered how we should understand the Constitution's allocation of war powers today. Practice, of course, cannot supplant or override the clear requirements of the Constitution, which gives the power to declare war to Congress. Furthermore, of the dozen major wars in American history, five were formally declared by Congress and six were authorized by other legislative measures. There is, to be sure, a pattern of practice involving more limited presidential uses of force falling short of major national conflicts, a substantial number of which involved the protection or rescue of U.S. nationals caught up in harm's way. For example, of the 200 or so cases sometimes cited as examples of unilateral commitments of force by the President, nearly 70 involved the protection or rescue of U.S. nationals, actions far short of deliberate war against foreign countries and reasonably covered by the President's authority to respond to sudden threats. A number of other operations were interventions or peace enforcement actions that aimed at limited goals. Others involved more far-reaching objectives, however, even if the risks were relatively low. In some of these cases, like Haiti, for instance, Congress protested unilateral actions taken by the President and made clear its view that its authorization should have been sought in advance. My basic point is this: one must be very cautious in drawing broad conclusions about presidential power from a numerical list of cases. These instances each have to be examined carefully, and the authority claimed by the President and Congress's reaction fully assessed. Ultimately, however, whatever conclusions one comes to concerning the constitutional implications of small-scale presidential actions undertaken without congressional authorization, the fact remains that major wars have been authorized by Congress.

Where exactly does a global war on terrorism fall on the spectrum between major war and smaller scale military actions? If it were purely a police action against hostile non-state actors, akin to operations against pirates or to other small-scale operations with limited objectives, a case can be made that historical practice indicates a record of presidential deployments without advance congressional authorization. The President, after all, clearly possesses authority to repel and to forestall terrorist attacks against the United States, its forces, and citizens.

Yet, this global campaign is much more ambitious than apprehending terrorists. It aims to destroy a multi-state terrorist infrastructure and potentially defeat or overthrow sponsoring regimes. While military force is not the only, or even indeed the main, instrument for waging this war, the range of military activities that we have mounted to date is very diverse—combat operations, continuous air patrols, maritime interception of shipping, the training and equipping of foreign militaries for combat operations, operational assistance to post-conflict stability operations, just to name a few. Given that the current campaign is focused against a global terrorist network that is based in over sixty countries, that has the capacity to inflict massive casualties, and that requires or depends upon the sponsorship or acquiescence of various countries for its training and safe-harbors, the scope and complexities of this military campaign would appear to defy any commonsense notion of a limited police action.

## CONGRESS'S POST-SEPTEMBER 11 AUTHORIZATION OF FORCE: SCOPE AND LIMITS

Congress's authorization for the use of force against those responsible for the attacks of September 11 is an express recognition that Congress and the President both have a critical constitutional role to play in the war on terrorism. Mindful of the centrality of congressional war powers in a campaign against terrorism that will be long-term and far-reaching, Congress sought to craft an authorization that both allowed for appropriate executive flexibility but at the same time is not a blank check.

Though not restricted geographically, Congress's post-September 11 authorization does contain some clear limits. The Joint Resolution authorizes the President:

> to use all necessary and appropriate force against those nations, organizations, or persons he determines planned, authorized, committed, or aided the terrorist attacks that occurred on September 11, 2001, or harbored such organizations or persons, in order to prevent any future acts of international terrorism against the United States by such nations, organizations or persons.

The joint resolution, in essence, authorizes (a) necessary and appropriate force, against those states, organizations, or persons who (b) planned, authorized, committed, or aided the September 11th attacks, or (c) harbored such organizations or persons, (d) in order to prevent future acts of international terrorism against the United States by such nations, organizations or persons. Thus, the force must be directed against those responsible in some way for the September 11th attacks, or those who harbored such organizations or persons; and the purpose of using force is focused and future-oriented: to prevent additional terrorist acts against the United States by the states, organizations, or persons responsible for the September 11th attacks or who harbored those responsible. The President determines whether the necessary link to the September 11th attacks is established, and presumably Congress expected he would make his determination

and the basis for it known to Congress in some fashion, perhaps through a war powers report or through briefings, e.g., to the intelligence committees. Moreover, in signing the Joint Resolution, President Bush made clear that he would consult closely with Congress as the United States responds to terrorism.

Congress' post-September 11th resolution was an unambiguous decision to authorize force. Like the Gulf War authorization in 1991, the authorization explicitly affirms that it "is intended to constitute specific statutory authorization within the meaning of section 5(b) of the War Powers Resolution." This removes any actions that fall within the scope of the authorization from the War Powers Resolution's 60-day time-clock provision. At the same time, Congress made clear that the requirements of the War Powers Resolution otherwise remain applicable.

### THE WAR POWERS RESOLUTION AND THE WAR AGAINST TERRORISM

For all the controversy it has spurred, key elements of the War Powers Resolution are constitutionally compelling and warrant broad support. First, its overriding purpose is to "insure that the collective judgment of both the Congress and the President" applies to the introduction of U.S. forces into hostilities and to the continued use of those forces. Second, it seeks to enable Congress to better fulfill its constitutional responsibilities by requiring the President "in every possible instance" to "consult with Congress before introducing" U.S. armed forces into hostilities or imminent hostilities and to continue to "consult regularly" with the Congress while U.S. forces are in those situations. Moreover, the legislative history of the War Powers Resolution makes clear that Congress expected consultations to be meaningful:

Rejected was the notion that consultation should be synonymous with merely being informed. Rather, consultation in this provision means that a decision is pending on a problem and that Members of Congress are being asked by the President for their advice and opinions, and in appropriate circumstances, their approval of action contemplated. Furthermore, for consultation to be meaningful, the President himself must participate and all information relevant to the situation must be made available.

Third, under the War Powers Resolution, the President is required to report to Congress within 48 hours in designated situations, and to make periodic reports to Congress at least once every six months if U.S. forces remain in hostilities or imminent hostilities.

Whatever conclusions one reaches about the more controversial provisions of the War Powers Resolution, such as the 60-day time clock, the consultation provisions are sound and reasonable efforts to ensure that both the President and the Congress fulfill their constitutional responsibilities concerning the commitment of U.S. forces abroad. Moreover, even when Congress has authorized the use of force, as it did after September 11, regular, meaningful consultations between Congress and the President remain vital in the ongoing war on terrorism. Such consultations are imperative to ensure that there is a frank exchange of views and a shared understanding between Congress and the President on future directions in the war on terrorism and broad support for the steps ahead. To give a counterexample: The experience in Somalia is a cautionary reminder that congressional authorization and support in the early phases of an operation does not replace the need for continued dialogue about the goals and risks of a changing mission. We cannot afford to make the same mistakes in the current context.

## CONSULTATIONS

How should a system of regular, meaningful consultations between Congress and the Administration be structured as the country faces up to what will likely be a long, complex campaign against terrorism? Clearly, a commitment by the President to hold regular consultations with the bipartisan congressional leadership would be invaluable. Second, as the War Powers Resolution expressly provides in section 4(b), Congress should request that a broader range of information be included in the periodic war powers reports provided by the Administration. Those reports, which have generally been perfunctory since the War Powers Resolution was first enacted, should, in the context of the war on terrorism, include a fuller discussion of the objectives and effectiveness of U.S. action, including our efforts to work closely with allies on multiple fronts. Congress may also wish to request that the reports be made more frequently, say every three months, and, in any event, invite Cabinet officials to testify on the state of the war on terrorism when those reports are submitted. The combination of fuller reports and high-level testimony could, in conjunction with meaningful consultations, make for a more significant and effective dialogue between Congress and the Administration regarding future goals and strategies in the war on terrorism.

## FUTURE AUTHORIZATION

As important as consultations are, however, they are not a substitute for congressional authorization if military action is contemplated that clearly implicates Congress's war powers. While the post-September 11 authorization is broad, it does contain limits, most notably the requirement of a clear link to the attacks of September 11. Other threats to U.S. security unrelated to those attacks may exist or arise in the future, and various military options may be considered, including options that go beyond measures to prevent future acts of terrorism by those responsible for the September 11th attacks. Whether and when additional congressional authorization is constitutionally required will depend on the facts of the situation and on the nature and objectives of the military action contemplated.

Constitutionally, the President clearly possesses the power to repel attacks and to forestall imminent attacks against the United States and its armed forces, and to protect Americans in imminent danger abroad. But the decision to go beyond this and commence a war belongs to Congress. Major military action with far-reaching objectives such as regime change is precisely the kind of action that constitution-ally should be debated and authorized by Congress in advance. The Constitution's "wisdom" on this point is compelling: Authorization, if provided by Congress, ensures that the risks and implications of any such action have been fully considered and that a national consensus to proceed exists. Congressional authorization also ensures American combat forces that the country is behind them, and conveys America's resolve and unity to allies as well as adversaries.

The war against terrorism will, unfortunately, be with us for a long time. However, as our nation moves ahead on various fronts, using a variety of tools and means, our response will be more effective and more sustainable if the Congress and the President continue to work together in the best tradition of our great Constitution.

# THE CONTINUING DEBATE:
## Presidential War Powers and Terrorism

### What Is New

The decision for war against Iraq in 2003 followed a familiar scenario. Some Bush administration officials opposed asking for a congressional resolution. "We don't want to be in the legal position of asking Congress to authorize the use of force when the president already has that full authority," said one such official. In the end though, Bush was mindful of polls showing, in one survey, that 80% of Americans wanted him to get authorization from Congress before launching an attack, while only 17% thought that an unnecessary step, and 3% were unsure. This and the urge to demonstrate broad support led Bush in October 2002 to seek a resolution, even while maintaining that legally he did not need one. And as has also usually been true, Congress complied by large majorities: in this case, 296 to 133 in the House and 77 to 23 in the Senate. Even in signing the joint resolution, though, Bush asserted his unilateral authority. In his words, "While I appreciate receiving…support, my request for it did not, and my signing this resolution does not, constitute any change in the long-standing positions of the executive branch on either the president's constitutional authority to use force to deter, prevent, or respond to aggression or other threats to U.S. interests or on the [un]constitutionality of the War Powers Resolution."

As has occurred during many recent U.S. conflicts, there was a legal challenge. Six members of Congress and the families of several soldiers being sent to Iraq filed a suit charging that the congressional resolution was an unconstitutional delegation of the authority by Congress to declare war to the president. And, following the established pattern, a federal judge dismissed the suit on the grounds that the lawsuit engaged "political questions in the legal sense that are beyond the jurisdiction of the court."

### Where to Find More

One recent study is Ryan C. Hendrickson, *The Clinton Wars: The Constitution, Congress, and War Powers* (Vanderbilt University Press, 2002). An article that advocates repealing the WPR on the grounds that its 60-day provision gives the president too much power is Louis Fisher and David Gray Adler, "The War Powers Resolution: Time to Say Goodbye," *Political Science Quarterly* (Spring 1998). To find a copy of the War Powers Resolution go to the Web site of Yale Law School's Avalon Project at: http://www.yale.edu/lawweb/avalon/warpower.htm. For background on the use of the War Powers Resolution, see the Congressional Research Service report, "The War Power Resolution: Presidential Compliance," March 16, 2004 on the State Department Web site at: http://fpc.state.gov/fpc/31784.htm. Also good is the CRS report, "Response to Terrorism: Legal Aspects of the Military Use of Force," September 13, 2001 at: http://fpc.state.gov/documents/organization/6217.pdf.

### What More to Do

Clear up the confusion about Congress' authority to declare war and the president's authority as commander in chief. Write and debate in class an amendment to the Constitution that will specify when (if ever) presidents can use military force or send U.S. forces into harm's way on their own authority and when (if ever) doing so would require a declaration of war or other form of congressional authorization.

# BUREAUCRACY

## THE DEPARTMENT OF EDUCATION AND TITLE IX:
### Champion of Equality *or* Overzealous Crusader?

### CHAMPION OF EQUALITY

**Advocate:** Judith Sweet, Vice-President for Championships and Senior Women Administrator, National Collegiate Athletic Association

**Source:** U.S. Department of Education, Secretary's Commission on Opportunity in Athletics, Hearings, August 27, 2002

### OVERZEALOUS CRUSADER

**Advocate:** Amanda Ross-Edwards, Visiting Professor of Political Science, Fairfield University

**Source:** "The Department of Education and Title IX: Flawed Interpretation and Implementation," an essay written especially for this volume, October 2003

We tend to think that elected representatives serving in Congress and, to a degree, the elected president, make federal rules. However, in terms of sheer volume, non-elected agency officials make most government rules. Off these functionaries, the president appoints about 600, with career civil servants making up the rest of the 2.8 million civilian federal employees.

One measure of the deluge of bureaucratic rules is the *Federal Register*, the annual compilation of new rules, rule changes, and other authoritative bureaucratic actions. Just for 2003, the *Federal Register* was an immense 75,795 pages of regulations addressing almost every conceivable subject. So great is the impact of the rule-making and implementation authority of the bureaucracy that some analysts refer to it as the fourth branch of government.

Administrators make binding rules in two ways. One is by issuing regulations that, in theory, simply add detail to the general intent of laws passed by Congress. In practice, many analysts say, agency-made rules take laws in a direction that Congress did not anticipate or even want. The second way that bureaucrats make rules is by how they implement the law. As with regulations, implementation is supposed to follow the intent of the law, but whether that is true is sometimes controversial. You will see presently that advocate Amanda Ross-Edwards charges that the Department of Education has both formulated rules and implemented them in a manner that has subverted Congress' original intent when it enacted Title IX of the Education Amendments (Act) in 1972. This legislation declared that no one "shall, on the basis of sex, be...subjected to discrimination under any education program or activity receiving Federal financial assistance." It is language that covers most activities at all levels of education, although here we will focus on athletics in higher education.

The legislation also, as most acts do, authorized and directed agencies "to effectuate the provisions of [this act]...by issuing rules, regulations, or orders of general applicability which shall be consistent with achievement of the objectives of the statute."

What is not in dispute here is the value of the basic law. It was enacted to protect girls and women from discrimination by schools and colleges, which was widespread as late as the 1960s. For example, after Luci Baines Johnson, the daughter of President Lyndon Johnson, married in 1966, Georgetown University's nursing school denied her re-admission on the grounds that school regulations barred married women (but not married men) from being students. And it was not until 1970 and a federal court order that the University of Virginia even admitted undergraduate women, much less let them play sports.

There can also be no argument that since the passage of Title IX there has been a dramatic increase in the number of women participating college sports and in the percentage of student athletes who are women. Judith Sweet attributes these changes to the enforcement of Title IX, but Amanda Ross-Edward contends that the expansion of women's athletics was already underway and that the changes reflect social norms more than the legislation.

What is very much in dispute here is whether the Department of Education's Office for Civil Rights, which since 1994 has been responsible for enforcing Title IX, has followed congressional intent when interpreting the law and formulating regulations and policies. Also at issue, albeit less directly so, is the matter of how equal opportunity should be measured. In this sense, this debate is distinctly related to Debate 17 on education policy and affirmative action admissions. Critics of both the way that Title IX has been enforced and many aspects of affirmative action charge that numerical quotas are used overtly or covertly and that they are neither legal nor just.

## POINTS TO PONDER

➢ Amanda Ross-Edwards argues men are being subjected to reverse discrimination. What is the basis of the charge, and do you agree?
➢ Currently, only 45.8% of college students are men. Should this mean that 54.2% of all college scholarship athletes should be women?
➢ If not by proportionality, how would you evaluate a school's compliance with Title IX?

# The Department of Education and Title IX:
## Champion of Equality

Judith Sweet

I've loved sports all my life. As a young girl I dreamt of representing my high school and college on a sport team. I never had that opportunity because there were no teams at either the high school or college level.

While I would welcome the opportunity to share my perspective based on those life and campus experiences that Cynthia alluded to, my remarks today will focus on the NCAA.

On behalf of the National Collegiate Athletic Association and its more than 1200 member colleges, universities, conferences, and affiliated organizations, I'm pleased to have the opportunity to provide the Commission with comments about the impact of Title IX on intercollegiate athletics from the Association's perspective.

For those of you who may not be as familiar with the NCAA as others of you are, allow me to briefly note that the NCAA is a membership driven association. The NCAA derives its authority, including all national policy, entirely from the will of the membership through the vote of institutional or conference representatives.

The vast majority of decisions regarding athletics programs, including which sports to sponsor or to cease sponsoring, are made at the campus level. Member institutions have complete autonomy over their programs except where the broader membership has set standards through national policy.

Allow me also briefly to describe the role of intercollegiate athletics for women 30 years ago when Title IX was signed into law. There were no college athletic scholarships to speak of for women, no NCAA championships for women, and very few opportunities for competition.

In 1971/72 a survey of the NCAA member institutions showed that only 29,977 women were participating in sports and recreational programs compared to over 170,000 men, more than five times as many men as women.

The athletics opportunities for women were few, and the prospects for growth were dismal. With numbers like that, it might be fair to wonder what college woman would show any interest at all in athletics.

What a difference 30 years of legislative impetus, opportunity and support make. Today nearly 150,000 women are competing in sports at NCAA member schools.

While some individuals suggest that women do not have a strong interest in sports participation, the numbers prove otherwise. In the last ten years alone female NCAA participants have increased by more than 55,000. The number of collegiate women's soccer teams has grown from 80 in 1982 to 824 in 2002.

The number of girls participating in sports at the high school level exceeds 2.7 million. As opportunity has increased, interest has increased. Of the 87 championships in 22 sports conducted by the NCAA, 43 are exclusively for women, and bowling will be added to the women's championship in 2003/04.

And...the Committee on Women's Athletics has also indicated that they will look at the number of scholarships being provided in all of our sports. The NCAA membership has demonstrated a commitment to both men's and women's Olympic sports through legislation that allows the continuation of championships in Olympic sports even if the number of sponsoring institutions does not meet minimum requirements for championship events.

Clearly Title IX has promoted opportunities for female athletes over the last 30 years, but there is much more still to be done to ensure that men and women who attend NCAA member schools have equitable access to athletics participation.

Although women comprise 54 percent of the undergraduate student population at NCAA member schools on average, as you have heard, they account for only 4 percent of the athletics participants. They receive only 40 percent of the scholarships; they receive only 36 percent of the operating dollars, and have only 32 percent for recruiting budgets.

Like any social legislation designed to change the deeply imbedded status quo, Title IX has had and still has its critics. Over the last 30 years the voices of dissent have been less strident regarding the law itself and have grown more concerned with the standards used to measure compliance.

The Department of Education standards consider an athletics program to be in compliance with Title IX if its student athletes by gender are in proportion to the make-up of the undergraduate student body or if the program can demonstrate a history of expanding its program to meet the needs of the underrepresented gender or if the program can demonstrate that it has fully and effectively accommodated interests and abilities of the underrepresented gender.

Critics argue that the focus of courts and the Office of Civil Rights has been on a proportionality test and that it has become the de facto single test used to determine compliance. The unintended consequence of Title IX they say has been the cutting of the so-called nonrevenue men's sports in order to get the number of athletics participants

for an institution more in line with the undergraduate population by gender.

Others have claimed that increased expenses in providing opportunities for women to comply with Title IX have resulted in a reduction of spending for men's sports. In fact, financial reports from 1972 to 1993 show that in Division 1-A for every new dollar spent on women's sports, three new dollars were spent on men's sports.

Before I discuss the findings of the report on this issue from the United States GAO [General Accounting Office, an investigate agency of Congress] in March 2001, allow me to share with you a message from the NCAA executive committee, one of the primary decision making bodies within the government structure and comprised of university Presidents and Chancellors.

In a discussion about the work of the Commission at their meetings earlier this month, the President spoke strongly of the value of Title IX and urged the Office of Civil Rights to apply consistent Title IX enforcement and interpretations in all regions of the country.

Regarding decisions by member institutions to cut men's sports, this group of college and university CEOs noted that institutions have dropped sports for various reasons, such as institutional philosophy, program priorities, finances, infractions, safety, lack of conference opportunities, inadequate facilities, insurance costs, and others, but the single most important message that they wanted me to deliver on their behalf was this: Don't blame Title IX for institutional decisions to cut programs.

The President's position is supported by findings of the GAO report. The United States Congress included provisions in the higher education amendments of 1998 that required the GAO to study participation in athletics, including schools' decisions to add or discontinue sports teams. They examined the membership of both the NCAA and the NAIA. Among the GAO's findings are these: Athletics participation for both men and women have increased since 1981. The total number of teams has increased for both men and women.

Since 1992, 963 schools added teams and 30 discontinued teams. Most were able to add teams, usually women's teams, without discontinuing any teams.

The report found that the level of student interest was the factor schools cited most often as greatly or very greatly influencing their decisions to add or discontinue both men's and women's teams.

The conclusions are clear. The decisions to discontinue specific sports are made at the institutional level for a variety of reasons.

If the decision is made to eliminate sports for gender-equity reasons, it is because institutions have chosen this path rather than pursuing other options, not because Title IX dictates such action.

The task before the Commission is an important one. In a perfect world Title IX would not be necessary. There would be enough resources and the will to do the right thing and thus meet everyone's needs. Social legislation exists, of course, because we do not live in that perfect world.

In the charge to this commission the Department of Education acknowledges that extraordinary progress has resulted from the passage of Title IX. While we like to think that this progress would have taken place without Title IX because it was the right thing to do, the fact is that opportunities and support for girls and women in athletics are still not equitable with those provided for men, even though it was 30 years since the law was passed.

Your charge appears to bear more on the federal standards for measure of compliance than on the necessity for the law. The degree to which the Commission can give direction to colleges and universities in achieving compliance with Title IX, emphasizing application of any of the three prongs, would remove the misunderstanding that proportionality is the only way to comply. The law is clear; the intent is to correct inequities.

The NCAA stands ready to assist the Commission any way it can as you deliberate. The ultimate test for compliance with Title IX may have been summed up best by an NCAA gender-equity task force in 1992. It defined gender equity in the following manner: An athletics program can be considered gender equitable when the participants in both men's and women's programs would accept as fair and equitable the overall program of the other gender. No individual should be discriminated against on the basis of gender, institutionally or nationally, in intercollegiate athletics.

As I conclude my comments, I urge you to consider the following: Would participants in both our men's and women's programs accept as fair and equitable 40 percent of the participation opportunities, 36 percent of the operating dollars, and 32 percent of the recruiting dollars? Would we expect that of them?

# The Department of Education and Title IX:
## Overzealous Crusader

AMANDA ROSS-EDWARDS

In 1973, one year after passage of Title IX, tennis professional Billie Jean King received a congratulatory call from President Nixon for being the first female athlete to win one hundred thousand dollars in prize money in a single year. In 2003, Justine Henin-Hardenne received one million dollars in prize money for winning a single event, the U.S. Open in Women's Tennis. It is clear that women's opportunities in sports have increased in the 31 years since Title IX was enacted. It is also clear that in the past ten years Title IX's interpretation and implementation have become flawed. Contrary to Title IX's original aim of equal opportunity for women in education, the courts and the Office for Civil Rights at the Department of Education have equated equal outcomes in the form of statistical proportionality as their primary means of measuring compliance with Title IX statute.

Title IX prohibits sex discrimination in education by institutions that receive federal funding. Although Title IX passed in 1972, it was not until 1975 that the Department of Health, Education and Welfare published implementing regulations. These regulations, however, were vague and thus provided very little guidance on how schools should enforce the law against sex discrimination in athletics. It was not until 1979 that the department's Office of Civil Rights (OCR) established its Title IX Athletics Policy Interpretation. According to Jessica Gavora, a senior policy advisor at the Department of Justice, "although this interpretation lacks the legal status of an official government regulation, it has been treated by succeeding adminis-

trations and by the courts as the government's final word on implementing Title IX in athletics." This document declares that schools may comply with Title IX in one of three ways: 1) proportionality; 2) showing a recent history of adding women's athletic teams; or 3) proving that the interests of the student body were being met. Gavora notes in her book, *Tilting the Playing Field*, that "Officials in the OCR insist that the three-part test is progressive; compliance they say, is measured in stages. If a school is unable to comply under the first test, it may do so under the second and, failing there, it has a final opportunity under the third test. In any case, a school need pass only one of the three tests to be in compliance with the law." Historical evidence, however, demonstrates that this isn't true; statistical proportionality has become a requirement for compliance under Title IX statute.

The Office for Civil Rights has never explicitly defined proportionality; however, the courts have generally agreed at this point that proportionality is an athletics participation rate that is within plus or minus five percent of the sex ratio of the student body. Proportionality, thus, does not count the number of opportunities available to men and women, but rather the actual number of individual men and women competing in sports. In order to comply under the proportionality rule, the percentage of women participating in athletic programs should be proportional to the percentage of women enrolled in the college or university. If 51 percent of the student body is made up of women, but only 45 percent of the athletes are women, then the college or university would not be in compliance with Title IX.

As noted, in theory a school must only meet one of the three prongs. In practice, however, as the result of significant court cases and executive interpretation, the proportionality rule has become a "safe harbor" for a school's compliance with Title IX. In 1991, Brown University cut two women's teams and two men's teams for budgetary reasons. At the time, Brown University had 15 sports teams for women, compared to the average 8.3 for other NCAA Division I schools. In fact, the number of women's varsity teams at Brown outnumbered the men's. Only Harvard had a broader and more generous women's athletic program.

Despite Brown's exemplary program of women's athletics, Amy Cohen, along with seven other women from the teams that had been cut, filed a lawsuit against Brown charging non-compliance with Title IX. They argued that the proportion of women participating in sports at Brown was less then the proportion of female students. At the time the lawsuit was filed, 51 percent of Brown students were women, while only 39 percent of Brown's athletes were women. According to the plaintiffs, if 61 percent of the athletes at Brown were male, then cutting two men's teams and two women's teams merely perpetuated a preexisting inequality.

The relevance of this case is the context within which it was decided and the impact of its outcome on the future actions of other schools regarding men and women and sports. In 1992, the Supreme Court decided the case of *Franklin v. Gwinnett County Public Schools*, which involved Christine Franklin's claim that the Gwinnett County Public School district owed her punitive damages for not protecting her from her teacher's repeated harassing behavior even after she reported the incidents. The Supreme Court ruled in her favor and thus set precedent for women to receive monetary compensation for Title IX violations.

By the time the Brown case arose, lawyers, such as Arthur Bryant, executive director of the Trial Lawyers for Public Justice (TLPJ), had fully recognized the possibilities associated with Title IX statute. In the early 1990's, Bryant and TLPJ had filed a number of successful Title IX actions against colleges and universities. Their strategy involved filing a case against a university or college that had cut a women's team and demanding that the team be reinstated. The case usually never made it to court because college administrators wanted to avoid the publicity and the legal costs. The women's teams were thus reinstated and Bryant received his attorney's fees.

Aside from the issue that a primary motive behind these cases was monetary gain for Bryant, there is also the question of how Bryant found out about these cases. In the Brown case, a woman named Kathryn Reith, a Brown alumna and director of advocacy for the Women's Sports Foundation, was responsible for creating the case. As a representative of an interest group interested in women's athletics, she wanted female athletes to file federal complaints under Title IX. It was not until the Franklin decision that money provided the needed added incentive for individuals to file complaints. Reith and Bryant thus looked for the ideal client in the Brown University case and chose Amy Cohen, the former captain of the Brown gymnastics team. In the Brown case, therefore, it was not female athletes pressuring the school and the government for more opportunities; instead it was pressure group incentive and monetary interest that led to the creation of this case. Women were not demanding more athletic opportunity; money and organized interests motivated policy reinterpretation.

Unlike the other suits filed by Bryant, Brown University administrator Vartan

Gregorian refused to settle. In court, Cohen's lawyers argued that Brown could correct the discrimination against women by refunding the women's gymnastics and volleyball teams and continuing to create teams for women until proportionality was reached. Brown's lawyers responded that this was a complete misapplication of the law. The three prong test was clearly a misrepresentation of congressional intent. The authors of Title IX legislation stated clearly in the congressional record that Title IX did not mean quotas. Furthermore, athletics is only one part of Title IX's larger applicability to the academic realm. For instance, dance programs have proportionately more women than men, and engineering programs have proportionately more men than women. So why is disproportionate involvement in sports targeted as an indication of discrimination?

In 1995, the lower courts found in favor of Amy Cohen. Brown University immediately filed an appeal. In January 1996, while waiting for the decision of the first circuit of the U.S. Court of Appeals, Norma Cantu, head of the Office of Civil Rights (OCR), issued a clarification of the three part test in which she reinterpreted the third prong. Appointed as President Clinton's Chief Title IX enforcer, Cantu had established a proactive approach to Title IX enforcement. According to Gavora, within the first nineteen months of Cantu's tenure, "OCR began 240 reviews of schools from which no civil rights complaints had been filed." This was in sharp contrast to the Reagan and Bush administrations that waited to initiate investigations until complaints were filed against schools and universities.

Prior to Cantu's reinterpretation, schools were required to meet the interests and abilities of women only to the same degree as they met the interests and abilities of men. Cantu's directive instructed that the interests of only the underrepresented sex be ful-

ly accommodated. This reinterpretation served as an indication that compliance with Title IX required more than the provision of equal opportunity for women in athletics; it required remedial action. Cantu also put both the NCAA and its member institutions on notice that the federal government backed the Title IX compliance evolving in the courts. Ten months later, the First Circuit of the U.S. Court of Appeals confirmed the lower courts decision and in April 1997, the Supreme Court denied review thereby letting the lower court's ruling stand. The message was not lost on other schools and their lawyers. Since then, the safest and surest way to comply with Title IX has been by ensuring that statistical quotas are met.

As a result, colleges have proceeded to cut men's teams as the surest means of complying with Title IX. For instance, in the hearings before the U.S. Department of Education, Secretary's Commission on Opportunity in Athletics, Christine Stolba, a senior Fellow with the Independent Women's Forum, testified that between 1993 and 1999, 53 men's golf teams, 39 men's track teams, 43 wrestling teams and baseball teams have been eliminated. The University of Miami's diving team, which had produced 15 Olympic athletes, has also been eliminated. Furthermore, in 2001, the General Accounting Office, reported that between 1981 and 1999, 171 men's wrestling programs, 83 men's tennis teams and 56 men's gymnastics teams, had been eliminated.

These men, whose opportunities to play sports are being denied, have a valid argument that they are victims of reverse discrimination. Men's teams are being cut and opportunities to play are being denied in order to create the required number of male and female athletes. Not only is this inequitable, but it may also have an impact on the Olympic movement in the United States. College athletics is a primary source for our nation's Olympic athletes; therefore, as the number of men's teams is reduced, the number of potential Olympic athletes is also reduced.

Some argue that this is a spending choice. Colleges and universities facing budget cuts choose to cut men's teams rather than cut money and players to sports like football that bring revenue and name recognition to the school. On the one hand, large division 1-A football programs could do a lot to alleviate some of the division between the two sides of this debate by curbing some of the excesses in their programs. On the other hand, division 1-A football programs are more of an exception to the rule. According to Bill Curry, a former college football coach and ESPN game analyst, in 2002, only 17.2% of college football teams were Division 1-A. These are the teams that need the large number of scholarships to field championship teams. Two-thirds of these programs produce revenue for their universities.

When it comes to complying with Title IX under the proportionality rule, however, it is not a budget issue; it is a Title IX issue. Money is beside the point; Title IX deals with the number of bodies on the playing field. As an example, in 1994, Marquette University cut its men's wrestling team. There was no budget issue. At the time, it was the alumni who funded the wrestling team. The real issue was that the number of male wrestlers, more than 30, skewed the overall number of male-to-female athletes at Marquette. Women made up 54% of Marquette's student body compared to only 46% of its student athletes. Marquette University, thus, dropped wrestling in order to comply with Title IX and remain NCAA certified. Furthermore, Marquette University does not have a football team, so football cannot be blamed as a blanket issue.

Also relevant is the number of male versus female walk-on athletes. Studies show

that men's team rosters are bigger than women's because more men walk-on than women. If it was really about budget issues then schools wouldn't be turning away non-scholarship, walk-on athletes who don't cost the school very much. Cost has nothing to do with it. Instead, it has to do with a quota over which men's participation cannot go and under which women's participation cannot go. Why should men be penalized because they walk on and women don't?

In response, supporters of the current method of implementation argue that women's demonstrated interest in sports is not a true measure of equality because it fails to consider the potential for female athletic participation. They contend that women turn out to play sports at a lower rate than men as a result of past discrimination against female athletes. It is true that, culturally, in the past women were not encouraged to play sports. Only recently have women athletes become truly accepted role models for future generations. The UCONN women's basketball team, for instance, only began charging for its games in 1993. By the late 90's, every game was sold out. According to this argument, therefore, Title IX needs to ensure that the opportunity exists for women to achieve their full athletic potential. If the opportunities are created, women will want to play these sports. In other words, if you build it, they will come.

Congress, however, did not pass a law thirty years ago that said it was the responsibility of colleges and universities to create interest in athletics. It passed a law that barred discrimination based on sex. The point is not whether or not making sure women reach their full athletic potential is a good idea or not. It's about interpreting the law correctly. If we want schools and universities to create athletic opportunities for women then we need to pass a law for that purpose. Title IX isn't that law. Furthermore, Congress has never amended Title IX in the years since 1972; instead, the executive branch has progressively changed Title IX's meaning through successive reinterpretations of its implementation policy. The eventual consequence of the U.S. Department of Education's Secretary's Commission on Opportunity in Athletics will be further development in Title IX's meaning.

Those who oppose changing the current interpretation of Title IX, such as Judith Sweet, argue that Title IX policy has been directly responsible for changing women's opportunities in education and sport. Title IX's compliance standards should, therefore, not be changed because athletic opportunities for girls and women in athletics are not yet equitable. Evidence suggests, however, that by the time Title IX passed in 1972 the revolution in women's sport had already begun. Women's participation in sport began to increase significantly before Title IX's passage in 1972 and well before the executive enacted Title IX's final policy interpretation in 1979 which established

Title IX's enforcement guidelines. For instance, according to Cavora, "between 1971 and 1972, the number of girls playing high school sports jumped almost threefold, from 294,015 to 817,073." Furthermore, the number of women participating in intercollegiate athletics doubled in the five years *before* Title IX from around 15,000 to 30,000. Although it was the government that created the statute and regulations to enforce the principal of not using the people's money to deny access, it was the changing social environment that led women to seek such access in the first place.

It is clear that Title IX is still needed as a means of ensuring equal opportunities for women in education and athletics. There must be, however, a better way of implementing this law. If courts and policy makers recognize that Title IX guarantees equal opportunity, but does not necessarily guarantee equal outcomes, then they can return to the original intent of Title IX and restore the integrity of this policy's interpretation and implementation.

## THE CONTINUING DEBATE:
## The Department of Education and Title IX

### What Is New

In June 2002, the ongoing uproar over the application of Title IX prompted Secretary of Education Secretary Roderick Paige to create the Commission on Opportunity in Athletics to examine the implementation of Title IX. The 18-member panel was divided evenly between men and women and included individuals with backgrounds in government, academia, and athletics. On February 26, 2003, the Commission submitted several recommendations to Paige, two of which were highly controversial. These drew furious dissent from some of the commissioners, numerous interest groups, and several prominent members of Congress, both Democrat and Republican. One was that the Secretary of Education be allowed to formulate a "reasonable variance" from existing Title IX standards to measure compliance. Opponents of this change argued that "close enough" was not a satisfactory benchmark. The second controversial recommendation was to authorize the secretary to establish "additional ways of demonstrating equity." Proponents of Title IX fretted this vaguely worded standard could be used to gut enforcement. Whether he agreed with these criticisms or was averse to a political donnybrook, Paige announced in July 2003 that he would not act on either of the controversial recommendations.

### Where to Find More

Information about Title IX and the Commission on Opportunity in Athletics is available on the Department of Education site: http://www.ed.gov/about/bdscomm/list/athletics/qsandas.html. Two articles that take opposing views on Title IX are Michael Lynch, "Title IX's Pyrrhic Victory," *Reason*, April 2001 (http://reason.com/0104/fe.ml.title.shtml); and Mariah Burton Nelson, "And Now They Tell Us Women Don't Really Like Sports?" *Ms. Magazine*, January 2003 (http://www.mariahburtonnelson.com/WomenSportsMsTitleIX.html). For a group that criticizes Title IX, go to the Web site of the Independent Women's Forum at http://www.iwf.org/ and click "issues" on the top. The opposite stance is taken by the National Women's Law Center. Among other things, its Web site (http://www.nwlc.org/) lists 30 colleges which it charges are not in compliance with Title IX.

### What More to Do

One thing to do is to visit the Web site of the National Women's Law Center to see if your school is on the list of 30 colleges the Center says are in particular violation of Title IX. Look at the data provided at the site. Assuming it is true, do you agree with the Center? You can also contact the office of your school's athletic department to get comparable data for your college. How does it stand? Also, you can help Secretary of Education Paige come up with Title IX enforcement standards with which everyone can agree. Draft a department regulation detailing how compliance will be measured.

# JUDICIARY

## LEGAL PHILOSOPHY AS A QUALIFICATION FOR THE BENCH:
### Judicious Standard *or* Obstructionist Barrier?

### JUDICIOUS STANDARD

**ADVOCATE:** Laurence H. Tribe, Professor, Harvard Law School

**SOURCE:** Testimony during hearings on "Judicial Nominations, Filibusters, and the Constitution: When a Majority Is Denied Its Right to Consent," before U.S. Senate Committee on the Judiciary, May 6, 2002

### OBSTRUCTIONIST BARRIER

**ADVOCATE:** Todd F. Gaziano, Senior Fellow in Legal Studies and Director, Center for Legal and Judicial Studies, The Heritage Foundation

**SOURCE:** Testimony during hearings on "A Judiciary Diminished Is Justice Denied: The Constitution, the Senate, and the Vacancy Crisis in the Federal Judiciary" before U.S. House of Representatives, Committee on the Judiciary, Subcommittee on the Constitution, October 10, 2002

The power of federal judges to make policy underlies this debate. As Supreme Court Chief Justice Charles Evans Hughes once put it, "We are under a Constitution, but the Constitution is what the judges say it is." This ability to make policy has two sources. One is the power of interpretation, the ability to find meaning in the words of the Constitution and legislative acts. There is considerable controversy about whether judges should follow "original intent," but many judges adhere to the alternative philosophy of Justice Oliver Wendell Holmes, Jr. that the Constitution should be interpreted "in the light of our whole experience and not merely in that of what was said a hundred years ago."

The courts also make policy through the power of judicial review: the determination of whether state and federal laws and actions taken by officials are constitutional. The policy implications of this power are evident in the cases of *Plessy v. Ferguson* (1896), in which the Supreme Court ruled that separate but equal racial accommodations (in this case in railroad cars) was constitutional, and *Brown v. Board of Education* (1954), in which the court reversed itself and ruled that separate but equal accommodations (in this case in schools) was unconstitutional. U.S. policy changed because nine justices in 1954 saw things differently than nine justices had in 1896.

The powers of judicial review and interpretation that federal judges, particularly Supreme Court justices, possess means that their appointments have important policy ramifications. This is intensified by the rarity of Supreme Court vacancies. Since 1789, there have been 44 presidents but only 18 chief justices, and there have been nearly 12,000 members of Congress, compared to 108 chief and associate justices.

Historically, the willingness of the Senate to usually confirm Supreme Court nominees Court has ebbed and flowed. At first, legislative challenges were common.

From 1789 to 1900, the Senate did not confirm 23 individuals, or about one-third of all nominees to the Supreme Court. Partisanship was often the reason. For example, George Washington's nomination in 1795 of John Rutledge as chief justice was defeated by Federalist Party senators who were offended that Rutledge had opposed the Jay Treaty with Great Britain.

By contrast, during the first half of the 20th century, senators rejected only one nominee to the high court. Many nominees, including Earl Warren, did not even appear before the Senate Judiciary Committee. This was changed by the surprisingly liberal record established as chief justice by Warren, a Republican governor of California appointed by Republican President Dwight Eisenhower. Since 1955, all nominees have testified during the confirmation process. Moreover, the process has become more contentious, with six Supreme Court nominees rejected since 1968. Especially during the terms of Bill Clinton and George W. Bush, resistance to appointments has also increasingly affected nominations to lower courts.

It is important to point out that the issue is not simply presidents appointing members of their own party to the bench. That has been the overwhelming historical norm, which only makes sense given the data that shows, among recent appointments, Democratic judges tend to take liberal positions and Republican judges are more apt to take conservative positions in their rulings.

Compounding the debate, there is controversy over the process. Particularly contentious is the practice in the Senate of members sometimes using a filibuster (a tactic of halting business by speaking continuously) to block confirmation. A filibuster can be halted by a cloture vote, but that is difficult to actuate because it takes 60 votes to pass.

## POINTS TO PONDER

➤ Laurence Tribe explains why he opposed the nomination to the Supreme Court of Robert Bork, a nominee of impressive experience (judge of the U.S. Circuit Court of Appeals, Yale law professor, Solicitor General, Acting U.S. attorney general). What is Tribe's reasoning? Do you agree?

➤ Todd F. Gaziano argues "the confirmation process…needs to be fixed somehow." Why does he think it is broken? Who does he hold responsible?

➤ Can the inherently political nomination and confirmation process be expected to create a neutral, apolitical judiciary?

# Legal Philosophy as a Qualification for the Bench: Judicious Standard

## Laurence H. Tribe

I am honored to have been invited...to shed whatever light I can on the extremely important, and hopefully not too timely, topic of the Senate's role in the consideration of presidential nominations to the Supreme Court of the United States. I say "hopefully not too timely" because I think it wise of the Senate...to focus its attention now—not when a vacancy arises or a name is put forward—on the criteria to be applied in the confirmation process, and particularly on the role of ideology in that process.

There is a difficult trade-off here, to be sure. In Washington, as elsewhere, the squeaky wheel gets the grease. Focusing meaningful attention on an issue before it becomes a problem, much less a crisis, is difficult in the best of circumstances. Doing so when the issue is as abstract and complex as that of confirmation criteria for Supreme Court Justices is more difficult still. Yet waiting until the matter is upon us, complete with a name or a short list of names, with interest groups and spinmeisters formidably arrayed on both sides, assures that the discussion will resemble a shouting match more than a civil conversation, and that every remark will be filtered through agenda detectors tuned to the highest pitch. On balance, I believe that addressing the question of the Senate's proper role under a veil of ignorance—ignorance as to precisely when a vacancy will first arise, which of the sitting justices will be the first to depart, and which name or names will be brought forth by The White House—seems likeliest to lead to fruitful reflection on how to

proceed when the veil is lifted and we are all confronted with the stark reality of specific names and all that they might portend for the republic.

It is understandable that, partly because of the seemingly abstract and speculative character of such a discussion in the absence of any actual nominee, and partly because the more immediate question actually facing the Senate Judiciary Committee is how best to evaluate a group of nominees already put forward by the President to fill various vacancies in the federal courts of appeals, [you have] chosen to cast its inquiry more broadly than a focus on Supreme Court nominations would indicate and has decided to include in its charge the question of what role ideology should play in considering federal judicial nominations generally. For that reason, at the conclusion of my observations about my principal topic that of Supreme Court nominations I will offer a few thoughts about the broader question....But because I want to preserve to the degree possible the distinct advantages of separating the general question of criteria from any particular nominee or set of nominees, I will carefully avoid saying anything about any pending nomination and will, until the end of my remarks, discuss only the matter of nominations to the Supreme Court.

When my book *God Save This Honorable Court* was published in 1985 defending an active role for the Senate in the appointment of Supreme Court Justices, the Court was delicately balanced, with liberals like William Brennan and Thurgood Marshall offsetting conservatives like William Rehnquist and Antonin Scalia.

Yet, on the inevitable book tour, I found quite a few otherwise well-informed people wondering why the composition of the Supreme Court was all that big a deal, and why it shouldn't suffice for the Senate simply to make sure that the President wasn't packing the Court with cronies and with mediocrities. Having satisfied itself of the professional qualifications and character of the President's nominee, some people wondered, why should the Senate be concerned with that nominee's philosophical leanings or ideological predispositions?

People seemed to view things differently when they were exposed to the historical background showing that the Framers contemplated a much more central role for the Senate in this process, and when they learned that it was mostly the unwieldiness of having a collective body like the Senate make the initial nomination that led the Framers [of the Constitution], at the last minute in the drafting process, to entrust the nomination to the President and to leave the Senate with the task of deciding whether to confirm or reject; that, even in the final version of the Constitution as ratified in 1789, the Senate's task was not left wholly passive (deciding between a thumbs-up and a thumbs-down) but was cast as the role of giving its "advice and consent;" and that, with the exception of an uncharacteristic lull in the last century, the Senate has traditionally exercised its advice and consent function with respect to the Supreme Court in a lively and engaged manner, concerning itself not simply with the intellect and integrity of the nominee but with the nominee's overall approach to the task of judging, and often with the nominee's substantive views on the burning legal and constitutional issues of the day. Those who initially assumed the Senate need not concern itself with a nominee's ideology tended to view the matter in a new light when reminded that, both in

the formative days of our nation's history, under presidents as early as George Washington, and in recent decades, there has been a venerable tradition in which the Senate has played anything but a deferential role on Supreme Court nominations.

All of that registered with people back in 1985, but it wasn't until the 1987 resignation of [Justice] Lewis Powell and the confirmation battle later that year over Robert Bork that the concrete stakes in this otherwise abstract controversy came to life for the great majority of the American public. In retrospect, although one can lament the ways in which some interest groups and politicians—on both sides of the question, frankly—exaggerated the record bearing on Judge Bork's views and bearing on what kind of Supreme Court Justice he would have made, the fact is that his confirmation hearings represented an important education for large segments of the public on such fundamental matters as the meaning of the due process and liberty guarantees of the Fifth and Fourteenth Amendments to the Constitution, the relevance and limits of the Ninth Amendment's reference to unenumerated rights, the connection between various ways of approaching the Constitution's text and history and such particular unenumerated rights as personal privacy and reproductive freedom, the relationship between a tightly constrained and literalist reading of the Constitution in matters of personal rights and a more open-textured and fluid reading of the Constitution in matters bearing on state's rights, and a host of other topics of enduring significance.

For my own part, as one of the expert witnesses called to testify about Judge Bork's constitutional philosophy and about the consequences for the nation were he to gain an opportunity to implement that philosophy as a Supreme Court

Justice, I make no apology for anything I said at the time. Knowing full well that my testimony would put me on the enemies' lists of some extremely powerful people with very long memories, I felt it my duty to testify to the truth as I understood it. I would do the same thing again today. When the Senate finally rejected the nomination of Robert Bork, many of his allies cried "foul" and have since practiced decades of payback politics. Indeed, they have even succeeded, with the aid of some revisionist history, in adding to the vocabulary the highly misleading new verb, "to Bork"—meaning, "to smear a nominee with distorted accusations about his or her record and views"—as though the predictions of the sort of justice Robert Bork would have become were in some way misleading or otherwise unfair.

But the truth, as Judge Bork's post-rejection writings made amply clear, was just as his critics had indicated. Unless being confirmed would have caused him to undergo a radical conversion—something on which the nation has a right not to gamble—his rejection, and the subsequent confirmation of Justice Kennedy in his stead, meant one less member on the far right wing of the Court and left Justice Scalia (later with Justice Thomas) holding down the starboard alone. The nation had held a referendum on the Borkian approach to reading the Constitution of the United States, and the Borkian approach had decisively lost. And, lest it be supposed that I review this history simply to reprise a political episode that was painful for all concerned, I should make plain that my purpose is altogether different. It is to remove the fangs from the verb "to Bork" and to restore some perspective, lest anyone be misled into beginning the debate over the Senate's proper role with the erroneous premise that the Senate should be less than proud of the last

instance in which it rejected a Supreme Court nominee on ideological grounds.

Today, it takes very little effort to persuade any informed citizen that the identity of who serves on the Supreme Court of the United States matters enormously—matters not simply to the resolution of these large questions of how the Constitution is to be approached and how its multiple ambiguities are to be addressed, but as well in the disposition of the most mundane, and yet basic, questions of how we lead our lives as Americans. Whether laws enacted for the benefit of the elderly or the disabled are to be rendered virtually unenforceable in circumstances where the violator is a state agency and the victim cannot obtain meaningful redress without going to federal court; whether people stopped in their cars for minor offenses like failing to have a seatbelt properly attached to a child's car seat may be handcuffed and taken by force to the police station where they are arrested and booked and held overnight; whether police may use sense-enhancing technologies like special heat detectors to peer through the walls of our homes in order to detect the details of what we do there; whether, having recognized that everything we do in the privacy of our homes counts as an intimate detail when it comes to protecting us from various kinds of search and surveillance, judges will nonetheless continue to let state legislatures regulate the most intimate sexual details of what we do behind closed doors with those we love; whether government may forbid the kind of research that might prove essential to the prevention and cure of devastating degenerative diseases whenever that research uses stem cells or other tissues from embryos created in clinics for infertile couples—embryos that would otherwise be discarded without making such life-generating new knowledge possible; what kinds of campaign finance restrictions are to be permitted when the broad values of democracy seem pitted against the specific rights of individuals and corporations to use their wealth to purchase as much media time as money can buy; who is to be the next President of the United States—these are just some of the questions whose answers have come to turn on a single vote of a single Supreme Court Justice.

The battle that was fought over the nomination of Judge Bork to become Justice Bork was fought because the general approach to constitutional interpretation that he seemed to represent attracted him to some but frightened an even larger number. Most dramatic among the anticipated consequences of his confirmation would have been the addition of his vote and voice to the far right wing of the Court on such issues as reproductive freedom, which the Constitution of course never mentions in so many words. His confirmation, people came to recognize despite his avowals of open-mindedness on all such matters, would have meant the certain demise of *Roe v. Wade* [1973, permitting abortions], a decision whose most recent application, in last year's "partial birth abortion" case from Nebraska, was, after all these years, still 5 to 4—as are a large number of crucial decisions about personal privacy, gender discrimination, sexual orientation, race-based affirmative action, legislative apportionment, church-state separation, police behavior, and a host of other basic issues.

After the Supreme Court's highly controversial and I believe profoundly misguided performance last December in the case of *Bush v. Gore* [2000, regarding the Florida electoral vote]—in which I should acknowledge I played a role as author of the briefs for Vice President Gore and as oral advocate in the first of the two Supreme Court arguments in the case—it's difficult to find anyone who any longer

questions why it matters so much who serves on the court. The significance of *Bush v. Gore* in this setting doesn't depend on anybody's prediction of who would have won the vote-count in Florida had the counting gone on without the Supreme Court's dramatic and sudden interruption on December 9, 2000, or of who would have been chosen the next President by Congress this January 6 if the Supreme Court had let the constitutional processes operate as designed and if competing electoral slates had been sent from Tallahassee, Florida to Washington, D.C. The great significance of the case is to underscore that, by a margin of a single vote, the branch of our government that is least politically accountable—wisely and designedly so, when matters of individual and minority rights or of basic government structure are at stake—treated the American electorate and the electoral process with a disdain that a differently composed Court would have found unthinkable. So it was that, when push came to shove, and the Supreme Court's faith in democracy was tested, the Supreme Court blinked. It distrusted the people who were doing the counting, it distrusted the state judges, it distrusted the members of Congress to whom the dispute might have been thrown if it hadn't pulled down the curtain. And the Court could get away with it, partly because nobody in the House or Senate, to be brutally honest, relished the thought of discharging the constitutional responsibility of deciding which electoral votes to count and then facing his or her own constituents—and because the people were growing weary of the no longer very sexy or novel topic of dimpled ballots and hanging chads, and Christmas was just around the corner, and, after all, everyone knew that the election was basically too close to call anyway. Lost for some in all of that realism, I fear, was the high price our democracy paid for the convenience of a Court that was willing—no, not just willing, positively eager—to take those burdens from our shoulders and simply decree a result. Among the results is an unprecedented degree of political polarization in the Court's favorability rating with the public—a rating that now stands roughly twice as high among Republicans as among Democrats, surely an ominous gap for the one institution to which we look for action transcending politics.

This isn't the time or place to debate the details of *Bush v. Gore*, a subject about which I have written elsewhere; I stress the case because it shows at least as dramatically as any case possibly could just how much may depend on the composition of the Court; how basic are the questions that the Court at times decides by the closest possible margins; and how absurd are the pretensions and slogans of those who have for years gotten away with saying, and perhaps have deceived even themselves by saying, that the kinds of judges they want on the Court, the "restrained" rather than "activist" kinds of judges, the kinds of judges who don't "legislate from the bench," are the kinds exemplified by today's supposedly "conservative" wing of the Court, led by Chief Justice Rehnquist and supported in area after area by Justices O'Connor, Scalia, Kennedy, and Thomas. Those are, of course, the five justices who decided the presidential election of 2000. They are, as well, the five justices who have struck down one act of Congress after another—invalidating federal legislation at a faster clip than has any other Supreme Court since before the New Deal—on the basis that the Court and the Court alone is entitled to decide what kinds of state action might threaten religious liberty, might discriminate invidiously against the elderly or the disabled, or might otherwise warrant action by Congress in the discharge of its solemn constitutional power under Section 5 of the Fourteenth Amendment to determine what legislation is necessary and appropriate to protect liberty and equality in America.

Some might be tempted, after watching the Court perform so poorly in the pit of presidential politics, and after witnessing it substitute its policy judgments for those of Congress in one legislative arena after another, to imagine that, if we could only wave a magic wand and remove all ideological considerations from judicial selection—both on the part of the President in making nominations and on the part of the Senate in the confirmation process—somehow the Olympian ideal of a federal judiciary once again above politics and beyond partisan reproach could be restored. For several reasons, that is a dangerous illusion. First, there's no way for the Senate to prevent the President from doing what Presidents from the beginning of the republic have asserted the right to do, and what some Presidents have done more successfully than others: pick nominees who will mirror the President's preferred approach to the Constitution's vast areas of ambiguity. Second, in dealing with those areas of ambiguity, there may or may not be any right answers, but there most assuredly are no unique or uncontroversial answers; invariably, in choosing one Supreme Court nominee rather than another, one is making a choice among those answers, and among the approaches that generate them. And third, with a Supreme Court that is already so dramatically tilted in a rightward direction, anything less than a concerted effort to set the balance straight would mean perpetuating the imbalance that gave us not only *Bush v. Gore* but the myriad decisions in the preceding half-dozen years in which the

Court thumbed its nose at Congress and thus at the American people.

In an accompanying memorandum that I prepared for distribution this April to a number of members of the Senate, I explore in greater detail how these recent Supreme Court encroachments on congressional authority have come about and what they signify. For purposes of my statement today, suffice it to say that such encroachments are the antithesis of judicial restraint or modesty; that the justices who have engineered them are the most activist in our history; that holding them up as exemplars of jurists who would never dream of "legislating from the bench" is, to put it mildly, an exercise in dramatic license; and that the judgments the Senate will have to make about the inclinations and proclivities of prospective members of the Supreme Court must be considerably more nuanced than the stereotypical slogans and bumper stickers about activism vs. restraint, and even liberalism vs. conservatism, can possibly accommodate.

Some scholars, including most prominently University of Chicago Law Professor Cass Sunstein,...have powerfully argued that an active, nondeferential, role for the Senate in evaluating Supreme Court nominees is called for, quite independent of *Bush v. Gore*, by the way in which the federal judiciary in general, and the Supreme Court in particular, have been systematically stacked over the past few decades in a particular ideological direction—a direction hostile, for example, to the enactment of protective congressional legislation under Section 5 of the Fourteenth Amendment, and hostile as well to other ostensibly "liberal" or "progressive" judicial positions, on topics ranging from privacy to affirmative action, from states' rights to law enforcement. For Professor Sunstein,...the active role the Senate ought to play is exactly as

it would have been had *Bush v. Gore* never been decided.

Other scholars, most prominently Yale University Law Professor Bruce Ackerman, argue that *Bush v. Gore* has thrown the process of judicial appointment into what Professor Ackerman calls "constitutional disequilibrium," so that, instead of two independent structural checks on a necessarily unrepresentative and politically unaccountable Supreme Court, we are now down to just one. Because, in his view, the current Court must be acknowledged to have "mediated" the "President's relationship to the citizenry"—by helping put him in office by a 5 to 4 vote—"only the Senate retains a normal connection to the electorate," and this demands of that body, as Professor Ackerman sees it, that it shoulder an unusually heavy share of the burden of democratic control, by the people acting through the political branches, of the judicial branch to which we ordinarily look to hold the balance true. Translated into an operational prescription, the Ackerman position would recommend that the Senate simply refuse to confirm any new justices to the Court before President Bush, as Professor Ackerman puts it, "win[s] the 2004 election fair and square, without the Court's help." As a fallback, Professor Ackerman would urge the Senate to consider any nominations President Bush might make to the Court during his current term on their own merits, but without what Ackerman describes as "the deference accorded ordinary presidents."

Although I am intrigued by Professor Ackerman's suggestion, it seems to me the wrong way to go, either in its strongest form or in its fallback version. The strongest form would make sense, I think, only if we were convinced that the justices who voted with the majority in *Bush v. Gore* acted in a manner so corrupt and illegitimate, so devoid of legal justification, that one could say they essentially installed George W. Bush as president in a bloodless but lawless coup. But if we believed that, then the remedy of not letting the leaders of that coup profit from their own wrong of denying them the solace of like-minded successors as they depart the scene—would be far too mild. If we thought the Bush majority guilty of a coup, we should have to conclude that they were guilty of treason to the Constitution, and that they should be impeached, convicted, and removed from office.

Believing that what the *Bush v. Gore* majority did was gravely wrong but not that it amounted to a coup or indeed anything like it— believing that the majority justices acted not to install their favorite candidate but out of a misguided sense that the nation was in grave and imminent peril unless they stopped the election at once—one would have to look to the Ackerman fallback position. But all it tells us is something that I argued was the case anyway as early as 1985— that the Senate should not accord any special deference to nominations made by any President to the Supreme Court. Indeed, I go further than does Professor Sunstein in this respect. As I understand his position, he would have the Senate withhold such deference for reasons peculiar to the recent history of the nation and of appointments to the federal bench and especially to the Supreme Court over the past few decades. Had we not lived through a time of Republican Presidents insistent on, and adept at, naming justices who would carry on their ideological program in judicial form, sandwiching Democratic Presidents uninterested in, or inept at, naming justices similarly attuned to their substantive missions, Professor Sunstein would apparently urge that the Senate give the President his head in these matters and serve only in a backseat capacity, to pre-

vent rogues and fools, more or less, from being elevated to the High Court.

In a world in which each position on the Supreme Court might be given to some idealized version of the wisest lawyer in the land—the most far-sighted and scholarly, the most capable of clearly explaining the Constitution's language and mission, the most adept at generating consensus in support of originally unpopular positions that come to be seen as crucial to the defense of human rights—perhaps we could afford in normal times to accept a posture of Senatorial deference, with exceptions made in special historical periods of the sort some believe we have been living through. But if we ever lived in a world where such a universal paragon of justice could be imagined, and in which the kinds of issues resolved by Supreme Court Justices were not invariably contested, often bitterly so, between competing visions of the right, that day has long since passed.

Today, regardless of whether past Presidents have acted or failed to act so as to produce a Supreme Court bench leaning lopsidedly in a rightward direction, and regardless of whether a majority of the current Court has acted in such a way as to render the President whom it helped to elect less entitled to deference than usual in naming the successors of the Court's current members, the inescapable fact is that the President will name prospective justices about whom he knows a great deal more than the Senate can hope to learn—justices whose paper trail, if the President is skillful about it, will reveal much less to the Senate than the President thinks he knows. Given his allies and those to whom he owes his political victory, as well as those on whom he will need to depend for his re-election, the incumbent President, if those constituencies expect him to leave his mark and therefore theirs upon the Court, will try to name justices who will fulfill the agenda of those constituencies—in the case of President Bush, the agenda of the right—without seeming by their published statements or their records as jurists to be as committed to that agenda as the President will privately believe them to be. Presumably, the incumbent President will look for such nominees among the ranks of Hispanic jurists, or women, or both, in order to distract the opposition and make resistance more painful. And certainly this President, like any other in modern times, will select nominees who have already mastered or can be coached in the none too difficult game of answering questions thoughtfully and without overt deception but in ways calculated to offend no-one and reveal nothing.

In this circumstance, to say that the burden is on those who hold the power of advice and consent to show that there is something disqualifying about the nominee, that there is a smoking gun in the record or a wildly intemperate publication in the bibliography or some other fatal flaw that can justify a rallying cry of opposition, is to guarantee that the President will have the Court of his dreams without the Senate playing any meaningful role whatsoever. Therefore, if the Senate's role is to be what the Framers contemplated, what history confirms, and what a sound appreciation for the realities of American politics demands, the burden must instead be on the nominee and, indeed, on the President. That burden must be to persuade each Senator—for, in the end, this is a duty each Senator must discharge in accord with his or her own conscience—that the nominee's experience, writings, speeches, decisions, and actions affirmatively demonstrate not only the exceptional intellect and wisdom and integrity that greatness as a judge demands but also the understanding of and commitment to those constitutional rights and values and

ideals that the Senator regards as important for the republic to uphold.

On this standard, stealth nominees should have a particularly hard time winning confirmation. For proving on the basis of a blank slate the kinds of qualities that the Senate ought to demand, with a record that is unblemished because it is without content, ought to be exceedingly difficult. Testimony alone, however eloquent and reassuring, ought rarely to suffice where its genuineness is not confirmed by a history of action in accord with the beliefs professed. And testimony, in any event, is bound to be clouded by understandable reservations about compromising judicial independence by asking the nominee to commit himself or herself too specifically in advance to how he or she would vote on particular cases that might, in one variant or another, come before the Court. Interestingly, we do not regard sitting justices as having compromised their independence by having written about, and voted on, many of the issues they must confront year in and year out; the talk about compromising judicial independence by asking about such issues sometimes reflects unthinking reflex more than considered judgment. But on the assumption that old habits die hard, and that members of the Senate Judiciary Committee will continue to be rather easily cowed into backing away from asking probing questions about specific issues that might arise during the nominee's service on the Court, it should still be possible to formulate questions for any nominee, including tough follow-up questions, at a level of generality just high enough so that the easy retreat into "I'm sorry, Senator, I can't answer that question because the matter might come before me," will be unavailing. And, to the extent such slightly more general questions yield information too meager for informed judgment, the burden must be on the nominee to satisfy his or her interlocutors that the concern underlying the thwarted line of questioning is one that ought not to disturb the Senator. That satisfaction can be provided only from a life lived in the law that exemplifies, rather than eschewing, a real engagement with problems of justice, with challenges of human rights, and with the practical realities of making law relevant to people's needs. When a nominee cannot provide that satisfaction—when the nominee is but a fancy resume in an empty suit or a vacant dress, perhaps adorned with a touching story of a hard-luck background or of ethnic roots—any Senator who takes his or her oath of office as seriously as I know, deep down, all of you do, should simply say, "No thanks, Mr. President. Send us another nominee."

What this adds up to is, of course, a substantial role for ideology in the consideration of any Supreme Court nominee. It would be naive to the point of foolhardiness to imagine that the President will be tone-deaf to signals of ideological compatibility or incompatibility with his view of the ideal Supreme Court justice; ideology will invariably matter to any President and must therefore matter to any Senator who is not willing simply to hand over to the White House his or her proxy for the discharge of the solemn duty to offer advice and consent.

As a postscript on the distinct subject of circuit court nominees, it seems worth noting that, although such nominees are of course strictly bound by Supreme Court precedents and remain subject to correction by that Court, and although there might therefore seem to be much less reason for the Senate to be ideologically vigilant than in the case of the Supreme Court, three factors militate in favor of at least a degree of ideological oversight even at the circuit court level.

First, well under 1% of the decisions of the circuit courts are actually reviewed by the Supreme Court, which avowedly declines to review even clearly erroneous decisions unless they present some special circumstance such as a circuit conflict. Especially if the circuit courts tend toward a homogeneity that mirrors the ideological complexion of the Supreme Court, that tribunal is exceedingly unlikely to use its discretionary power of review on certiorari to police lower federal courts that stray from the reservation in one direction or another; it will instead focus its firepower on bringing the state courts into line and resolving intolerable conflicts among the lower courts, state and federal.

Second, there are a great many gray areas in which Supreme Court precedents leave the circuit courts a wide berth within which to maneuver without straying into a danger zone wherein further review becomes a likely prospect. Even though no individual circuit court judge is very likely to use that elbow room in order to move the law significantly in one direction or another without a check from the Supreme Court, the overall balance and composition of the circuit court bench can have a considerable effect, in momentum if nothing else, on the options realistically open to the Supreme Court and thus to the country.

Third, in the past few decades, the circuit courts have increasingly served as a kind of "farm team" for Supreme Court nominations. On the Court that decided *Brown v. Board of Education* in 1954 there sat not a single justice who, prior to his appointment to the Supreme Court, had ever served in a judicial capacity. Governors, Senators, distinguished members of the bar, but no former judges. Today, however, rare is the nominee who has not previously served in a judicial capacity, most frequently on a federal circuit court. On the current Court, only the

Chief Justice lacked prior judicial experience when he was first named a justice; and, of the other eight justices, all except Justice O'Connor, who had served as a state court judge, were serving on federal circuit courts when appointed to the Court. The reasons for this change are many; they include, most prominently, the growing recognition that ideology matters and that service on a lower court may be one way of detecting a prospective nominee's particular ideological leanings. Whatever the reasons, the reality has independent significance, for it means that any time the Senate confirms someone to serve on a circuit court, it may be making a record that, in the event the judge should later be nominated to the Supreme Court, will come back to haunt it. "But you had no trouble confirming Judge X to the court of appeals for the Y circuit," supporters of Supreme Court nominee X are likely to intone. Keeping that in mind will require the Senate to give fuller consideration to matters of ideology at the circuit court level than it otherwise might.

The primary ideological issue at the circuit court level, however, should probably remain the overall tilt of the federal bench rather than the particular leanings of any given nominee viewed in isolation. In a bench already tilted overwhelmingly in one direction—today, the right—a group of nominees whose ideological center of gravity is such as to exacerbate rather than correct that tilt should be a matter of concern to any Senator who does not regard the existing tilt as altogether healthy.

And one needn't be particularly liberal to have concerns about the existing tilt. Just as a liberal who recognizes that people who share his views might not have all the right answers ought to be distressed by a federal bench composed overwhelmingly of jurists reminiscent of William J. Brennan, Jr. or William O. Douglas—or

even by a federal bench composed almost entirely of liberals and moderates and few conservatives—and just as such a liberal should doubt the wisdom, in confronting such a bench, of adding a group of judges who would essentially replicate that slant, so too a conservative who is humble enough to recognize that people who share her views might not have a lock on the truth should feel dismayed by a federal bench composed overwhelmingly of jurists in the mold of Antonin Scalia or Clarence Thomas—or even by a federal bench composed almost entirely of conservatives and moderates and few liberals—and ought to doubt the wisdom, in dealing with such a bench, of adding many more judges cut from that same cloth. The fundamental truth that ought to unite people across the ideological spectrum, and that only those who are far too sure of themselves to be comfortable in a democracy should find difficult to accept, is that the federal judiciary in general, and the Supreme Court in particular, ought in principle to reflect and represent a wide range of viewpoints and perspectives rather than being clustered toward any single point on the ideological spectrum.

Indeed, even those who feel utterly persuaded of the rightness of their own particular point of view should, in the end, recognize that their arguments can only be sharpened and strengthened by being tested against the strongest of opposing views. Liberals and conservatives alike can be lulled into sloppy and slothful smugness and self-satisfaction unless they are fairly matched on the bench by the worthiest of opponents. It may even be that the astonishing weakness and vulnerability of the Court's majority opinion in *Bush v. Gore*, and of the majority opinions in a number of the other democracy-defying decisions in whose mold it was cast, are functions in part of the uniquely narrow spectrum of views—narrower, I think, than at any other time in our history—covered by the membership of the current Court—a spectrum which, on most issues, essentially runs the gamut from A through C. On a Court with four justices distinctly on the right, two moderate conservatives, a conservative moderate, two moderates, and no liberals, it's easy for the dominant faction to grow lazy and to issue opinions that, preaching solely to the converted, ring hollow to a degree that ill serves both the Court as an institution and the legal system it is sup-

posed to lead. It is thus in the vital interest of the nation as a whole, and not simply in the interest of those values that liberals and progressives hold dear, that the ideological imbalance of the current Supreme Court and of the federal bench as a whole not be permitted to persist, and that the Senate take ideology intelligently into account throughout the judicial confirmation process with a view to gradually redressing what all should come to see as a genuinely dangerous disequilibrium.

# Legal Philosophy as a Qualification for the Bench: Obstructionist Barrier

## Todd F. Gaziano

### A DIMINISHED JUDICIARY: CAUSES AND EFFECTS OF THE SUSTAINED HIGH VACANCY RATES IN THE FEDERAL COURTS

The topic of today's hearing is certainly worthy of this Committee's attention. That you took the time to conduct this hearing so soon before you must recess for the election is further proof that the subject matter is important....

I concur in the statement contained in the hearing title, "A Judiciary Diminished is Justice Denied: the Constitution, the Senate, and the Vacancy Crisis in the Federal Judiciary." Nevertheless, the situation in the federal courts is uneven. There is not yet a crisis across-the-board, even though judicial emergencies have been declared for many courts. On close examination, the consequences of the high vacancy rate are partially ameliorated by the hard work of the judicial branch itself. That said, many federal appellate circuits have had such sustained high vacancy rates that it is straining the justice system mightily and has contributed to at least the perception of judicial manipulation in some very important cases.

The obvious cause of the vacancy crisis is the U.S. Senate's conscious refusal to act in a timely manner on many of the President's judicial nominations. The near complete breakdown in the judicial confirmation process as it relates to United States court of appeals nominees is worthy of special attention and concern. It is simply not possible to justify the stonewalling and other improper committee action on the grounds of payback or any other excuse. In 1997 when the vacancy rate on the appellate courts was less than half of what it is now the current Chairman of the Senate Judiciary Committee, Patrick Leahy [D-VT] said the situation was a "crisis" that interfered with the administration of justice. The current state is nothing less than a dramatic failure of the Senate's constitutional duty to provide its advice and consent to presidential appointments. It is also a violation of the Senate's obligation of comity to the executive and judicial branches of government, which is a vital aspect of the separation of powers.

The result is not just limited to shame on the Senate, however. The Senate's actions have begun to impair the judicial branch's ability to perform its constitutional functions. That impairment is limited at this point, but the impairment grows steadily as the period of sustained judicial vacancies is extended. The House Constitution Subcommittee is right to explore the implications of the Senate's failure.

### THE CONSTITUTIONAL FRAMEWORK OF ANALYSIS

The United States Constitution provides that the President "shall nominate, and by and with the Advice and Consent of the Senate, shall appoint...Judges of the Supreme Court, and all other [Principal] Officers of the United States, whose Appointments are not herein otherwise provided for." That clause further provides that "Congress may by Law vest the Appointment of such inferior Officers, as they think proper, in the President alone, in the Courts of Law, or in the Heads of

Departments." All federal judges below the Supreme Court are inferior in the judicial sense.

Lower court judges might also be "inferior Officers" for Appointments Clause purposes for whom Congress could vest the appointment in either the President or the Supreme Court alone. But Congress (or the Senate) has chosen to retain its power to pass on all judicial nominations. That is its prerogative. Yet, that choice underscores the Senate's duty, which extends to the other two branches of government and to the citizens who rely on the justice system, to provide its advice and consent in good faith and in a timely manner.

Scholars of the founding period have examined the historical record to illuminate some issues that I will only briefly address here. For example, there is evidence [in *Federalist* Nos. 76–77] that the framers of the Constitution expected every presidential nominee to be voted on by the entire Senate and feared the arbitrary exercise of appointment power by a small committee. That seems clear, but I am unsure whether the text of the Appointments Clause, which confers the advice and consent role to the entire Senate, requires the Senate to act on every nomination. Those I respect have opined that the Constitution does not permit a committee of the Senate to block a nomination, but I am still dubious of that proposition. The Rules Clause that allows the Senate to make its own rules of procedure may permit the entire Senate to delegate its agenda-setting function to a committee.

Others have interpreted the Senate Rules to require a full-Senate vote on presidential nominations regardless of what the relevant committee recommends. In my view, Senate Rule XXXI is ambiguous. It requires referral of all presidential nominations to "appropriate committees," and it further states that "the final question on

every nomination shall be, 'Will the Senate advise and consent to this nomination?'" Does that simply specify what the final question shall be on "every nomination" that is referred back to the full Senate or does that imply that the final question must be asked for "every nomination?" The Senate parliamentarians have given it the first construction.

I have not studied in depth either the constitutional question or the related question regarding the Senate rules in part because there is ultimately no remedy—apart from shame—for the violation of such a requirement. Assuming a disappointed nominee with standing filed a suit to force a full-Senate vote on his nomination, the courts would almost surely rule that the case presented a "political question" and decline to rule on the matter under its "political questions" doctrine. As for the tactic of urging shame, many other aspects of the confirmation process should have generated more shame. But it is still appropriate for citizens to add their voice to the chorus.

In that vein, the full Senate ought to vote on each one of the President's nominees to high office. The Senate should do so as a matter of prudence and in keeping with the comity that is required of each branch of government to the others, whether the Constitution or the Senate's current rules require such a vote or not. This is particularly true for those who have been nominated for a lifetime post in the judicial branch. The procedures the Senate adopts for such nominations affect more than just the business of the Senate; they also touch on the constitutional obligations of both other branches of government. The President has the obligation to nominate and appoint judges to fill up vacancies in the federal courts, and confirmed judges are the only individuals who can exercise the power conferred in Article III of the Constitution.

A full-Senate vote is even more appropriate where it is fairly clear that a majority of the Senate would vote to confirm the nominees, which is still the case with Charles Pickering and Pricilla Owen [both nominated by President George W. Bush to the Fifth Circuit Court of Appeals]. Both Pickering and Owen received well-qualified ratings from the American Bar Association (ABA) review panel. In April 2001, Senator Leahy described a positive rating by the ABA as the "gold standard." Gold does not tarnish, so it is unclear why Senator Leahy and other Democrats on his committee have now abandoned their high regard for the ABA review panel.

No Republican senator announced opposition to either Pickering or Owen, and at least one senator from the majority [Democrats] announced support for both of them. Democratic senators who expressed their support for Pickering and Owen are not on the Judiciary Committee, but they sought the opportunity to vote on the nominations. Yet, the Senate Judiciary Committee [at that point controlled by the Democrats] refuses to forward these nominations to the full Senate—even with a negative recommendation, and Majority Leader Tom Daschle [D-SD] does nothing to bring the nominations to the Senate floor. Whether or not the Constitution or the Senate rules require such a full-Senate vote, it is still undemocratic for the current Senate leadership to block a presidential nomination from even being debated on the Senate floor. Ten senators are currently dictating the composition of the federal bench. Even a filibuster by a minority of the Senate would be less cowardly than the current practice.

## THE CAUSE OF SUSTAINED HIGH VACANCIES IN THE FEDERAL COURTS

The most serious problem with the confirmation process is not the Senate Judiciary Committee's refusal to forward nominations that it has acted on to the full Senate, but its refusal to complete its action on most court of appeals nominations. Over the past several decades, the Senate sometimes has slowed down the confirmation process toward the end of a presidential term if the President and Senate majority are from different parties. Although some of President Clinton's judicial nominations were confirmed at the end of the 106th Congress [1999–2000], a slowdown in the last few months and the October adjournment of the 106th Congress contributed to a slightly higher than normal vacancy rate at the beginning of President George W. Bush's administration. (An even more severe slowdown took place at the end of President George H.W. Bush's administration.)

There is always some delay in the judicial nomination process at the start of a new presidential administration. The President possibly could have begun sending judicial nominations to the Senate in March of 2001, but the delayed transition period for President Bush pushed back the normal FBI background check and clearance process for cabinet and sub-cabinet nominees. Some of these officials also help vet potential judges. The pace of President Bush's judicial nominations since early May of 2001 was record setting. Within a year of announcing his first nominees, the President had sent more than 100 judicial nominations to the Senate. The ABA completed its review and supplied its recommendation within about three weeks of each nomination. With one exception, so far the ABA has rated every one of President Bush's nominees either qualified or well-qualified.

Two judges who had received an earlier appointment from President Bill Clinton and a sitting district judge who was acceptable to Louisiana's Democratic senators were promptly confirmed for life-time seats on the appellate courts. Almost all of the remaining nominations languished in the Senate without hearings even being scheduled. For months, the rate of confirmation of all federal judges barely kept pace with retirements. The pace of confirmation of federal district judges has picked up in the past year, but the confirmation process for court of appeals nominees has been set at a glacial pace.

## 1. THE VACANCY STATISTICS AND PERIODS OF UNREASONABLE DELAY BY THE SENATE

In the past, confirmation battles were waged over certain Supreme Court nominees and a very few lower court nominees. As mentioned above, the Senate sometimes slowed down the confirmation process toward the end of a presidential term, but this slowdown was the exception rather than the rule. What's dramatically different now is the systematic refusal to act on many of President Bush's initial nominees, particularly his appellate court nominees. The number of vacancies on the federal courts has actually increased by about fifteen percent since the end of the last Congress. And during this Congress, most of President Bush's initial group of judicial nominees have been waiting for more than 17 months without so much as a hearing and a committee vote.

Based on the practice of many federal judges in announcing their retirement in advance and my review of recent confirmation statistics, I believe that a vacancy rate of about three to four percent represents the "full employment" level (to borrow a term from economists) for the federal judiciary. Yet, the Senate Judiciary Committee's inaction and the Senate's overall slow pace on most of the President's appellate court nominees have resulted in much higher vacancy rates. On the federal district courts, 50 of

665 judge seats (or 7.5%) are vacant. On the federal appellate courts, 27 of 179 judgeships (or 15.1%) are vacant.

Retired Judge (and former U.S. Senator) James Buckley [R-NY] concluded [in a newspaper op-ed piece] that "the Senate's willful failure to act upon a president's judicial nominees can only be described as an obstruction of justice." Judge Buckley pointed out that, when he was a senator, nominees of the caliber nominated by President George W. Bush "would have been confirmed within weeks after their names had been submitted." Yet, it appears that a majority of President Bush's first eleven court of appeals nominees will not even have a committee vote 20 months after they were nominated.

Whether they all deserve to be confirmed or not (and the ABA thinks they are deserving), the Senate's conscious refusal to schedule hearings for most appellate court nominees is a shocking dereliction of duty. There may not be a committee vote by the end of this year for such distinguished professors, Supreme Court advocates, and judges as Deborah Cook, John Roberts, Jeff Sutton, Michael McConnell, Miguel Estrada, Terrence Boyle, and Timothy Tymkovich. That's inexcusable. Moreover, the two who did receive a hearing this fall (Michael McConnell and Miguel Estrada) may have to start the process all over again in 2003 if the full Senate does not vote on their nominations before the end of the current Congress. [The need to start again is because all pending business dies at the end of each two year Congress.]

With regard to court of appeals nominees, the delays are many times worse than at any recent time. These delays strain the judiciary and are unfair to individual nominees. To the extent that an intentionally prolonged delay can damage a law practice and keep individual nominees in professional and personal limbo, it becomes cruel. As explained further below, those who rely on the federal justice system may suffer as well.

The American Bar Association (ABA) has consistently urged the Senate to act promptly to confirm judicial nominees. In August of 2002, however, the ABA House of Delegates approved an especially strong statement that for the first time specifically identified the Senate Judiciary Committee as a "cause of blockage in the confirmation process" and urged the Committee to take prompt action on nominations. The ABA said that: "The notion that the Committee, by the simple expedient of refusing to hold timely hearings may avoid confirmation proceedings in the full Senate, is simply unacceptable to our notion of an appropriate and constitutional nomination process."

A persistent but low vacancy rate is unavoidable, reflecting a small number of vacancies that are promptly filled. Most federal judges are appointed at the prime of their professional career, or slightly later. Statutes provide comfortable benefits for federal judges who assume a semi-retirement status at age 65 (and after they have served 15 years). Most judges assume this "senior status" soon after they become eligible. Some judges announce their retirement date (colloquially, it is referred to as "going senior") with enough advance notice to allow the President time to nominate a replacement, but other judges do not. Serious illness, death, and other unanticipated events cause some vacancies to arise without notice. Accordingly, there will always be some vacancies in the federal courts.

In recent decades, when the confirmation process is running smoothly, the vacancy rate has dropped to around five percent. Chief Justice William Rehnquist has still admonished past Presidents and past Senates to act more expeditiously in nominating, confirming, and appointing judges to fill anticipated or actual vacancies. By comparison, a congressional seat is not left vacant for long before a special election is held (in the case of a House seat) or a temporary appointment is made (in the case of a Senate seat). When government officials are willing to spend a lot of time and money for a special election to fill 1/435th of the seats in the U.S. House of Representatives, Congress should make more of an effort to promptly fill numerous vacancies in the federal judiciary.

There were 67 judicial vacancies at the end of the 106th Congress and 77 now near the end of the 107th Congress, proving that the Senate is not even keeping pace with new retirements. Dueling statistics have unfortunately become commonplace in this debate, but there is one set of statistics that simply cannot be explained away. The stalling is undeniable when you consider the court of appeals nominations by themselves. The chart below shows the average number of days the first eleven circuit court nominees had to wait for final Senate action, and the respective confirmation rate by President.

| President | Average Number of Days Initial 11 Court of Appeals Nominees Waited for Final Senate Action | Court of Appeals Confirmation Rate |
| --- | --- | --- |
| Reagan | 39 | 100% |
| G.H.W. Bush | 95 | 100% |
| Clinton | 115 | 100% |
| G.W. Bush | approx. 400 (and counting) | 27% (thus far) |

If you eliminate the judges nominated by President George W. Bush who were first appointed by President Clinton, the picture looks even worse. Only one of the nine non-Clinton judges has been confirmed, a total of 11%. The average wait approaches 500 days for the remaining nine nominees, and is in excess of 500 days for eight of them. As this testimony is being prepared, seven of them have not had a committee vote and four have not even had a hearing.

Recently, Judge Buckley urged that the Senate rules be changed to allow the Judiciary Committee a few months to review the qualifications of judicial nominees and make its recommendation. Judge Buckley argued that the full Senate should vote after a few months whether or not the committee had acted. The current Chairman of the Senate Judiciary Committee, Patrick Leahy, proposed similar procedures just a few years earlier. Senator Leahy sponsored a bill in 1998 that would have required the Senate to act on all nominations pending for more than 60 days before it took a ten-day or longer recess.

Pursuant to his own legislative plan, Senator Leahy should at least have finished committee action on Miguel Estrada, Deborah Cook, John Roberts, Jeff Sutton, Michael McConnell, Dennis Shedd, Terrence Boyle, Timothy Tymkovich, Charles Pickering, and Priscilla Owen before the Senate took its August recess in 2001. Each of the nominees received a well-qualified rating from the ABA. Each of their nominations had been pending in his committee for over 60 days by then, most for over 80 days. But Leahy did not complete committee action on any of the above nominees by the August 2001 recess. Of those listed above, only Pickering, Owen, and Shedd were given hearings by the August 2002 recess—one year later. Many other court of appeals candidates nominat-ed during the summer of 2001 have not had a committee hearing either.

Although the federal courts of appeals have an overall vacancy rate of over fifteen percent, some circuits have had a sustained vacancy rate of between thirty and fifty percent. The situation in the U.S. Sixth Circuit Court of Appeals is the most dramatic. During the Clinton Administration, the Chief Judge of the Sixth Circuit wrote to the Senate Judiciary Committee to express his deep concern regarding four vacancies in the sixteen-member court. He wrote that his court was "hurting badly" and that the situation was "rapidly deteriorating due to the fact that 25% of the judgeships are vacant."

The Sixth Circuit was operating for most of this past year with only half of its authorized judges. It still has seven vacant positions today, a 44% vacancy rate. President Bush made seven nominations to that court in 2001, two of whom were in the very first batch sent to the Senate on May 9, 2001. (President Bush sent an additional nomination a few months ago.) But Senator Leahy has held a hearing on just two of them, and only one has been confirmed. As explained below, the Senate's complete inaction on the circuit with the highest vacancy rate has caused some particular hardships and led to some questionable judicial practices.

## 2. THE SENATE JUDICIARY COMMITTEE IS NOT PROVIDING ITS ADVICE AND CONSENT IN A MANNER CONSISTENT WITH THE CONSTITUTION OR THE RULE OF LAW

In addition to the intentionally prolonged delay in voting on most of the President's judicial nominations, several of the hearings that were conducted by the Senate Judiciary Committee were not only irrelevant to the merits of individual nominees, they instead attempted to lay the predicate for improper questioning at later confirmation hearings. In keeping with this agenda, hearings that were conducted for appellate court nominees during this Congress have been intentionally confrontational and focused on matters that are not properly the subject of such a hearing.

The few hearings that were conducted for appellate court nominees focused on a nominee's supposed political beliefs rather than his or her qualifications or philosophy of judging. Texas Supreme Court Justice Priscilla Owen was cross examined for seven hours in one hearing this past July, despite her obvious qualifications to join the U.S. Fifth Circuit Court of Appeals. Justice Owen received a unanimous well-qualified rating from the ABA. Justice Owen's reelection to the Texas Supreme Court in 2000 was endorsed by every major newspaper in Texas, and Owen won the support of a record number of voters in Texas. Yet, on a party-line vote, the Senate Judiciary Committee voted in early September to block her confirmation based on supposed ideological concerns. Last month, committee Democrats also tried to discredit and bully Miguel Estrada over his purported personal ideological leanings.

This conduct is based on a fundamental misconception some senators have regarding the proper role of judges and our judicial system. There is a crucial difference between political ideology, which is a set of political beliefs or goals, and a nominee's judicial philosophy, which is a theory of, or approach to, judicial decisionmaking. Political beliefs ought to play no role in a judge's judicial philosophy.

The rule of law is premised on the following bedrock principle: law can be objectively determined and fairly applied to all no matter what judge or other official is in power. The rule of law is an ideal, and every ideal is imperfect. Yet, American school children learn that this is an essential characteristic of our system of government. Ours is a nation of laws and not men, we are told. This is another way of saying that the application of the law does not vary depending on who is in charge. The law can be, and for the most part is, applied consistently and fairly to all. Any deviation from this norm is to be condemned, not encouraged.

Accordingly, the founding generation believed that the federal judiciary would be "the least dangerous" branch—in large part because they understood that the "judiciary power" was fundamentally different than that exercised by the political branches. In *Federalist* 78, [Alexander] Hamilton argued that legal traditions would cabin a judge's role and mode of decisionmaking. A judge, he maintained, would exercise "judgement" not "will." His argument presupposed that such a distinction was intelligible and readily understood. That conception of law—that judges can objectively discern what the law is, rather than what it should be—was the governing orthodoxy for over 130 years.

Rule by the party embodies a different ideal—one practiced by many communist nations. In that system, all judicial rulings are supposed to conform to the then current dictates, plans, agenda, or beliefs of the governing party. What is desired more than anything else in a judge or other government official is the proper political ideology, because that best informs all other action. Since there is thought to be no objective truth, the correctness of a ruling may change if the party line changes. Generally, only long-time party members who have proven their personal allegiance to the party's teachings are entrusted with high government power.

Antecedents of this thinking in America can be found in post-civil war nihilism, but the legal realists of the 1920s were the first to significantly undermine the rule of law. Legal realism, mingled with strains of pragmatism, relativism, and deconstructionist thought, captured the legal academy between the 1920s and 1960s. It began to bear substantial fruit in the courts thereafter. It is an oversimplification, but the orthodox thought of this era—running at least through the mid-1980s—is that law is just politics by another name.

This development is profoundly misguided and destructive. Yet, it is not surprising that its adherents increasingly urged the courts to become instruments of social change in overtly political ways. The courts' rulings ending government discrimination were (and are) necessary, but the tools the courts developed to fight the massive resistance to civil rights were also invoked to promote more amorphous social goals without clear constitutional foundations.

For a judge, such a seductive request is difficult to resist, even more so if the dominant legal culture has eliminated the traditional moral constraints on judging. With differences of style rather than content, the courts began to assume the role of another political branch to which dissatisfied citizens could turn to have their personal preferences, their will, enacted into law.

In this climate, it is easy to see why judicial confirmation battles might develop for Supreme Court justices. Unfortunately, the confirmation battles themselves further politicize the courts and reinforce the caustic notion that the courts are little more than a political plum. This notion was expressly stated by Abner Mikva [former member of Congress and Chief Judge of District of Columbia Circuit of the Court of Appeals] and many liberal academics, who argue that Bush's Presidency is illegitimate. Still brooding about the correct Supreme Court ruling in *Bush* v. *Gore*, Mikva and others who should know better

have urged the Senate to confirm no Bush nominee to the Supreme Court and encourage all means of thwarting his legitimate nominees to the appellate courts.

Hearings conducted by Senator Charles Schumer [D-NY] last fall on "whether ideology matters" in judicial selection and more recently in connection with the D.C. Circuit Court are an outgrowth of that dangerous thinking. Perhaps ideology matters a great deal for a nominee or senator who believes that there is no meaningful difference between law and politics. But that belief would demonstrate to me that the nominee has an unacceptable judicial philosophy. No further inquiry into the nominee's political beliefs is necessary. Testimony offered by President Clinton's former Counsel, Lloyd Cutler, and President George H.W. Bush's former Counsel, C. Boyden Gray, urged the Senate not to focus on political ideology in judicial selection. They both also agreed that extensive partisan inquiry is harmful to an independent judiciary.

A nominee with an appropriate judicial philosophy is one truly dedicated to the rule of law. Senators should be free to probe a nominee's theory of judging, *i.e.*, the methodology he would use when deciding cases, as long as the question does not ask the nominee to take a position on a matter that may come before him. Thus, I do not think that it is always enough for a nominee for a lower court judgeship to simply pledge that he will follow the law as set forth by the higher courts without explaining what that means. A record of scholarship or prior opinions, or a discussion of venerable old cases might help the committee to determine if the nominee appreciates what the rule of law requires.

I also think nominees reasonably could be asked to explain their general theory of various clauses of the Constitution. A competent grasp of the Constitution is necessary for any judge, and a discussion about its provisions might also be a good window on the nominee's approach to law and legal reasoning. Once again, however, senators must be careful not to ask the nominee about a particular subject matter or legal issue that might come before the nominee. Not only does the Code of Judicial Ethics require current and prospective judges to refuse to pledge how they might rule in the future, the American people want independent judges who have not committed themselves to a particular ruling.

Unfortunately, the argument that political ideology should not matter, and that extensive inquiry about it is destructive of an independent judiciary, is based on an understanding of law (i.e., the rule of law) that many senators seem to reject. The prevailing attitude is that the ideological stakes are high, and to the victor go the spoils. Modern-day legal realists, and their judicial activist advisers, desperately want judges who will impose a liberal or progressive will, not law. This is how the political branches were designed to operate, but not the courts.

A senatorial litmus test on an open or evolving legal issue is even more destructive to an independent judiciary than an improper inquiry about the nominee's general political beliefs. Senators who admit that they are applying such a single-issue litmus test know this full well. Their clear purpose is to eliminate any shred of judicial independence with regard to some controversial legal issue like abortion that is largely settled in the law but still permits some limited room for legislative action. Urged on by special interest groups that are influential in their states, these senators want only activist nominees who will strike down legislation that is permissible under Supreme Court cases, such as parental notification statutes with judicial bypass mechanisms.

These same senators express strong opposition to recent Supreme Court decisions (and lower court judges who would follow them) that enforce any limit in the Constitution on Congress's power to legislate. The senators denounce decisions interfering with any law they sponsored on the ground that it was passed with majority support. But requiring parents to be notified when their minor child seeks an abortion (absent special circumstances) is supported by an overwhelming majority of Americans. The difference, which educated senators should know, is that judges sometimes are required to enforce limits on legislative action and sometimes they are forbidden to do so, according to the Constitution. Lower court judges must follow the rulings of the Supreme Court on these matters, but some liberal senators who pretend to stand on principle really just want progressive outcomes: they want judges to ignore liberal legislation that exceeds Congress's authority and strike down other legislation that is permissible but that they, and their interest group supporters, simply don't like.

In contrast, modern-day federalists sincerely want judges who will fight the temptation to act on political biases, and instead, adhere to a mode of judging that minimizes such influences, including careful adherence to the text and the intent of those who enacted the governing text. Some senators and liberal activists may actually believe such a code cannot be followed. To them, nominees who pledge fidelity to the rule of law are, at best, dupes who will not advance the progressive cause. At worse, such nominees are seen as dissemblers who will become "conservative judicial activists" on the court.

Senator Schumer is at least honest about his view and objectives, and there is something to be said for that. If I were a nominee, I think I would probably rather be bullied by senators over my supposed political beliefs than have my character assassinated over some trumped-up offense—as was the case with Brooks Smith and Charles Pickering. Nevertheless, both practices are destructive to the individual nominees, to the confirmation process, and to the rule of law. And both lines of inquiry fuel the tit-for-tat mentality that helps keep the confirmation wars alive.

A significant change in our collective view of the proper role of the courts is desperately needed (which should also lead to contraction in the judiciary's improper exercise of power). As difficult as that may be to foster, the federalist view is steadily gaining ground again and hearings like this one will help educate the general public about what is at stake. Men of good faith on the right and left have spoken out that ideology should not matter.

Even if it is not possible to alter senators' understanding of the proper role of the courts, the confirmation process still needs to be fixed somehow, perhaps as the result of a political truce. In my view, the President has acted with great restraint so far, perhaps too much restraint. He has a lot more tools at his disposal that he has not employed to bring attention to the judicial vacancy crisis. He could communicate to the Senate that he will call the Senate back into special session if they do not act on a sufficient number of his nominees by its next recess. Indeed, I think he should have delivered such a message last fall, when the Senate's plan of obstruction was already clear.

In addition, the President could fill the longest-standing vacancies with recess appointments under the Recess Appointments Clause, which appointments last until the end of the Senate's "next Session." A President must not abuse his power under that clause, but he needs to take some action to help the courts and change the incentives the Senate faces in doing nothing. I would advise the President to give recess appointments to qualified individuals who are not then nominated for the life-time position. This would allow the Senate to displace the recess appointee at any time it acts to confirm a regular appointee. Such action would not interfere with the Senate's deliberations, but it would undermine the liberal activists who urge the Senate majority to inaction.

If nothing changes in the confirmation process, the legal realists' understanding may become more and more of a self-fulfilling prophesy: only those who behave as political ideologues will be appointed. These are the seeds the Senate majority is sowing now.

## EFFECTS OF PROLONGED JUDICIAL VACANCIES ON THE COURTS AND THE ADMINISTRATION OF JUSTICE

The sustained number of judicial vacancies, particularly in the federal appellate courts, is straining the judiciary as never before. In short, the political process and partisan delays risk substantial harm to our justice system.

Although the effect of prolonged judicial vacancies on the courts and the administration of justice is obviously related, it is possible in theory for the remaining judges and their staffs to simply work much harder and more efficiently in an attempt to ensure that the administration of justice is not affected by the Senate's bad faith. This is certainly what the courts have attempted to do. Their level of success is hard to evaluate for some reasons that are explained below, but also because there is a qualitative aspect of administration of justice that is exceedingly difficult to measure.

That said, the federal judiciary is a thoroughly professional institution which is supervised by the very able Chief Justice of the United States. It is aided by many career staff attorneys, judicial law clerks, and administrative personnel. The judicial system can adequately handle a relatively low number of vacancies on a circuit court as well as a district court vacancy in a judicial district where there are many other district judges. (A district court vacancy in a one- or two-judge judicial district, however, presents severe problems.) Likewise, the larger district and circuit courts can adequately handle a short period when there are more than a few vacancies.

When vacancy rates increase in a given court, the Judicial Conference of the United States may declare a judicial emergency for that court (based on guidelines it has developed). This has been done increasingly over the past several years. Nearly 40% of the current judicial vacancies have been classified by the Judicial Conference of the United States as "judicial emergencies." Pursuant to court rules in effect in many judicial districts or circuits, this permits certain emergency rules to operate within that court.

For example, an appellate court must generally decide cases in three-judge panels. Most appellate courts sit to hear oral argument once per month for about four days in randomly-shuffled three judge panels. A sixteen member court with only nine judges (as is the case in the Sixth Circuit, which covers all of Michigan, Ohio, Kentucky, and Tennessee) can form only three panels per month instead of five if it sticks to its active judges alone. Court rules normally in effect allow panels to be formed with two active members of the court and one senior or visiting judge—assuming the court can find visiting and senior judges willing to regularly take on that burden. Emergency rules may allow a panel to be formed with only one active judge and two senior or visiting judges.

The Ninth Circuit panel that decided the "Pledge of Allegiance Case," *Newdow* v.

*U.S. Congress*, (2002), was composed of one active judge and two senior judges. Circuit rules may also allow the senior or visiting judge that sat on the original panel to sit on the "en banc" panel if the entire court reconsiders the decision. In the Ninth Circuit, where the entire court does not sit on "en banc" rehearing panels, this may further skew the jurisprudence of the court.

Another change the emergency rules may allow is for two judges to rule on motions panels and certain types of summary dispositions if they both agree on the result. At first blush, it may not be clear why this presents a problem since two judges can overrule a third judge who might be assigned in the normal course of events. But there is a reason why three judges are on normal motions and summary disposition panels. The third judge may spot an issue that the first two judges may not notice, and he may convince one of them to change his mind or send the case to the oral argument calendar. In the Fifth Circuit, where I served as a law clerk, any one judge on a summary disposition "screening" panel could send the case to the oral argument docket. A third judge obviously increases the likelihood of that happening.

It is impossible to quantify how often the emergency rules might affect the outcome or handling of a case in the federal courts, but several prominent federal judges are concerned about interference with their normal procedures. Chief Judge Douglas Ginsburg of the D.C. Circuit Court of Appeals explained a few months ago that the court's "ability to manage [its] workload in a timely fashion will be seriously compromised" if it has to operate with only eight of its twelve members for much longer. Chief Judge Ginsburg then catalogued the reduced number of oral argument cases that will be heard in the circuit in the 2002–2003 term and the change in composition and duration of emergency panels. He concluded his remarks with a somber note: "[I]t is clear that the delay [in confirmations] has begun to jeopardize the administration of justice in this Circuit."

The Circuit Judge I had the great pleasure to serve early in my career, Edith Jones, recently published a novel type of workload study in the *Texas Tech Law Review* [in 2002] that provides some additional and interesting insights. Judge Jones's study is not intended to catalogue all of the work she did during the study period of three months, because she excludes many categories of work she performs. For this reason, it is not intended to show the total number of hours she worked—as a lawyer does in private practice. Instead, Judge Jones set out to categorize the type of cases she handled during the study period, note the number of cases in each category and relative time she spent on each type (excluding some periods of time such as oral argument). She also explained the methods her circuit has developed to expedite the relatively repetitious or easy cases so that the court could stay on top of its docket.

To her great credit, Judge Jones does not complain about her workload (which she downplays in her article despite the tremendously long hours I know she works), and she believes her court can manage fairly well with at least fifteen active judges on the seventeen-member court. Yet, her article still highlights some problems with the few vacancies on her court and suggests graver problems for other circuits.

For example, Judge Jones confirmed that the average number of oral argument cases heard by each judge in a year has not varied significantly in over fifteen years. That number is approximately 140. These are the hardest cases, or at least those where the judges believe that a lawyer's argument may be critical. Judge Jones confirms that the "lawyers' appearance has

been critical to our decisionmaking" in a significant number of the oral argument cases. Senior judges are used whenever possible in the Fifth Circuit already. So, even with only two vacancies on the court, the total number of cases that can be scheduled for oral argument is substantially decreased. A fair number of those cases decided without oral argument might have been resolved differently.

Judge Jones explained further that "[w]hat has increased phenomenally during [her] tenure is the volume of the summary calendar." The circuit has come up with some novel and interesting ways of expediting these cases that are determined to be less complicated, legally or factually. One method used in several circuits is for the circuit staff attorneys to prepare memos on the cases that appear to them to be routine. Those cases are distributed randomly to different "screening" panels. If the first judge on the distribution list agrees that it is a routine case, she drafts an opinion and presents it to the other judges in turn. The two other judges on that screening panel do the same thing with their third of cases. Any judge on the panel may review the entire record in the case and send it to the oral argument calendar, but that happens with few cases. No doubt this is principally because the circuit staff attorneys and first reviewing judge got it right, but it is probably also due in part to the fact that the cases placed on the screening panels receive less attention.

Given that the average number of oral argument cases per judge is fixed and the volume on the summary calendar has increased phenomenally, that means an increasing percentage of the circuit's caseload is decided on the summary calendar. Academics have criticized many of the case handling techniques like the one described above. Although I believe the academic criticism is largely uniformed, it is hard to deny that less attention is paid to these cases. (We all must prioritize our work, except perhaps in academia. Would the academics prefer the courts to fall further and further behind on their dockets?) Yet, the only way for a circuit to handle the extra workload that additional vacancies pose is to increase even further the percentage of cases disposed of on the summary calendar.

Judge Jones acknowledges this point with a warning:

> [T]he addition or subtraction of a single screening panel affects a large percentage redistribution of the summary calendar among the active judges. Such a redistribution may occur, for good or ill, as a group of Fifth Circuit judges begins to take senior status in the next few years. If replacements are not speedily confirmed, the per-active-judge burden of the summary calendar will escalate and begin seriously to impinge on the time necessary to address the oral argument docket cases.

The situation in other circuits has already passed the point at which oral arguments are canceled and judges must spend less time on those that are held. The D.C. Circuit has a 33% vacancy rate. The Ninth Circuit has an 18% vacancy rate. And the Sixth Circuit has the highest vacancy rate at 44%.

There are approximately 55,000 appeals filed in federal courts of appeals per year, and the circuit courts generally do not have the discretion to refuse to take such cases. Fifteen percent of that total is 8,250. Who will handle those appeals? How will the work get done? Through the increased use of the summary calendar and emergency procedures, a court may attempt to keep up with its normal flow of cases. But sustained periods of high vacancy on some courts overwhelm even the most diligent courts.

One disturbing possibility is that the emergency rules in place in some circuits also permit judicial manipulation of the docket. The emergency rules may bypass the normal random assignment of judges, and often allow the chief judge to assign visiting and senior judges to panels of his choosing. The rules also increase the chance that cases will not be assigned randomly either. There have been questions raised in several circuits regarding possible manipulation of the rules. Even the appearance of judicial manipulation is disturbing.

One judge in the Sixth Circuit took the extraordinary step of questioning the timing of the en banc [the entire court] hearing of the two University of Michigan racial preference cases in an appendix to his dissent in the first of the cases [*Grutter v. Belligner*] to be decided....The chief judge waited before he circulated the en banc request until two judges who were appointed by Republicans had taken senior status and would be ineligible to sit with the full court. With the circuit court at half its normal complement of judges, the case was then scheduled and heard. It was decided months later while the Senate Judiciary Committee refused to schedule any hearings for the judges who had been nominated to fill the vacancies.

Part of the Sixth Circuit controversy is related to the fact that the court reached a result in the *Grutter* case in conflict with every other circuit. In an extraordinary writ, the students who are challenging the racially preferential admissions policy asked the Supreme Court last week to take the remaining case, *Gratz v. Bellinger*, away from the Sixth Circuit and decide both cases without further action by that court. Hopefully, the Supreme Court will hear the two cases and remove the cloud that hangs over the proceedings in the Sixth Circuit.

[These cases were heard by the Supreme Court. See Debate 17.] But the Senate's inaction with regard to the Sixth Circuit has allowed such a cloud to develop. At its worst, the Senate intended this result. At best, the Senate has enabled such a controversy to arise through its sloth or callous refusal to act. Neither indictment is particularly attractive.

## CONCLUSION

The judicial confirmation process is at a new and disturbing low. Ten Democrats on the Senate Judiciary Committee and the current Senate leadership are holding numerous judicial nominees hostage in an attempt to undue the consequences of the last presidential election, and apparently, in an attempt to hold vacancies open for liberal judicial activists.

The immediate harm to the administration of justice is hard to quantify, but it is real, and evidence of it is growing as the judicial confirmation delays stretch on. The long-term harm from the politicized confirmation process to the courts as an institution is even more grave. If the rule of law is to survive in its traditional form, the judicial confirmation process must be radically changed.

# THE CONTINUING DEBATE:
## Legal Philosophy as a Qualification for the Bench

### What Is New

The tension between President Bush and Senate Democrats over judicial nominations continues. As the minority party in the Senate, the Democrats have used the filibuster to block a number of the president's nominees. One of the most well-known of these was Miguel Estrada, who Bush nominated in 2001 for a seat on the District of Columbia Circuit Court of Appeals. What made Estrada a focal point was the widespread speculation that Bush was positioning him to later be the first Latino Justice of the Supreme Court. No one disputed Estrada's solid legal background. An immigrant from Honduras, he graduated from Harvard Law School, clerked for Supreme Court Justice Anthony Kennedy, and was an attorney in the Justice Department under Presidents George H.W. Bush and Bill Clinton. Suspecting that Estrada was very conservative, Democrats pressed Estrada to state his position on controversial issues, such as abortion. He declined to do so on the grounds that each case is different. The Democrats also asked for internal documents on Estrada's views from the Justice Department. President Bush rejected the request as violating the separation of powers. The Democrats then filibustered to block a confirmation vote. Finally, in mid-2003, a frustrated Estrada withdrew his name from consideration. Overall, though, the number of blocked nominations have been small. Of Bush's judiciary choices, 198 had been confirmed as of July 2004 and only 10 had been blocked by filibusters.

### Where to Find More

The Supreme Court Historical Society at http://www.supremecourthistory.org is a good place to begin. Then turn to Lee Ryan, "United States Supreme Court Research—Getting Started," University of San Francisco Law Library site at: http://www.usfca.edu/law_library/supres.html. Two good studies of the appointment process are David Yalof, *Pursuit of Justices: Presidential Politics and the Selection of Supreme Court Nominees* (University of Chicago Press, 1999) and Joyce A. Baugh, *Supreme Court Justices In The Post-Bork Era: Confirmation Politics and Judicial Performance* (Peter Lang, 2002). For a group that would support the opposition to Miguel Estrada and similar nominees, go to http://www.pfaw.org/pfaw/general/, the site of the People for the American Way. The opposite view is held by the Committee for Justice at http://www.committeeforjustice.org/

### What More to Do

The issues in this debate are apt to become even more intense when the next Supreme Court vacancy occurs. When that happens, decide what you think and get involved by contacting your senators or, even better, by getting active with one of the many groups that will be involved on one side or the other. More immediately, think about whether blocking otherwise qualified (legal training, experience) judicial nominees based on their political philosophy is acceptable. Whatever your view, react to Todd Gaziano's view that "the confirmation process…needs to be fixed somehow." What, if anything, would you do?

# ECONOMIC POLICY

## CONSTITUTIONALLY REQUIRE A BALANCED BUDGET:
### Fiscal Sanity *or* Fiscal Irresponsibility?

### FISCAL SANITY

**ADVOCATE:** William Beach, Director, Center for Data Analysis, Heritage Foundation

**SOURCE:** Testimony during hearings on the "Balanced Budget Amendment" before the U.S. House of Representatives Committee on the Judiciary, Subcommittee on the Constitution, March 6, 2003

### FISCAL IRRESPONSIBILITY

**ADVOCATE:** Richard Kogan, Senior Fellow, Center on Budget and Policy Priorities

**SOURCE:** Testimony during hearings on the "Balanced Budget Amendment" before the U.S. House of Representatives Committee on the Judiciary, Subcommittee on the Constitution, March 6, 2003

In a moment of candor, U.S. budget director David Stockman confessed in 1981, "None of us really understands what's going on with all these numbers." Today's budgets are even more daunting, given that they are three times larger (revenue: $1.8 trillion; expenditures: $2.1 trillion) than the one that perplexed Stockman. A few questions and answers about the budget will help provide a foundation for thinking about a balanced budget amendment. Unless noted, all data relates to the fiscal year (FY) 2003 budget (October 1, 2002 to September 30, 2003).

**How important is the budget to the U.S. economy?** It is the most important aspect of the economy. Budget outlays account for 19.5% of the U.S. gross domestic product (GDP, the value of the wealth produced within a country).

**How much has the budget grown?** The budget has outpaced inflation and the population. At $1.8 trillion, the FY2000 budget outlays were almost 3.5 million times larger than the 1792 budget ($5.2 million). Even controlled for inflation, the FY2000 budget was 1,101 times larger than in 1792. On a per capita basis, and again controlling for inflation, the $6,406 per U.S. resident that the federal government spent in FY2000 was 196 times more than in 1792.

**Where does the money come from?** Individual income taxes are the biggest source (49%). Other sources are corporate taxes (10%), payroll taxes (*e.g.*, social security and Medicare, 36%), and miscellaneous taxes (5%).

**Where does the money go?** Human resources (*e.g.*, health, welfare, and social security) consume 65% of the budget. Other outlays are national defense (17%), physical resources (*e.g.*, environment and transportation, 5%), interest on the national debt (8%), and other functions (5%). The most important shift in spending in recent decades has been the relative decrease in defense spending (48% of outlays in FY1963) and increase in human resources spending, (28% that year).

**What are some relevant budget concepts?** One set is the *discretionary budget* and the *mandatory budget*. The first involves programs that receive specific annual appropriations. The second involves "entitlement" programs funded by a formula (*e.g.*, food stamps) and also expenditures the government is legally obligated to make (*e.g.*, paying interest on the national debt). Discretionary programs make up 37% of expenditures. Note that Congress, at its discretion, can change the formulas and thus the costs of entitlement programs or even abolish them. The second set of concepts is *on-budget* and *off-budget* receipts and expenditures. On-budget accounts are those that flow in and out of the U.S. Treasury. Off-budget accounts either go through special "trust funds," such as the social security account, or through such corporate-like activities as the U.S. Postal Service. On-budget accounts equal 74% of receipts and 83% of expenditures.

**What is the history of budget surpluses and deficits?** Since 1900, there has been a budget deficit about 70% of the years, including every year since 1970 except FY1998–FY2001. The estimated budget deficit for FY2003 is $304 billion, about $1,050 per U.S. resident.

**How does the government fund the deficit?** It borrows money. The government borrows some from itself by, for example, dipping into the social security trust fund. The rest it borrows by selling bonds to the public. In late 2001, the national debt was $5.8 trillion ($20,500 per American). Of that the government owed itself $2.5 trillion and the public $3.3 trillion. Interest on the public debt was $108 billion. Foreign investors hold 30% of the bonds. The national debt is 56% of the GDP, the same proportion as in 1960.

**What is the history of trying to control the budget?** In recent decades, attempts to legislatively control the budget began amid the perennial and mounting deficits between FY1970 and FY1997. They peaked in FY1992 at $290 billion, equal to about 21% of the budget. During these years, Congress passed several budget control acts. Each had some impact on restraining the budget, but none has provided a permanent solution. The surplus achieved during FY1998–FY2001 was more the result of revenues generated by one of the most prosperous decades in U.S. history than budget control. Attempts to add a balanced budget amendment to the Constitution have failed. The House passed such an amendment in 1997, but it was defeated in the Senate by one vote.

## POINTS TO PONDER

➤ Think about who favors and opposes a constitutional balanced budget amendment. Is the idea inherently conservative or liberal?
➤ Compare the dangers William Beach argues result from deficit spending and those Richard Kogan sees if a balanced budget amendment is adopted.
➤ Consider politics and ask yourself why president and Congress have such a difficult time balancing the budget.

# Constitutionally Require a Balanced Budget:
## Fiscal Sanity

WILLIAM BEACH

There are many things that the 108th Congress [2003–2004] can do for the long-term well being of those represented by the members: among them are strengthen our national and domestic security, provide tax relief that yields a stronger economy, and enact needed reforms to key programs that affect the country's neediest citizens. However, this Congress certainly would secure its place in history and fulfill its obligation to govern for the general good if it referred to the states for ratification an amendment to the Constitution that requires the federal government to operate within a balanced budget.

My testimony today is divided among three headings: 1) the constitutional importance of vigorous debate over competing priorities; 2) the statistical evidence that supports a rapid movement toward a balanced budget amendment; and 3) the role that dynamic revenue estimation plays in the process of achieving annual budget balances.

## THE PLACE OF SPENDING DEBATES IN THE HEALTH OF THE CONSTITUTION

I know that many fiscal conservatives view the balanced budget amendment as justified principally on financial grounds. It is virtually uncontroversial that governments at all levels should practice the spending disciplines of well-run businesses. This practice is especially important at the federal level, if for no other reason than the enormous influence that federal spending has on other governments and the economy generally. Spending limitations encourage better accounting controls and auditing

processes, which assure that the monies allocated to address the priorities of voters are, indeed, well spent.

However, I believe that a larger, constitutional goal is served by amending the constitution to require a balanced budget: representative government works only as well as it allows a full airing of its citizens' divergent views, particularly in open debates over competing public policy priorities. Without a way to limit spending, such debates are unlikely to occur.

Suppose an extreme situation in which there exist no limitations on the ability of the federal government to spend taxpayers' funds except the capacity of taxpayers to produce revenues. In such a world, no one's spending goals would go unachieved in the short run. There would, as a consequence, be no debate over the direction the nation should go in meeting the needs of its elderly citizens, its educational systems, or its national defense. And, without debate and the deep social, economic, and policy inquiry such debate engenders, we would likely be unable to sustain our republican form of government.

Of course, such an extreme world cannot exist for long, if for no other reason than boundless spending by government inevitably destroys the economy out of which revenues flow. The point of this scenario, however, applies equally well to more realistic gradients of the extreme case. The ability of a government to avoid hard decisions about priorities because it can borrow to meet its revenue shortfalls also diminishes debate over competing views of our country's future and current priorities. This borrowing ability may, as well, enable organizations with powerful lobbying capabilities to squeeze millions of dollars in subsidies from Congress and the Administration with the public scrutiny that debate can produce.

## ARE THERE REASONS FOR BEING CONCERNED?

These constitutional considerations should be justification enough to adopt a balanced budget amendment, even if reality had yet to catch up with the possibilities outlined above. However, the evidence is mounting that those fiscal disciplines that may once have protected these vital constitutional processes have yielded utterly to growth in spending that far exceeds required levels.

Let me highlight a few facts:

• The outlays of the federal government today are slightly more than 23 times greater than they were in 1960.

• Government spending after adjusting for inflation has increased by nearly five fold since 1960, while the population has grown by a factor of 1.6.

• Per capita federal spending now stands at $7,600. In 1960, per capita federal spending stood at $510.

• Per capita share of publicly held federal debt now stands at $13,720. In 1960, this share stood at $1,310.

• Total publicly held debt in 1960 was about $236.8 billion. In 2003 it equals about $3.88 trillion.

• Worse news on the debt is on the way. By 2020, most of the baby boom generation will be retired and drawing monthly checks from Social Security. By 2030, the total Medicare enrollment will be more than double the current Medicare population. Neither Medicare nor Social Security is expected to survive the onset of the baby boom

without massive infusions of additional cash or major structural reform. The unfunded liabilities of Social Security alone are now in excess of $21 trillion over the next 75 years.

The recent Congresses have shown little will to reverse or even slow this explosion in federal spending. The 107th Congress completed a four-year spending spree that exceeds every other four-year period since the height of World War II. Between 2000 and 2003, federal spending grew by $782 billion. This growth in spending is equivalent to $73,000 in household spending, which, again, was exceeded only during the darkest hours of the Second World War.

If the spending record of the period 1960 through 2000 fails to convince members of Congress that spending growth is beyond their collective abilities to control, the past four years should abundantly make the case.

## THE ROLE OF DYNAMIC REVENUE ESTIMATION IN THE BUDGET PROCESS

Exceptionally rapid growth in government spending, such as we've seen in the last four years, bears down heavily on the general economy and, thus, on federal revenue growth. The consumption of goods and services by government generally comes at the expense of consumption and investment by private companies. This redirection of economic resources should be a concern to policy makers because private companies generally use identical resources more productively than government. When government uses economic resources instead of private firms, the growth of the economy slows below its potential, which reduces potential employment and tax revenue growth.

Members of Congress and the general public do, however, change public policy from time to time in order to achieve a specific end, like winning a war or encouraging an expansion of economic activity that call for spending above revenues. When the public and the Congress begin considering these policy changes, a better, more informed debate will be had if those involved in the decision process are able to see estimates of how their proposed changes would affect budget outcomes.

For reasons well beyond this hearing, Congress has resisted the adoption of dynamic tax and budget analysis in the past. However, the 107th Congress made great progress in bringing macroeconomic analysis into the tax policy debate, and a beginning also was made in introducing this analytical discipline into the preparation of the annual budget.

I raise this emerging capability here because it relates directly to the constitutional and fiscal importance of evaluating competing budget priorities. If the budget committees and those other bodies that propose tax policy changes were to use macroeconomic analysis as a routine part of their deliberations, I am confident the Congress would make better decisions between competing budget priorities than they do now.

Let me briefly illustrate how dynamic economic analysis could inform the annual debate over the federal budget. The Center for Data Analysis at The Heritage Foundation recently completed an econometric analysis of President Bush's proposed economic growth plan. This plan contains a number of major changes to current tax law, including the end to the double taxation of dividends. We introduced these tax law changes into a model of the U.S. economy that is widely used by Fortune 500 companies and government agencies to study such changes. Here are few of the interesting effects we found that would likely stem from adopting the President's plan:

- Employment would grow by nearly a million jobs per year over the next ten years, which adds significantly to the tax base of federal and state governments.

- The drop in the unemployment rate reduces government outlays for unemployed workers at all levels of government.

- Investment grows much more strongly under a tax regime without the double taxation of dividends than with such a policy, which expands the growth rate of the general economy, thus offsetting some of the deleterious effects of rapidly growing federal spending.

- The payroll tax revenues grow more rapidly with President Bush's plan than without, thus adding about $60 billion more to the trust funds than currently forecasted.

- Most importantly, the forecasts of fiscal doom made by many of the plan's critics fail to materialize. The additional economic growth produced by the plan reduces the ten-year "cost" to about 45 percent of its static amount.

- This economic feedback also reduces the growth of new publicly held debt that the plan's critics expect. Instead of a trillion dollars in new debt, the economic growth components of the plan produce significantly under 50 percent of that amount. In fact, the plan supports the creation of $3 in after-tax disposable income for every $1 of new debt, while still reducing all publicly held debt by 28 percent between 2004 and 2012.

While this testimony has touched on only a few of the many arguments that can be advanced in support of a balanced budget amendment, I trust that the thrust of my interest in this constitutional outcome is clear. We need the amendment not only to contain the growth in spending (a worthy goal all by itself), but also to protect our constitutional process of vigorous public debate over important policy alternatives. A budget process constrained by a balanced budget amendment and accompanied by the routine use of standard macroeconomic analysis would be more likely to produce the size and quality of government that most Americans desire.

# Constitutionally Require a Balanced Budget:
## Fiscal Irresponsibility

### Richard Kogan

The question before us today is whether the Constitution should be amended to require that the federal budget be balanced every year....

First, let me very briefly explain how restrictive the text of the current proposed amendment really is. By requiring that each year's expenditures be covered by that year's income, the amendment would preclude borrowing, even during times of unusual duress, such as wars or recessions; moreover, it would effectively preclude saving for the future, because the money saved in the present *could not be used* to cover future costs.

No state or local government, no family, and no business is required to operate under such restrictions. Every family borrows to finance the purchase of a house—that's what a mortgage is—and many borrow to finance higher education; every state, city, or county borrows to pay for school, road, or hospital construction or parkland acquisition; and most growing businesses borrow to finance new capital construction or acquisition.

Moreover, the amendment would prohibit dipping into past savings, since under the amendment *this* year's costs must be covered entirely by *this* year's income. Yet most families dip into savings to pay for a child's college education and certainly to cover costs during retirement; every state that "balances" its budget in fact can use its rainy day fund to help cover costs during a recession; and businesses often use retained earnings from prior years to finance expansions. This amendment makes saving for the future

pointless because the saved money could never be used: it would be unconstitutional to use rainy day funds, or to use the accumulating assets in the Social Security trust fund to help cover the costs of the baby boomers' retirement. In effect, it would prohibit this generation from building up public savings, or paying down public debt, for the express purpose of providing assets to make the burden on future generations lighter.

Second, such a restrictive amendment is truly inferior economics—it would require the government to reduce consumption during recessions, thus slowing the economy even further, throwing more people out of work, and in some cases running the risk of turning a recession into a full-blown depression. This Administration is exactly right when it says that Congress should not raise taxes during a recession. By the same token, Congress should not cut public spending during a recession. Either action takes purchasing power out of the hands of consumers at exactly the wrong time. In effect, the amendment would ban automatic stabilizers, such as unemployment compensation. Likewise, the amendment would give the seal of approval to over-stimulating the economy during an inflationary boom, risking an acceleration of inflation that could be seriously destabilizing.

Even though the states operate under much less restrictive rules, the actions states are forced to take during the current recession—raising taxes and cutting education, health care, social services, and infrastructure—are harming the economy and slowing the recovery; this fact makes it doubly important to maintain robust automatic stabilizers at the federal level.

Third, the experience of the last twenty years illustrates that setting targets for a budget surplus, or deficit, or balance, is not workable but that limiting the cost of legislation works far better. From the mid 1980s through 2000, three Presidents and many Congresses gradually worked to undo the damage of the first half of the 1980s, mostly by taking hard votes but partly by writing statutory rules or rules of House and Senate procedure providing guidance that Congress very largely followed. Especially after Gramm-Rudman-Hollings I and II were replaced by the far more workable system of appropriations caps and a rule of budget neutrality for tax and entitlement legislation—the so-called PAYGO rule— the budget moved from deficit to surplus. The relative failure of GRH I and II is important because those laws, like the amendment before us, attempted to set a specific fiscal target for the budget. The relative success of caps and the PAYGO rule illustrates that targeting the *cost of legislation*—rather than the overall level of the surplus or deficit—is a far superior road to the desired result. If this subcommittee is truly concerned about future deficits, it should work with the Budget and Rules Committees and the Administration to re-impose reasonable appropriations caps and the rule of budget neutrality. More importantly, Members should eschew any new tax cuts or entitlement increases, such as a prescription drug benefit, except to the extent that they are fully offset.

Fourth, almost every state has a political system in which the governor is inherently much more powerful than the legislators, most of whom are part-time legislators with other jobs. This is a logical consequence of allowing governors great freedom to implement or not implement elements of the budget, depending on circumstances, given

various state balanced-budget requirements. By analogy, this amendment could lead to a vast strengthening of presidential powers and a weakening of congressional authority. This worries me; Congress is not very efficient, but its very inefficiency was deliberate, to minimize hasty and ill-considered actions. This has worked well for a few centuries, and I see no need to fundamentally change the balance of power.

Fifth, it is possible that power won't be shifted from the Congress to the President, but rather from the Congress and President to the courts. My guess is that the courts would find the amendment unenforceable, making this exercise mere show. But if the courts believed the Constitution prohibited an unbalanced budget except to the extent Congress voted by supermajority to approve it, then the risks of this amendment would be profound. We have absolutely no way of knowing what a court would do to balance the budget when Congress refused, or more likely, when the budget fell out of balance despite Congress' best efforts. I have attached a paper raising many of the legal avenues that can be imagined—court-ordered surtaxes or benefit cuts; court-ordered enactment of tax increases or spending cuts that the President had vetoed; court-ordered enactment of tax increases or benefit cuts that Congress had designed but had been defeated; court-ordered invalidation of appropriations bills, entitlement increases, and tax cuts; or contempt citations.

Sixth, whether the Courts will enforce the balanced budget amendment or not, there are a wide variety of gimmicks Congress can use to evade it. Among these are borrowing by another name, e.g. lease-purchase contracts; paying for costs through contingent liabilities, e.g. loan guarantees or insurance contracts; timing shifts that move costs from the present to the future, e.g. back-loaded IRAs and the new so-called "savings account" proposals; off-loading federal programs onto nominally independent "government-sponsored enterprises" such as REFCORP [Resolution Funding Corporation: an agency created in 1989 to issue bonds needed to raise funds to deal with the crisis caused by the collapse of numerous savings and loan institutions.]; and the perennial favorite, unfunded mandates on states, localities, businesses, and individuals. In fact, if this amendment were enacted, it could ultimately be referred to as the Unfunded Mandates Act of 2003. [Unfunded mandates are requirements to act without providing funding to carry out the mandated actions].

Seventh, let us leave aside the constitutional question for the moment and ask the public policy question. *Should* the Federal Government aim to balance its budgets? Clearly not during a recession, as I have said. How about on average over the business cycle? Even here, I think that a balanced budget would be the wrong general target. A better target would be to run surpluses, not balance, for the remainder of the decade, in an attempt to pay off much or all of the debt before the baby boom generation retires. The purpose, in this case, is to reduce or eliminate future federal payments for interest on the debt and thereby allow future tax revenue to be used entirely to pay for public benefits and needs, such as Social Security or defense. Because the federal government is a major supporter of people in retirement and because there will be a bulge in retirees at the end of the decade, federal costs will inevitably grow starting in about a decade. If we can reduce federal costs for interest at the same time that the federal costs of Social Security and Medicare are growing, we can afford *part* of the increased costs of Social Security and Medicare without having to raise taxes.

Thus, the question is whether we should pay somewhat higher taxes now (when I am paying them) in order to pay off the debt, or wait a decade or more to raise taxes, when I will be retired but my children will be paying taxes. It seems to me only fair that I and my generation be willing to reduce the tax burden on my children and their generation by being willing to pay somewhat higher taxes now so that we can reduce or eliminate the debt before we retire.

In short, if we are discussing budget policy rather than artificial budget rules, we happen to be in one of the rare decades in which surpluses are generally a better goal than balanced budgets. A surplus doesn't mean we are collecting "extra, unneeded" taxes; it merely means that the taxes we are collecting now will be needed for our future retirement.

This policy discussion illustrates one reason the constitutional amendment is a bad idea: circumstances change over time. During some decades, balance might be generally a good goal, but one should also take into account the private saving rate and needs of the future. In the particular circumstance we are in, where we can predict with certainty that the need for public expenditures will increase in the future compared with current needs, it makes sense for the nation to save for the future by paying down debt. Unlike the right to free speech or the right to a lawyer (which can be viewed as a permanent right), the appropriate general target for fiscal policy depends on circumstances, so it is inherently wrong to enact any such target into the Constitution.

Finally, a constitutional balanced budget amendment is fundamentally unworthy of a democracy. Our Constitution currently allows *every* public policy question—war versus peace, the levels and types of taxes, the purposes and amount of public expenditures, what constitutes a federal crime, whether to admit a new state to the Union—to be decided by majority vote. (True, the rights of individual citizens are protected against a majority decision to discriminate, and it takes a 2/3 vote to override a presidential veto. But these aspects of the Constitution do not favor one set of public policy preferences over any other.) Under a constitutional Balanced Budget Amendment, citizens with one preference on public policy (let us say, those who favor a tax cut or an increase in unemployment benefits during a recession, or merely allowing revenues to fall naturally and the normal unemployment compensation law to continue to operate) would have fewer legal rights than citizens with the opposite viewpoints because they would need more votes to win. This is so inherently unfair that it should be rejected out of hand. Equal legal rights, including the right to have our votes count the same amount as anyone else's votes, is fundamental.

## THE CONTINUING DEBATE:
## Constitutionally Require a Balanced Budget

### What Is New

Concern over chronic budget deficits was quieted for a time by the cumulative $558 billion budget surplus of FY1998–FY2001. Then the budget plunged back into deficit spending. Lagging revenue was one cause. Congress enacted significant tax cuts at the request of President Bush. Also, the economy slowed. Rising unemployment decreased income taxes, and the downturn in the stock market cost the government billions of dollars in lost capital gains and dividends taxes. The net result is that revenue for FY2003 was $162 billion less than for FY2000. Increased spending was the other cause of renewed budget deficits. The Bush administration's responses to the September 11, 2001 terrorist attacks added about $100 billion to the budget between FY2000 and FY2003 to increase military and homeland security spending. Human resource outlays also grew during these years, adding $200 billion to the budget. The net result was a return to deficit spending (–$159 billion) in FY2002 which grew to $422 billion in FY2005. Moreover, the Office of Management and Budget (OMB) projects a cumulative deficit for FY2002–FY2009 of $2.4 trillion. For those years, the Congressional Budget Office (CBO) puts the cumulative deficit at $2.6 trillion.

### Where to Find More

The budget, budget history, and projected budgets are available at the OMB site (http://www.whitehouse.gov/omb/) and the CBO site (http://www.cbo.gov/). The balanced budget amendment introduced in the House of Representatives in 2003 was bottled up in its Judiciary Committee and died there. However, new proposals will almost surely be introduced in the 109th Congress beginning in 2005. These can be located at http://thomas.loc.gov. Further information is available on the Web sites of the two advocates' centers: Richard Kogan's Center on Budget and Policy Priorities (http://www.cbpp.org/) and William Beach's Center for Data Analysis, Heritage Foundation (http://www.heritage.org/research/).

### What More to Do

There are few if any painless budget choices. It is easy to say, "Slash welfare spending and make those people get jobs" or "Vastly increase taxes on those fat-cat rich people and corporations and make them pay their fair share." But such statements do not make real budgets. To "get real," do two things. One, in your class take the FY2003 budget and revise it. If you want to balance it, you will need to hike taxes or cut spending. So decide who gives and who gets. Second, debate and, if you wish, amend House Joint Resolution 22, the proposal in the 108th Congress to add a balanced budget amendment to the Constitution. While you are at it, tell your members of Congress what you think.

# 16 CRIMINAL JUSTICE POLICY

## THE DEATH PENALTY:
### Racially Biased *or* Justice Served?

### RACIALLY BIASED

**ADVOCATE:** Julian Bond, Professor of History, University of Virginia and Distinguished Professor-in-Residence, American University

**SOURCE:** Testimony during hearings on "Race and the Federal Death Penalty," before the U.S. Senate Committee on the Judiciary, Subcommittee on Constitution, Federalism, and Property Rights, June 13, 2001

### JUSTICE SERVED

**ADVOCATE:** Andrew G. McBride, former U.S. Associate Deputy Attorney General

**SOURCE:** Testimony during hearings on "Race and the Federal Death Penalty," before the U.S. Senate Committee on the Judiciary, Subcommittee on Constitution, Federalism, and Property Rights, June 13, 2001

Murder and capital punishment share four elements. They are: (1) a planned act (2) to kill (3) a specific person who (4) is not immediately attacking anyone. Should then murder and capital punishment be judged just or unjust by the same standard?

The first question is whether killing is ever justified. The doctrine of most religions contain some variation of the commandment, "Thou shalt not kill." For moral absolutists and pacifists, this prohibition is unbendable. They would not kill another person under any circumstances. Most people, however, are moral relativists who evaluate good and evil within a context. They do not condemn as immoral killing in such circumstances as self-defense and military combat.

What about premeditated acts by individuals? Most societies condemn these as murder even if the other person has harmed you. To see this, assume that a murderer has killed a member of your family. You witnessed it and thus are sure who is guilty. If you track down the murderer and execute him or her, by law now you are also a murderer. Yet 67% of Americans favor capital punishment, which is the state carrying out roughly the same act.

Arguably the difference is the willingness of most people to apply different moral standards to individuals acting privately and society acting through its government. This distinction is an ancient one. For example, God may have commanded "Thou shalt not kill" for individuals (Exodus 20:13), but in the very next chapter God details "ordinances" to Moses, including, "Whosoever strikes a man so that he dies shall be put to death" (Exodus 21:12). The point here is not whether you want to accept the words that Exodus attributes to a deity. After all, just two verses later, God also decrees death to "whoever curses his father or his mother." This would leave few teenagers alive today. Instead, the issue to wrestle with is whether and why it is just or unjust for a government, but not an individual, to commit an act with the four elements noted in the first paragraph. For those who see no moral distinction between actions by individuals and a society, capital punishment is wrong no matter how heinous the crime is, how fair the legal system is, or what the claimed benefits of executing criminals are.

There are others, though, who do not argue that capital punishment is inherently immoral. Their view is that executions have no positive effect. To think about this point, you have to first decide what it is you want capital punishment to accomplish. One possibility is to deter others from committing similar crimes. The other possibility is punishment as a way of expressing the society's outrage at the act. A great deal of the debate at this level is about whether capital punishment is a deterrent. It is beyond the limited space here to take up that debate, but to a degree it misses the point of why most Americans who favor capital punishment do so. When asked in a 2001 poll why they support it, 70% replied it is "a fitting punishment" for convicted murders, while only 25% thought, "the death penalty deters crime," and 4% were unsure.

Yet another line of attack on capital punishment is that the system is flawed. Some contend that mistakes get made, and innocent people are sometimes convicted and executed. Then there is the argument represented in this debate made by Julian Bond and disputed by Andrew McBride that, as conducted in the United States, the process from investigation, through trial and sentencing, to the carrying out of the death penalty is racially tainted. There can be little doubt that the demographic characteristics of those executed are not in proportion to their group's percentage of the society. Between 1977 and 2001, African Americans (about 12% of the population) made up 36% of those executed. Because federal criminal justice statistics classify Latinos as "white," it is hard to find the impact of executions on that group. However, Texas and California give some clues. Combined the two states' population is 49% white, 9% African American, 28% Latino, and 16% other identifiers. The two states' combined death row population is 37% white, 38% African American, 22% Latino, and 4% others. It must be said that the disproportionate number of blacks executed does not by itself prove racial bias. Fully 98% of all those executed are men, yet there is little to argue the system is biased against males. Instead, consider the arguments of Bond and McBride carefully.

## POINTS TO PONDER

➤ What evidence does Julian Bond provide to support his claim that "the death penalty serves as a shield for attitudes on race" in the United States.
➤ Given the disproportionate percentage of blacks executed. how does Andrew McBride justify his argument that "there is no credible statistical evidence of racial bias in the enforcement of the federal death penalty"?
➤ What, if anything, would make you change your view on capital punishment?

# The Death Penalty:
# Racially Biased

## JULIAN BOND

Thank you for inviting me to offer my perspective as Chairman of the Board of the National Association for the Advancement of Colored People (NAACP) and as a member of Citizens for a Moratorium on Federal Executions (CMFE).

The NAACP is the nation's oldest and largest civil rights organization. We have long been opposed to the death penalty and are horrified by its all too frequent and easily documented racially discriminatory application. We do not believe it deters crime. It targets and victimizes those who cannot afford decent legal representation. It is used against the mentally incompetent. It tragically sends the innocent to death.

The death penalty serves as a shield for attitudes on race. It is used most often in states with the largest African-American populations and disproportionately used when the accused is black and the victim is white. In addition to being bad domestic policy, it increasingly alienates the United States from our allies and lessens our voice in the international human rights arena.

I am also a member of Citizens for a Moratorium on Federal Executions (CMFE). CMFE is a coalition of dozens of American public figures who joined together last fall when Juan Raul Garza was scheduled to be the first individual executed by the United States Government in nearly 40 years. Some members of CMFE support the death penalty in specific circumstances; others are unalterably opposed. Nonetheless, we spoke with one voice in urging President Clinton to declare a moratorium on federal executions.

Among the 40 people who signed CMFE's first letter to President [Bill] Clinton, delivered on November 20, 2000, were former high-ranking members of the Justice Department, former Clinton administration officials, the Dean of the Yale Law School, a Nobel Laureate, Congressional Gold Medal and Presidential Medal of Freedom recipients, civil rights, religious and civic leaders, former U.S. Senators, and prominent individuals in the world of arts and entertainment. Since last November, CMFE's roster has expanded to include an even broader spectrum of civil rights and religious leaders, the Founder and President of the Rutherford Institute, the Editor of the *American Spectator*, and a former United States Ambassador.

There can be no question that CMFE was able to assemble this cross-section of prominent U.S. citizens to call for a moratorium on federal executions because the public is prepared to carefully re-examine the use of capital punishment in this nation. At no time since the death penalty was reinstated by the Supreme Court in 1976 have Americans voiced such grave doubts about the fairness and reliability of capital punishment. At the state level, those doubts are reflected in the unprecedented moratorium on executions put into place by Governor Ryan of Illinois, in death penalty moratorium bills introduced and enacted in state legislatures, and in studies commissioned by Governors in other states. At the national level, Senator [Dianne] Feingold [D-CA] has introduced a bill calling for a moratorium on federal executions and Senator [Patrick] Leahy

[D-VT] has introduced legislation that would require greater protections for those prosecuted for capital crimes at the state and federal levels. Professional, community and civil rights organizations, including the League of United Latin American Citizens (LULAC), the National Urban League, the NAACP, the Black Leadership Forum, the Leadership Conference on Civil Rights and the American Bar Association, have called on the Executive Branch to suspend federal executions, and religious organizations have intensified their long-standing calls for a death penalty moratorium.

When CMFE addressed President Clinton on November 20, we were responding to the September 12 release of the Department of Justice survey that documented racial, ethnic and geographic disparities in the charging of federal capital cases. The CMFE wrote: "Unless you take action, executions will begin at a time when your own Attorney General has expressed concern about racial and other disparities in the federal death penalty process. Such a result would be an intolerable affront to the goals of justice and equality for which you have worked during your Presidency. Consequently, we urge you to put in place a moratorium until the Department of Justice completes its review of the federal death penalty process."

As I speak to you today, of course, the first federal execution in almost 40 years has been carried out. The man put to death was not Mr. Garza, who now faces execution in less than a week's time, on June 19 [Garza was executed that day at the U.S. Penitentiary in Terre Haute, Indiana].

Mr. Garza did not precede Timothy McVeigh to the death chamber in Terre Haute because, on December 7, 2000, President Clinton stayed Mr. Garza's execution for six months. While the President announced that he was not prepared to

halt all federal executions, he nonetheless told the nation that further examination of possible racial and regional bias in the federal death penalty system "... should be completed before the United States goes forward with an execution in a case that may implicate the very questions raised by the Justice Department's continuing study. In this area there is no room for error."

Nothing has transpired since President Clinton's December 7 statement and grant of reprieve that warrants going forward with Mr. Garza's execution nor with carrying out the death sentence of any of the other 19 individuals on federal death row. We reject any suggestion that the report released by Mr. Ashcroft on June 6 constitutes a reliable or thorough study of possible racial and regional bias in the federal death penalty system. Nor does it answer the troubling questions raised by the Justice Department's September 12 survey.

On December 8, the day following the President's decision to stay Mr. Garza's execution, I was one of several CMFE representatives, who, along with Congressman John Conyers, met with former Attorney General Reno, former Deputy Attorney General Holder and other Justice Department attorneys to discuss President Clinton's announcement and plans for a more comprehensive investigation of the federal death penalty, which would include the participation of outside experts. Members of the Department of Justice acknowledged that this critical task could not be accomplished by the end of April of this year, the timetable set by President Clinton when he announced the December reprieve for Mr. Garza.

The result of that discussion with Attorney General Reno and Deputy Attorney General Holder was memorialized in the CMFE's letter to President Clinton, dated January 4, 2001.

We next learned that on January 10, 2001, the National Institute of Justice assembled a group of experts from within and without the Department of Justice to discuss the parameters of the comprehensive investigation that the Attorney General, Deputy Attorney General and the President had announced was needed.

At his confirmation hearing, then-Attorney General-designate John Ashcroft stated that evidence of racial disparities in the application of the federal death penalty "troubles me deeply." Acknowledging he was "unsure" why more than half the federal capital prosecutions were initiated in less than one-third of the states, the Attorney General asserted that he was also "troubled" by this evidence.

He expressed his approval of a "thorough study of the system," and proclaimed, "Nor should race play any role in determining whether someone is subject to capital punishment."

On June 4, 2001, CMFE wrote to President Bush, reiterating our call for a moratorium on federal executions. We raised the concern that the Attorney General's actions and statements subsequent to his confirmation hearing "cast doubt" on "the Administration's commitment to the principles he set forth at his confirmation hearing." We noted that "[t]here has been no indication that the Department intends to continue the necessary independent investigation of racial and geographic bias in the death penalty, which was to have been administered by the National Institute of Justice. Moreover, Attorney General Ashcroft's statements to members of Congress, including his testimony before the House Appropriations Committee in early May, suggest that even the internal inquiry that the Department of Justice embarked upon will consist of little more than a re-analysis of the same data already examined and found to demonstrate 'troubling' racial and geographic disparities." Just two days later, on June 6

2001, the Department of Justice released a flawed study purporting to demonstrate that federal administration of the death penalty was bias-free.

Now, Attorney General Ashcroft claims that "there is no evidence of favoritism towards white defendants in comparison with minority defendants." But such evidence does exist, and its existence raises serious doubts about fairness in our criminal justice system.

Without guarantees of fairness, there can be no public confidence in the administration of justice.

That lack of confidence is heightened and the guarantees of fairness are lessened by the Department of Justice's recent report on the Federal Death Penalty System.

Evidence of race-of-victim discrimination was ignored. Differences among geographical regions in which the penalty is sought by United States' Attorneys, approved by the Attorney General, and imposed by juries were ignored. Stark racial differences in death-penalty avoidance by whites and minorities who enter a plea to a non-capital charge were not fully examined or explained. The entrance of racial disparities at discrete stages in decision-making was evaded. Arguments for further study by researchers assembled by the Department of Justice were ignored.

Before Tuesday [June 11, 2001, the day Timothy McVeigh was executed], the United States had not executed anyone for nearly 40 years. What is the hurry, especially when life and liberty are at stake? When asked at his confirmation hearing, "Do you agree with President Clinton that there is a need for 'continuing study' of 'possible racial and regional bias' because 'in this area there is no room for error?'" the Attorney General unequivocally answered, "Yes!"

Attorney General Ashcroft has broken his pledge to the United States Senate. There has been no "thorough study of the system." It has fallen to you to assure Americans that, at least when it comes to the ultimate penalty in our federal system, justice is blind to race and ethnicity.

You cannot fix everything that is wrong in our justice system, but you can do this.

# The Death Penalty: Justice Served

## ANDREW G. MCBRIDE

### INTRODUCTION

I am honored to appear…today on the important subject of the fair and even-handed enforcement of the federal death penalty.…

I believe that the death penalty serves an important role in the spectrum of penalties that the federal criminal justice system has available. Recent studies indicate the death penalty does in fact play a role in the general deterrence of capital crimes. We know the death penalty accomplishes specific deterrence, for it eliminates the possibility that a known-killer will kill again in prison or upon eventual release. The death penalty offers an additional measure of protection for our federal law enforcement officers—who are often faced with the prospect of arresting violent felons who are already facing life imprisonment. Most importantly, the death penalty sends a message of society's outrage and resolve to defend itself against the most heinous of crimes. As we have seen most recently in the [Oklahoma City federal building bomber Timothy] McVeigh case, it gives survivors a sense of justice and closure that even life imprisonment without parole cannot accord. As a former prosecutor who has tried capital cases, and as a citizen, I share the concern [everyone here] that the death penalty be enforced in a fair, even-handed, and race-neutral manner. At the same time, I am wary of the misuse of race and racial statistics as a "stalking horse" for those who are opposed to the death penalty in all circumstances. Honest opposition to capital punishment on moral grounds is one thing, throwing charges of racism at federal law enforcement officers and federal prosecutors in order to block enforcement of a penalty the Congress has authorized and the American people clearly support, is another. I fear that some of my fellow panelists today have let vehement opposition to all capital punishment blind them to some simple facts about enforcement of the federal death penalty.

### THERE IS NO CREDIBLE STATISTICAL EVIDENCE OF RACIAL BIAS IN THE ENFORCEMENT OF THE FEDERAL DEATH PENALTY

The dangers of statistical analyses are perhaps best captured in the old saying "Figures never lie but liars often figure." [We] should be very wary of the results of regression analysis or other statistical devices applied to capital punishment. No two capital defendants are the same. No two capital crimes are the same. Federal law and the Eighth Amendment require that juries be allowed to consider every aspect of the crime, the background and competence of the defendant, and even impact evidence regarding the victim, in arriving at the correct punishment. Regression analysis posits that each factor relevant to the imposition of the death penalty can be identified and then given an assigned weight, such that very different cases can be meaningfully compared. This premise is simply false. There are literally millions of legitimate variables that a prosecutor or jury could consider in seeking or imposing capital punishment. If we truly believed that they could all be identified and weighted, we would allow computers to deliberate and impose penalty. Instead, we quite properly rely upon human judgment, the judgment of the prosecutor, the death penalty committee in the Department of Justice, the Attorney General, the district court judge, and a fairly-selected jury from the venue where the crime occurred. In my opinion, and in my experience for seven years as a federal prosecutor, I saw no evidence that the race of defendants or victims had any overt or covert influence on this process. I believe the charge is fabricated by those who wish to block enforcement of the federal death penalty for other reasons.

I would ask [you] to keep four points in mind as it evaluates these very serious, but, in my opinion, wholly unsupported charges. First, pointing to statistical disparities between racial percentages of capital defendants and racial percentages in the population at large is utterly specious. The population at large does not commit violent felonies—only a small percentage of both the white and non-white communities are ever involved in violent crime. The sad fact is that non-whites are statistically much more likely to commit certain crimes of violence that might lead to death penalty prosecutions. African Americans make up approximately 13 percent of the nation's population. Yet, according to the FBI's 1999 uniform crime reports, there were 14,112 murder offenders in the United States in 1999, and of those offenders for whom race was known, 50 percent were black. Given that most murders are intra-racial, it is not surprising that of the 12,658 murder victims in 1999, 47 percent were black.

Capital crimes also are more likely to occur in urban areas that are more densely populated and tend to have higher minority populations. According to the FBI data, 43 percent of murders in 1999 were recorded in the South, the most heavily populated area of the country. The same data shows that the Nation's metropolitan areas reported a 1999 murder rate of 6 victims per 100,000 inhabitants, compared to rates of 4 per 100,000 for rural counties and cities outside metropolitan areas.

One cannot simply ignore these facts in evaluating the performance of our criminal justice system. Indeed, if the numbers of federal capital defendants of each race precisely mirrored their representation in society as a whole, that would be truly a cause for alarm. It would suggest real "racial profiling" in the death penalty.

Second, the federal government does not have general jurisdiction over all violent crimes committed within its jurisdiction. From 1988 to 1994, the only federal death available was for murder in relation to certain drug-trafficking crimes. This period coincided with the worst drug epidemic in our Nation's history—the spread of crack cocaine from New York and Los Angeles to all our major urban centers. Most of the participants in the drug organizations that distributed crack cocaine were black, and most of the homicides connected with this drug trade were black-on-black homicides. Approximately half of the defendants presently on federal death row were convicted of a drug-related homicide.

The Department of Justice study released last week indicates that the Eastern District of Virginia [a federal district court area] is a prime example of an area where the type of crime at issue and the needs of state and federal law enforcement have shaped the statistics. I was a prosecutor in that district for a period of seven years, and I can assure [you] that I never saw any racial bias in the investigation or charging stages by federal agents or prosecutors during my tenure there.

Drug-related homicide was a major problem in the urban areas of Richmond, Norfolk, and Virginia Beach. Many of these homicides were unsolved and had in fact been committed by interstate drug gangs with roots as far away as New York, Los Angeles, and even Jamaica. Joint task forces, composed of federal agents, state police, and local detectives investigated these cases under the supervision of federal prosecutors. Local leaders and politicians, including leaders of the African American community, welcomed this effort to focus federal resources on inner-city crimes and the unsolved murders of African-American citizens. These prosecutions were a classic example of the federal government lending support where support was needed and requested and the crimes had a significant interstate element. The results of aggressive federal prosecutions have included cutting the murder rate in Richmond, Virginia in half from its high in the early 1990's.

Third, the available statistical evidence indicates that whites who enter the federal capital system (both pre- and post-1994) are significantly more likely to face the death penalty than minority defendants. Thus, even opponents of the federal death penalty seem to concede that there is no racial bias in the Department of Justice procedures for determining whether or not to seek the death penalty. Instead, they posit racial bias in the decision to make a case federal in the first place. It is obvious that these critics have never served as a state or federal prosecutor. The same federal prosecutors who make the initial intake decision regarding state or federal prosecution also make the initial decision on the death penalty and prepare the recommendation memorandum to the Attorney General's standing committee. The proposition that they are severely racially biased in the former (the intake decision when capital status is unsure) but are not biased in the latter (when the decision to seek the death penalty is actually

made) is absurd. Intake decisions are made by supervisors in the United States Attorney's Offices, who often have fixed protocols with their state counterparts regarding certain crimes. The fact that a group of bank robbers is multi-jurisdictional, or that an organization's trafficking level of cocaine has gone above 10 kilograms of crack are factors likely to result in federal prosecution. Race is never a factor and the notion that federal law enforcement agents are making "racist" intake decisions (by themselves) is a baseless charge that displays a shocking lack of knowledge of how our federal/state criminal justice system actually works.

Fourth, [you] should not place any stock in statistical patterns or comparisons. A "pool" of approximately 700 federal capital cases is too small a cohort for any serious statistician to produce any reliable conclusions. Moreover, all such studies suffer from the flaw noted above—they assume that all the factors that influence capital punishment can be quantified. It is clear that they cannot be. Rather than focus on largely meaningless statistical games, we should focus on continuing and improving the procedures in place at the Department of Justice to ensure that every capital eligible crime is submitted and reviewed, and that every decision to seek the death penalty is fully justified by the facts and circumstances of the case.

## CONCLUSION

In my opinion as a former federal prosecutor, there is no racial bias in the federal capital system. The decision to seek federal prosecution itself is made by federal prosecutors based on largely fixed criteria regarding the interstate nature of the crime or other objective, non-racial factors. The decision to actually seek the death penalty for a capital eligible crime has several layers of review and includes a standing committee that ensures fairness and continuity. Statistical evidence is of little or no probative value in this area and is, in my opinion, being manipulated by those who simply oppose the federal death penalty for any crime. The American people overwhelmingly support capital punishment and Congress has made it available for a limited set of federal crimes. I believe that the Department of Justice has enforced these laws in an unbiased manner to date and that it will continue to do so under the leadership of Attorney General [John] Ashcroft.

# THE CONTINUING DEBATE:
## The Death Penalty

### What Is New

Globally, about half the world's countries have a death penalty, and about 40% use it at least occasionally. The United States is among the countries most likely to execute prisoners. According to Amnesty International, there were 1,146 known executions in 28 countries in 2003. Of these, 84% occurred in just four countries: China (726), Iran (108), the United States (65), and Vietnam (64).

The number of death row inmates in U.S. prisons has grown from 692 in 1980, to 2,246 in 1990, to 3,577 in 2003. The racial composition of the condemned is 44% African American, 44% white, 10% Latino, 1% Asian American, and 1% unclassified.

### Where to Find More

To review the legal background of capital punishment, including the U.S. Supreme Court's suspension of the death penalty in *Furman v. Georgia* (1972) and its reinstatement of capital punishment in *Gregg v. Georgia* (1976), go to Cornell University's Legal Information Institute at http://www.law.cornell.edu and enter "death penalty" in the search function. Also read the anti-death penalty article, William S. McFeely, "Trial and Error: Capital Punishment in U.S. History," January 2001 at http://historymatters.gmu.edu/d/5420/; and the more neutral review, Donna Lyons "Capital Punishment on Trial," *State Legislatures* (May 2000) at http://www.ncsl.org/ programs/cj/cappun.htm. For a group on each side of the issue, visit the Web sites of Pro-Death Penalty.com at http://www.prodeathpenalty.com/ and the Death Penalty Information Center at: http://www.deathpenaltyinfo.org/. Also visit the site that lists the more than 300 prisoners executed in Texas since 1982. What makes the site at http://www.tdcj.state.tx.us/stat/executedoffenders.htm worth visiting is that you can hyperlink from the name of each executed individual to a picture, personal information, and a description of the crime each committed. It puts a "face" on the data about both those convicted of murders and the victims.

### What More to Do

Discuss all the various permutations of the death penalty debate, including whether it is ever justified under any circumstances and, if so, under what circumstances; whether it is only justified by utilitarianism (if it deters later murders) and/or as punishment per se, and whether the fact that executions are not proportionate among various demographic groups is evidence that capital punishment should be abolished. Also, get active. The federal government and 38 states have death penalty laws on the books; 12 states and the District of Columbia do not. Find out the law in your state and support or oppose it.

# EDUCATION POLICY

## AFFIRMATIVE ACTION ADMISSIONS:
### Promoting Equality *or* Unfair Advantage?

### PROMOTING EQUALITY

**ADVOCATE:** 41 College Students and 3 Student Coalitions

**SOURCE:** Amicus Curiae brief to the U.S. Supreme Court in *Grutter v. Bollinger* (2003)

### UNFAIR ADVANTAGE

**ADVOCATE:** 21 Law Professors

**SOURCE:** Amicus Curiae brief to the U.S. Supreme Court in *Grutter v. Bollinger* (2003)

Surveys show that nearly all Americans support the idea of equal opportunity, but the data on the circumstances of various groups casts doubt on whether the country has yet to achieve it. Economically, for example, the average household income of whites is 63% greater than that of African Americans and 69% greater than that of Hispanics. The 24% poverty rate among black and Latino households is triple that for white households. There are also income gaps for the employed. For every dollar made by the average white worker, blacks make 72 cents, and Latinos make 65 cents. As for unemployment, the spring 2004 rate of white unemployment was about 4.3%, compared to 9.8% for blacks and 5.8% for Latinos. Moreover, significant disparities in poverty, income, and unemployment have persisted as far back as the data goes.

To address such gaps, the federal government began to promote affirmative action in 1961 when President John F. Kennedy issued Executive Order 10925 requiring that federally financed projects "take affirmative action to ensure that hiring and employment practices are free of racial bias."

Later, state and local governments also adopted affirmative action programs, and they and the federal government extended them to education and other areas. Title IX, featured in Debate 16, was part of that effort. Whether because of these policies or more general social changes, the position of women and minorities in education has improved somewhat. Women now make up a majority of college undergraduates and 44% of graduate students. Asian Americans are a greater percentage of both undergraduate and graduate students than they are in the general population. However, improvement for blacks and Latinos has been slower. Between 1980 and 2000, African Americans rose from 9.9% to 13.4% of undergraduates, and Latino enrollment went from 3.7% to 8.6%. This enrollment gap has created a large disparity in college graduates, with 28% of whites over age 25 having a bachelor's degree, compared to 16.5% of African Americans, and 10.6% of Hispanics. At the professional school level, white enrollment between 1980 and 2000 dropped from 81% to 73.9%, while black enrollment grew from 5.8% to 7.2%, and Latino enrollment climbed from 3.9% to 4.7%. This leaves minorities particularly underrepresented in law, medicine, and other professions. Among lawyers, 5.4% are blacks, and 3.9% are Latinos. African Americans are 6.5% of the physicians, and Hispanics are 3.4%. As a reference point, the population in 2000 was 69% white, 12.3% African American, 12.5% Hispanic, and 3.3% Asian American, with other groups making up the balance. Women were 51.9% of the population.

While Americans strongly support the theory of equal opportunity, many have disagreed with the application of affirmative action programs in education and other areas. As a result, there have been a number of court challenges alleging unconstitutional "reverse discrimination." The first significant education case was *Regents of the University of California v. Bakke* (1978), which involved the rejection of a white applicant to medical school that reserved 16% of its places for minority students. In a 5–4 decision, the Supreme Court ruled somewhat confusingly that (a) numerical quotas were not constitutional but that (b) race could legitimately be considered during the admissions process. The following articles trace the legal background more, but the ambiguities in the *Bakke* ruling created disagreements among various Circuit Courts of Appeals over what could and could not be done with respect to affirmative action admissions. This set the groundwork for two "companion" cases involving the University of Michigan. One, *Gratz v. Bollinger,* focused on undergraduate admission and involved the university giving minority students 20 points on a 150-point admissions score. The second, *Grutter v. Bollinger,* related to law school admissions but did not involve a stated quota or a point scheme, only the goal of achieving a "critical mass" of minority students.

The articles below relate to *Grutter,* although most of its underlying rationale also applied to *Gratz.* The two articles are *amicus curiae* (friend of the court) briefs filed by those who were not direct parties to the case but who the court agreed had an important concern. The first, supporting the university's affirmative action program, was filed by a coalition of three student groups and 41 individual students. The second, opposing the university, was written by 21 law professors.

## POINTS TO PONDER

➤ Read the briefs as a Supreme Court justice. What is your decision in *Grutter v. Bollinger* and why?

➤ Assuming the only difference *Gratz v. Bollinger* is the explicit use of a point system, would you make the same decision as in *Grutter* and why?

➤ What should affirmative action mean as a policy directive?

# Affirmative Action Admissions:
## Promoting Equality

### 41 COLLEGE STUDENTS AND 3 STUDENT COALITIONS

## STATEMENT OF THE CASE

When plaintiff filed suit in *Grutter v. Bollinger* in 1997, 41 individually named black, Latino, Native American, Arab American, Asian Pacific American, other minority and white students and three coalitions—United for Equality and Affirmative Action (UEAA), Law Students for Affirmative Action, and the Coalition to Defend Affirmative Action and Integration & Fight for Equality By Any Means Necessary (BAMN), sought and eventually won the right to present our defense of the Law School's affirmative action plan.

Beginning on the 16th of January 2001, a day after the Martin Luther King holiday, the *Grutter v. Bollinger* case went to trial. One month later, after 15 days of trial, and 24 witnesses, the case concluded. The student intervenors fought for the district court trial in order to disprove the plaintiff's claim of "reverse discrimination" and to lift the profound stigma that the attack on affirmative action has placed on the shoulders of minority students. We presented the overwhelming majority of evidence at trial: 15 of the 24 witnesses were called by us, and we used 28 hours and 48 minutes of the 30-hour limit imposed by the district court.

As the student intervenors will show, the plaintiff has not proved that she has been a victim of discrimination—and the United States has not offered a viable alternative to affirmative action. The facts show that if the plaintiff prevails in this Court, the Law School will quickly and inevitably resegregate. That conclusion is confirmed by the resegregation of the universities that has resulted from the end of affirmative action in California, Texas, and Florida. If the plaintiff prevails, gains toward integration will be reversed and replaced by a massive return to segregation starting in the most selective universities and spreading throughout higher education and into the society as a whole.

## I. RACE AND THE LAW SCHOOL APPLICATION POOL

For two-thirds of black students and 70 percent of Latino students, the path to the future leads through segregated elementary and secondary schools. The worst segregation, which was once in the South, is now in the major industrial states of the Northeast and Midwest. Michigan [has] 83 percent of its black students attending segregated schools. For Latinos, segregation by race and ethnicity is compounded by segregation by language, with 50 percent of the Latinos in California speaking Spanish at home. For Native Americans, over half live in cities where they face segregation like that faced by blacks and Latinos, while just under half remain in impoverished government-run reservations and boarding schools.

The segregation concentrates and compounds the effects of poverty. While poverty disadvantages the poor of all races, poor whites are more dispersed residentially, and their children are far more likely to enroll in schools that have a substantial number of middle-class students. That is far less likely for black, Latino, and Native American students.

Even for black students from middle- and upper-middleclass families, substantial disadvantage exists. For equivalent incomes, black families have less wealth, less education, and fewer relatives who can provide financial and other assistance in times of trouble. Even when middle class black people or Latinos move to nearby suburbs, the suburbs are, or quickly become, segregated and the school systems quickly decline. Even for the very few black families who move to stable white, upper-middleclass suburbs with good school systems, there remain racial isolation, stereotyping, tracking, and stigma.

In testimony at trial [in the Federal District Court] on behalf of the student defendants, Professor Gary Orfield of the Harvard University School of Education summarized the impact of segregation:

> There never was a separate but equal school system. That's because of many things. It's because the poverty levels in segregated schools are much higher....[T]here are fewer minorities in teacher training. There are many fewer teachers who choose to go to work in schools of this sort. Most teachers who start in segregated schools leave faster. The curriculum that is offered is more limited. The probability that the teacher will be trained in their field is much more limited. The level of competition is less. The respect for the institution in the outside world is less. The connections to colleges are less. There are more children with health problems....The population is much more unstable....The kids don't have books....There [are] no facilities....[I]t is like a different planet, a different society.

Segregation—separate and unequal schools—means that there are far fewer black, Latino, and Native American students who graduate from college. The national

pool of students who could apply to a school like Michigan is disproportionately white—and many of the comparatively small number of black, Latino, and Native American students in that pool attended segregated elementary and secondary schools.

## II. BIAS IN MICHIGAN'S ADMISSIONS SYSTEM WITHOUT AFFIRMATIVE ACTION

### A. A Segregated School in a Segregated Profession

Before the advent of affirmative action, there were very few black students who graduated from college, fewer still who applied to law school, and almost none who were admitted to law school.

In the 1950s and early 1960s, except for the law schools at the historically black colleges and universities, the nation's law schools were essentially all white and all male. In 1960, the nation had 286,000 lawyers, of whom 2180 were black and not more than 25 were Native American. The number of Latinos was not recorded but was unquestionably minuscule. Before 1968, each year there were about 200 black law graduates in the nation.

From 1960 through 1968, the Law School graduated 2687 law students, of whom four were black and none were Latino or Native American

### B. The LSAT

In the early 1960s, the University of Michigan Law School admitted students based on a rigid index that combined undergraduate grades with an LSAT score. At that time, the School was not nearly as selective as it would become. But as more students went to college—and as affirmative action began to open the doors to minorities and to women of all races—the number of applicants to all law schools expanded dramatically. The schools became more selective and the LSAT became far more important.

The plaintiff and the United States call the LSAT "objective"—but they offer no proof to support the claim that it is an "objective" measure of anything important or that it is "race-neutral" in any way. In fact, all the evidence at trial showed the reverse.

The uncontested evidence presented at trial by the student defendants also demonstrated that test scores had little predictive value. In an uncontested study, Professor Richard Lempert, a member of the committee that drafted the 1992 policy, testifying for the students at trial, established that an applicant's LSAT score did not correlate with later success as a lawyer, measured by income, stated satisfaction, or political and community leadership.

### C. Undergraduate Grades

The other major "objective" criterion in the traditional Law School admissions system is the undergraduate grade point average (UGPA). While the racial gap on that average is much smaller than the LSAT gap, the gap is still significant when admissions are very competitive, as they have been at the Law School for many years.

The racial segregation in K–12 education causes part of the racial gap in UGPAs; but the conditions on the nation's campuses also contribute to the gap. Black, Latino, and Native American students feel and are isolated; and the cumulative effect of a daily run of slights and profiling takes its toll on black and other minority students. As the district court conceded, while the effect cannot be quantified for each student, racial prejudice depresses the undergraduate grades and overall academic performance of minority students who apply to Law Schools.

The grids prepared by the plaintiff's chief witness, Dr. Kinley Larntz, reflect the gap in test scores and grades and stand as a measure of the cumulative effect of discriminatory tests, segregated education, social inequality, and the depressing effect of racial prejudice on the undergraduate grades and overall academic performance of minority students.

### III. THE LAW SCHOOL AFFIRMATIVE ACTION PROGRAM

Under pressure from students on the campus and the civil rights movement, the law faculty began an intense series of debates that stretched from the 1960s through the current date about how to deal with the realities outlined above.

In the course of those debates, faculty members repeatedly recognized that numerical credentials discriminated against black and other minority applicants, "caus[ing] [their] actual potential...to be underestimated, especially when gauged by standard testing procedures...thought to be 'culturally biased.'"

In 1973, the [University of Michigan] Law School graduated 41 black students and its first Latino student. In 1975, it graduated its first two Asian-Americans, followed by its first Native American in 1976. The increasing number of black and other minority students cleared the way for the admission of increasing numbers of women of all races.

After this Court handed down its decision in *Bakke* in June 1978, the faculty formulated a policy to comply with the decision.

In 1992, the faculty adopted the plan that is now in effect. The plan calls for consideration of each applicant as an individual; attempts to seek many forms of diversity; and states the School's commitment to enrolling a "critical mass" of black, Latino, and Native American students, who would not be admitted to the Law School in significant numbers without that commitment.

## IV. WHAT ENDING AFFIRMATIVE ACTION WOULD MEAN

In ruling for the plaintiff, the district court conceded that the elimination of affirmative action at the Law School would result in an immediate reduction in underrepresented minority enrollment of over 73 percent. But this would only be the start. The end of affirmative action at selective colleges would dramatically reduce the pool of minority applicants to the Law School, driving the number of minority law students down still further. Within a few years at most, the Law School would again be nearly as segregated as it was in the 1960s.

In 1997, the ban on affirmative action announced by the University of California (UC) Board of Regents went into effect. The following year, only one black student enrolled at Boalt Hall. Minority enrollment at the UCLA School of Law dropped dramatically.

The few black and other minority students who remain at California's most selective campuses have faced increased racism caused by the elimination of affirmative action.

Dr. Eugene Garcia, the Dean of the Graduate School of Education at Berkeley, testified that black, Latino, and Native American students have been forced from the flagship campuses of the UC system onto its two least selective campuses. As the state's population continues to grow, the "cascade" will continue until the vast majority of black, Latino, and Native American students are forced out of the UC system altogether.

The UC faculty and administrations opposed the ban and sought to undo its effects. At Berkeley, the school downplayed the importance of grades and test scores; at UCLA, the school attempted to substitute the consideration of socio-economic status for the consideration of race. Because neither approach could serve as a substitute for affirmative action, both schools found it impossible to enroll a class including more than token numbers of black and other minority students.

## SUMMARY OF THE ARGUMENT

In this case, the plaintiff is asking the Court to reinterpret the American Constitution to the dramatic detriment of black, Latino, and other minority people and women of all races. If the Court does what [the] plaintiff asks, it will resegregate, divide, and polarize our country. The authority of the Court would be compromised.

Segregation and inequality are increasing in education. Irrespective of the legal forms used to enforce, to maintain, or passively to justify the separate and unequal condition of education at virtually every level, the fact stands as a profound insult and provocation to the minority youth of America and to the best of the nation's legal and political traditions. Minority children are, in their increasing majority, relegated to second-class, segregated schools—today's version of the back of the bus. The very small handful of black, Mexican American, and Native American students who have made it to the front of America's education bus—institutions like the University of Michigan Law School—are now being told by the plaintiff to get out of their seat and move to the back of the bus.

The demographic fabric of America is changing. By the middle of this century, no racial grouping will be in the majority. America will be a more diverse society; it must not become a more segregated society. We must strive to make equality more, not less, of a reality, or we will surely face renewed social convulsions.

The movement to defend affirmative action and integration has awakened and stirred into action every sector of this society. What unites these many peoples in defense of affirmative action is the conviction that the Constitution's pledge of equality should have meaning and currency in our collective American future. Our progress as a nation depends on the realization of this prospect.

# Affirmative Action Admissions:
## Unfair Advantage

### 21 LAW PROFESSORS

### INTEREST OF *AMICI CURIAE*

*Amici curiae* are law professors with a professional interest in promoting learning environments free from the taint of racial discrimination. *Amici* are committed to the principles of equality under law embodied in the Constitution, and oppose invidious racial discrimination of any kind. In particular, *amici* oppose as unconstitutional the race-based admissions policies employed by the University of Michigan School of Law and many other institutions of higher learning. A list of the *amici* and their institutional affiliations is provided as an appendix to this brief. The institutional affiliations are for identification purposes only. The views expressed in this brief are those of the individual *amici* and do not necessarily reflect the views of the institutions at which they teach.

### SUMMARY OF ARGUMENT

This Court should hold that "diversity" is not a compelling state interest sufficient to justify race-based discrimination. First, "diversity" is employed by universities as a shorthand term for discrimination on the basis of race, is indistinguishable from the use of quotas, and is not a remedial interest. Second, racial "diversity" in the classroom does not constitute academic diversity; to the contrary, it is based on racial stereotyping and fosters stigmatization and hostility. Furthermore, even stereotypically assuming it resulted in a greater diversity of views and information, such a result is not a compelling interest that would outweigh constitutional rights in this or other contexts. Finally, "diversity" is a race-balancing inter-

est that would, by its own terms, require race discrimination for eternity.

### ARGUMENT

The Court has held repeatedly that racial classifications are *"presumptively invalid and can be upheld only upon an extraordinary justification."* (*Shaw v. Reno*, 1993) Race-based classifications can survive strict scrutiny only if they are narrowly tailored to serve a compelling state interest.

The University of Michigan School of Law ("Michigan") employs race-based classifications in its admissions policies, and race often is the deciding factor between the admission of one applicant and the rejection of another with equal or better qualifications. The questions for this Court, therefore, are whether Michigan's asserted interest is constitutionally "compelling" and whether its admissions program is narrowly tailored to serve that interest.

*Amici* [we] respectfully submit that this Court should state in words so clear that they cannot be misunderstood by university administrators that the use of racial preferences, classifications, or "pluses" for the purpose of achieving a racially diverse student body is prohibited by the Fourteenth Amendment. The failure of the Court to address the "diversity" question head-on could have devastating consequences for the rights of individuals of all races who participate in the admissions process. Since *Bakke* [*University of California v. Bakke*, 1978], the "diversity" principle in practice has been used to create a loophole through which universities continue to discriminate broadly and openly on the basis of race.

## I. MICHIGAN'S DIRECT PURSUIT OF RACIAL DIVERSITY NECESSARILY ENTAILS RACIAL CLASSIFICATIONS

The pursuit of "diversity" in general is a broad and potentially varied exercise that can turn on any number of characteristics or traits. Universities can seek geographic diversity, intellectual diversity, athletic and artistic diversity, and even socio-economic diversity. Those qualities are directly relevant to the educational mission and are not themselves constitutionally suspect. But the direct pursuit of *racial* diversity as an end unto itself, and as a supposed means of creating other types of diversity, is quite different. That pursuit involves taking a single characteristic—race—that the Constitution and this Court have declared unrelated to legitimate bases for distinguishing among individuals, and relying upon it not withstanding such admonitions.

### A. Pursuit of "Diversity" Is a Euphemism for Race-Based Decisionmaking

Making disingenuous use of Justice Powell's lone dictum regarding "diversity," [in the *Bakke* decision], universities such as Michigan have adopted the seemingly benign language of pursuing diversity in general as a misleading euphemism for decision-making processes and goals based overtly on race. It is the view and experience of *amici* here that whatever nods of the head universities make toward more general notions of diversity, their affirmative action programs, such as the one in this case, remain targeted at a narrow vision of *racial* diversity *regardless* of the consequences of such programs for other types of diversity.

Numerous experienced law professors, including even those who support racial preferences in admissions, have recognized and acknowledged that the language of educational diversity in the admissions context is generally used as a cover for direct racial decision-making. Such professors speak not merely as academics who have studied the issue, but as first-hand observers within law school communities and administrations, and often as direct participants of the very admissions processes they describe. Professor Alan Dershowitz of Harvard has been forthright about the deceptive use of the "diversity" label in connection with race-driven admissions programs:

> The *raison d'être* for race-specific affirmative action programs has simply never been diversity for the sake of education. The checkered history of "diversity" demonstrates that it was designed largely as a cover to achieve other legally, morally, and politically controversial goals. In recent years, it has been invoked—especially by professional schools—as a clever post facto justification for increasing the number of minority group students in the student body.

Professor Samuel Issacharoff, of Columbia and formerly of Texas, makes a similar point. One of the attorneys who defended the University of Texas School of Law's racedriven admissions policy, has nonetheless has acknowledged that "diversity" is the current jargon for racial discrimination: "[O]ne of the clear legacies of *Bakke* has been to enshrine the term 'diversity' within the legal lexicon to cover everything from curricular enrichments to thinly-veiled set-asides."

Other experienced law professors with diverse views of the affirmative action issue in general have recognized the same truth.

Professor Jed Rubenfeld of Yale, who defends "affirmative action" on non-diversity grounds not advanced by Michigan in this case, notes the disingenuousness of the claim that race-driven admissions advance true "diversity" measured by any criteria *other than* race. "[T]he pro-affirmative action crowd needs to own up to the weaknesses of 'diversity' as a defense of most affirmative action plans. Everyone knows that in most cases a true diversity of perspectives and backgrounds is not really being pursued.

In the end, even the proponents of affirmative action, if they are being candid, recognize that the "diversity" pursued by programs such as Michigan's is directly race-based in both its means and its ends, favoring or disfavoring particular races for their own sake without concern for diversity of qualities other than race. While such programs may pay lip-service to intellectual or experiential qualities other than race, they invariably collapse back to using race for its own sake, or as a proxy for other, pertinent, qualities without regard to whether such racial stereotyping is true or permissible.

### B. Direct Pursuit of Racial Diversity Is Functionally Indistinguishable from Racial Quotas

"Diversity"-based admissions policies such as the one at Michigan necessarily begin and end with some perceived level of optimal diversity among the characteristics —in this case race—that they use to classify candidates. In order to achieve its claimed interest in diversity, Michigan must have at least some sense of what constitutes the proper representation of each race before it can decide that certain racial groups are "under-represented" and the student body thereby insufficiently diverse. Professor Issacharoff candidly acknowledges the point:

> The problem with diversity as a justification for a challenged affirmative action program is that it is an almost incoherent concept to opera-

tionalize, unless diversity means a predetermined number of admittees from a desired group....[S]elective institutions must approach the applicant pool with predetermined notions of what an appropriately balanced incoming class should look like.

The only way to ensure adequate "representation" among the races at the end of the admissions process is to begin with an institutional definition of "diversity" that necessarily produces the desired proportions of racial representation in a class of admitted students. Michigan's "diversity" policy is symbolic of the numbers game that has become synonymous with admissions policies that employ racial preferences. For example, members of Michigan's admissions staff receive "daily reports," which track applicants by race. Dennis Shields, the former director of admissions at Michigan, has acknowledged that "as an admissions season progressed, he would consult the daily reports more and more frequently in order to keep track of the racial and ethnic composition of the class." Mr. Shields said that he did this to ensure that a "critical mass" of minority students were enrolled. "Diversity in education" through race-driven admissions is meaningless without quotas or something constituting the functional equivalent of a quota system.

The district court determined after careful consideration of all of the facts that the "critical mass" concept is functionally equivalent to a quota system. The district court explained:

> [O]ver the years, [critical mass] has meant in practice that the law school attempts to enroll an entering class 10% to 17% of which consists of underrepresented minority students. The 10% figure, as a target, has historical roots going back to the late 1960s. Beginning in the 1970s.

the law school documents begin referring to 10–12% as the desired percentage. Professor Lempert testified that critical mass lies in the range of 11–17%. Indeed this percentage range appeared in a draft of the 1992 admissions policy, and it was omitted from the final version despite Professor Regan's suggestion that it remain for the sake of "candor."

"Diversity" policies must be described as what they are—means of implementing racial quotas. That such quotas might be informal or hidden under a cloak of rhetoric does not change that essential fact.

### C.  "Diversity" Is Not a Remedial Interest

Thus far, the only constitutionally compelling interest recognized by this Court as satisfying strict scrutiny for racial classifications is the remediation of the effects of past race discrimination.

Michigan's "diversity" policy is not, and does not purport to be, remedial. The question for this Court then is whether "diversity" should be added as a "compelling," not merely valid or permissible, state interest that can be used to justify direct and intentional racial discrimination.

Because the Court has "strictly" limited the use of racial classifications to the remedial context, respondents must demonstrate that there is something so special, so *compelling,* about marginal differences in the educational experiences of post-secondary students that universities, alone among our government-sponsored institutions, should be allowed to practice what the Constitution prohibit[s]—naked race discrimination. Although the question properly posed seems to answer itself, an examination of the realities of "diversity" in the classroom also leads to the conclusion that this so-called justification for discrimination does not pass constitutional muster.

### II.  RACIAL "DIVERSITY" IS NOT A COMPELLING INTEREST

Because the pursuit of racial diversity for its own sake is an affront to the Fourteenth Amendment, the defenders of "diversity" ultimately resort to some version of the argument that bringing together persons of different "backgrounds"—as defined by their skin color or national origin—will "enhance" the educational experience of students by creating academic or viewpoint diversity. But Michigan's admissions policy, and other "diversity" policies like it, cannot be defended on the ground that racial diversity promotes academic diversity. The defense of "diversity" programs on the ground that they expose people of different races to one another, thereby facilitating learning, respect and appreciation among the races, does not relate to a true "interest in intellectual diversity—diversity of 'experiences, outlooks and ideas' that would otherwise be left out—but specifically in racial and ethnic diversity as such."

### A.  Interests in "Diversity" That Assume Stereotyping Cannot Have Compelling Weight

The "diversity" rationale suggests that it is permissible to use race as a proxy for experiences, outlooks or ideas, and that the use of race as a proxy will ensure that different viewpoints are brought to the classroom. But however desirable a diversity of *ideas* may be, there is no basis for categorizing it as "compelling," rather than merely acceptable or substantial for purposes of analyses *other than* strict scrutiny. The abhorrent essential predicate to the interest—governmental stereotyping of different races as to their views—also assures that the interest in racial diversity for its secondary viewpoint effects cannot count as compelling.

Common sense and classroom experiences demonstrate that "viewpoint diversity" and "academic diversity" in the classroom are not affected by the racial composition of a student body. Dean and long-time professor at Michigan, Professor Terrance Sandalow, wrote in the *Michigan Law Review*:

"My own experience and that of colleagues with whom I have discussed the question, experience that concededly is limited to the classroom setting, is that racial diversity is not responsible for generating ideas unfamiliar to some members of the class. Students do, of course, quite frequently express and develop ideas that others in the class have not previously encountered, but even though the subjects I teach deal extensively with racial issues, I cannot recall an instance in which, for example, ideas were expressed by a black student that have not also been expressed by white students. Black students do, at times, call attention to the racial implications of issues that are not facially concerned with race, but white and Asian-American students are in my experience no less likely to do so."

Racial diversity is not required to foster a full discussion of issues and viewpoints in the classroom. If a white applicant and a black applicant each have the same view on an issue, and their respective race is ignored as it must be under the Constitution, there is no true "intellectual" or "academic" reason for admitting one of the students over the other.

Any "diversity" policy that is premised on the notion that people of different races bring particular viewpoints to the classroom solely because of their race should be struck down. If schools truly think that viewpoint diversity enhances education, they can pursue it directly rather than using race as a proxy.

Apparently realizing the difficulty of defending its admissions policy on the ground that race defines viewpoint, Michigan attempts an alternative claim that racial diversity in the classroom is required to *dismantle* stereotypes.

[The University of] Michigan argues in essence that, because it assumes individuals generally believe that members of a "minority" race all share the same viewpoint on all issues, the educational experiences of members of the benighted majority will be "enhanced" by interaction with a "critical mass" of minority students. This argument merely shifts the stereotyped assumptions over to the majority racial group, but is no less offensive therefore.

Moreover, Michigan hardly needs racial preferences to teach the obvious—that not all members of any given minority think alike. If, miraculously, something more were needed to make this point to students, surely a sufficiently diverse *reading list* would suffice. Michigan's self-contradictory treatment of individuals as members of groups, purportedly in order to demonstrate that individuals are *not* members of groups, is closer to being incredible than it is to being compelling.

### B. Discrimination Resulting from Racial Stereotyping Results in Stigmatization and Hostility

Even if one were to hypothesize that a compelled increase in racial diversity would increase educationally valuable viewpoint diversity to some degree, it would also generate educationally detrimental stigma and hostility based on precisely the same type of stereotyping regarding race employed by the University. Indeed, policies that seek diversity through race are [according to one scholar] a "statement by government that certain persons identified by race are in fact being placed in positions they may be presumed not likely to hold but for their race."

"Diversity" admissions programs, such as Michigan's, foster rather than minimize the focus on race. The policy treats preferred minorities as a group, rather than as individuals. Although Michigan purports to consider other types of diversity—such as unusual employment experiences and extracurricular activities—race is the most identifiable diversity factor that separates one applicant from another.

*Amici's* collective experiences support the conclusion that both students who are admitted, and those who are not admitted, recognize that race indisputably plays an important role in admissions. Applicants from races that do not benefit from Michigan's preferences, who have high LSAT scores and GPAs, but who nonetheless are denied admission, will likely conclude that race determined their fate in the admissions process. Similarly, members of all races who gain admission may believe that their minority classmates would not be their classmates but for their race. Because of the lowered expectations that accompany racial preferences in admissions, members of minority groups are and will be stigmatized—sometimes self-stigmatized—as inferior.

The racial hostility and stigmatization that is bred in universities as a result of racial preferences is felt both in our classrooms and throughout all of society. If not stopped now, the hostility and scarring that can result from racial preferences based on "diversity" could take generations to heal. At a minimum, however, such consequences cut against any claimed benefits and render Michigan's asserted interest in the educational benefits of racial diversity necessarily less than compelling.

### C. Government-Defined Viewpoint Diversity Is Not a Compelling Interest

Regardless whether racial classifications generate viewpoint diversity and accepting that viewpoint diversity is, in general, a valuable thing in an educational environment, that does not even remotely satisfy the requirement that it must be a "compelling"

interest sufficient to justify otherwise unconstitutional conduct. The difficulty in too-easy a transition from merely desirable to constitutionally compelling seems apparent: We would not authorize state universities to violate students' right to free speech or free exercise of religion on the ground that doing so would, in the view of academics, create a better educational environment or a greater "diversity" of views.

But if it is a compelling interest to discriminate on the basis of race in order to promote an educational atmosphere with a supposedly more diverse set of student views, then it is unavoidably a compelling interest for all other constitutional purposes. The notion that the government might impose a myriad of speech restrictions and compulsions in the name of "diversity" demonstrates the absurd premise that marginal differences in educational diversity rise to the level of "compelling" state interests.

### D. The "Diversity" Rationale Is Limitless

"Diversity" also fails as a "compelling interest" because it has no logical stopping point. The Court has repeatedly rejected alleged "compelling interests" that extend indefinitely into the future.

By definition, a "diversity" interest supports indefinite discrimination on the basis of race in university admissions because there will always be a need to engage in race-based decisionmaking to ensure a "properly diverse" student body. "Diversity"—with its concomitant quotas and careful monitoring of racial admissions—indeed would *require* unending use of race in admissions.

For this reason, and for all of the other reasons set forth above, "diversity" does not constitute an extraordinary justification sufficient to overcome the presumptive invalidity of government-sponsored race discrimination.

## THE CONTINUING DEBATE:
### Affirmative Action Admissions

### What Is New

In 2003, the Supreme Court upheld the University of Michigan's position in *Grutter v. Bollinger* and rejected it in *Gratz v. Bollinger*. By a 5 to 4 vote in *Grutter*, the court permitted the law school's use of race as one factor in determining admissions on the grounds that a "compelling state interest" existed in promoting diversity at all levels of society. But by 6 to 3 in *Gratz*, the justices rejected the undergraduate admission process that gave automatic points to minorities on the admissions scale. These decisions reconfirmed *Bakke*, but thereby also left some of that decision's uncertainties in place about how to judge an affirmative action program without resorting to numbers when establishing goals or monitoring progress.

Perhaps reflecting the fine line the court walked in the two decisions, public opinion about affirmative actions varies with the way the question is asked. For example, consider the wording and results of three polls taken in 2003. The first asked Americans if they "generally favor or oppose affirmative action programs for racial minorities? A plurality (49%) replied, "favor," 43% said "oppose," and 8% were unsure. The second poll introduced a reason for affirmative action, asking, "In order to overcome past discrimination, do you favor or oppose affirmative action programs…[for minorities]?" With that prompt, support for affirmative action was much higher (63% in favor, 29% opposed, 8% unsure). By contrast, support declined to 38% (with 51% opposed, and 10% unsure) in a poll whose question included the word "preferences" ("Do you favor or oppose affirmative action programs that give preferences to…minorities?").

### Where to Find More

For an extensive legal and policy review of affirmative action, turn to Samuel Leiter and William M. Leiter, *Affirmative Action in Antidiscrimination Law and Policy: An Overview and Synthesis* (State University of New York Press, 2002). You can read the decisions and the dissents for both *Grutter v. Bollinger* and *Gratz v. Bollinger* by going to the Supreme Court Collection Web page of Cornell University's Legal Information Institute at http://supct.law.cornell.edu/supct/ and entering the case names in the search function. The Web site of the Coalition to Defend Affirmative Action and Integration & Fight for Equality By Any Means Necessary (BAMN), one of the student groups who filed an amicus curiae brief in *Grutter*, is at http://www.bamn.com/. An organization with an opposing point of view is American Civil Rights Institute at http://www.ACRI.org/.

### What More to Do

Write an admission policy for your university that addresses the demographic component. Then find out what your school's written policy is (if any) and interview admissions officials to find out how they implement affirmative action. How does the school's policy compare with your views?

# FOREIGN POLICY

## TORTURING TERRORISTS:
### Sometimes Justified *or* Always Abhorrent?

### SOMETIMES JUSTIFIED

**ADVOCATE:** Robert G. Kennedy, Professor of Management, University of St. Thomas

**SOURCE:** "Can Interrogatory Torture Be Morally Legitimate?," paper presented at the Joint Services Conference on Professional Ethics, U.S. Air Force Academy, January 2003

### ALWAYS ABHORRENT

**ADVOCATE:** Lisa Hajjar, Professor of Sociology, Law and Society Program, University of California-Santa Barbara

**SOURCE:** "Torture and the Future," *Middle East Report Online*, May 2004

Torture. Now there is a nasty word. Or is it always? *Can the ends ever justify the means?*

Many Americans expressed shock when the media revealed in 2004 that U.S. military guards had tortured and otherwise degraded prisoners at the Abu Ghraib prison in Iraq. Similar stories surfaced about alleged mistreatment of al-Qaeda and Taliban prisoners in Afghanistan and at the U.S. naval base at Guantánamo Bay, Cuba. There is no dispute that torture inflicted solely to cause suffering violates every standard of humanity and that the abuse of the Iraq prisoners of war was criminally wrong. Terrorists may be a different matter, though.

Moral absolutists hold that ends never justify means. Taking that position in *Groundwork on the Metaphysics of Morals* (1785), philosopher Immanuel Kant contended that we all should "do what is right though the world should perish [because of it]." Few people are absolutists, though. Instead, most of us implicitly practice moral relativism and judge actions by their context. For example, true pacifists are moral absolutists who would not kill for any reason, even to save their own life. A moral relativist is apt to believe that it is acceptable to kill someone in self-defense and perhaps in certain other circumstances, such as military service. The never-ending problem with moral relativism is where to draw the line.

Because most people equate terrorists with evil, the moral permissibility of torturing them as a means to achieve the laudable end of combating terrorism is a topic that Americans have begun to confront in recent years. The plot of the 1998 movie, *The Siege*, centered on the conflict between two officials sent to New York City after Muslim terrorists launched a series of strikes and the president declared marshal law. One is General William Deveraux played by Bruce Willis; the other is FBI agent Anthony "Hub" Hubbard, portrayed by Denzel Washington. To uncover terrorist cells and prevent more attacks, Deveraux tortures and even kills prisoners whom he believes are terrorists or have information about them. Hubbard is aghast at these tactics. In its climactic scene, the film condemns Deveraux, who is arrested by the heroic Hub and led away. Neatly given the film's moral viewpoint, the terrorist threat was defused anyway. But what if violence had continued? What if after the arrest of Deveraux, gentler interrogations had failed to uncover information that would have saved the lives of hundreds, even thousands of Americans who later perished. Would Hub have still been the hero?

*The Siege* was a clear reference to the 1993 terror attack that killed six people when a bomb planted by Muslims exploded in the underground garage of New York City's World Trade Center. No polls exist from that period to indicate how people felt about using torture to prevent terrorism. Clearer is that Hub was legally right at the time. Then torture violated several international treaties to which the United States is a party, including the United Nations Convention against Torture and Other Cruel, Inhuman or Degrading Treatment or Punishment (1984). That treaty makes it illegal for a country to use official torture, which it defines as:

> Any act by which severe pain or suffering, whether physical or mental, is intentionally inflicted on a person for such purposes as obtaining from him or a third person information,…when such pain or suffering is inflicted by or at the instigation of or with the consent or acquiescence of a public official or…person acting in an official capacity.

Now torture also violates U.S. law, including the Federal Anti-torture Statute (1994) and Executive Order No. 13107 (1998), by which President Clinton directed federal officials to abide by the convention against torture and other international treaties. Laws and executive orders can be changed, though, and so the debate here should focus on what the standard should be for the future, not on what has occurred.

## POINTS TO PONDER

➤ Consider where Kennedy and Haijar agree and disagree about using torture on common criminals and military prisoners of war, as well as about torturing proven or suspected terrorists.

➤ Think about the differences in the ways that Kennedy and Haijar consider the range of physical and psychological duress used on prisoners. Are distinctions between stress, abuse, and torture meaningful?

➤ Torturing an enemy military prisoner of war might extract information that would save American lives, just as torturing a terrorist might. If torture is sometimes justified, is it the status of the individual (captured soldier, captured terrorist) or what that person knows that legitimizes the torture?

# Torturing Terrorists: Sometimes Justified

## ROBERT G. KENNEDY

The immediate problem in this paper is the question of whether the imposition of severe pain or discomfort on a subject in a process of interrogation is always wrong. There should be no doubt that it can be wrong and probably quite often is wrong, but must it always be so? Proponents of the absolute position that it is always and everywhere wrong appeal to human dignity, human rights, and to a common sense revulsion at the thought of deliberating harming another human being. Fair enough, but the concept of human dignity (and its expression as a set of human rights) cannot merely be used as a trump card that ends discussion. It must be examined more carefully to determine what its concrete requirements are. Moreover, common sense, while it can be a good intuitive first step, can never be a substitute for systematic ethical analysis.

The task before us, then, is to think through the requirements of human dignity (and so human rights) and to use these requirements to evaluate the moral status of interrogation and interrogatory methods.

## WHAT DOES HUMAN DIGNITY REQUIRE?

The problem posed by the urgent need for successful interrogations and the ancient and understandable hostility to torture is but a species of a larger issue. This larger issue is the question of when, if ever, human persons may legitimately be coerced to act against their wills and, more particularly, whether physical force of one sort or another may be used as an element of coercion. Other species of this larger issue include the disciplining of children, the defense of persons or property by private individuals, police actions, and war. Each of these involves instances in which (physical) force might be required to bring about legitimate ends. Would the use of force in any of these categories necessarily constitute a violation of human dignity and human rights?

The idea that human persons are endowed with a value or a dignity (from the Latin *dignus* = value, worth) is an ancient one. As it is derived from the Judaeo-Christian theological tradition, it has not been a universal feature of Western civilizations. At the root of the idea is the conviction that persons share equally in this dignity and that certain sorts of actions may never be chosen by others because they would constitute a violation or denial of that dignity. For example, the life of an innocent person may never be directly and intentionally taken, nor may a person ever be sodomized or raped. Each such act would reduce the person to the status of a thing and deny the value of that individual's personhood. This is what Kant meant when he said that persons must always be regarded as ends and never treated by others as mere means to ends chosen by those others.

The twentieth century, which witnessed some of history's most gruesome violations of human dignity, also was the century in which a commitment to human dignity was widely embraced, from the United Nations' *Universal Declaration of Human Rights* (1948) to the proliferation of human rights groups worldwide. This is undoubtedly a very good thing, but it also has brought with it a sort of rhetorical excess that can serve more to obscure than to promote. This can happen in two ways.

First, we often hear human dignity and human rights described as "inalienable" or "inviolable" or "absolute." This is misleading because it tends to merge two dimensions of human dignity into one. Human dignity is inalienable or inviolable but only if we are talking about the *existence* of the characteristic. To put it another way, the moral doctrine of human dignity insists that it is a characteristic that belongs to every person without exception, that it is permanent, and that it cannot justly be denied or extinguished. None of this pertains to the *extent* of human dignity.

Consider this simple example. It is widely agreed that human dignity requires respect for the right to own property. In the sense that no human person can be denied the right to own property as a matter of principle, the right is inviolable and absolute. However, this right to own property, as an expression of human dignity, does not by itself substantiate a claim to own this or that piece of property. Nor does it justify a limitless claim on pieces of property in the face of the overwhelming need of others. As regards its existence only, the right to own property is inalienable and inviolable; as regards its extent, the right may be justly qualified in a variety of ways and for a variety of reasons. Not least of these reasons will be the requirements of the common good of the society.

This distinction between existence and extent is obscured in discussions about human dignity and human rights when the absoluteness of the first category is carelessly applied to the second. As suggested above, some human rights are absolute, but most are not. Human dignity is both

protected by and governed by justice. One person's right to acquire property, for example, is limited by the right of others to hold their property in peace and safety.

A second category of confusion about human dignity has to do with what qualifies as a human right. There is an endless list of claims that can be dressed up in the language of human rights. Convicted criminals serving a prison sentence can claim that failing to provide them with pornography or Internet access is to deny them their human rights; same-sex partners (soon to be followed by polyamorous groups) can claim that the failure of states to recognize their relationship as a marriage is to deny their human rights; and so on. Such claims are rarely followed by tight arguments explaining why they should be considered human rights. Too often they are trump cards played to discourage further discussion by implicitly labeling opponents of the claims as potentially willing violators of human dignity.

These claims are frequently left unchallenged, however, because we are unclear about what a human right really is and how it may properly be limited.

Human rights are distinct from created or contingent rights. Created rights are not rooted in what it means to be a person but instead derive from some contingent event or relationship. They may be brought into being (and defined) by promises or contracts, legislation, relationships (family, friendship, etc.), or by some other event. By contrast human rights are defined by human nature and by the general requirements of a fulfilling human life. The catalogue of human rights would follow from a catalogue of basic human capacities and from the requirements of human well-being.

By way of example, a summary of human rights might be divided into four categories (though there could certainly be other ways to organize our thinking about the kinds of human rights). One would include rights related to the human capacity to reason, such as a right to the truth, to education, and to free inquiry. A second would include rights related to the human capacity to choose, such as (among many others) the liberty to choose an occupation, a spouse, or a place of residence. A third would concern individual well-being or, we might say, bodily integrity. Rights in this category would include the right to life, as well as rights to safety and freedom from intentional physical and psychological harm. The final category would be related to the social nature of the human person. Rights here could be the right to belong to a community, to form a family, and to participate in governance and culture.

Human dignity requires that the rights in each category be respected, but it does not require that each right be treated as if it were absolute in extent. Indeed, to demand this would be an absurdity, for to treat every right as if it were absolute in extent would create an impossible world. Every person possesses a right to know the truth but this cannot be absolutized in such a way as to extinguish the human right to privacy. We respect the human right to truth by not telling lies; we do not have a duty to be completely candid and to share every secret. Similarly, individuals have a human right to choose an occupation, but this is limited by their capacities and by the nature of the occupation. For example, there is no violation of rights if someone who cannot sing is denied a starring role with an opera company, nor is anyone free to choose robbery or blackmail as an occupation.

Furthermore, the full set of human rights, qualified though they may be in many general ways, are also qualified in individual instances by the requirements of justice. For example, individuals have a general right in their movements and in the way in which they structure their lives. Some régimes arbitrarily and unreasonably restrict the movement of their citizens and so violate that human right. However, individuals who abuse their freedom by engaging in criminal activity may justly forfeit some of this freedom to the state, or they may suffer some other penalty that may constitute a diminishment of their rights (e.g., a fine, mandatory community service, restitution, prohibition from working in a certain occupation, etc.). Assuming that the penalty is proportionate to the offense, it would not constitute a violation of a human right.

On the other hand, we have yet to consider whether the use of force, including the intentional imposition of pain or discomfort, is a necessarily violation of human rights, or whether it may sometimes be a justified exception.

## HUMAN RIGHTS AND THE USE OF FORCE AGAINST PERSONS

The human capacity to choose freely points us in the direction of a set of human rights that are both fundamental and extensive. Perhaps the most fundamental right in this set is the right to be free from coercion in making choices. The exercise of free will is one of the defining characteristics of the human person and so the most appropriate way to bring about a change in someone's plans or behavior is to use arguments (not to be confused with quarrels) and other forms of persuasion. The attempt to coerce someone to act against his will is ordinarily, therefore, a far more serious matter than simply restricting his freedom in some external way. If such a use of force is unjust it constitutes an immediate attack on human dignity and so must be avoided. The questions that we must address are whether the use of force or the imposition of pain may be justifiable and whether such justifiable coercion could occur in the context of interrogation. To this end we will try to tease out the broad outlines of a theory of the just use of force.

Can coercion be just? On the one hand, it would seem that coercion is never justified because coercion always aims to produce behavior that is contrary to the will of the person coerced. A moment's reflection, however, should make it clear that there is a major qualification to the right not to be compelled to act against one's will. This qualification is that one must will what is good, or at least that one cannot will what is harmful to others, to the good of the community, or, strictly speaking, to oneself.

Consider some examples in categories of action apart from interrogation in which force or pain might be used. For example, parents must discipline their children, which is to say that at minimum parents must shape habits in their children that will give them the capacity to avoid harming themselves and others. To this end parents legitimately restrict the freedom of their children to choose whatever pleases them, and sometimes the restrictions are physical and forceful. When these actions are done for the sake of the child's well-being (or for the well-being of others) and are proportionate to the achievement of that well-being, they are justified.

On rather a different level we have the private defense of persons and property. Few people would deny that individuals may justly use proportionate force to defend themselves, their families, and their property from unjust assault. This would be true even if, in cases where serious harm to the innocent were threatened, the defensive force resulted in severe harm or death to the attacker.

Or consider examples from the category of police action. Until relatively recently most police officers had a very limited range of options from which to choose when confronting a person engaged in a criminal act that threatened serious harm to persons or property. They could confront the person verbally, they could strike him or attempt to constrain him physically, or they could shoot him. Given the volatile situations in which officers could find themselves, most police departments have encouraged them to adopt fairly low thresholds for resorting to firearms. Though the rule may not be "When in doubt, shoot!" it is not too far from this. Within the last few years, however, a range of intermediate weapons has become available. These weapons are normally less-than-lethal, but they are capable of causing discomfort, significant pain, or even serious injury. Nevertheless, they are widely regarded as welcome additions to the police arsenal because they provide options better proportioned to most police incidents than the use of deadly weapons. Implicit in this acceptance is the recognition that some people behave in ways that cause them to forfeit their right not to be physically harmed. Another way of saying this is to say that people engaged in certain kinds of bad behavior can no longer assert their human right not to be harmed if force is necessary to deter or frustrate that behavior.

Of course, the most obvious example of this principle has to do with war and military action. While many specific actions in war may well be immoral, it is widely acknowledged that some deliberate actions that harm or even kill soldiers are morally justified. Combatants—those engaged in the business of war—may rightly be subject to violent force whose object is to prevent them from achieving their objectives.

All of these cases share some common elements and the following set of principles is proposed as a general theory of the just use of force intended to apply to these and all similar situations.

We may begin with the assumption that argument and persuasion aimed at changing the plans and behavior of human persons are the means most respectful of human dignity. This dignity is most fully respected when persons are helped to see the truth and freely to choose the good. However, it is also common human experience that virtually all of us on some occasions in our lives, and some of us on many occasions and in very serious ways, make plans and choose behavior that harms the dignity and property of others. While it would be better for us to amend our choices freely, we are not always willing to do so. Therefore, on some occasions, as noted above, it will be morally legitimate for others to frustrate our plans and take steps to change our behavior. My further contention is that the use of force, not excluding the imposition of pain, injury, or even death, can be justifiable, according to the following principles.

First, the person or group employing force must have **Standing to Act.** This means that the person or group must have some responsibility for the good to be protected by the use of force. The principle will be applied as a matter of prudence and so more broadly in some cases than in others. For example, we are likely to apply it narrowly with regard to the disciplining of children, limiting Standing to Act to parents and perhaps other close relatives. On the other hand, almost anyone witnessing, say, an assault on an elderly woman would have Standing to Act to protect her. In other cases, such as the use of some kinds of force (especially deadly force) by the police or the military, we would define Standing to Act narrowly again.

Second, the person or group employing force must have **Sound Reason to Act**. Sound Reason to Act exists when real harm may be done or actually is being done to persons or their property and when at least four additional criteria are met.

1. The criterion of *Discrimination*, which is to say that force may only be directed against a person who is know to be acting badly or to be planning to act badly, especially when the bad action is directed against the person or property of others. In some special cases (e.g., children, persons who are severely depressed or mentally incompetent), force might be employed to prevent someone from harming himself.

2. The criterion of *Necessity*, which is satisfied when there is a legitimate need for action to be taken and no non-coercive means are reasonably available.

3. The criterion of *Proportionality*, which requires that the potential or actual harm to others or their property is sufficiently serious that the use of force is warranted, and also that any force employed be reasonably proportioned to the harm caused and to the status of the perpetrator.

4. The criterion of *Prospect for Success*, which limits the use of force to situations in which there is ample reason to believe that the force employed will bring about the hoped-for change in plans or behavior.

Third, the person or group employing force must have **Right Intention in Acting**. In general, this means that the person or group must intend primarily to prevent the harm being caused or about to be caused by the perpetrator. The principle is violated if the prevention of harm takes second place to a desire to exact vengeance, to exercise power, or to obtain some sort of advantage over others.

The use of force, whether it be a matter of restraint or threat, or the actual imposition of pain, injury, or death, always marks a breakdown in the peace and harmony that ought to characterize human relationships. It causes damage that may not be immediately apparent and sometimes that damage later fuels still further erosions of peace and harmony. It can never be chosen lightly and it must always be employed to restore an authentic and just peace. While force is sometimes a necessary tool, it is also a dangerous one for families and communities to employ. We need to consider now whether and to what extent it may legitimately be used in the context of interrogation.

## TORTURE AND INTERROGATION

Torture is an ugly word, and the practice of torture in all its forms has a particularly ugly history. It is for good reason that civilized communities, from ancient times, have severely limited or abolished torture as an instrument of the state. The word "torture," however, is used to name a number of different practices that involve the use of force to change plans or behavior. Some of these practices are rightly condemned as gross violations of human dignity, but must this be true of all?

We can begin to answer this question by sorting out the principal kinds of situations in which torture is said to be involved. First of all, torture may be used as a punishment or in the context of interrogation. For purposes of this paper, we will not be concerned with the morality of punitive torture and so we may set it aside to concentrate on interrogatory torture.

Interrogatory torture, which in general aims to elicit information or consent from the subject, may also be broadly divided into three categories: judicial torture, probative torture, and defensive torture. Judicial torture is the name I will give to situations where torture is employed to compel a subject to confess to a crime, to accuse another person of a crime, or otherwise to give evidence about a crime for use in legal proceedings.

Probative torture is a practice that has probably been universally abolished by which a person accused of a crime is subjected to an ordeal as a test of his innocence or guilt.

Defensive torture describes a situation in which a person is subjected to one form of force or another in an effort to compel that person to cooperate in frustrating or curtailing a harmful act. The relevant act may be one in which the person himself is engaged or it may be one of which he has knowledge. In either case there is a serious harm that can be prevented but the subject refuses to offer the cooperation necessary to prevent the harm.

For the sake of argument, we will stipulate that judicial torture and probative torture are violations of human dignity and cannot be morally legitimate. We will further stipulate that torture, of whatever sort, is not constituted merely by the use of force but only by the use of severe force. That is to say, modest physical or emotional discomfort and other mild uses of force do not rise to the level of torture.

The question that remains is: Can defensive interrogatory torture ever be morally legitimate? For example, could a terrorist who has knowledge of an imminent bombing be justly subjected to torture in an effort to compel him to reveal what he knows about the attack? Could a kidnapper be tortured in an attempt to learn the whereabouts of his victim? Could a confessed murderer be forced to reveal the location of the victim's body?

To answer this we need to appeal to the principles governing a just use of force as discussed above. Defensive interrogatory torture may be legitimate if some instances of it can satisfy all of the criteria enumerated.

Two of the principles can be easily satisfied, or at least it can be easily determined whether a particular situation can satisfy them. They are the principles of Standing to Act and Right Intention to Act. Torture, as it is ordinarily defined, is a public act. That is to say, it is the act of a state authority, working through those persons properly delegated to act on behalf of the state. Police, for example, are authorized to do things to protect the common good that private citizens are not permitted to do. Similarly, persons generally authorized to use force for the sake of the common good (i.e., the police and the military) may be assumed in principle to have Standing to Act. It may however come to be the case, as some have suggested, that the employment of torture (if it were morally legitimate) would be reserved to certain persons explicitly empowered to use it. Others, except perhaps in very serious emergencies, would not have Standing to Act.

Right Intention to Act merely requires that persons employing force do so for the sake of preventing harm to innocent persons or their property. As mentioned above, this principle is violated if force is used for revenge, for personal gain, and so forth.

The real difficulty with defensive interrogatory torture has to do with whether instances of it can ever satisfy all of the criteria associated with Sound Reason to Act.

The first of the criteria, Discrimination, could be satisfied if the subject of the interrogation were known beyond reasonable doubt to possess the information necessary to frustrate the bad act and if he were unwilling to reveal that information.

The criterion would not be satisfied if the subject were merely suspected of possessing information.

The second criterion, Necessity, could be satisfied if time was short and no means of compelling cooperation short of force were available, which brings to mind something like a "Ticking Bomb" scenario.

The third criterion, Proportionality, requires something quite serious to be at stake. In the present world situation, with the wide concern about further terrorist attacks, one can readily imagine that some severe risk to innocent persons could be at stake. If so, the criterion of Proportionality would probably be fulfilled. However, we must be careful not to be so unimaginative that we cannot conceive of less serious uses of force than torture to accomplish our ends, or so complacent that we are too readily prepared to fall back on torture if other means are not rapidly successful. The use of torture has implications beyond the immediate suffering of and harm to the subject, and these implications ought to be considered in the context of Proportionality.

The final criterion, Prospect of Success, plays a larger role in the question of interrogatory torture than it normally does in other instances of the use of force. This criterion can be satisfied only when there is very good reason to believe that the force applied will result in the cooperation needed. It is not satisfied—and the use of force cannot be justified—when it is reasonably believed that a proportionate use of force will not compel cooperation or when the level of force deemed likely to succeed is disproportionately severe.

Another consideration comes into play here as well. Judicial interrogatory torture has generally fallen into disuse in one culture or another because it is an unreliable way of arriving at the truth. Subjects have a strong incentive to say what the interrogator wishes to hear, whether that be an accusation or a confession; anything to bring the torture to an end. The cases where torture was commonly used were often those in which no adequate corroborating evidence was available. As a result, where genuine success would be a determination of the truth, a phony success—an accusation or a confession that could not be independently verified—was accepted as a substitute.

Therefore, the criterion of Prospect of Success, with regard to defensive interrogatory torture, should also entail, the condition that the information obtained from the subject be able to be readily verified. In this way, the subject, knowing that the information he reveals can be promptly checked for accuracy, will be much more likely to tell the truth.

In sum, defensive interrogatory torture may be morally legitimate if imposed by persons properly authorized to do so, who act with the intention of protecting the innocent, and if there is a sufficiently grave risk to the well being of these innocent people (or their property). Furthermore, the subject must be known beyond a reasonable doubt to possess the capacity or the information needed to frustrate the bad act and be unwilling otherwise to exercise that capacity or reveal that information; time constraints or other conditions must make alternate methods of obtaining cooperation unreasonable; the harm at issue must be grave and the means used to obtain cooperation must proportionate to that harm; and there must be good reason to believe that such interrogatory methods would be successful and that information received could be promptly verified.

While these conditions may actually be fulfilled in some cases, this probably would happen rarely. It is quite likely that most instances in which interrogatory torture is employed would not conform to these principles and so would be immoral.

## SHOULD JUSTIFIABLE INSTANCES OF TORTURE STILL BE AVOIDED?

The purpose of this paper has been to examine more closely the question of whether some sort of interrogatory torture might be morally legitimate in some cases. I have argued that in some narrow range of cases the use of force, including the intentional imposition of severe pain, may be morally justified. Nevertheless, even if such legitimate instances exist, there may still be compelling reasons why the United States should choose never to use torture.

One reason is that we have entered into international agreements which, in some cases, seem to entail a commitment not to employ torture, and in one case at least this commitment seems to be exceptionless. It may be that such agreements are not considered to be binding on nations in the same way that criminal laws and contracts are binding on individuals. I will leave that to the experts in international law to determine. However that may be, two considerations may be relevant. First, it is hard to imagine that a commitment to refrain from a morally legitimate action can be binding in the face grave risk to the innocent. One of the most fundamental and solemn obligations of the rulers of a nation is to protect the innocent, and it seems unimaginable that a nation can be legally bound to refrain from doing what its moral obligations might require it to do. Second, from the way torture is defined and treated in the international declarations and covenants of the twentieth century one might reasonably conclude that either punitive torture or some immoral category of interrogatory torture is intended, but not defensive interrogatory torture as it has been discussed in this paper. In any event, fidelity to international law and agreements may be a reason to avoid all uses of torture.

A second reason may be to avoid what moralists call scandal. By this we mean not a shocking or startling event, but an act that provokes or encourages others to act badly. For the United States to employ torture, even in sharply limited cases, might set an example that would encourage less restraint in other parts of the world. The delicate distinctions of moral philosophy may not mean much to an oppressive régime which could attempt to justify its own immoral use of torture by pointing to the example of the United States.

A third reason, and one that should not be dismissed lightly, is the effect of employing torture on both the interrogator and the character of the nation. Both war and torture are nasty affairs, and even if the acts carried out in war are morally justified, they may still have deep psychological effects on those who fight. Similarly, the employment of torture cannot fail to affect the interrogator, regardless of how clearly he or she sees the good to be achieved. Furthermore, the lines between interrogation and revenge or punishment can easily be blurred, both by the individual and by the nation.

A fourth reason to avoid torture is that it may lead the nation and its leaders to be more willing to employ immoral uses of force, both within and without the context of war. The analysis presented here of interrogatory torture does not rely on utilitarian or consequentialist calculations of benefits and harms. In times of crisis, though, we are tempted to adopt "any means necessary" to protect what we value, but in doing so we may damage what we value after all. The use of torture, the justification of which would not be understood or accepted by everyone, might provoke many people to be prepared to endorse other, immoral actions on the basis of a flawed utilitarian analysis that they wrongly believe to justify defensive interrogatory torture.

Finally, it may be the case (though I think it is not) that interrogatory torture is actually futile, i.e., it simply doesn't work. During the Second World War it was widely believed that strategic bombing of population centers (London, Berlin, Tokyo) would so weaken the resolve of civilians to continue the war that their leaders would be compelled to sue for peace. This proved not to be true, as civilians generally demonstrated an amazing endurance; bombing seemed to strengthen their determination rather than erode it. By the same token, we may find that the use of torture is counter-productive. Those upon whom we may think to use it may be able to resist it in many cases. Or its use might inflame others to even more acts of terrorism. Or it may fail for other reasons. If this were to prove to be so, then the use of torture in interrogations would fail the criterion of Prospect of Success, and its use would therefore be unjustified and immoral.

The world in which we live has always been a messy place. In recent years, with the spread of terrorism, the increased prospect of asymmetric warfare, and the development of more portable weapons of mass destruction, it has become much messier. The wars of the twentieth century made civilians more vulnerable. Both police and the armed services will need to adapt their strategies and tactics for the new realities. No one can be an enthusiastic advocate for the use of torture, even in critical situations. Nevertheless, the protection of the innocent may justify aggressive means of interrogation that we had hoped we had left behind.

## Torturing Terrorists:
## Always Abhorrent

LISA HAJJAR

There is a popular belief that Western history constitutes a progressive move from more to less torture. Iron maidens and racks are now museum exhibits, crucifixions are sectarian iconography and scientific experimentation on twins is History Channel infotainment. This narrative of progress deftly blends ideas about "time," "place" and "culture." In the popular imagination, "civilized societies" (a.k.a. "us") do not rely on torture, whereas those societies where torture is still common remain "uncivilized," torture being both a proof and a problem of their enduring "backwardness."

George W. Bush epitomizes and mines the American popular imagination with his mantra of "spreading freedom," which carries a strong implication of stopping torture. Saddam Hussein's horrific legacy of mass torture was one of the arguments deployed to justify preemptive war against Iraq, and torture has become retroactively more important since weapons of mass destruction have failed to materialize. On April 30, 2004, Bush said, "A year ago I [gave a] speech saying we had achieved an important objective, accomplished a mission, which was the removal of Saddam Hussein. As a result, there are no longer torture chambers or mass graves or rape rooms in Iraq."

Even as Bush spoke those words, he and millions of newspaper readers and television viewers across the world were aware that torture chambers, rape and sexual abuse of detainees in Iraq are not a thing of the past. The public exposure of torture of Iraqi detainees by U.S. soldiers,

working in interrogation wings run by military intelligence and American "security contractors," at Abu Ghraib prison outside of Baghdad—as well as allegations of torture of other Iraqis by British soldiers—are headline news. The shocking revelations and photographs provide stark proof that torture is not a relic of "our past." Nor does torture provide a meaningful geographical or cultural demarcation between "civilized" and "uncivilized" societies.

### IMPLICATORY DENIAL

The fact is that, today, people are being tortured in two thirds of the world's countries. Yet if one were to accept the rhetoric of the world's states at face value, there is no torture in the world. No torturing regime defends or even acknowledges its own torture as torture. Stanley Cohen, author of *States of Denial* [Polity Press, 2000], identifies three common forms of denial of torture and other atrocities. "Literal denial" is when a state accused of torture responds by saying that nothing happened and that those who claim something happened are liars or "enemies of the state." "Interpretative denial" is when a state refutes allegations by saying that what happened is not torture but "something else"—like "moderate physical pressure" or "stress and duress." "Implicatory denial"—that is, denial by implicating others—occurs when a state acknowledges torture but blames it on "aberrant agents," claiming that rogue elements have breached official norms and policies. Official U.S. responses to the Abu Ghraib prison photos are a classic example of implicatory denial.

In the story on CBS "60 Minutes II" that exposed the abusive U.S. practices in Abu Ghraib, Brig. Gen. Mark Kimmitt said, "All of us are disappointed by the actions of the few. Number one, this is a small minority of the military, and number two, they need to understand that the army is a values-based organization. [The] acts that you see in these pictures may reflect the actions of individuals, but by God, it doesn't reflect my army." Secretary of State Colin Powell agreed with Kimmitt when he condemned the six soldiers who have been arrested in the Abu Ghraib incidents: "But I want to remind the world it was a small number of troops compared to the hundreds of thousands who have served around the world, who have come to build hospitals and schools and restore civil society." These implicatory denials were echoed, with a grander sweep, by Defense Secretary Donald Rumsfeld, who in Congressional testimony described the abuses depicted in the now infamous photos as "un-American."

Many Americans can doubtless relate to Rumsfeld's attempt to relegate the Abu Ghraib torturers—all, apparently, Americans—to another discursive time, place and culture. But before Rumsfeld spoke, investigative journalist Seymour Hersh, writing in the *New Yorker,* had already rebutted the implicatory denials so ambient in the Pentagon and the media sphere. Hersh obtained a copy of a report from another U.S. army general, Antonio Taguba, who investigated prisons and interrogation centers in Iraq between October and December 2003, and found "sadistic, wanton and criminal abuses" that were systemic and rampant. According to Hersh, "Taguba saved his harshest words for the military intelligence officers and private contractors." Brig. Gen. Janis

Karpinski, who oversaw 16 prisons in Iraq and has been relieved of those duties because of the scandal, said, "The [Abu Ghraib] prison, and that particular cell block where the events took place, were under the control of the MI (military intelligence) command." Karpinski sought to defend herself and lay the blame elsewhere when she noted that military intelligence officers went "to great lengths to try to exclude the International Committee of the Red Cross from access to that interrogation wing."

Denial of torture is articulated in many ways, but all states deny it for the same reason. Torture must be practiced in secret and denied in public because, in the mid-twentieth century, torture became an international crime. Irrespective of what penalties the arrested soldiers may face under the Uniform Code of Military Justice, the pictures from Abu Ghraib—whose authenticity no one has denied—document offenses of an especially heinous kind.

## LAW AND (INTERNATIONAL) ORDER

The international criminalization of torture is inextricable from the history of human rights. The unprecedented horrors and violence of World War II provided the negative inspiration for a revolution in international law to forge the principle that people should have rights as humans, and not merely as protected classes of subjects, such as citizens, civilians or prisoners of war. However, the creation of international human rights did not undermine or substantially alter the power of states. Rather, it entailed the elaboration of new internationalized norms of government to which all states would be expected to adhere, while preserving states' sovereign rights. Human rights obtained their "universalizing" character from the fact that people are subjects of states and states are subjects of international law.

The right not to be tortured became a human right when international law prohibited the practice, and established legal liabilities and penalties. The right not to be tortured is one of many human rights, but it is stronger than almost any other human right because the prohibition of torture is absolutely non-derogable and because the law recognizes no exceptions. What this means is that no one—ever, anywhere—has a "right" to torture, and that everyone—always, everywhere—has a right not to be tortured. It also means that anyone who engages in or abets torture is committing a crime.

The international prohibition of torture illuminates something very important about the rights of human beings. The right not to be tortured represents an ideal type of human rights norm because it invests people, regardless of their social status, their political identity or affiliations, with a kind of sovereign right over their bodies and minds, albeit limited to situations that fall within the legal definition of torture. In contrast, the right of persons not to be exterminated through genocide hinges on a collective identity as members of a national, religious or ethnic group. The right not to be deliberately targeted in war hinges not on one's humanity but rather on one's status as a civilian or non-combatant, or a surrendered or captured soldier.

The prohibition of torture is customary international law and therefore attaches universal jurisdiction. Universal jurisdiction means that if a perpetrator is not prosecuted in his or her own country, he or she can be prosecuted in any competent legal system anywhere in the world. Therefore, the right not to be tortured is accorded greater weight in law than the sovereign rights of states because torture is prohibited under all circumstances, including the "ticking bomb" scenario. In the words of the UN Convention Against Torture and Other Cruel, Inhuman or Degrading Treatment or Punishment (1984), "No exceptional circumstances whatsoever, whether a state of war or a threat of war, internal political instability or any other public emergency, may be invoked as a justification for torture." The U.S. ratified this convention in 1994.

## SHADES OF PINOCHET

Perhaps the most vivid illustration of the strength of the prohibition on torture and the universal jurisdiction that attaches to it is the case of former Chilean dictator Augusto Pinochet. Pinochet was arrested in 1998 in London when the British government conceded to act on an indictment by Spanish judge Balthazar Garzon. The Spanish indictment charged Pinochet with genocide and other forms of murder, but the only charge that held up as the case made its way through the British legal system was torture. Although Pinochet ultimately was released from British custody because of "ill health," the "Pinochet precedent"—holding that he was indictable—was a landmark. No *raison d'etat* could be invoked to justify torture, and no one, not even a former head of state, could claim legal immunity from prosecution on charges of torture.

Of course, the Pinochet case did not solve or even alter the problem of torture. But the Pinochet precedent does illustrate that the right not to be tortured is stronger—substantially stronger—than the right to life. There are many circumstances under which people legally can be killed, but none under which people legally can be tortured. Even forms of killing that constitute international crimes do not have the same robust non-derogability [inability to be mitigated or excused] as torture. War crimes are no less illegal than torture, but the obscuring effects of the "fog of war" make it difficult to ascertain liability. And unlike war crimes and genocide, the "chain of command" is irrelevant to bringing a case against a torturer, though the chain of command can be used to broaden the scope of legal liability. This last factor is crucial for understanding why states whose agents are caught torturing people resort to implicatory denial. Blaming "aberrant agents" is a means of trying to prevent legal action against those further up the chain of command. Pinochet probably never tortured anyone personally, but he was responsible—and liable—for torture by his jailers.

Indeed, the lawyers of the six American soldiers who are facing court martial for torturing Iraqis are saying that their clients, who are reservists, are "scapegoats." Their defense will seek to put into evidence those responsible for interrogation at the Abu Ghraib prison. One soldier, Staff Sgt. Ivan "Chip" Frederick, has said that when he asked for some guidelines on the treatment of prisoners because he was disconcerted by how they were being treated, a military intelligence officer told him that this was "how things are done." Frederick continued that he and other military police were encouraged to abuse and humiliate detainees to soften them up for interrogation.

## WHY IS THE PROHIBITION OF TORTURE SO STRONG?

Torture refers to purposefully harming someone who is in custody—unfree to fight back or protect himself or herself and imperiled by that incapacitation. Other violent practices, like domestic violence and battery, also involve the purposeful causing of pain, and in some ways these practices might "look like" torture. But they lack the public dimension of custodi-

anship. The distinction does not turn on what happens, because if it did, torture would be difficult if not impossible to distinguish from domestic violence and battery. Pain and suffering, humiliation and injury are common to all. But, legally, severe pain, suffering, humiliation and injury constitute torture only if they serve some public purpose and if the status and role of the torturer emanates from a public authority and if the person being harmed is in custody.

Contrary to the implications of some, the forced public nakedness, forced public masturbation and forced simulation of homosexual acts depicted in the Abu Ghraib photos do not qualify as torture or as "especially" torturous because the Iraqi detainees are Arab and, presumably, Muslim. Hersh himself implies that maltreatment crossed the line to become torture because, "such dehumanization [as is shown in the photos] is unacceptable in any culture, but it is especially so in the Arab world." Would persons of any ethnicity or culture find such abuse anything other than severely and sadistically humiliating? What was done to the Iraqi detainees was torture because the detainees were in the custody of the U.S. military and private contractors, because they were compelled by their captors to assume the humiliating positions and because they were powerless to resist their humiliation. While the detainees' cultural sensitivities were undoubtedly offended, the relevant point is that the most inalienable of their human rights was violated by their American jailers.

Notwithstanding these qualifications, there is no bright line empirically distinguishing torture from "everything else." Rather, torture is like a core within layers of violence. For example, being beaten while being arrested changes from "cruel treatment" to "torture" only when "custody" has been achieved, obviously a very blurry and contestable line. The combination of "torture" and "cruel, inhumane and degrading treatment" in the same laws contributes to this confusion, which is further compounded by the exclusion of painful—but lawful—punishments such as floggings, amputations or the death penalty. Many forms of violence may lead to torture and many forms of violence may result from torture, but the core violence that is torture—and what makes torture a "core international crime"—is violence (physical or psychological) against a person already in the custody of an authority.

An "authority" is a category that obviously would include states and their agents, but it would not exclude non-state groups and their agents, or civilians. Torture is not contingent on legitimacy, jurisdiction or international recognition. It is contingent on an organized rather than individualized capacity to take people into custody and then harm them for a purpose that is public rather than personal.

On this point, the use of private contractors to run prisons and conduct interrogations in Afghanistan and Iraq has been a subject of confusion. American media are reporting, and many people are assuming, that because these private contractors are civilians, they are not subject to military or international laws. Peter W. Singer of the Brookings Institution, writing in the May 2 *Los Angeles Times,* quotes Phillip Carter, a former Army officer now at UCLA Law School as saying that, "Legally speaking, [military contractors in Iraq] actually fall into the same gray area as the unlawful combatants detained at Guantanamo Bay." Carter may be correct in some respects, but the contractors have been hired and authorized to fulfill a public function of handling and interrogating

detainees on behalf of the U.S. government. As another military analyst, Paul C. Forage, told the *Baltimore Sun* on May 4, the private contractors could be prosecuted under either the Military Extraterritorial Jurisdiction Act of 2000 or a 1996 federal law. "I think it's a pretty clear case," Forage concluded. "It's not an area of legal limbo."

## TORTURE AND TERROR

If torture is so strongly prohibited, and denied by all states because it is fundamentally illegitimate, then why is it so common in today's world? While states torture people for numerous reasons, one common reason invoked by many states is that they claim to be engaged in conflicts with "terrorists."

Terrorism is a broad and flexible concept, and there is no clear, internationally accepted definition. It is used, variously, to describe certain kinds of actions, including attacks on civilians, hijackings, organized resistance or repression, and to identify certain types of actors. In U.S. national security discourse, the term terrorism typically is used to refer to non-state actors or organizations engaged in attacks or struggles against the state, emphasizing but not necessarily limited to violence, to which the state responds with "counter-terrorism."

Terrorism is not a figment of the politically paranoid imagination. The September 11, 2001 attacks were indisputably terrorist attacks, and al-Qaeda operates as a terrorist organization. Any and every instance of deliberately targeting civilians or civilian infrastructures as a tactic in the furtherance of some cause, whatever the political or ideological motivation and whomever the targeting agents, is terroristic. If the deliberate targeting of civilians constitutes terrorism, then we must acknowledge that states can be as culpable as non-state groups. However, as Richard Falk explains:

> With the help of the influential media, the state over time has waged and largely won the battle of definitions by exempting its own violence against civilians from being treated and perceived as "terrorism." Instead, such violence was generally discussed as "uses of force," "retaliation," "self-defense" and "security measures."

National security is a legitimate interest of any state, and states have a responsibility to provide for the security of their citizens. But the tendency to characterize and treat all "enemies" as "terrorists" or "terrorist sympathizers" contributes to the delineation between "legitimate" and "illegitimate" communities, leaving the latter vulnerable to state violence, and enabling the state to justify that violence as a necessary reaction to terror. Pointing out the limits and obfuscations of national security discourse is not an apologia for terrorism. Rather, it is an effort to understand, evaluate and criticize violence in a manner that is not glazed by partisan or statist ideology. [Statism is a belief that the state (country and its government) should play a powerful social and economic role.]

Around the world, some of the most egregious human rights violations have been perpetrated by states in the name of counter-terrorism. Terrorism is, by definition, a violation of human rights. Michael Ignatieff, director of the Carr Center of Human Rights Policy at Harvard, writes:

> The two terms—human rights and terror—look like a simple antithesis: human rights good, terror bad. [But] the antithesis is not so simple. Of course, human rights and terror stand opposed to each other. Terrorist acts violate the right to life, along with many other rights. But equally, human rights—notably the right to self-determination—have

constituted major justification for the resort to violence, including acts of terror.

Ignatieff correctly points out that it is not international human rights law—which is inherently pacifist—but rather, international humanitarian law that obtains in any war, including a war on terrorism. The Geneva Conventions, which compose the main body of international humanitarian laws, are agnostic about the causes of war or the justness of the aims of adversaries. Rather, they govern what is legally permissible in war. Their aim is to minimize suffering and destruction, and to provide guidelines for the detention and treatment of enemy civilians and combatants. International humanitarian law is not pacifist, but on the issue of torture it concurs with human rights law. Even in war, the right not to be tortured is absolutely non-derogable, and the use of torture in the context of conflict can constitute a war crime.

Since September 11, the Bush administration has articulated positions and pursued policies that blatantly contravene the Geneva Conventions, on the grounds that terrorists do not deserve legal rights and protections. These policies include the invention of a category, "unlawful combatants," that does not exist in international law. These unlawful combatants are being held incommunicado, at Guantánamo Bay and other locations, and subjected to years of interrogation with no judicial oversight, no public accountability and virtually no visitation by representatives of the International Committee of the Red Cross. Although the U.S. government claims that no torture is used in the interrogation of these detainees, these clandestine and extralegal conditions are an invitation for abuse. The Abu Ghraib images are a piece of hard evidence indicating that the U.S. has joined the list of countries—

Egypt, Israel, Uzbekistan—that are fighting wars on terrorism partly through the use of torture.

Still, because torture is illegal, it remains necessary for states to deny torture, even the torture of terrorists. In the U.S., the terrorist attacks of September 11 have raised for debate several vexing and related questions: should "terrorists" have a right not to be tortured? Is torture a necessary and effective tactic in the fight against terrorism? If so, why deny torture?

## A DISTINCTION IS BORN

Israel was the first state in the world to break the "torture taboo" by publicly authorizing interrogation practices that constitute torture. Israel has been in an official state of emergency and war since it was established in 1948. In the 1967 Arab-Israeli war, Israel captured and occupied the West Bank and Gaza and established a military administration to rule the Palestinians residing in these areas. A military court system was established to prosecute Palestinians suspected of violating Israel's military and emergency laws. These laws criminalized not only violence, sabotage and militancy, but also a vast array of political and non-violent activities. Israel used prosecution as one of its key strategies to rule Palestinians and to thwart and punish resistance to the occupation. Since 1967, over half a million Palestinians have been prosecuted in the military court system, out of a population that now numbers 3.2 million. There have been periods when incarceration rates in the West Bank and Gaza were among the highest in the world.

For two decades, allegations that Israeli soldiers and interrogators were routinely torturing Palestinian detainees were consistently refuted by Israeli officials as lies and fabrications of "enemies of the state." Then in 1987, for reasons unconnected to

the interrogation of Palestinians, the Israeli government established an official commission of inquiry to investigate the General Security Services [GSS].

The report produced by the Landau Commission was path-breaking in a number of ways. It confirmed that, in fact, GSS agents had used violent interrogation methods routinely on Palestinian detainees since at least 1971, and that they had routinely lied about such practices when confessions were challenged in court on the grounds that they had been coerced. The Landau Commission was harsh in its criticism of GSS perjury, but adopted the GSS's own position that coercive interrogation tactics were necessary in the struggle against "hostile terrorist activity." The Landau Commission accepted the broad definition of terrorism utilized by the GSS, which encompassed not only acts or threats of violence, but virtually all activities related to Palestinian nationalism.

The most path-breaking aspects of the Landau report were its conclusions and recommendations. The report's authors argued that national security requires physical and psychological coercion in the interrogation of Palestinians, and that the state should sanction such tactics in order to rectify the problem of perjury. The Landau Commission's justification for this recommendation was based on a three-part contention: that Palestinians have no right to legal protections given their predisposition for terrorism, that the GSS operates morally and responsibly in discharging its duties to preserve Israeli national security, and that GSS interrogation methods do not constitute torture. The Landau Commission offered a way for the state to engage in torture while simultaneously denying it by renaming it as "moderate physical pressure."

This euphemism traces back to British torture of Irish prisoners in Northern

Ireland, but the Landau report adds a distinctive wrinkle. A legal challenge was mounted against Britain's "five techniques" in the interrogation of suspected Irish Republican Army members on the grounds that they violate the European Convention on Human Rights. The majority decision by the European Court of Human Rights ruled that the five techniques (wall standing, hooding, subjection to noise, sleep deprivation, and deprivation of food and drink) do not amount to "torture" but to the lesser—and also prohibited—category of "inhumane and degrading treatment." But the British government accepted the minority opinion of the Court that the techniques constitute (or come close to) torture, and decided to forego their use. The Landau Commission, noting that Israeli interrogation tactics resembled the five techniques, embraced the Court's majority decision that they do not constitute "torture." Thus was born the euphemization of "moderate physical pressure" as "not torture."

The Israeli government adopted the Landau Commission's recommendations to "legalize" torture, and this stimulated enormous debate and criticism in Israel. Since 1987, there has been a concerted campaign by Israeli lawyers and human rights organizations to end Israeli interrogation practices that constitute torture. One of the main sites of struggle was the Israeli High Court of Justice which, in 1999, finally issued a ruling prohibiting the routine use of "pressure" tactics (though not calling these tactics "torture") while preserving the option to use such tactics in "exceptional circumstances."

In the U.S. today, many of the people who point to Israel as a model for good interrogation tactics are pointing implicitly to the Landau Commission report, rather than the struggles, scandals and changes that have emanated in its wake. The

Landau Commission had adopted an apocalyptic view of the world where nothing less than survival of the Israeli state and the Jewish nation were deemed to be at stake in the interrogation of "hostile terrorists." It concluded that survival and security trump other valued considerations, including due process and the right not to be tortured. Read on its own terms, the Landau Commission report is a blueprint for "absolute security" in a war on terror.

### "STRESS AND DURESS"

In a sense, the U.S. already has its own Landau Commission report. On December 26, 2002, Dana Priest and Barton Gellman published a lengthy story in the *Washington Post* revealing that U.S. security agents were utilizing "stress and duress" tactics in the interrogation of people captured in Afghanistan and elsewhere. The tactics they described are identical to Israeli "moderate physical pressure." Priest and Gellman wrote that: "Those who refuse to cooperate inside this secret CIA interrogation center [at the Bagram air base in Afghanistan] are sometimes kept standing or kneeling for hours, in black hoods or spray-painted goggles, according to intelligence specialists familiar with CIA interrogation methods. [The article noted that,] "At times, they are held in awkward, painful positions and deprived of sleep with a 24-hour bombardment of lights—subject to what are known as 'stress and duress' techniques."

Priest and Gellman also reported that detainees who could not be broken by the "restrained" stress and duress tactics might be given mind-altering drugs or "turned over—'rendered,' in official parlance—to foreign intelligence services whose practice of torture has been documented by the U.S. government and human rights organizations." They continued, "While the U.S. government publicly denounces the use of torture, each of the current national security officials interviewed for this article defended the use of violence against captives as just and necessary. They expressed confidence that the American public would back their view. The CIA declined to comment."

Like the Landau Commission report when it was published in Israel in 1987, this *Washington Post* story dramatically altered both what is known about American interrogation and how torture is talked about in the U.S. Human rights advocates assailed official admissions of "stress and duress" as defenses of torture. On January 11, 2003, in a letter to the *Washington Post*, two former Justice Department officials who served under Presidents Ronald Reagan and George Bush cited the European Court ruling as evidence that "stress and duress" is not torture. "Indeed," they retorted to the human rights advocates, "to say these practices do [constitute torture] ultimately trivializes the torture that does take place in so many areas of the world." So far, the pictures of grinning American soldiers forcing nude Iraqis into sexual positions seem to have dimmed the vigor of this particular defense for the "stress and duress" at Abu Ghraib. However, an ex-U.S. Army interrogation instructor named Tony Robinson, appearing on the Fox News Channel's "Hannity and Colmes" show on April 30, did say of the pictures that "frat hazing is worse than this."

More to the point, the use of tactics by U.S. officials that arguably constitute torture, and the rendering of prisoners to states with well-established records of torture—including Jordan, Egypt, Syria, Morocco, Pakistan and the Philippines—illuminate the conundrum of what to do about terrorism. Priest and Gellman recounted the testimony of Cofer Black, former head of the CIA Counterterrorist

Center, before Congress on September 26, 2002, to the effect that the CIA and other security agencies need "operational flexibility," and therefore cannot be held to the "old" standards. Black said, "There was before 9/11, and there was an after 9/11. After 9/11 the gloves come off."

## TALE OF TWO CLICHÉS

Taking the gloves off in interrogation is a thinly veiled reference to torture, but calling torture "stress and duress" or "abuse" is the homage paid to the still current imperative of denial. The presumptions that torture is both necessary and effective, and the implications of breaking the torture taboo by legalizing torture are shaping debates in the U.S. This debate circles around two clichés: the slippery slope and the lesser evil.

Jeremiads against the slippery slope argue that no cause or crisis justifies the erosion of the absolute prohibition against torture. Variations on this theme include: there is no such thing as just a "little torture," once you start torturing "terrorists" you open the door to torturing anyone in the future and using torture makes you no better than your enemy. Defenders of the lesser evil argue that the absolute prohibition on torture is immoral if it ties the hands of security agents from finding that "ticking bomb" and saving innocent lives. On CNN's "Crossfire," conservative commentator Tucker Carlson said, "Torture is bad. [But] some things are worse. And under some circumstances, it may be the lesser of two evils. Because some evils are pretty evil."

Interestingly, the example of Israel is invoked to bolster each case. The slippery slopers point the realities of torture in Israel—Palestine, where torturing tens of thousands of people has neither ameliorated the conflict nor enhanced Israeli security; rather it has exacerbated conflict and thus contributed to Israeli insecurity.

According to Yael Stein, a researcher at the Israeli human rights organization B'tselem, "Israel's experience shows you can't stop the slippery slope: they tortured almost all the Palestinians they could. It was in the system. The moment you start, you can't stop." The "lesser-evil"-ers argue that Israel has preserved its "democratic character" by bringing torture "into the law" and that its security services have a fabulous success rate of averting many "ticking bombs" by torturing terrorists.

While coercive Israeli interrogation tactics have provided information about militant organizations and arms caches and foiled plans of some would-be bombers, there is no public record that the use of torture has ever averted an actual ticking bomb in Israel—that is, a bomb that was imminently set to explode. American lesser evilers who invoke the Israeli example either misunderstand or misrepresent the fact that Israeli officials use the "ticking bomb" scenario loosely, not literally. But American "lesser-evil"-ers like Alan Dershowitz invoke the literal ticking bomb—not the future bomb, not the general danger, not the malevolent enemy—to argue that the U.S. should follow Israel's example and legalize torture. Dershowitz writes:

> If American law enforcement officers were ever to confront the law school hypothetical case of the captured terrorist who knew about an imminent attack but refused to provide the information necessary to prevent it, I have absolutely no doubt that they would try to torture the terrorist into providing the information. Moreover, the vast majority of Americans would expect the officers to engage in that time-tested technique for loosening tongues, notwithstanding our unequivocal treaty obligations never to employ torture, no matter how exigent the circumstances.

The real question is not whether torture would be used—it would—but whether it would be used outside of the law or within the law. Dershowitz offers a suggestion as to how torture can be brought "into the law": "torture warrants" issued by judges. He also offers a helpful suggestion for tactics: sterilized needles under the fingernails. He told an interviewer for Salon.com: "I wanted to come up with a tactic that can't possibly cause permanent physical harm but is excruciatingly painful. [T]he point I wanted to make is that torture is not being used as a way of producing death. It's been used as a way of simply causing excruciating pain. I want maximal pain, minimum lethality."

"Lesser-evil"-ers like Dershowitz criticize the "slippery-slopers" as human rights fundamentalists who would sacrifice innocent civilians to preserve a legal principle. They are not suggesting that we forsake the principle that torture is illegal, but rather that we suspend that principle in the handling of some people on the grounds that they are necessarily and legitimately "torturable." The implicit rationale is that terrorists are not human, and therefore are undeserving of inclusion in the universe of human beings covered by international and constitutional law that categorically prohibits torture. But the most glaring problem with this argument, as many critics have pointed out, is the implausibility of knowing with absolute certainty that the torture candidate possesses information about an imminent threat. The speculation would translate into a license to use violence on a person assumed to be guilty. Following Dershowitz's suggestion to involve judges in the dispensing of torture warrants would, at best, narrow the pool of candidates.

Oren Gross [director, Center for Legal Studies, University of Minnesota] refines the lesser evil position by arguing for what he terms an "extralegal model." This model would uphold the illegality of torture while enabling it to be used at the discretion of authorities. They would then be potentially subject to punishment, which they could avoid by gaining the approval of the public *ex post facto.* In some ways, this "extralegal model" already characterizes U.S. policies in the war on terrorism. Depending on how the Supreme Court rules in the cases of José Padilla, Yasser Hamdi and the Guantánamo Bay detainees, it might very well become the controlling norm for executive power. The extralegal model proposes that the U.S. have its rule of law cake while eating its unfettered executive power, too. Many legal issues are at stake, including *habeas corpus,* incommunicado detention, the right to counsel, and the transparency and accountability of government agents and agencies. But torture is a distinct issue of concern because the prohibition against it is so strong.

## NO ROOM FOR MISTAKES

The slippery slopers present a valuable and worthy defense of taking the moral and legal high road. Those who invoke the slippery slope tend to focus on the tortured and worry—with good cause, as the Abu Ghraib photos have shown—that they are defenseless and susceptible to abuse in custody. But making slippery slope arguments against torture to a public gripped by fear of "evildoers" and willing to sacrifice the rights of "enemies" is not an effective rebuttal to advocates of torture as a lesser evil.

Those who invoke the lesser evil tend to focus on the public that is vulnerable to terrorism and violence. Their arguments have appeal because many people are will-

ing to accept the legitimacy of torturing terrorists as necessary and effective. Much of the public is willing to trust that government agents empowered to decide whom to torture are capable of discerning real from imagined threats, and restricting torture to the former. But at least 22 Guantánamo Bay detainees—people described as "the worst of the worst" by Rumsfeld—have been released, an implicit acknowledgment that their very detention in a place where torture is likely being used had been a mistake. On May 5, the *New York Times* published an interview with an Iraqi advancing a credible claim to be the man infamously pictured naked and hooded in Abu Ghraib prison, a female soldier pointing jokingly at his genitalia—was the torture that he is now compelled to relive also a "mistake"? Without effective oversight by a judicial body, the public cannot know or trust that other such "mistakes" will not be made. When it comes to torture, there is no room for a mistake.

Naturally, it is important to focus both on the tortured and on the vulnerable public, but the case of Abu Ghraib shows that it is most important to focus on the torturers. They are representatives of the public they serve. If torture is practiced by agents of a state that claims to be a democracy, then "we the people" are responsible for torture. Citizens of a democracy cannot or at least should not be comforted by blaming a few "aberrant agents" if torture is systemic and routine. Those citizens cannot or should not be quiescent as democratic values and laws are being trampled in a panic. "We the people" are responsible for stopping, protesting and preventing torture.

Keeping torture illegal and struggling to enforce the prohibition are the front lines, quite literally, of a global battle to defend the one core right that all human beings can claim. If torture is legitimized and legalized in the future, it is not "the terrorists" who will lose but "the humans." Should proponents of torture as a lesser evil succeed in regaining legitimacy for the execrable practice, there would be no better words than George Orwell's from 1984: "If you want a picture of the future, imagine a boot stamping on a human face—forever."

# THE CONTINUING DEBATE:
## Torturing Terrorists

### What Is New

Many revelations have surfaced about U.S. policy toward and treatment of prisoners. Several U.S. soldiers and civilians have been charged with abusing prisoners of war in Iraq and Afghanistan, and some have pled guilty or have been convicted. There have been no arrests for mistreating suspected terrorists, whom the Bush administration have classified as falling outside the protections provided by the Geneva Conventions. Documents indicate that while President Bush told officials to "treat detainees humanely, including those who are not legally entitled to such treatment," Secretary of Defense Rumsfeld had earlier authorized interrogation methods at Guantánamo Bay that included stripping prisoners naked, using "stress positions," hooding, the "fear of dogs," and "mild non-injurious physical contact." The documents also contained a U.S. Department of Justice memo arguing that "torture as defined and proscribed [by U.S. law] covers only extreme acts....Of the kind difficult for the victim to endure."

How do Americans feel about torture? They do not support its wholesale use on terrorists, but a 2004 poll found that only 32% of them believed that torture was "never justified." Another 21% thought it was "rarely justified," while 28% thought torture was "sometimes justified, and 15% believed it as "often justified." Four percent were unsure.

### Where to Find More

Another view supporting the limited use of torture is Andrew C. McCarthy, "Torture: Thinking About the Unthinkable," *Commentary*, July–August 2004. Taking the opposite view is Michael Ignatieff, "Evil Under Interrogation: Is Torture Ever Permissible?" *The Financial Times,* May 15, 2004, at http://www.ksg.harvard.edu/news/opeds/. There are no organizations that, as such, support torture, but there are many that oppose it, including Human Right Watch at http://www.hrw.org/. On June 22, 2004, the White House released hundreds of pages of documents related to the U.S. treatment of prisoners in Iraq and elsewhere. They are not available on the Web, but important information can be gathered by looking at the archives of news sources on that date and the next.

### What More to Do

Watch the movie *The Siege* in class. Have one or more class members act as prosecutors and draw up a list of charges against General Deveraux. Other class members should be appointed to defend the accused. Yet members of the class might even assume the roles of Deveraux, Hubbard, and others. Then conduct a trial, with the rest of the class sitting as jurors, and the instructor acting as judge. In the case of the *United States v. Deveraux*, what is the verdict of you, the jurors? During your deliberations about combating terrorism, ask yourself whether you want your country to abide by the view of Socrates (*Gorgias*, 380 B.C.): "There are these two evils, the doing of injustice and the suffering of injustice...; to do injustice is a greater, and to suffer injustice a lesser evil."

# CREDITS

Amicus Curiae brief to the United States Supreme Court in *Grutter v. Bollinger* (2003).

Aultman, Kathi A. Testimony during hearings on the "Partial-Birth Abortion Ban Act of 2002" before the U.S. Senate Committee on the Judiciary, Subcommittee on the Constitution, July 9, 2002.

Beach, William. Testimony during hearings on the "Balanced Budget Amendment" before the U.S. House of Representatives Committee on the Judiciary, Subcommittee on the Constitution, October 10, 2002.

Best, Judith A. Testimony during hearings on "Proposals for Electoral College Reform: H.J. Res. 28 and J.J. Res. 43" before the U.S. House of Representatives Committee on the Judiciary, Subcommittee on the Constitution, September 4, 1997.

Bond, Julian. Testimony during hearings on "Race and the Federal Death Penalty," before the U.S. Senate Committee on the Judiciary, Subcommittee on Constitution, Federalism, and Property Rights, June 13, 2001.

Breyer, Stephen G. Opinion in *Ashcroft v. American Civil Liberties Union*, U.S. Supreme Court, June 29, 2004.

Cain, Becky. Testimony during hearings on "Proposals for Electoral College Reform: H.J. Res. 28 and J.J. Res. 43" before the U.S. House of Representatives Committee on the Judiciary, Subcommittee on the Constitution, September 4, 1997.

Casse, Daniel. "An Emerging Republican Majority?" Reprinted from *Commentary*, January 2003, by permission of the publisher and the author. All rights reserved.

Center for Reproductive Rights. Excerpt from "Unconstitutional Assault on the Right to Choose: 'Partial-Birth Abortion' Ban Is an Affront to Women and to the U.S. Supreme Court," February 2003. Reprinted by permission of the Center for Reproductive Rights. (www.reproductiverights.org).

Farber, Daniel A. From "Disarmed by Time: The Second Amendment and the Failure of Originalism," *Chicago-Kent Law Review*, Vol. 76, No. 1 (2000). Reprinted by permission of the author.

Gaziano, Todd F. Testimony during hearings on a "Judiciary Diminished Is Justice Denied: The Constitution, the Senate, and the Vacancy Crisis in the Federal Judiciary," before U.S. House of Representatives, Committee on the Judiciary, Subcommittee on the Constitution, October 10, 2002.

Hajjar, Lisa. "Torture and the Future," *Middle East Report Online*, May 2004. Reprinted by permission of MERIP (The Middle East Research and Information Project).

Hanson, Victor Davis. "I Love Iraq, Bomb Texas." Reprinted from *Commentary*, December 2002, by permission of the publisher and the author. All rights reserved.

Hatch, Orin. From *Congressional Record*, July 9, 2004, Vol. 150, No. 94.

Hibbing, John R. Testimony during hearings on "Limiting Terms of Office for Members of the U.S. Senate and U.S. House of Representatives," U.S. House of Representatives, Committee on the Judiciary, Subcommittee on the Constitution, January 22, 1997.

Jacob, Paul. Testimony during hearings on "Limiting Terms of Office for Members of the U.S. Senate and U.S. House of Representatives," U.S. House of Representatives, Committee on the Judiciary, Subcommittee on the Constitution, January 22, 1997.

Judis, John B., and Ruy Teixeira. "America's Changing Political Geography: Where Democrats Can Build a Majority," from the September/October 2002 issue of *Blueprint: Ideas for a New Century*, journal of New Democrats Online. http://www.ndol.org/blueprint. Reprinted by permission.

Kennedy, Anthony M. Opinion in *Ashcroft v. American Civil Liberties Union*, U.S. Supreme Court, June 29, 2004.

Kennedy, Robert G. From "Can Interrogatory Torture Be Morally Legitimate?" in the paper presented at the Joint Services Conference on Professional Ethics, U.S. Air Force Academy, January 2003. Reprinted by permission of Robert G. Kennedy.

Kmiec, Douglas. Testimony during hearings on "Applying the War Powers Resolution to the War on Terrorism," before the U.S. Senate Committee on the Judiciary, April 17, 2002.

Kogan, Richard. Testimony during hearings on the "Balanced Budget Amendment" before the U.S. House of Representatives Committee on the Judiciary, Subcommittee on the Constitution, October 10, 2002.

Leahy, Patrick. Statement during hearings on "A Proposed Constitutional Amendment to Preserve Traditional Marriage," before the U.S. Senate Committee on the Judiciary, March 23, 2004.

Malcolm, Joyce. "Infringement," *Common-place*, Vol. 2: No. 4, July 2002. http://www.common-place.org/. Copyright © 2002 by Common-place: The Interactive Journal of Early American Life. Reprinted by permission.

McBride, Andrew. Testimony during hearings on "Race and the Federal Death Penalty," before the U.S. Senate Committee on the Judiciary, Subcommittee on Constitution, Federalism, and Property Rights, June 13, 2001.

McInturff, Bill and Lori Weigel. "Servants of the People: Political Leadership and the Public Voice," *Public Perspective*, July/August, 2001. Reprinted by permission of the Roper Center for Public Opinion Research at the University of Connecticut.

O'Sullivan John. "Who Are We?" from *The American Conservative*, July 19, 2004. http://www.amconmag.com. All rights reserved. Reprinted with permission of Valeo IP, 800-271-7874.

Robertson, Lori. "Poll Crazy," *American Journalism Review*, January/February 2003. Reprinted by permission of American Journalism Review.

Ross-Edwards, Amanda. "The Department of Education and Title IX: Flawed Interpretation and Implementation," an essay written for this volume, October 2003.

Shain, Yossi. From "For Ethnic Americans, The Old Country Calls," *Foreign Service Journal*, October 2000. Reprinted by permission of Yossi Shain.

Sleeper, Jim. Review of Samuel Huntington's *Who Are We: The Challenges to America's National Identity*, History News Network, May 3, 2004. Originally appeared in the *Los Angeles Times*. Reprinted by permission of the author.

Stromseth, Jane. Testimony during hearings on "Applying the War Powers Resolution to the War on Terrorism," before the U.S. Senate Committee on the Judiciary, April 17, 2002.

Sweet, Judith. U.S. Department of Education, Secretary's Commission on Opportunity in Athletics, Hearings, August 27, 2002.

Tribe, Laurence H. Testimony during hearings on "Judicial Nominations, Filibusters, and the Constitution: When a Majority Is Denied Its Right to Consent," before U.S. Senate Committee on the Judiciary, May 6, 2002

Vidal, Gore. "We Are the Patriots." Originally appeared in *The Nation*, June 2, 2003. Reprinted by permission of the author.

Wheatcroft, Geoffrey. "Hyphenated Americans," *Guardian Unlimited Online*, April 25, 2000. Reprinted by permission of the author.